Springer Series in Supply Chain Management

Volume 11

Series Editor
Christopher S. Tang
University of California
Los Angeles, CA, USA

Supply Chain Management (SCM), long an integral part of Operations Management, focuses on all elements of creating a product or service, and delivering that product or service, at the optimal cost and within an optimal timeframe. It spans the movement and storage of raw materials, work-in-process inventory, and finished goods from point of origin to point of consumption. To facilitate physical flows in a time-efficient and cost-effective manner, the scope of SCM includes technology-enabled information flows and financial flows.

The Springer Series in Supply Chain Management, under the guidance of founding Series Editor Christopher S. Tang, covers research of either theoretical or empirical nature, in both authored and edited volumes from leading scholars and practitioners in the field – with a specific focus on topics within the scope of SCM.

Springer and the Series Editor welcome book ideas from authors. Potential authors who wish to submit a book proposal should contact Ms. Jialin Yan, Associate Editor, Springer (Germany), e-mail: jialin.yan@springernature.com

More information about this series at http://www.springer.com/series/13081

Volodymyr Babich • John R. Birge • Gilles Hilary
Editors

Innovative Technology at the Interface of Finance and Operations

Volume I

Editors
Volodymyr Babich
McDonough School of Business
Georgetown University
Washington, DC, USA

John R. Birge
University of Chicago Booth
School of Business
Chicago, IL, USA

Gilles Hilary
McDonough School of Business
Georgetown University
Washington, DC, USA

ISSN 2365-6395 ISSN 2365-6409 (electronic)
Springer Series in Supply Chain Management
ISBN 978-3-030-75728-1 ISBN 978-3-030-75729-8 (eBook)
https://doi.org/10.1007/978-3-030-75729-8

This Springer imprint is published by the registered company Springer Nature Switzerland AG
The registered company address is: Gewerbestrasse 11, 6330 Cham, Switzerland

Foreword

Technology has always gone through recurring breakthroughs. At the moment, artificial intelligence (AI), distributed ledger technologies (DLT) such as blockchains, and Internet of Things (IoT) are receiving significant attention and funding. Other technologies, such as quantum computing and 5G networks, are emerging. New sensors, integrated into "smart" objects, generate greater volume, variety, and velocity of data. Blockchain facilitates the secure storage and dissemination of these data through multiple agents, organizations, and markets. AI enables effective processing of data streams and analytics tools process ever larger data sets. Robots implement AI and analytics decisions in the digital and physical worlds. These technologies create synergies and foster the creation of "systems" (elements that interact with each other automatically and intelligently) and of new economic models. All parts of the economy and all corporate functions are likely to be influenced by technology breakthroughs. In this two-volume book, we aim to understand the effect of technology on finance, operations, and their interface specifically. We hold the view that greater integration between finance and operations through technology will occur. With this goal in mind, we invited a group of experts to contribute their perspectives, explain complex technologies in simple terms, and outline both operational and financial implications in a rigorous way.

The first volume starts with tutorials that offer overviews of emerging technologies, followed by additional tutorials that cover the integration of new technologies with broader issues for operations, finance, and accompanying transactions. We then offer two series of chapters on specific disruptive technologies and their applications: AI in the first volume and DLT in the second one. Volume II concludes by considering emerging economic models first in operations and then in finance that are heavily influenced by new technologies.

Specifically, Chap. 1, "Blockchain and other Distributed Ledger Technologies, an Advanced Primer," by Gilles Hilary, provides an overview of blockchain and other technologies that enable multiple locations to independently record and update information while preserving validity through their collective actions. The overarching technology of combining autonomous agents' actions to achieve overall consistent organization is explored in Chap. 2, "Operational and Financial

Implications of Transactionalizing Multi-Machine Maneuvers in Self-Organizing Autonomous System," by Karl Wunderlich.

The second part of Volume I provides tutorial material to give readers a broad background on issues concerning operations, finance, and technology issues. Chapter 3, "Interface of Operations and Finance: A Tutorial," by Volodymyr Babich and John R. Birge, highlight several essential ideas and results in operations for finance audiences, and conversely, several essential ideas and results in finance operations audiences. This tutorial emphasizes the interface between two disciplines and reduces entry cost for research at this interface. Chapter 4, "The Past, Present, and Future of the Payment System as Trusted Broker and the Implications for Banking," by Joseph Byrum, provides a history and overview of payment systems, their bases in enabling trusted transactions, and the effects of changing technology on the future evolution of these systems.

The rest of Volume I considers AI and machine learning applications as breakthrough technologies across finance and operations. Chapter 5, "Machine Learning in Healthcare: Operational and Financial Impact," by David Anderson, Margret V. Bjarnadottir, and Zlatana Nenova, focuses on applications in healthcare with financial and operational consequences, such as predicting demand, managing hospital readmissions, and improving diagnostic accuracy. Chapter 6, "Digital Lean Operations: Smart Automation and Artificial Intelligence in Financial Services," by Robert N. Boute, Joren Gijsbrechts, and Jan A. Van Mieghem, uses the framework of lean operations to explore the expansion of automating transactions to include decision-making capabilities such as credit checks. Chapter 7, "Applied Machine Learning in Operations Management," by Hamsa Bastani, Dennis J. Zhang, and Heng Zhang, provides an overview of supervised, unsupervised, and reinforcement learning methods and their uses in a variety of operational contexts. Chapter 8, "Artificial Intelligence and Fraud Detection," by Yang Bao, Gilles Hilary, and Bin Ke, examines how machine learning methods can be used in fraud detection, particularly for financial statement manipulation or accounting fraud. Chapter 9, "AI in Financial Portfolio Management: Practical Considerations and Use Cases," by Joseph Byrum, considers the use of artificial intelligence in three areas of portfolio management: optimizing investment, increasing operational efficiency, and enhancing customer experience. Finally, Chap. 10, "Using Machine Learning to Demystify Startups Funding, Post-Money Valuation, and Success," by Yu Qian Ang, Andrew Chia, and Soroush Saghafian, investigates a particular example of using machine learning to predict the success of startup funding after the latest round of investment (i.e., a post-money valuation).

The first part of Volume II focuses on aspects of distributed ledger technologies, particularly blockchains. Chapter 11, "Blockchain Intra- and Interoperability," by Alexander Lipton and Thomas Hardjono, considers the issues of exchanging assets on a single blockchain as well as those that concern exchanges across different blockchains and proposes vehicles to facilitate these operations. Chapter 12, "Distributed Ledger Technology and Fully Homomorphic Encryption: Next-generation Information-sharing for Supply Chain Efficiency," by Daniel Hellwig and Arnd Huchzermeier, describes the use of DLT along with fully homomorphic encryption, which enables the preservation of sensitive private information while sharing results on that data, and their applications in improving supply chain efficiency. Chapter 13, "Tutorial on Blockchain Applications in Supply Chains," by Volodymyr Babich and Gilles Hilary, reviews applications of blockchain technology to supply chains management and supply chain finance and reflects on whether the COVID-19 pandemic increase the importance of such applications. Chapter 14, "Impact of Blockchain-Driven Accountability in Multi-Sourcing Supply Chains," by Yao Cui, Ming Hu, and Jingchen Liu, also considers the applications of the blockchain technology to supply chains, but focuses on multi-sourcing situations where a buyer purchases from an arbitrary number of suppliers. Chapter 15, "Enterprise Payments with Central Bank Digital Currency," by Alan King, Francis Parr, and Martin Fleming offers an exploration of the opportunities and challenges of real-time payments and distributed ledger from an end-to-end technology point of view.

The second part of Volume II considers emerging operational models and applications. Chapter 16, "Integrated Framework for Financial Risk Management, Operational Modeling and IoT-Driven Execution," by Stephan Biller and Bahar Biller, describes a framework for analyzing project management in industrial companies in the context of development in business analytics. Chapter 17, "Market Equilibrium Models in Large-Scale Internet Markets," by Nicolas Stier-Moses and Christian Kroer, describes the function of markets for determining prices and allocations of goods and in particular the functioning of Fisher markets, in which buyers are constrained by budgets. Chapter 18, "Large-scale Price Optimization for an Online Fashion Retailer," by Hanwei Li, David Simchi-Levi, Rui Sun, Michelle X. Wu, Vladimir Fux, Torsten Gellert, Thorsten Greiner, and Andrea Taverna, analyzes how a global online fashion retailer, Zalando, can utilize a massive amount of data to optimize price discount decisions over a large number of products in multiple countries on a weekly basis.

Lastly, the third part of Volume II considers emerging financial models and applications. Chapter 19, "Microbanks in Online Peer-to-Peer Lending: A Tale of Dual Roles," by Jussi Keppo, Tuan Q. Phan, and Tianhui Tan examines the development of microbanks, peer-to-peer lending platforms that connect borrowers to lenders. Chapter 20 "FinTech Econometrics: Privacy Preservation and the Wisdom of the Crowd," by Steven Kou, offers an overview of the FinTech sector and discusses econometric issues related to the emergence of that sector, especially privacy and transparency issues. Chapter 21, "The Impact of Technology Choice on Capital Structure," by Peter Ritchken and Qi Wu, explores how new technologies can affect the timing of investment and their financing.

Washington, DC, USA — Volodymyr Babich
Chicago, IL, USA — John R. Birge
Washington, DC, USA — Gilles Hilary

Contents

Contributors

David Anderson Villanova University, Villanova, PA, USA

Yu Qian Ang Massachusetts Institute of Technology, Cambridge, MA, USA

Volodymyr Babich McDonough School of Business, Georgetown University, Washington, DC, USA

Yang Bao Antai College of Economics and Management, Shanghai Jiao Tong University, Shanghai, People's Republic of China

Hamsa Bastani Wharton Business School, University of Pennsylvania, Philadelphia, PA, USA

John Birge University of Chicago Booth School of Business, Chicago, IL, USA

Margret V. Bjarnadottir University of Maryland, College Park, MD, USA

Robert N. Boute KU Leuven and Vlerick Business School, Ghent, Belgium

Joseph Byrum Principal Financial Group, Des Moines, IA, USA

Andrew Chia Harvard University, Cambridge, MA, USA

Joren Gijsbrechts Católica Lisbon School of Business and Economics, Lisbon, Portugal

Gilles Hilary McDonough School of Business, Georgetown University, Washington, DC, USA

Bin Ke Department of Accounting, NUS Business School, National University of Singapore, Singapore, Singapore

Jan A. Van Mieghem Kellogg School of Management, Northwestern University, Evanston, IL, USA

Zlatana Nenova University of Denver, Denver, CO, USA

Soroush Saghafian Harvard University, Cambridge, MA, USA

Karl Wunderlich Noblis, Washington, DC, USA

Dennis J. Zhang Olin Business School, Washington University in St. Louis, St. Louis, MO, USA

Heng Zhang W. P. Carey School of Business, Arizona State University, Tempe, AZ, USA

Chapter 1
Blockchain and Other Distributed Ledger Technologies, an Advanced Primer

Gilles Hilary

1.1 What Is a Blockchain?

Although there are many versions of blockchain technology today, it was first introduced in 2008 as the technology supporting Bitcoin, the first successful virtual currency system that eschewed a central authority for issuing currency, transferring ownership, and confirming transactions. Yet in and of itself, blockchain technology is much more than the underpinning for Bitcoin (and other cryptocurrencies) and has found many applications beyond its initial purpose.

Blockchain is based on a peer-to-peer network of nodes (i.e., machines actively participating in a network), collectively adhering to a protocol for validating new blocks of data, thus enabling the transfer and preservation of digital files without relying on a central authority. Thus, blockchain is essentially a new form of database technology known as a "distributed ledger."

Traditional centralized databases hold only one master version of a database at any given time; naturally, there can be multiple copies, but only one "real" (or better "active") version of the database exists at any given point. In contrast, a distributed database involves multiple nodes that cooperate under one umbrella to maintain the integrity of the database should one of the nodes fail (e.g., a hardware problem). It is "fault-tolerant." However, even though the nodes do not necessarily trust information received from parties outside the umbrella (i.e., the database), they

---

I would like to thank the numerous professionals with whom I had conversations on this topic. In particular, I would like Richard Jones for providing comments on this draft. Naturally, all errors remain mine.

G. Hilary (✉)
McDonough School of Business, Georgetown University, Washington, DC, USA

V. Babich et al. (eds.), *Innovative Technology at the Interface of Finance and Operations*, Springer Series in Supply Chain Management 11,
https://doi.org/10.1007/978-3-030-75729-8_1

need to trust each other. The approach assumes that no node will alter or manipulate content (Brown, 2016).

Distributed ledgers (such as blockchains) go a step beyond what distributed databases achieve. They replicate the database, meaning each node has a copy. These versions can temporarily diverge from one another, but the technology constantly ensures that the different versions converge to a consensus version. They allow for the possibility for nodes to generate any kind of arbitrary data while posing as an honest actor. In other words, they remove the need for nodes to trust each other. The goal is for the system to be "Byzantine Fault Tolerant" (BFT), i.e., to display the ability to handle component failure when there is uncertainty about the behavior of a component and its failure. Distributed ledgers can either be decentralized (granting equal rights within the protocol to all participants) or centralized (giving certain users particular rights, Rutlan (2017)).

1.2 Blockchain Versus Other Forms of Distributed Ledger Technologies (DLTs)

A blockchain is a specific form of distributed ledger that has a specific data structure. Other forms of distributed ledgers also exist. For example, IOTA, Byteball, and DagCoin are based on the concept of Directed Acyclic Graphs (DAG). Hedera is based on a hashgraph, a DAG with specific features (Baird, 2018).[1] Unlike blockchain (which is a sequential list of blocks, as explained further subsequently), a DAG is a data structure that resembles a tree-like flow chart where all points head toward one direction (see Fig. 1.1).

A blockchain is a sequential list of records distributed over a network where each block in the chain contains a cryptographic hash of the previous block, along with a timestamp and transaction data. A hash value is the output of a hash function, a mathematical function that takes an input (or "message") and returns a fixed-size alphanumeric string. A hash function is deterministic (it will always yield the same output for a given input) but highly chaotic (a small change in the input yields widely divergent solutions for slightly different inputs).[2] Hashing provides the foundation for a cryptographic audit trail that is validated by different nodes. A blockchain is also replicated (usually a large number of times, at least for public blockchains). This implies that there are multiple versions of the database at the same time, requiring a mechanism to ensure constant convergence for the blockchain. This consensus mechanism needs to incorporate the fact that nodes may have altered the data. There are different implementations of this mechanism, and some examples are discussed subsequently.

---

[1]Interested readers can find more information on Hedera at https://www.hederahashgraph.com/

[2]Interested readers can experiment with hash functions on sites such as FileFormatInfo (https://www.fileformat.info/tool/hash.htm)

Blockchain structure

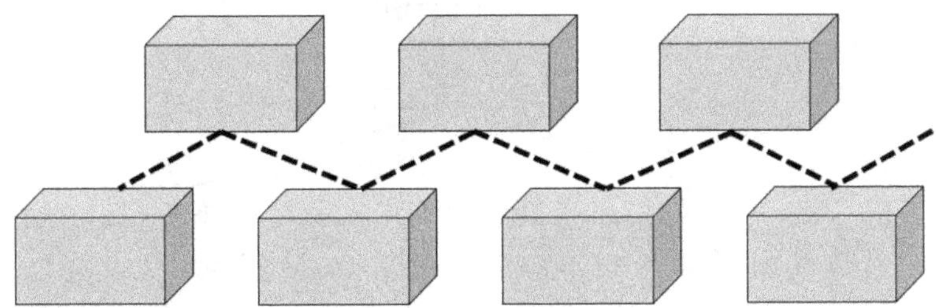

Directed Acyclic Graph (DAG) structure

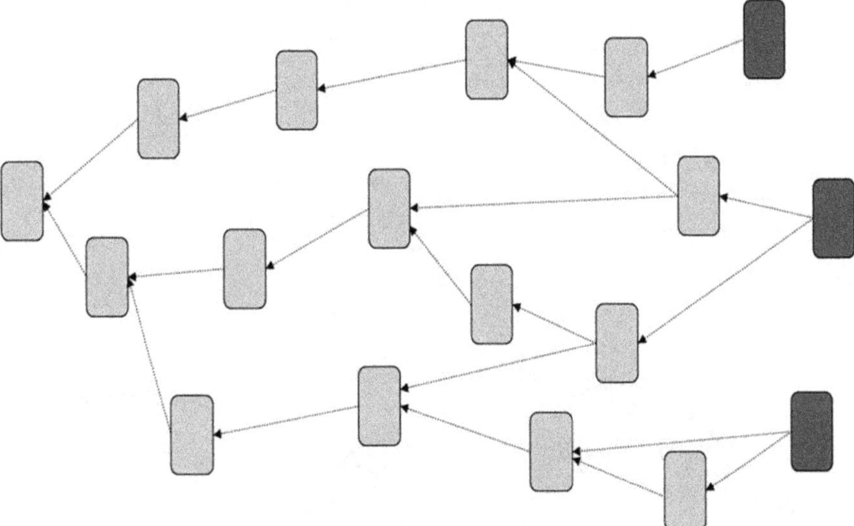

Fig. 1.1 Blockchain versus DAG

Data from a block are often encoded into a single hash using a structure known as a "Merkle tree" (represented in Fig. 1.2).[3] This is the case for common platforms such as Bitcoin, Ethereum, and Hyperledger, and the mechanism improves data storage efficiency. Merkle trees allow phones, laptops, and even the internet of things (IoT) devices to be powerful enough to run a blockchain. IoT represents the network of physical objects (trucks, toys, cameras, etc.) that exchange electronic data. Another solution to improve data storage efficiency is the use of a "light client," a technology that allows one only to download the chain of block headers

[3]Merkle trees are created by repeatedly hashing pairs of nodes until there is only one hash left (this hash is called the Root Hash, or the Merkle Root). They are constructed from the bottom up, from hashes of individual transactions (known as Transaction IDs) (see Ray (2017) for more details).

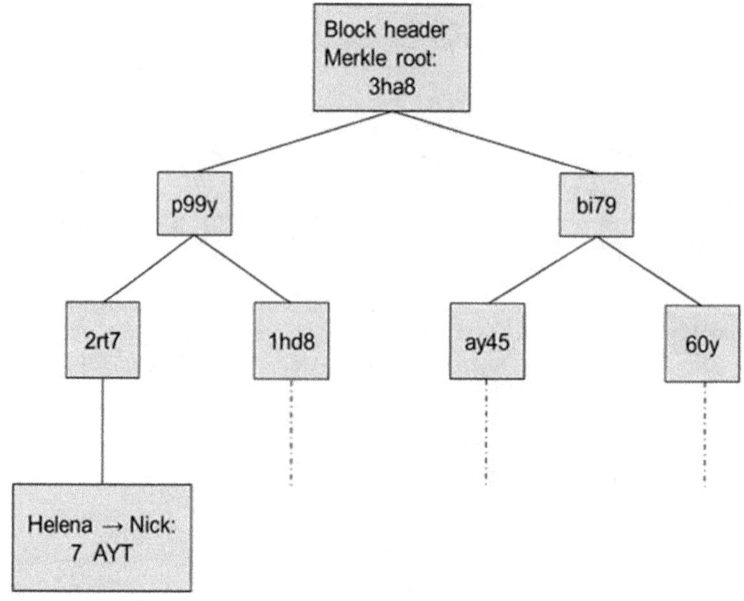

Fig. 1.2 Merkle tree

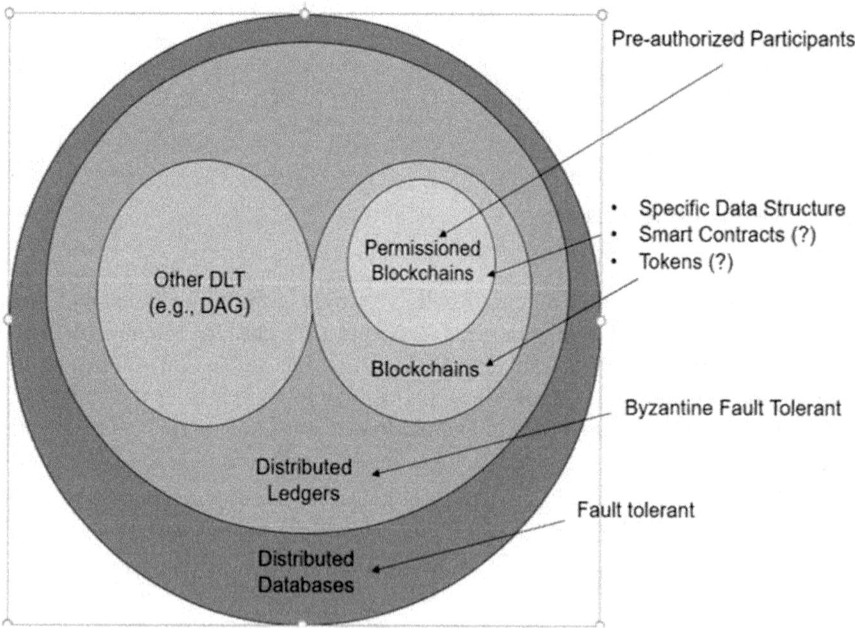

Fig. 1.3 Summary of distributed ledger technology

and verify that the hashing for a branch is consistent all the way up the tree; thus ensuring that the given transaction is in the correct position in the tree.

Blockchains are either public or private. Everyone can join a public blockchain, but participants in a private blockchain must be vetted. Most cryptocurrencies (e.g., Bitcoin) are based on a public blockchain, while many enterprise applications rely on private blockchains. Figure 1.3 summarizes these different categories.

1.3 The Bitcoin Example[4]

For concreteness and historical reasons, it is probably useful to continue our description of the blockchain technology by focusing on its original application, Bitcoin. Bitcoin was the first public blockchain. It enables a distributed digital ledger to record transactions between two parties in a verifiable and permanent way. Bitcoin blockchain is essentially the combination of peer-to-peer (P2P) software (comparable to BitTorrent) with a public key cryptographic tool (comparable to PGP).[5] The core of the programming is written in C++, a common programming language. As in other blockchain technologies, it is consensus based to protect its integrity. Records cannot be altered retroactively without the alteration of all subsequent blocks and the collusion of the network. The blockchain contains two kinds of records: transactions and blocks. Blocks hold batches of valid transactions and additional information necessary for the system to work. To give an example, each block includes information necessary to link it to the previous block.

The normal process flow for updating the blockchain ledger is as follows. A party requests a transaction involving the transfer of Bitcoins to another party. The requested transaction is then broadcast over a P2P network, and the nodes validate the transaction in terms of compliance with the blockchain's rules, the digital signature, and any conflicts with previously seen transactions. If a transaction is validated, it enters that node's local list of provisional unconfirmed transactions. Transactions that are not validated are rejected.

To perform this validation, nodes employ specific algorithms. When a new account is created, the owner receives a private key associated with the account. When there is a transaction, the text from the transaction and the private key is combined through a cryptographic function (Elliptic Curve Digital Signature Algorithm, ECDSA for short). Thus, the signature is unique to each transaction. Another function allows other people to decode the signature and to verify that the

[4]The original white paper describing Bitcoin can be found here: https://bitcoin.org/bitcoin.pdf. The author is Satoshi Nakamoto, a pseudonym for the person or people behind the development of the platform. The identity of Nakamoto has not been conclusively confirmed to this day.

[5]Pretty Good Privacy (PGP) is a software that provides cryptographic privacy and authentication for data communication. PGP enables the signature, encryption and decryption of files and messages for a greater level of privacy and security of electronic communications.

message was sent from a legitimate source. The signature of the transaction is then used as an input in the next transaction, where each input includes an amount of Bitcoin and an address, ensuring that all individual transactions are linked to each other. Each individual bitcoin address is not linked to any one person in a registry, but all transactions can be tracked, mapped, and followed. This property is known as pseudo-anonymity. However, the procedure by itself does not guarantee that double-spending is impossible. Double-spending occurs when a bad actor spends the same funds twice by sending multiple orders at the same time. Centralized databases can easily prevent this, but the fact that the ledger is distributed may prevent this immediate verification.

To address this issue, transactions are grouped in blocks that are time-stamped. Blocks contain a block header storing metadata: the current version of the block structure, the previous block header hash (a reference to the block's parent block), a Merkle root hash (a cryptographic hash of all of the transactions included in the block), the time that the block was created, nBits (the current "difficulty" that was used to create the block, a concept defined subsequently), and a "nonce" ("number used once," a random value that the creator of a block is allowed to manipulate however they so choose). The rest of a block contains transactions.[6]

These blocks are ordered in a single chain that is replicated over the entire network. Once verified, the transaction is combined with other transactions to create a new time-stamped block of data for the ledger. The new block is then added to the existing blockchain in a way that is meant to be permanent and unalterable (each block contains a link to the previous block). This addition is done by consensus. It takes about 10 minutes to produce a Bitcoin block (with a maximum size of 1 MB).[7] As of June 2020, the overall size of the Bitcoin database is approximately 280 GB, but this is constantly increasing.[8] Three to seven transactions can be added to a block per second. Transactions are pending until they are confirmed, but they are not lost. At worst, the stamping of these transactions is delayed until another block becomes available.

The current consensus mechanism in the Bitcoin blockchain uses the Proof-of-Work (PoW) approach to stamp the blocks. In this approach, the node (or "miner") that is the fastest to complete a block can add it to the consensus. Bitcoin blockchain determines the order of the blocks by using a mathematical lottery based on solving a mathematical problem (a "cryptographic hash"). The lottery is based on SHA256, a deterministic but highly chaotic function. This implies that it is easy to check that a problem has been solved by inputting the proposed solution in SHA256 but makes it extremely difficult to reverse-engineer it. One analogy may be as follows. Suppose

---

[6]Interested readers can obtain more information at https://www.pluralsight.com/guides/blockchain-architecture

[7]An old CD may have a size of 700 MB.

[8]Interested readers can follow the evolution of the blockchain size at https://www.blockchain.com/charts/blocks-size

that you have to find the phone number of a person without a directory, and the only solution is to call a very large number of people until you obtain the right number. Once you find it, it is easy for other people to verify this. Thus, the only way to solve the problem is to try an extraordinarily large number of inputs before coming arbitrarily close to the required solution (the minimum "closeness" is known as the "difficulty"). The difficulty is chosen in proportion to the total amount of hashing power at work across the network so that a new block is published approximately every 10 min. The target is adjusted every 2016 blocks (approximately every 2 weeks) so that mining the next 2016 blocks should take exactly 2 weeks, if the total network power does not change (Mercer, 2016). However, solving the hash function problem is costly. Among other things, it requires computer time, bandwidth, and electricity. These costs are nontrivial. The cumulative amount of electricity needed to operate the Bitcoin network, for example, approximates electricity consumption in Israel.[9]

To incentivize miners to incur these costs, the first node that solves the problem (and thus adds a block to the chain) receives a financial reward in the form of newly minted Bitcoins. However, the reward for mining is declining in a predictable way (it is divided by two every 210,000 blocks).[10] As the rewards for mining decline, there should be fewer miners; however, there is a mechanism to mitigate this problem. Adding transactions costs a small fee. Mining a block earns the fees associated with all transactions included in the block. Once a miner solves the problem, the block is added to her own version of the database, and she propagates its results. Upon notification, other miners check the consistency of the database against their own version, verify that the problem has been solved, and realize they have no further incentive to solve it. They add the block to their own version of the ledger and move on to the next problem. A node can read data for free.

Theoretically, an agent could alter blockchain history, but with PoW, they would also need to have the majority of computational power in the network to verify it. Because the Bitcoin network benefits from a colossal amount of computation power at this point, it would be extremely difficult for an attacker to break the network by brute force. This protects the immutability of the record. PoW is expensive in terms of computational cost, but this cost is precisely what makes the network attack resistant. Moreover, each additional block makes the chain more robust by exponentially increasing the number of computations necessary to break the network.

To summarize, Bitcoin blockchain is censorship-resistant (i.e., anyone can transact on the blockchain and a transaction, once made and paid for, cannot be stopped), Byzantine fault-tolerant (i.e., there is imperfect information about the failure of network components), pseudo-anonymous (it operates in a state of stable

[9]Interested readers can follow the Bitcoin energy consumption at https://digiconomist.net/bitcoin-energy-consumption consulted on June 7, 2020.

[10]As of May 2018, the reward is 12.50 bitcoins per block.

disguised-user identity) but fully traceable (i.e., not fully anonymous), auditable (both the code and the database are public), immutable,[11] accountable (time-stamping), and cannot be repudiated (signature) at the transaction level. Many of these features are common to other distributed ledgers, but most of them (e.g., pseudo-anonymization, traceability, auditability, immutability) are not ontological characteristics of distributed ledgers.

1.4 Consensus Mechanisms

Various blockchain platforms have made different implementation choices that bring their own advantages and drawbacks. We list some examples in Table 1.1. For example, Bitcoin blockchain is permissionless (everyone can join and mine). In fact, it strives on this openness as additional miners make it more robust. In this case, no single agent dominates the network (although, as we discuss subsequently, a coalition could theoretically reach 51% of the nodes and control it). By contrast, private blockchains vet participants and may allow a single agent to dominate the network. In this case, the PoW approach is ineffective as nodes do not have incentives to incur the mining costs, and the lack of depth prevents the mining costs from proving immutability. Hyperledger Fabric, an alternative blockchain technology used in private blockchains, uses different consensus mechanisms including the so-called Practical Byzantine Fault Tolerance (PBFT) protocol in which a sufficient number of node votes are required for the approval of a block to join the consensus. Some of the most popular consensus algorithms for private blockchains (e.g., Raft) are based on a leader-follower model wherein a leader who creates the blocks and adds to the blockchain is selected for each block. Other cryptocurrencies (such as Peercoin and Ethereum) rely on Proof-of-Stake (PoS) instead. In PoS, a deterministic algorithm chooses nodes based on the number of coins an individual has. In other words, nodes would have more chances of being selected to add a block to the chain and receive a reward if they "stake" more coins in the verification process. If they are caught cheating, they lose their tokens. Both PBFT and PoS do not require the consumption of significant resources to develop consensus and are not affected by a potential reduction in network depth caused by the declining benefit of mining. Possibilities also exist between the completely permissionless public blockchains and the completely permissioned private blockchains. For example, different agents may be able to receive different levels of permission to read or affect the consensus database.

[11] I discuss forks and Sybil attacks below.

Table 1.1 Examples of consensus mechanisms

Proof of work: Bitcoin, colored coins, DAG, Factom, Coin ERPsim
Proof of stake: Casper, Ethereum
Delegated proof of work: Graphene, Steem, BitShares
Leader-based consensus: Paxos, RAFT, ZAB, Mencius
Round Robin: Multichain, TenderMint
Federated consensus: Ripple, Stellar (Ripple Fork)
Proof of elapsed time: Sawtooth
Practical Byzantine Fault Tolerance: Tendermint, Openchain, ErisDB
N2N: Corda

1.5 Performance and Scalability

Public blockchains (and to a lesser extent, private blockchains) currently face performance and scalability issues. Bitcoin, for example, can handle approximately seven transactions per second but usually fewer (Vermeulen, 2017), while VisaNet can allegedly handle up to 56,000 transactions per second.[12] In 2017, digital "pets" called crypto-kitties "bred" on Ethereum (a popular blockchain platform) substantially clogged the network by consuming around 20% of computational power. Naturally, the more complex the data structure, the worse the problem. For example, blockchains can contain self-executable code (i.e., "smart contracts"),[13] which are harder to process than simple transactions. This scalability problem stems in part from the fact that in a basic blockchain platform, every fully participating node in the network must validate every transaction and seek agreement from other nodes on it. Other DLTs such as DAG offer the possibility of greater scalability but have not yet been extensively deployed and tested at this point.

Various approaches have been designed to mitigate this problem. One possibility is to increase the block size. The larger the block size, the fewer blocks to process. However, this increase in throughput comes with the cost of increasing the latency (the length of the propagation of mined blocks through the network) due to the use of larger blocks. In other words, mining is faster, but it takes longer for the network to realize that a block has been mined. Another approach is to optimize the consensus mechanism. LiteCoin, for example, a cryptocurrency derived from Bitcoin,[14] is able to improve the chain's efficiency by using PoS (instead of PoW) as a consensus mechanism.

Another option is to use overlay protocols to limit the amount of data processed by the nodes. For example, the bitcoin blockchain contains all transactions that have been carried out since the inception of Bitcoin in 2009. The Segregated

[12] See Vermeulen (2016). However, Visa baseline capacity is typically lower.

[13] I elaborate on smart contracts below.

[14] LiteCoin has been developed through a Bitcoin's fork. I elaborate below on what forks involve.

Witness (SegWit) approach removes data related to digital signatures from Bitcoin transactions to reduce the size of the database and the content of each block. Conversely, Plasma reduces the amount of unnecessary data in the Ethereum root chain by only broadcasting completed transactions to the public Ethereum chain. The integration of overlay protocols may create integration issues.

Another approach, called "sharding," is to partition the data in such a way that only a small subset of nodes has to verify a subset of transactions. In essence, this partitions the database into several pieces (the "shards") distributed on different servers. As long as there are sufficient nodes verifying each transaction, the system will still be secure, but will also allow for the system to process transactions in parallel. In principle, on-chain scaling via sharding and complementary off-chain scaling via channels can be used at the same time; however, a well-developed integration is yet to be implemented.

1.6 Smart Contracts and Oracles

A second issue is that records in blockchain databases can contain any number of elements, including executable software. For instance, in Ethereum, each record is a contract that carries a mini database that exposes methods for modifying the data, allowing for the automatic execution of "smart contracts."[15] A smart contract is a computer protocol intended to facilitate, verify, or enforce the negotiation or performance of a contract.[16] "Decentralized Apps," DApps, are applications relying on smart contracts. Smart contract code can be written in languages such as Go or Java for Fabric, Solidity for Ethereum, and Java or Kotlin for Corda (Corda is a platform designed for enterprise applications, particularly those in the financial sector). However, a self-executable set of instructions (lines of codes) does not necessarily translate into legally binding contracts. Consumer laws, for example, make certain contractual provisions illegal and thus unenforceable, even if the consumer explicitly agrees to them. Corda increases the likelihood for a contract to be legally binding by allowing the possibility of adding redacted material to the blockchain.[17]

In addition, many of these contracts need external validation which can be done by prespecified agents, but the interest in blockchain partly lies on removing the need for trusted intermediaries. In order to directly interact with the real world,

[15] Smart contracts are called "chaincodes" in the Fabric environment.

[16] The concept of smart contract was originally proposed by Nick Szabo.

[17] See Valenta and Sandner (2017) for more details on Corda. Interested readers can also find more technical details on Corda at https://docs.corda.net/key-concepts-tradeoffs.html

blockchains need sensors and actuators.[18] The development of the Internet of Things (IoT) should increase their relevance.

An "oracle" is an "agent" that finds and verifies real-world occurrences and submits this information to a blockchain for use by smart contracts. For example, an oracle can obtain electronic data from an external website (e.g., a currency price or a temperature level in a certain country). Alternatively, the oracle can obtain the information directly from a sensor. One example is Oraclize, which provides cryptographic evidence of the sensor's readings and anti-tampering mechanisms that render the device inoperable in the case of a breach. However, this particular oracle is centralized, which may create a point of vulnerability in the execution of smart contracts if the flow of information that triggers the smart contract can be manipulated (e.g., tampered with or delayed). Decentralized oracle services, such as ChainLink, are currently developing systems to communicate with off-chain systems and application programming interface (API) to mitigate this vulnerability (Town, 2018). Oracles such as Augur, Gnosis, or Polyswarm offer blockchain-based prediction markets, i.e., markets that are exchange-traded, created for the purpose of trading the outcome of events. Market prices can indicate what the crowd thinks the probability of an event is.

1.7 Tokens

Relatedly, the elements contained in the database may lead to "tokenization." In the context of blockchain, tokenization is the process of converting rights to an asset into a digital token on a blockchain (Cameron-Huff, 2017). Bitcoins and other cryptocurrencies are tokens. However, other assets can be similarly tokenized. One such approach facilitates the trading of illiquid assets and enables micro-payments. LAToken is an asset tokenization platform that allows users to convert tangible assets such as real estate or artwork into tokens, thereby making them sellable in fractions. Steemit is a social network that rewards users who participate in various ways: it uses tokens to reward content creators and curators of the best content on the site (Aru, 2017). Tokens enable Initial Coin Offering (ICO), a financial mechanism that takes advantage of blockchain technology to raise funds. For example, blockchain data storage network Filecoin raised more than $257 million in an ICO over a month of activity in 2017. Depending on the jurisdiction and on the specific characteristics of the issuance, ICO may be unregulated (at least in principle), or regulated like the issuance of regular securities, or may be completely illegal.

Sidechaining is any mechanism that allows tokens from one blockchain to be securely used within a completely separate blockchain (the sidechain) but allows

[18] An actuator is a component of a machine that is responsible for moving and controlling a mechanism or system, for example by activating a switch.

the token to move back to the original chain (the main chain) if necessary.[19] One application of this technology is the possibility of executing "atomic swaps." Traditionally, a trusted third party such as a cryptocurrency exchange is necessary to perform a swap of cryptoassets. An atomic swap system uses a hash time-locked smart contract to execute the transaction. There is the possibility of failed trade but no counterparty risk.

1.8 Data Structure and Immutability

A third issue is the nature of the "facts" in the database. There are currently three possible forms of data storage: full, partial, and pointer only. In the first case, the distributed ledger contains all data, including, for example, all documents related to a specific agreement. In the second case, some data (e.g., a large document) associated with the transaction are stored separately off-chain but referenced on the distributed ledger. In the third case, the distributed ledger only stores hashes that serve as pointers to the actual location of the data that is stored outside the blockchain.

It is important to note that blockchain uses cryptography to link the different blocks through a hash. However, the information contained in the blocks themselves is not necessarily encrypted (as it is in the case of the Bitcoin blockchain). Encryption provides a level of security that is needed in some applications, but the additional computational costs associated with the encryption may not be justified in other cases. It is also important to note that the data are not necessarily immutable. In some cases, this is a problem. In others, it may be a good thing (please see subsequently). As we note, the possibility that a bad actor can rewrite the Bitcoin database single-handedly by brute force is limited by the current computing power necessary to do this. Quantum computers may change this in the future, posing a potentially deadly problem for the platform, but this remains a speculative possibility at the moment (Gheorghiu et al., 2017).

Another possibility is a Sybil attack. In a Sybil attack, the attacker subverts the reputation system of a peer-to-peer network by creating a large number of pseudonymous identities, using them to gain a disproportionately large influence on the management of the network. This allows the bad actor to subvert the system and possibly rewrite the database. Sybil attacks are more likely to occur when nodes are fewer. As of June 2020, there are approximately 10,000 nodes on Bitcoin networks,

[19]Interested readers can obtain more details at https://ethereum.stackexchange.com/questions/379/what-is-a-sidechain

with a large proportion located in North America and Western Europe.[20, 21] By comparison, there are approximately 16,000 nodes on the Ethereum network. The depth (or liquidity) of these pools is important for providing robust and resilient networks. NEO, for example, another cryptocurrency with a multibillion-dollar market capitalization, relied on 13 validating nodes controlled by its development team (as of November 2017). The team was able to shut down the network with a moment's notice in October 2017, and the blockchain went down in 2018 when one node disconnected temporarily (O'Ham, 2018).[22]

Most public blockchains display a greater number of nodes. However, there is a trend toward greater concentration through "mining pools." These groups of miners pool their resources and split proceeds equally, based on the amount of computing power they contribute. This approach mutualizes the risk of mining and thus provides more predictable flows of rewards to participants. It allows miners with weaker machines to contribute meaningfully to the process (albeit less than those with more powerful setups). Indeed, the hardware required to mine efficiently has increasingly become elaborate and costly. Mining started with standard off-the-shelf central processing units (CPU), then moved to graphic processing units (GPU), and then to Application-Specific Integrated Circuits (ASIC), extremely fast chips designed to deal with specific problems such as solving SHA-256 hashes optimally. However, the centralization induced by these pools challenges the premise of a distributed public blockchain. In June 2020, for example, the distribution of "hashrate" (the computing power) on the Bitcoin network was very concentrated, with the top five mining pools controlling approximately 70% of the hashrate (the largest controlling approximately 20%).[23] This lack of depth can create security issues, for example, by making Sybil attacks easier to execute. This can be mitigated by changing the consensus method but remains a concern for public blockchains. Private blockchains typically have extremely concentrated pools but are in a better position to handle this lack of network depth through participant vetting and network governance.

Such examples are problematic for the integrity of the blockchain. However, the ability to change records collectively and retroactively is not necessarily a bad thing. In the case of Bitcoin, its database contains materials unrelated to cryptocurrency. Some are relatively harmless (e.g., a textbook, the original text providing the intellectual underpinning of blockchain), but others are much more sinister (e.g., malware, links to websites claiming to contain child pornography, see Matzutt et al.,

[20]The numbers were comparable in May 2017 (see https://bitnodes.earn.com/ for the current statistics).

[21]The number for Ethereum is close to 7500 (https://www.ethernodes.org/ consulted on June 7, 2020).

[22]The number of nodes decreased to seven (see https://neo.org/consensus to see the evolution over time).

[23]See https://blockchain.info/pools to follow the hashrate distribution.

2018). Removing these items easily and without damaging the structural integrality of the chain would be a good thing but is not technically possible at present.

Most changes to the databases happen through "forks." A fork is a technical event that occurs because diverse participants need to agree on common rules (See Castor (2017) or Light (2017) for more details on forks). At its most basic, a fork is what happens when a blockchain diverges into two potential paths forward. Many of the forks are addressed without any specific intervention. For example, forks happen any time two Bitcoin miners find a block at nearly the same time, but the protocol provides an automated solution to address this divergence. Forks can happen either because an issue arises regarding a network's transaction history or a new rule on transaction validity is enacted. These situations may involve an open-source code modification.

A soft fork is a change in the code that is backward compatible (and thus more benign). More specifically, it is a change in the protocol that restricts the ruleset enforced by full nodes. The Bitcoin blockchain has experienced several soft forks associated with technical software upgrades that did not alter the nature of the chain, for example.

A hard fork is a software upgrade that introduces a new rule to the network that is not compatible with the older code. For example, in 2017, the Bitcoin protocol split the network into two, and an alternative cryptocurrency (Bitcoin Cash) was created as a consequence. Substantial differences between community participants over the future development of the protocol motivated this schism.[24] LiteCoin (discussed earlier) is also a fork from the original Bitcoin. Another example occurred in 2016 when Ethereum split into two chains. In April 2016, a new company developed "The DAO," a venture capital firm that would have allowed investors to make decisions through smart contracts without human intervention, had its program not failed.[25] The venture raised $150 million before being hacked (Wong and Kar, 2016). The question then became whether the funds should have been returned to the rightful investors through an Ethereum hard fork (Kar 2016). Although the majority of community members accepted this, a substantial minority refused, leading to the creation of two versions of the blockchain, Ethereum (the modified chain) and Ethereum Classic (the original chain). In the first case, the hard fork did not change the blockchain (but created an incompatibility for subsequent transactions). In the second case, the hard fork retroactively changed the blockchain. One can argue the merits of each decision, but it exemplifies how blockchains are not immutable by construction. These hard forks were contentious in part because of the open permission-less nature of the platform, but it may be easier to implement with a more limited number of participants associated with permission blockchains.

---

[24]In this case, network participants receive both sets of crypto-assets.

[25]A decentralized autonomous organization (DAO) is a generic term for organizations that operate exclusively through smart contracts. "The DAO" was an example of such an organization that ultimately failed.

Both Sybil attacks and hard forks require the garnering of a sufficiently large percentage of participants to change the blockchain.[26] However, nothing prevents the development of codes that allows for editable blockchains. In fact, at least one case of such technology ("chameleon hashes") has been patented (in this case, changes are marked in the database (Accenture, 2016)). Naturally, this approach is not feasible in a completely open platform, but it may be useful in certain cases: correcting errors, removing illegitimate content, or compliance with privacy laws, for example (Matzutt et al., 2018).

1.9 Anonymity and Pseudo-Anonymity

A fourth issue is anonymity. Recall that initial blockchains such as the ones for Bitcoin and Ethereum guaranteed pseudo-anonymity but not complete anonymity.[27] Other tools are currently being developed to provide additional privacy. One such approach relies on zero-knowledge proofs, methods by which one party (the *prover*) can show conclusively to another party (the *verifier*) that she knows a value x, without revealing x or conveying any information apart from the fact that she knows this value. For example, a payer may prove that it has a proper authorization key without having to disclose it. zk-SNARK (Zero-Knowledge Succinct Non-Interactive Argument of Knowledge) is a specific implementation of the zero-proof approach that can be verified quickly ("succinct"), removing the need for a trusted intermediary ("noninteractive," see Greenspan (2016)).[28] Since 2017, Ethereum has included the feature through a pre-compiled (i.e., "ready to use") smart contract (Lundkvist, 2017). Currently, zk-SNARKSs are being considered for sidechains to increase privacy by allowing payments to occur in separate blockchains and then self-destruct following the transaction (Lundkvist 2017. Zcash, a cryptocurrency, relies on zk-SNARKSs to offer greater privacy. Interestingly, Zcash offers the option to "shield" the transaction (i.e., make it anonymous or not). As of December 2017, only around 4% of Zcash coins were in the shielded pool.[29] One possible explanation could be that the process of creating a transaction with zk-SNARKs remains slow and costly. Another issue with zk-SNARKs is that if a bad actor has access to the initial parameters necessary to set up the chain, they would be able to create false proofs that look valid to the verifier. For Zcash, this would mean the malicious party could create a potentially unlimited amount of counterfeit

[26] The required percentage varies and can be more or less than 50%.

[27] In fact, blockchains have been used to deanonymize other networks (e.g., Al Jawaheri et al. (2019), or Kalodner et al. (2017)).

[28] A more formal analysis of zk-SNARKs can be found in Ben-Sasson et al. (2019).

[29] Interested readers can find more information at https://en.wikipedia.org/wiki/Zcash

coins.[30] In contrast, zk-STARKs (zero-knowledge, Succinct, Transparent Argument of Knowledge) have been touted as a less costly and faster alternative to zk-SNARKs. Their biggest advantage is that no trusted setup is required. They are also expected to be more "quantum resistant" than zk-SNARKs. Zero-knowledge tools are not the only applications available to enhance privacy. Monero, for example, uses stealth addresses and ring signatures.[31] Stealth addresses are a technology that uses a one-time destination public keys address based on receivers' published addresses. It obscures a sender's IP address and uses a ring signature, which combines a sender's output address with a group of other possible sender addresses chosen randomly from the blockchain, making it impossible to determine who the original signer was. This approach appears to provide a lower level of privacy but offers a higher and greater computational speed (Mercer, 2016). Although Zcash and Monero are two of the leading privacy-oriented cryptocurrencies, they are not the only options. Dash is one example that promises privacy through the mixing of transactions. PIVX (Private Instant Verified Transaction) is the by-product of a DASH fork that led to some improvements, offering faster, more robust, and more private trade execution. Another example is Verge. Verge is not cryptographically private but simply obfuscates traffic and conceals a user's IP address when transacting through the use of TOR and i2P routing. Hyperledger Fabric offers options to create "channels," private "subnets" of communication between two or more specific network members for private and confidential transactions. Note that the different privacy features are becoming integrated. In the case of Jumblr, Komodo (a zero-knowledge fork of Zcash) is used to anonymize bitcoins through a series of atomic swaps. Although this conversation takes place in the context of cryptocurrencies, it is important in an enterprise context. Firms are unlikely to join a blockchain if access to the information cannot be protected.

1.10 Security

A fifth issue is security (Hilary, 2018). Security can be compromised in multiple ways in distributed ledgers. Naturally, code vulnerabilities can create issues. Perhaps the earliest example occurred in August 2010 when a developer found a bug that allowed for the massive creation of bitcoins.[32] The DAO failure is discussed previously. As projects grow in complexity, code size also increases. The code for Bitcoin core, for example, has increased from 3000 lines to several hundred

[30]The founder of Z-cash executed an elaborate "ceremony" to convince the rest of the world this was not an issue for the cryptocurrency (a video can be found at https://www.youtube.com/watch?v = D6dY-3x3teM).

[31]Naturally, no solution is fool-proof (see Tramer, Boneh and Paterson(2020)).

[32]The bug called CVE-2010-5139 was a number overflow error that led to the creation of at least 92 million irregular bitcoins. The bug was subsequently corrected.

thousand in 2020. Some projects require more than a million lines. Furthermore, the fluid nature of the technology and the desire to beat the competition may lead to some start-ups being careless in their code development.

Another source of concern is tied to the infrastructure of the chain. For example, Sybil attacks (discussed previously) can allow a bad actor to control the consensus mechanism. Nodes can also be subject to direct attacks, which are particularly concerning when there are a few (e.g., NEO discussed previously).

However, the main security concerns are probably located outside of the chains themselves. For example, we discuss oracles and sensors above. Another important vulnerability is located in cryptocurrency exchanges. These exchanges are platforms that enable the exchange of cryptocurrencies for other assets, such as conventional currencies or other digital currencies. Mt. Gox was the largest such platform at one point, handling 70% of all Bitcoin transactions in 2013 (Tanzarian, 2014). However, the site was hacked in 2014, and some 850,000 Bitcoins worth $450 million disappeared.[33] It is particularly easy for insiders to engineer hacks of these platforms. Although the distributed nature of blockchains allows them to deal with Distributed Denial of Service (DDOS) attacks more easily, this is not the case for these exchanges. Bitfinex, for example, one of the largest exchanges, was unable to operate for an hour because of such an attack in December 2017 (Cheng, 2017). Wallets create related vulnerabilities. Wallets (in this context) are devices that allow users to manage crypto-assets such as a bitcoin address. A bitcoin address is the hash of a public cryptographic key that is required for transactions to go through.[34] Wallets can either be located on a computer or a phone, on a dedicated mobile device, on the cloud, or even on a piece of paper. "Hot wallets" are connected to the internet while "cold wallets" are not. If one loses control of the wallet, one loses control of the crypto-assets, opening the possibility for ransomware and plain hacks if wallets are not well-protected.[35,36] For example, Gatecoin, a Hong Kong exchange, experienced an attack on its hot wallets, resulting in the loss of several millions of dollars. Cold wallets are harder to hack as they are not directly connected to the internet, but design flaws can allow bad actors to turn a cold wallet into a hot one. In 2016, Bitfinex was breached, causing 120,000 units of the cryptocurrency bitcoin, valued at $72 million at the time, to be stolen.

One possible line of defense against the theft of keys involves the use of dedicated equipment. Hardware security modules (HSMs), for example, are high-end crypto-processors that securely generate, protect, and store digital keys.[37] Another example

[33]The site was hacked for the first time in 2011 for a smaller amount (see Sharma (2017)).

[34]More specifically, the private key allows the verification of ownership for the public key and the assets connected to it. This allows for transfer of ownership to happen without the revelation of the private key to a third party.

[35]Ransomware is a form of malicious software that threatens to publish the victim's data or perpetually block access to it (usually by encrypting it) unless a ransom is paid.

[36]James Howells lost £4.2 million when he trashed a hard drive containing the private keys for 7500 bitcoins without realizing what it contained.

[37]Naturally, no system is fool-proof (see Steel (2019)).

is the use of HSMs by banks to validate PINs when customers withdraw cash from an ATM, or to validate transaction cryptograms when customers purchase goods at a merchant point-of-sale terminal. Instead of keeping the key on servers that can be vulnerable to network breaches, the keys are kept on an HSM. Chip manufacturers such as Intel have also designed security products that allow the operation of Trusted Execution Environment (TEE) (aka "safe enclaves"). Operating wallets in TEE mitigates the risks described previously (Thomsen, 2018).

1.11 Conclusion

A blockchain is essentially a database with a specific structure. Historically, databases were centralized entities with one owner (naturally, there could be multiple individuals representing this owner) and potentially many users. This basic technology started in the 1960s and now is very mature. For some applications, the blockchain approach still makes sense (e.g., a security exchange may want to centralize all transactions on one trading platform).

However, in many situations, there is a need for multiple actors with potentially diverging interests to share data. Two companies may need to share sales/purchasing records but have opposite interests. The traditional answer has been to establish separate databases that exchange information with each other. Electronic Data Interchange (EDI) solutions have been developed to facilitate these transactions, but for databases that interact infrequently (or operate in degraded environments), the exchange is likely to involve human intervention. Brokers dealing in illiquid products often trade over the phone, for example.

Of course, these data exchanges have costs like for any transaction. There is an initial cost to set up the database and marginal costs to process subsequent transactions. EDI systems are tied to specific processes, computer protocols, and document formats. The cost of integrating these different elements is significant and increases as the number of nodes in the network increase. Value Added Networks (VANs) are informational clearinghouses that are set up to facilitate EDI by centralizing and dispatching the data (through a hub-and-spoke system). They can mitigate some of these transaction costs but require to be trusted.

DLTs such as blockchain offer an alternative approach to data sharing problems by massively distributing the database and removing the notion of ownership. They make it easy to add nodes to the network and lower the cost of processing additional transactions. These marginal costs, however, remain higher than those associated with a centralized database that has been properly optimized for specific usage. Table 1.2 summarizes these different cost structures.

Although DLT removes the need for trusted intermediaries and offers additional features (such as added resiliency), the main benefit of DLT is to offer an alternative cost structure for databases. Most things accomplished with DLT can be done with an alternative technology, but many of these possibilities are not economically feasible.

Table 1.2 Summary of the costs

	Centralized Database	Network with EDI	Network without EDI	Blockchain
Owner	One	Many	Many	None
Setup cost	High to very high	High to moderate at the firm level but often redundant	Very low to low	Low to moderate
Cost of adding a node	Impossible	Moderate	High	Low
Cost of adding a transaction	Minimal	Low to medium	Very high	Medium to high

One framework for examining the optimality of a DLT approach is to consider the 4Vs of Big Data: Volume, Variety, Velocity, and Veracity. The core motivation of blockchain technology is to ensure that data cannot be easily manipulated (the database is BFT). However, we do not have much of a historical perspective on whether DLT can indeed provide security that is superior to a traditional database protected with state-of-the-art technology. DLT security can also be negatively affected by layers built around the DLT per se (e.g., wallets, API, etc.). DLT can aggregate heterogeneous systems and add value through tokenization and smart contracts; thus, DLTs hold the promise of better integration of IoT. This appears to be one of the main benefits of the technology. Improved integration can also acquire data faster, but processing is less efficient than with traditional systems at the moment. The effect on Velocity is therefore generally undetermined. Finally, efficiency and scalability are currently the two main problems of this emerging technology. DLT is, therefore, unlikely to help with the volume of data.

References

Accenture, Press Release, Sept. 20, 2016., https://newsroom.accenture.com/news/accenture-debuts-prototype-of-editable-blockchain-for-enterprise-and-permissioned-systems.htm.

Al Jawaheri, H., Al Sabah, M., Boshmaf, Y., Erbad, A. (2019). Deanonymizing Tor hidden service users through Bitcoin transactions analysis, working paper, https://arxiv.org/pdf/1801.07501.pdf

Aru, I. (2017). Tokenization: The force behind blockchain technology, from https://cointelegraph.com/news/tokenization-the-force-behind-blockchain-technology

Baird, L. (2018). Hashgraph consensus: Detailed examples, from https://www.swirlds.com/downloads/SWIRLDS-TR-2016-02.pdf.

Ben-Sasson, E., Chiesa, A., Tromer, E., and Virza, M. (2019). Succinct non-interactive zero knowledge for a von Neumann architecture, https://eprint.iacr.org/2013/879.pdf

Brown, R. (2016). On distributed databases and distributed ledgers, from https://gendal.me/2016/11/08/on-distributed-databases-and-distributed-ledgers/

Buterin, V. (2015). Merkling in Ethereum, https://blog.ethereum.org/2015/11/15/merkling-in-ethereum/

Cameron-Huff, A. (2017). How tokenization is putting real-world assets on blockchains, from https://bitcoinmagazine.com/articles/op-ed-how-tokenization-putting-real-world-assets-blockchains/

Castor, A. (2017). A short guide to bitcoin forks, from https://www.coindesk.com/short-guide-bitcoin-forks-explained/

Cheng, E. (2017). Cyberattack temporarily hits bitcoin exchange Bitfinex, from https://www.cnbc.com/2017/12/04/cyberattack-temporarily-hits-bitcoin-exchange-bitfinex.html

Gheorghiu, V., Gorbunov, S., Mosca, M., and Munson, B. (2017). Quantum-proofing the blockchain, from https://evolutionq.com/assets/mosca_quantum-proofing-the-blockchain_blockchain-research-institute.pdf

Greenspan, G. (2016). Understanding zero knowledge blockchains, from https://www.multichain.com/blog/2016/11/understanding-zero-knowledge-blockchains/

Hilary, G., Blockchain: Security and confidentiality. (December 1, 2018). French Military Police Journal (Revue de la Gendarmerie Nationale), Issue 4, 2018, 99-103, https://ssrn.com/abstract=3327248 or doi:https://doi.org/10.2139/ssrn.3327248.

Kalodner, H., Goldfeder, S., Chator, A., Möser, M., Narayanan, A. (2017). BlockSci: Design and applications of a blockchain analysis platform, working paper, https://arxiv.org/pdf/1709.02489.pdf.

Kar, I. (2016). The developers behind Ethereum are hacking the hacker that hacked it, from https://qz.com/713078/the-developers-behind-ethereum-are-hacking-the-hacker-that-hacked-it/

Light, J. (2017). The differences between a hard fork, a soft fork, and a chain split, and what they mean for the future of bitcoin, from https://medium.com/@lightcoin/the-differences-between-a-hard-fork-a-soft-fork-and-a-chain-split-and-what-they-mean-for-the-769273f358c9

Lundkvist, C. (2017). Introduction to zk-SNARKs with Examples, https://media.consensys.net/introduction-to-zksnarks-with-examples-3283b554fc3b

Lundkvist, C. (2019). SimpleMultiSig updates: EIP712 and security audit, from https://www.coindesk.com/zk-starks-new-take-on-zcash-tech-could-power-truly-private-blockchains/

Matzutt, R., Hiller, J., Henze, M., Ziegeldorf, J. H., Mullmann, D., Hohlfeld, O., and Wehrle, K. (2018). Quantitative analysis of the impact of arbitrary blockchain content on Bitcoin, Proc. 22nd International Conference on Financial Cryptography and Data Security 2018.

Mercer, R. (2016). Privacy on the Blockchain: Unique ring signatures, https://arxiv.org/abs/1612.01188

O'Ham, T. (2018). NEO blockchain goes down after a single node disconnects temporarily, from https://bitsonline.com/neo-blockchain-tanks/

Ray, S. (2017). Merkle trees, from https://hackernoon.com/merkle-trees-181cb4bc30b4

Rutlan, E. (2017). Blockchain Byte, R3 Research, https://www.finra.org/sites/default/files/2017_BC_Byte.pdf

Sandner (2017). Comparison of Ethereum, Hyperledger Fabric and Corda, http://explore-ip.com/2017_Comparison-of-Ethereum-Hyperledger-Corda.pdf

Sharma, M. (2017). 5 Bitcoin disasters of all time; why it's never safe to invest in virtual currency businesstoday.in/exclusive/rebrain-or-rot/bitcoin-disasters-virtual-currency-cryptocurrency-invest-in-bitcoin/story/265555.html

Steel, G. (2019). How ledger hacked an HSM, from https://cryptosense.com/blog/how-ledger-hacked-an-hsm

Tanzarian, A. (2014). #bitcoinfail: Top 10 Failures in Bitcoin History, from https://cointelegraph.com/news/bitcoinfail-top-10-failures-in-bitcoin-history

Thomsen, S. (2018). Ethereum wallet in a trusted execution environment/secure enclave, from https://medium.com/weeves-world/ethereum-wallet-in-a-trusted-execution-environment-secure-enclave-b200b4df9f5f

Town, S. (2018). Introduction to Chainlink (LINK)—The decentralized oracle network, from https://cryptoslate.com/chainlink/

Tramer, F., Boneh, D. and Paterson, K. G. (2020). Remote side-channel attacks on anonymous transactions, working paper, from https://crypto.stanford.edu/timings/

Valenta, M. and Sandner, P. (2017). Comparison of Ethereum, Hyperledger Fabric and Corda, FSBC Working Paper, http://explore-ip.com/2017_Comparison-of-Ethereum-Hyperledger-Corda.pdf

Vermeulen (2016). VisaNet—handling 100,000 transactions per minute, from https://mybroadband.co.za/news/security/190348-visanet-handling-100000-transactions-per-minute.html

Vermeulen (2017). Bitcoin and Ethereum vs visa and PayPal—transactions per second, from https://mybroadband.co.za/news/banking/206742-bitcoin-and-ethereum-vs-visa-and-paypal-transactions-per-second.html

Wong, J. I. and Kar, I. (2016). Everything you need to know about the Ethereum "hard fork", from https://qz.com/730004/everything-you-need-to-know-about-the-ethereum-hard-fork/

Chapter 2
Operational and Financial Implications of Transactionalizing Multi-Machine Maneuvers in Self-Organizing Autonomous Systems

Karl Wunderlich

2.1 Introduction

Autonomous machines are capable of sensing localized obstacles and performing tasks without human direction. Autonomous machines may also be *mobile*, that is, possess the ability to explore their immediate environment while fulfilling assigned tasks. Examples of autonomous machines include self-driving passenger vehicles, autonomous delivery drones, and unmanned boats or submersibles. Note that autonomy differs from teleoperation or remote piloting, where a human operator drives, flies, or directs a machine from a distance.

When multiple autonomous machines operate near one another, contemporaneous motions and actions of machines must be organized to encourage an efficient and collision-free operational environment. Machines may be organized by a centralized third party, a *controller*, who computes optimal paths and action and directs machines according to a system-wide plan. An example is current air traffic control systems where human air traffic controllers direct human pilots to follow specific flight paths to ensure safe distances are maintained aircraft.

Alternatively, systems of mobile entities may *self-organize*. In this case, autonomous machines independently determine concurrent motions and actions without direction from a controller entity. Decentralized self-organizing systems can range from unconstrained, pure ad hoc interactions to operations based on simple rule sets to complex coordination-based shared intent and negotiation (e.g., as described in Murata and Kurokawa (2012) in a general case, or in Toksöz et al. (2019) for drone swarms). A familiar example of a decentralized self-organization is roadway traffic operations, where simple rules (like driving on the right-hand

K. Wunderlich (✉)
Noblis, Washington, DC, USA
e-mail: kwunderl@noblis.org

V. Babich et al. (eds.), *Innovative Technology at the Interface of Finance and Operations*, Springer Series in Supply Chain Management 11,
https://doi.org/10.1007/978-3-030-75729-8_2

side of the road), are combined with supporting roadside control equipment (e.g., stop lights). Each driver operates their vehicle with the implicit understanding that all other vehicles will also obey established rule sets and control device indicators. Decentralized forms of control are logical in this case since there are millions of vehicles in motion at any time creating billions of instances of potential collision to be individually identified and deconflicted.

Increasingly capable, autonomous, and mobile machines—either deployed operationally or in development—are poised to augment, transform, or disrupt current forms of human activity in a wide range of physical environments. While a single, autonomous vehicle traversing a roadway may be a technological marvel, it is designed to operate within current norms. That is, it is restricted to maneuvers expected from a human-driven vehicle. Several million such autonomous vehicles in motion at the same time on the roadway pose deeper questions about whether legacy forms of general self-organization compensating for the limitations of human drivers are still practical, or even desirable.

This chapter examines the concept of a self-organizing, autonomous system presented as a series of related processes that can be adapted for a world of increasingly capable autonomous machines operating at scale. This chapter specifically concerns itself with systems of self-organizing machines with the following attributes:

- autonomous (i.e., capable of some form of imperfect sensing and maneuvering)
- heterogeneous (i.e., machines differ significantly in size, ability to maneuver, and ability to sense, as well as differences in desired trip path, urgency, and ownership)
- non-adversarial (i.e., no machine seeks intentional collisions or to damage other machines) and
- episodic (i.e., machines have many, time-limited, and varied small-group encounters drawing from a large pool of potential machine participants).

Modern transportation systems are excellent examples of such self-organizing systems when the notion of autonomy includes human driven, piloted, or remotely operated machines: roadway and rail systems, general aviation, near-surface aerial drone operations, and ship traffic operating on (or below) the surface of bodies of water. Other examples include machines operating collectively in orbit, space, or in extraterrestrial environments. Systems excluded from consideration are self-organizing systems of autonomous machines with adversarial intent (e.g., military applications) and single-purpose centralized systems (e.g., a factory floor or automated warehouse), where all the motions of all machines can be accurately observed and precisely directed.

Using a framework for classifying machine intent, autonomy, and capability to self-organize, this chapter examines how to create powerful new operational models that simultaneously derive and quantify the underlying value proposition related to machine motion and action. These revealed values, and the transactional nature of repeated machine-to-machine interactions, create an opportunity to link value contribution and distribution (i.e., system finance) more effectively with optimizing system safety and efficiency (i.e., system operations). Machine-centric, self-organizing systems need not resemble the legacy human-centric systems they are poised to replace. Instead, the new systems may hold the potential to resolve many of the seemingly intractable financial and operational issues inherent to current human-centric systems.

First, this chapter introduces some fundamental tactical aspects of self-organizing systems, including an initial discussion regarding machine *negotiation over shared space,* and a range of methods for deconflicting maneuvers. Next, we introduce the notion of machine trust and the critical interplay between *trust and priority* that is critical to the integrity of collective maneuver planning. *Collective maneuver planning* is systematized into an iterative process that includes conflict identification, negotiation, and priority determination—and when complete, transformed into a multi-machine transaction. The *multi-machine maneuver transaction* is examined in more detail to consider the full self-organizing ecosystem, including the role of fixed infrastructure and system maintenance. Finally, we explore the foundational requirement for transaction verification and the concept of *machine-earned trust.* We further examine machine-earned trust, including how it differs foundationally from the human concept of trust, and the role it can play in unlocking unrealized potential in system safety, efficiency, and finance. The chapter concludes with an examination of these principles as they apply to current models of *roadway operations and finance.*

2.2 Negotiation over Shared Space

Consider four autonomous machines operating in a two-dimensional constrained space (Fig. 2.1). There is a risk of collision as the machines (represented by alphabetically indexed circles) move among target waypoints (shown as numbered triangles) performing actions. Machines must stay within the boundaries of the space while avoiding collisions with any obstructions (indicated with rounded square shapes) or other autonomous machines. The next target waypoint for each machine is indicated by the shaded arrow next to each respective machine, pointed in the general direction of anticipated motion.

We assume each machine can sense (imperfectly) nearby fixed or dynamic obstacles but has limited or no information regarding obstacles beyond the limited range of their sensors. From sensor inputs, a machine can create a localized probability map of its surroundings that reflects the intrinsic collision risk of movement along any path in the space. In Fig. 2.1, Machine B is likely to create a map that shows a low chance of immediate collision on a path directly toward Waypoint 4, but a high chance on a direct course toward Waypoint 1 where there is a fixed obstruction. Machine B may have limited or no knowledge regarding the location of other fixed obstacles further away or other machines in locations hidden behind obstructions. In this case, Machine B may have no information regarding the current location of Machine A because of sensor interference from the obstruction located between Waypoints 1 and 3.

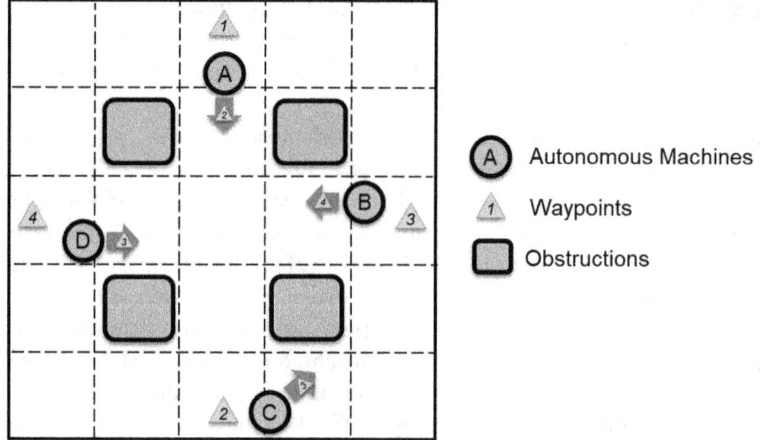

Fig. 2.1 Multiple autonomous machines in a constrained space

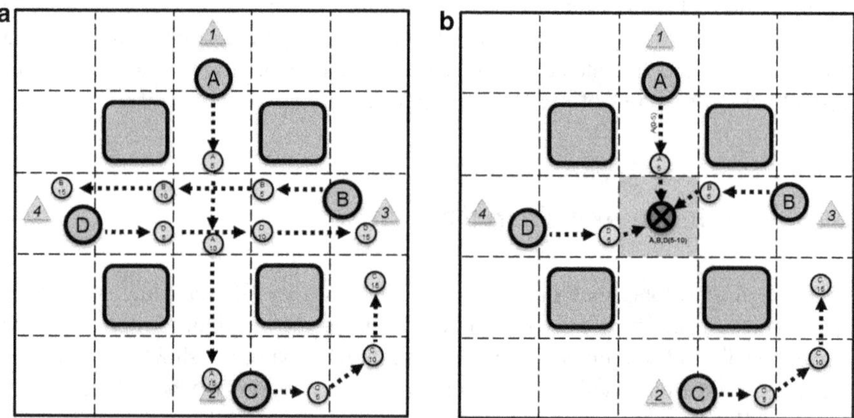

Fig. 2.2 (**a**) Unconstrained machine path planning. (**b**) Path conflict identification

Based on current information on obstacle location, each machine plans for upcoming motion with the eventual goal of reaching the next waypoint. This plan of motion is bounded by a *maneuver horizon*. In this case, consider a 15 s maneuver horizon. The set of unconstrained motion paths developed by each machine are shown in Fig. 2.2a. Note that the path is broken into three segments with smaller circles showing the expected location of the machine at 5 s intervals, that is, at times 5, 10, and 15 s (the end of the current maneuver horizon). Barring some inability to successfully maneuver along these paths, if there were no other machines in the space, each of the machines could reach or nearly reach their target waypoints within the maneuver horizon.

However, there *are* other machines in the constrained space. An examination of the unconstrained path plans between 5 and 10 s shows that three machines have a chance of collision near the center of the overall space (Fig. 2.2b). We may observe that this overlap of desired path plans represents a *conflict* in the system that must be *deconflicted* to reduce the risk of collisions among machines.

A critical assumption regarding the deconfliction of path plans regards whether the machines operate in *isolation* (i.e., they cannot communicate with each other) or in *coordination* (where machines can communicate with each other). If the machines are operating in complete isolation (no information shared among machines) the conflict will be unknown to Machines A, B, and D until they approach the center of the space and their individual sensor systems can detect each another. At this point, each of the machines may consider one of the four options:

- *Retreat* to their original positions, ending up no closer to their target waypoints
- *Wait* for the newly discovered dynamic obstacles to move away before continuing over the initial planned path
- *Replan* based on its current understanding of obstacle location or
- *Proceed*, or move forward, on the current path regardless of collision risk.

What cannot be known is the likelihood that any or all machines will wait, proceed, replan, retreat, or proceed. As a result, the system is either highly inefficient (machines continue to myopically maneuver and risk gridlock) or acutely unsafe (machines lurch into each other), or some combination of these two unfavorable attributes.

Common rule sets can be a useful tool in deconfliction. In our example, the machines might all have common programming to consider only clockwise motion around the edge of shared space, traversing waypoints {1,3,2,4} in order while keeping suitably distant from any detected obstacle (fixed or other machines). This reduces collision risk, but the system may be inefficient. Machines may have waypoint combinations that do not conform to this pattern. For example, if the counterclockwise sequence {4,2,3,1} were assigned to a machine, it would require each machine to traverse three-quarters of the total perimeter of the space to reach each waypoint. Meanwhile, the most efficient shortcut in the space, the center, would remain unused. Deconfliction through common rulesets limits adaptation to the specific risks and opportunities resulting from individual deconfliction scenarios. Another issue with common rule sets is the risk that heterogenous machines may not be programmed with a consistent ruleset—or may even have a different expected ruleset. An analogy is a human driver trained to follow right-hand of the road rule sets (e.g., like those used in North America) reverting to right-hand driving in a system where left-hand driving prevails (e.g., those used in the United Kingdom). Common rule sets are only practical in systems where they are observed with extremely rare exceptions.

Common rule sets reflect the ability of entities within the system to communicate with each other. When ability to communicate is limited, common rule sets are critical to system safety and operational efficiency. Human drivers share intent with other nearby human drivers using a turn signal indicator, making eye contact with other drivers, honking the vehicle horn, and other visual and auditory cues. Some signals are considered more urgent (e.g., honking) than others (e.g., the use of a turn signal). However, the human ability to communicate using visual and auditory signaling with other drivers is extremely limited in scope, speed, and precision when compared to the potential ability of autonomous machines. Autonomous machines, using wireless communications technology, have a significant advantage over humans in the capability to exchange data regarding situational awareness, indicate intent, and facilitate negotiation among machines. For example, this includes the ability to share complex data regarding known obstacles and intended motion paths. This implies that conflicts may be anticipated and avoided in a new transaction-driven method, if a common deconfliction process could be introduced. This new form of deconfliction designed around the strengths of wirelessly connected autonomous machines need not imitate limited human-centric deconfliction that compensate for limited communications with strong common rule sets. However, before introducing such a machine-centric deconfliction process, there are two foundational concepts in deconfliction to consider: *priority* and *trust.*

2.3 Priority and Trust in Collective Maneuver Planning

Deconfliction is impossible without establishing *priority*. Simply put, two machines cannot occupy the same space at the same time. If two machines do attempt to occupy the same space at the same time, the result is collision. Therefore, some form of priority access to the dynamic space is required. The machine which receives priority may simply maintain its current path plan. The machine which *yields* priority must replan and reject any new path which conflicts with the path plan of the machine with priority. Priority may be determined in various ways; however, how priority is determined in a system can create significantly different outcomes with respect to both system efficiency and equity.

Further, priority is meaningless without *trust.* If a machine agrees to yield priority, but then simply fails to yield, then a collision is likely to occur. In a system where machine adherence to priority mechanisms is unreliable, all machines will be required to move cautiously and ignore all signals of intent generated by other machines. We will return to the notion, dimensions, and quantification of *machine trust* later. For now, however, assume that the machines depicted in our example (Figs. 2.1 and 2.2a, b) have some rudimentary form of non-absolute trust that allows for the determination of priority. Fundamental methods of priority determination include:

- *Hierarchical priority*, in which priority is determined by a common rule set that assigns priority based on a classification of machine identity and the nature of the desired maneuver
- *Random priority,* in which priority is assigned to one machine by chance and
- *Negotiated priority,* in which priority is assigned to the machine making the highest bid.

Hierarchical priority. A hierarchical priority system requires a rule set covering all possible machines in all possible situations. For example, we may consider a common rule declaring that all vehicles conducting police or emergency response vehicles have priority over vehicles who are not performing these critical services. Priority is easily determined when vehicles from two different priority classes have conflicting path plans—the nonemergency vehicle yields priority. However, this approach cannot systematically determine priority among vehicles in the same priority class, e.g., in the case of conflict between a police vehicle and an emergency response vehicle.

Priority among vehicles of the same priority class may be resolved based on additional rules related to the nature of the desired maneuver. For example, we may consider a rule declaring that paths with right-hand turn maneuvers have priority or left-hand turning maneuvers, an analog of the "right-before-left" priority provisions in current human driver rule sets for stop-controlled intersections. Such rule sets may be situational (e.g., only in stop-controlled intersection) or general (all situations). Situational hierarchical prioritization requires a nearly limitless set of well-defined situations, carefully constructed to avoid overlap. General hierarchical prioritization rules may result in highly inefficient or inequitable operational scenarios. Consider the case of one vehicle attempting to turn left against the flow of many machines all turning right. The left-turning vehicle, if it cannot backup or otherwise maneuver, this would-be left-turning vehicle will wait indefinitely until there are no right-turning vehicles.

Random priority. A simple method of determining priority is to assign it randomly among machines with conflicting paths. Random priority resolves issues like the indefinitely waiting left-hand turning vehicle just discussed. Hybrid priority based on machine type (e.g., emergency response vehicles) and random assignment can also be considered. However, one limitation of random priority is that it often does not yield particularly efficient use of conflicted space. This is because random priority inherently implies that all parties in contention for the use of the space have identical urgency and that the value of the space is unconsidered (or considered to have no value). Yielding machines are not compensated in any individual transaction. Over time, all machines may receive priority at equal rates in a pure random system, but in the moment the act of *yielding* is an uncompensated action allocating some unmeasured value to the vehicle receiving priority.

Negotiated priority. Using negotiation to resolve contention over space provides critical information revealing the dynamic value of that space. What is the value of moving goods and/or people from one location to another? A ship delivering cargo is paid for the delivery of that cargo to a specific location according to a delivery contract. A train moving passengers from one city contains passengers who purchased tickets that reveal the value of that service versus competing alternatives. However, the value of the space in the cargo hold or the seat on the train depends on the willingness to pay of goods owners (in the case of the ship) or the passenger (in the case of the train). When there is high demand for that space (cargo hold section or seat) priority is determined by whoever is willing to pay the highest price for the space. The emergent value of the space is an important market signal—both to the shipowner and the train operator. This signal incentivizes either an increase in carrying capacity (e.g., more seats on the train), efficient allocation of fixed capacity (e.g., train passengers with flexibility opt to travel on other trains with lower demand), or some combination of both increased capacity and efficient allocation.

Reconsider our example with an identified conflict in the center of the shared constrained space (Fig. 2.3). First, let us introduce information regarding the inherent value of reaching the next waypoint for each machine (using some generic unit of value). For example, Machine A will receive 32 units of value for reaching Waypoint 2. In more complicated constructs, the value of reaching each waypoint may be dynamic, e.g., 32 units of value if reached before some deadline. However, for this example, we will consider value for reaching a specific waypoint that does not vary dynamically.

In terms of *urgency*, Machine A should be willing to pay the most for a direct path to Waypoint 2 because among Machines A, B, and D in contention for the center space, it will receive the highest reward for reaching the next waypoint compared to other machines. Priority access to the high-value center of the constrained space can thus be negotiated using an auction process among machines with conflicting paths.

In this case, let us assume that the machines negotiate using a simple *sealed-bid auction* system. Each machine submits a single bid. The winner of the auction is the highest bidder, with ties broken randomly and price set at the second highest bid plus one unit of value. Fig. 2.4 illustrates the process in our example, with Machine A winning the auction with a bid of 10 units. The revealed value of the center space between $t = 5$ and $t = 10$ is 8 units, equal to the second-highest bid submitted by Machine B plus one unit. In a shared collective maneuver plan resulting from the sealed-bid auction, Machines B and D agree to yield to Machine A and are entitled to some (or all) of the 8 units of value paid by Machine A for priority. Note that the bid of Machine C is not considered because it did not have a conflicting initial path in the path planning horizon.

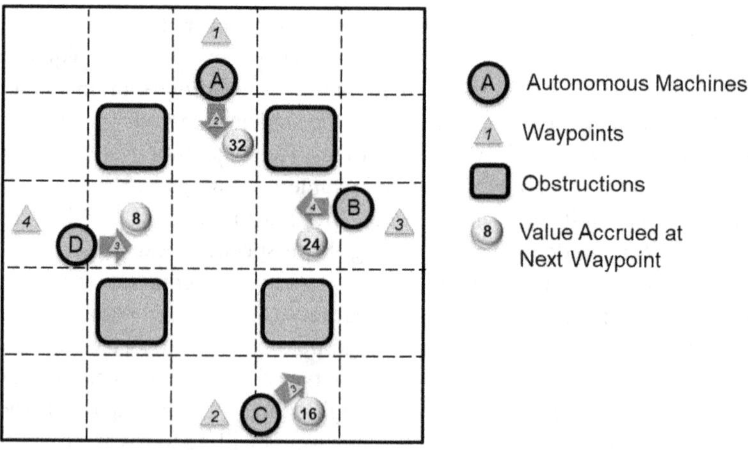

Fig. 2.3 Value of reaching waypoints for each autonomous machine

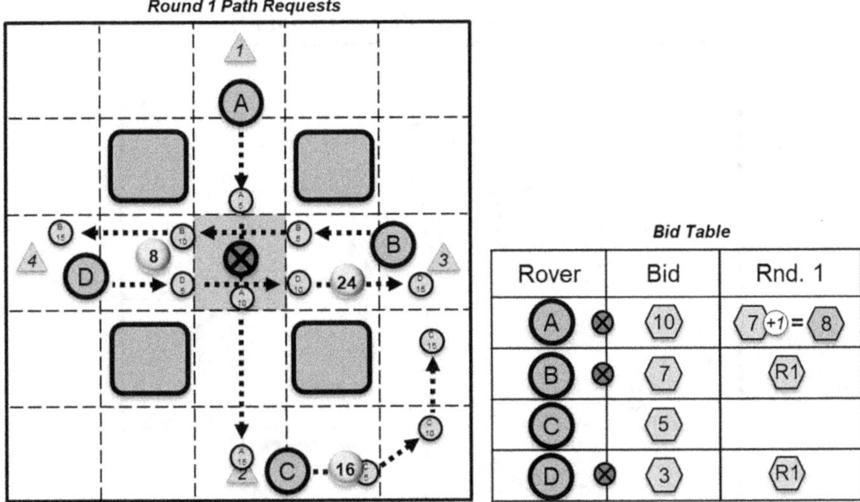

Rover	Bid	Rnd. 1
A	10	7 (+1) = 8
B	7	R1
C	5	
D	3	R1

Fig. 2.4 Sealed bid auction table

The result of the initial round of bidding establishes that Machine A will have highest priority. Before other machines can consider alternative paths, the maneuver plan must reflect the dynamic space now reserved for use by Machine A. Fig. 2.5 shows that Machine A will occupy some space between the two obstacles nearest to Waypoint 1 in the first 5 s, occupy some part of the center space in the following 5 s interval, and traverse some part of the space nearest to Waypoint 2 in the final 5 s interval. How much lateral and longitudinal space should be reserved for Machine A depends on how *trusted* that machine is to maneuver precisely along the projected path. We will revisit the notion of *maneuver precision trust* later. However, assume that no two machines can be reliably trusted to share any individual grid space in the same 5 s period. The result is that the space reserved for each machine encompasses all individual grid space traversed within each 5 s interval (reflected in Fig. 2.5). Now excluding from consideration the space reflecting the priority of Machine A, a second round of negotiated path planning can be conducted with the remaining three machines (Fig. 2.6). Here, Machine B and Machine D submit desired paths to advance to the edge of the center space by $t = 10$, wait for Machine A to clear, and then advance towards the target waypoint. However, this creates a conflict for the center space in the last 5 s time interval. Fig. 2.6 shows that Machine B has the highest bid in this round (Fig. 2.7).

Machine B receives priority over Machine D for the contested center space between $t = 10$ and $t = 15$ with a bid of 7 units and a revealed value of 4 units (one unit higher than Machine D's bid of 3 units). Machine D is noted as a yielding vehicle in Round 2 and is eligible for compensation. Note that once again, the desired path of Machine C is not in conflict, just as it was not in conflict in Round 1.

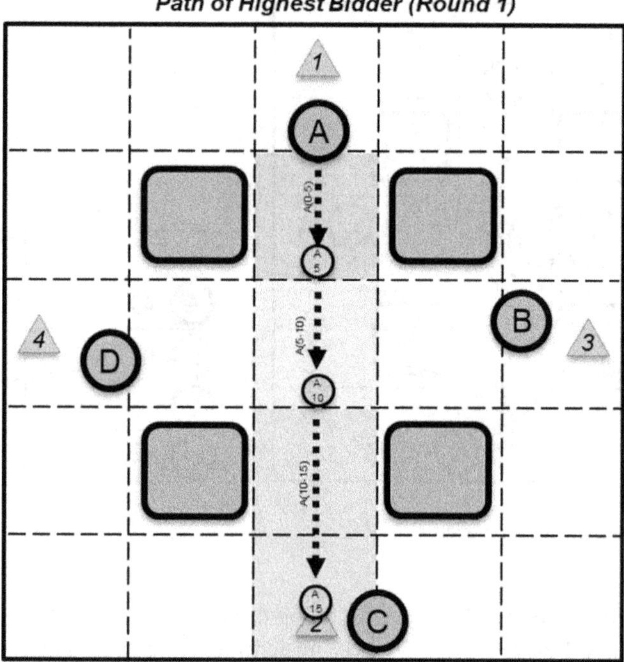

Fig. 2.5 Space reserved for highest priority machine

Machine B is allocated the dynamic space associated with the Round 2 priority path, including the deconflicted center space between $t = 10$ and $t = 15$ (Fig. 2.8a). In a third round of path planning, Machine D diverts toward Waypoint 1 to avoid the now fully reserved center space. Machine C again submits a plan to work toward Waypoint 3 using the edge of the permitted maneuver space (Fig. 2.8b). There is no conflict between the paths of Machine B and Machine D, so deconfliction is not needed, priority need not be determined, and any bids are disregarded.

We now have a complete collective maneuver plan (Fig. 2.9) that is both fully deconflicted and contains a clear record of machines designated as receiving priority (Machine A paying 8 units in Round 1 and Machine B paying 4 units in Round 2) or yielding (Machines B and D in Round 1, and Machine D in Round 2). These are the fundamental elements of a multiparty transaction among all machines that include an emergent valuation of dynamic space within the maneuver space. If all machines execute within prescribed tolerances, then the machines will have successfully self-organized simultaneously to deconflict motion (ensuring safety), maximizing value of motion (improving efficiency), and revealing the value of dynamic space.

Verifying maneuvers. This transaction is of little value unless the machines can be trusted to carry it out. Autonomous machines, like humans, are not deterministic in performance, even when conducting identical maneuvers in identical conditions

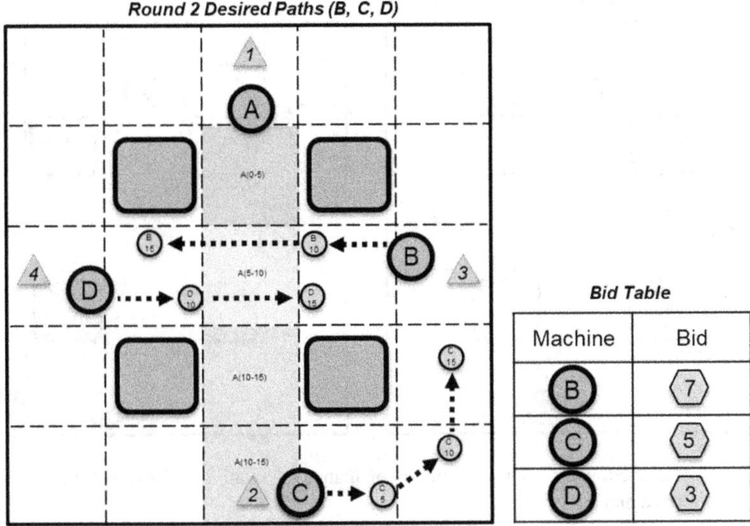

Fig. 2.6 Desired paths and bids in second planning round

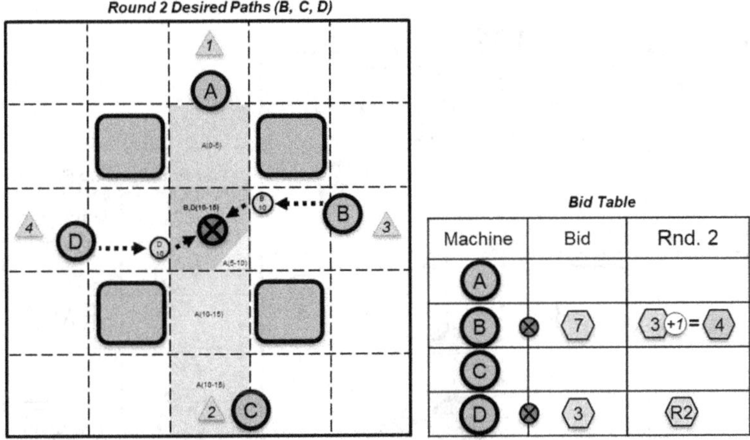

Fig. 2.7 Priority determination in second planning round

over time. The result is some variation in maneuver precision when machines attempt to follow the completed maneuver plan.

That said, by definition, autonomous machines can sense the position of objects near them, including other machines. This implies that all autonomous machines may also play a role in verifying that the collective transaction has been observed (within tolerances) by all participating machines. Consider our example where Machine A accelerates too quickly in the first 5 s and ends up overshooting the maneuver plan, entering the center grid element of the maneuver space prior to

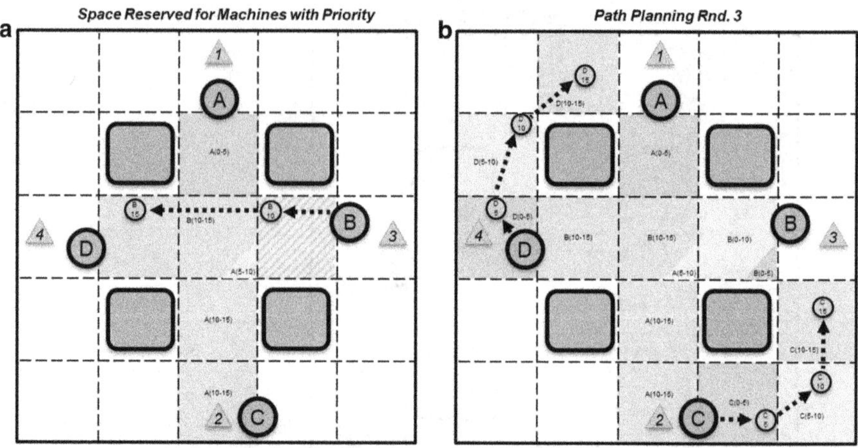

Fig. 2.8 (**a**) Reserved space after two rounds of maneuver planning. (**b**) Desired paths in third round of collective maneuver planning

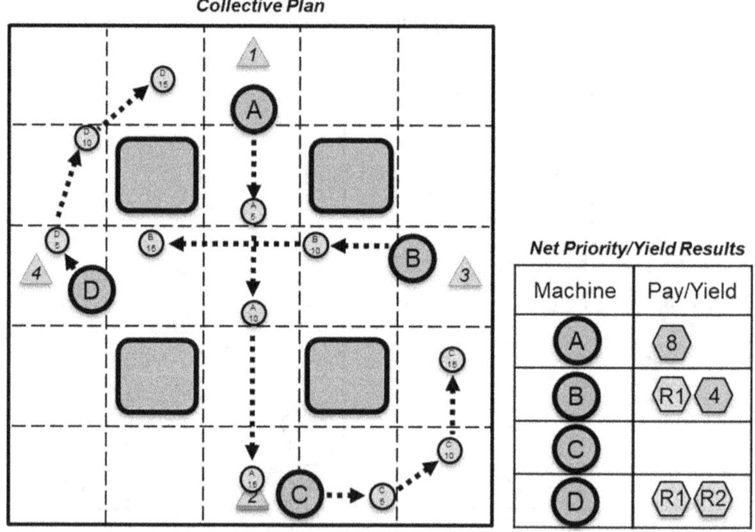

Fig. 2.9 Completed maneuver plan with priority/yield elements

time $t = 5$ (Fig. 2.10). Machine B may detect the premature arrival of Machine A and flag this deviation from the collective maneuver plan. In addition, Machine A may be required to self-report position as a requirement of collective maneuver planning. In either case, all future collective maneuver planning should be cognizant of the fact that Machine A may not be reliably trusted to execute against the maneuver precision assumed in this specific collective maneuver plan. Conversely, other machines able to remain within the tolerances of the maneuver plan have

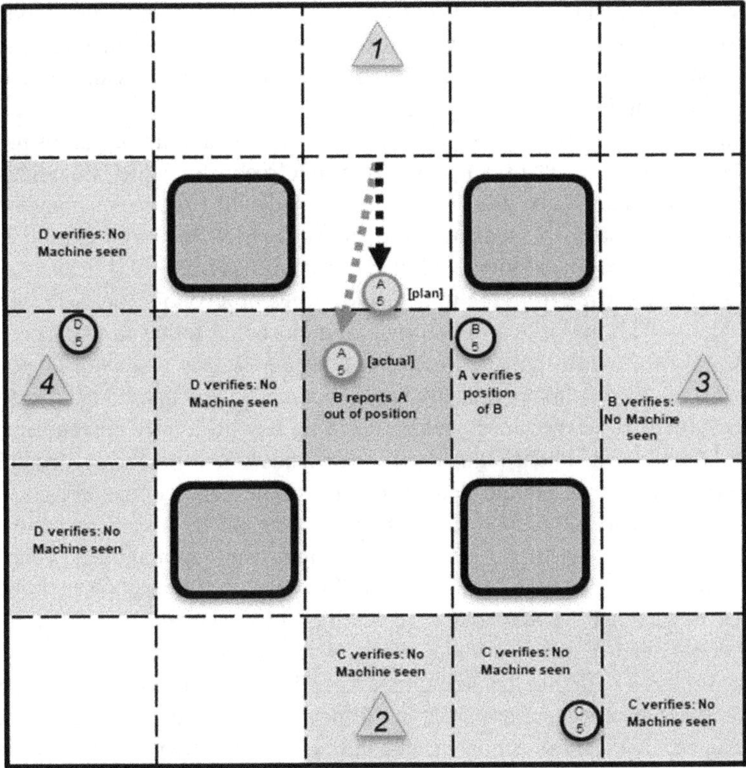

Fig. 2.10 Detected deviation from maneuver plan

demonstrated, at least in this specific instance, they have earned some incremental amount of trust that they could complete a similar maneuver in future interactions.

Another key outcome from the negotiation over shared space with verification is that the collective maneuver plan can serve as the basis for a *multi-machine transaction*. This transaction includes the determination of priority among machines, assigned paths, and tolerances, as well as pending compensatory payments. It is a smart contract in the sense that terms can be added to the transaction and can be verified, and machines that fail to adhere to or disrupt the terms of agreement face specific consequences (e.g., liability for additional payments and/or loss of earned trust).

2.4 Machine Trust

We have presented how a notional concept of trust is required to enable machine maneuver priority and multi-machine negotiation over shared maneuver space.

However, the notional concept of *machine trust* must be defined with additional dimension and precision to create a comprehensive ecosystem of multi-machine transactions that can both optimize long-term operations and provide a sustainable source of system finance.

Human trust provides a good reference point to begin a discussion of machine trust. Human trust in self-organizing system like roadway traffic is predicated on the assumption that other drivers understand and will follow the common rule sets regarding behavior in a shared system. We expect that, with extremely rare exception, other drivers encountered in the system will have valid licenses and be operating vehicles free from the influence of drugs or alcohol. That said, our trust lies primarily with the system of common rule sets being followed with some level of precision—not with individual drivers. Drawing from a vast pool of potential other drivers, we cannot practically log encounters with individual drivers and instantly recall past experiences before deciding how to jointly maneuver. Driver identity is unknown, intent signaling is rudimentary, and maneuver execution is rigidly channelized and controlled by common rule sets. Human driver trust is essentially a binary construct. That is, we expect other drivers to conform to common rules (e.g., turn right only from the right-hand lane) and act accordingly until we observe some egregious violation of that rule set. In this sense, individual vehicles can be treated as untrusted (e.g., a vehicle observed to be weaving aimlessly among lanes) and be given a wider berth. New drivers will even broadcast their untrusted status by affixing magnets emblazoned with such phrases as "New Driver" to alert others to expect actions from the vehicle that may not conform to common rule sets. Other drivers presumably take notice, closely observe untrusted vehicle behavior, and drive more cautiously near such a vehicle.

Machine trust is similar in concept to human trust but differs significantly in nature and representation from human trust. Wirelessly communicating autonomous machines need not be subject to the same limitations as humans. Fundamentally, wirelessly connected autonomous machines can represent trust with complexity, dimension, and precision that far exceed human capabilities.

First, machine trust can be represented using a *nonbinary, individualized* frame of reference. Machines that make relatively small violations in maneuver execution, for example, may be given slightly wider berth. Machines that make large violations or disregard maneuver plans may be treated with even more caution. Further, if persistent machine identity is known to all other machines engaged in maneuver planning, each *individual* machine can be differentiated and treated differently from each other, appropriate to the level of demonstrated reliability of that machine in past interactions.

Second, machine trust is *multidimensional*. We have introduced the dimension of maneuver trust in our example with machines negotiating over shared space. But maneuver trust is just one aspect of machine trust that can be represented and utilized in collective maneuver planning. Four fundamental aspects of machine trust include:

- *Identity trust.* Is the machine entering into collective maneuver planning the machine it purports to be? This is critical since machine trust is individualized. If a machine can easily spoof the identity (and earned trust) of another machine, then no aspect of machine trust can be trusted to be valid.
- *Reported position trust.* Autonomous machines can share current and projected position with each other to assist in maneuver planning. Complex and precise maneuver planning requires precise positioning as two machines cannot pass near to each other if positioning is highly imprecise.
- *Sensor trust.* How accurate are sensor readings shared by one machine with other machines? Another key advantage of machines over humans is that machines can share detailed maps of local obstacles with each other, practically extending the collective range and improving the situational awareness of all machines. When sensors overlap (one machine detects an obstacle and another does not) then relative machine sensor trust can be used to influence whether the collective plan will consider the obstacle to be more or less certain.
- *Maneuver trust.* How well does the machine adhere to the path assigned to it in collective maneuver planning? When trust is low, then larger tolerances must be allocated to that vehicle. Conversely, when trust is high, then paths with smaller tolerances can be safely allocated.

2.5 An Earned Machine Trust Ecosystem

In the introduction to this chapter, we focused our attention on self-organizing autonomous systems that are *episodic* in nature. This implies that an individual machine is likely to engage in multiple collective maneuver plans over a single trip, and thousands or even millions of such interactions over the serviceable lifetime of an individual machine. However, any individual machine is unlikely to encounter the same machine frequently in large open systems like roadway systems. Much like humans, individual autonomous machines cannot (in isolation) develop a useful log of multidimensional machine trust. However, the limitation for machines is specifically related to a sampling problem—that is, the probability that any individual machine will have a meaningful track record of interaction with all (or nearly all) other machines in a large machine population is tiny.

To solve this problem, a broader ecosystem that includes transaction and trust management is required (shown in Fig. 2.11). Machines engaged in collective maneuver planning *broadcast* information regarding identity, current sensor and position data, and intent (desired path)—here represented by the large truck. Other machines engaged in collective maneuver planning with the truck are *users* of this broadcast data. These machines are collectively interested in the trustworthiness of the truck broadcasting data as well as the accuracy of specific position, sensor, and maneuver data shared by the truck. The trust report for all vehicles (including the truck) is managed externally by a consortium of entities collectively managing trust and transactions. In this case, we specifically call out the use of distributed ledger

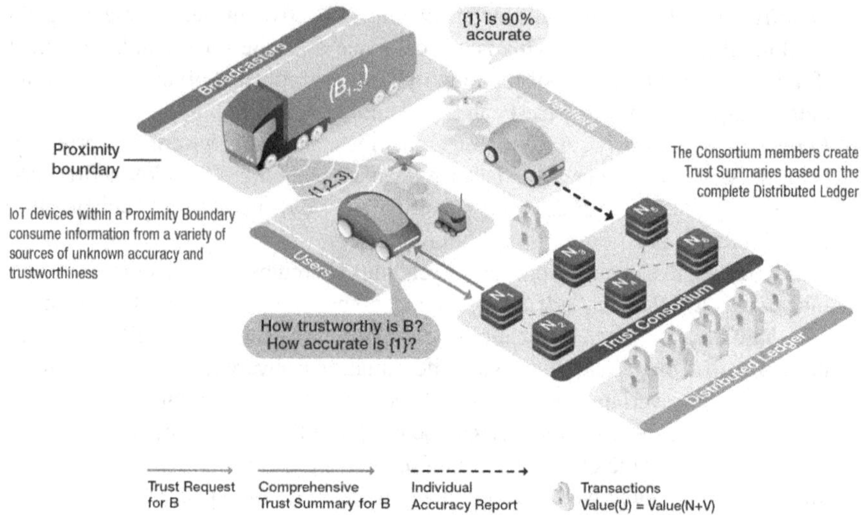

Fig. 2.11 Earned trust ecosystem enabling earned machine trust

technology (see Hilary, 2022) because it is particularly well-suited to the creation and enforcement of smart micro-contracts among machines.

Individual entities within a Trust Consortium compete to deliver trust reports rapidly to machines engaged in collective maneuver planning. This initiates maneuver planning since now all vehicles have the best-updated information on multidimensional machine trust for all other vehicles. Machines execute maneuvers that may or may not precisely conform to the collective plan. The machines themselves, other neighboring machines, or fixed infrastructure can verify adherence to the plan. The resulting transaction outcome (defined in the multi-machine smart contract), represented in Fig. 2.11 using the padlock icon is returned to the Trust Consortium. Consortium members compete again to encode the transaction as quickly as possible into a master distributed ledger containing the outcomes of all prior transactions. These outcomes include the transfer of value (here some form of cryptocurrency) among entities in the transaction and the adjustment of various dimensions of machine trust for each individual machine.

In our example, the effect of earned trust is planning maneuvers with close tolerances among machines only when all participating machines have a demonstrated capability to perform these maneuvers safely. Consider a case where Machines B and D have demonstrated in multiple prior collective maneuver planning encounters that they can safely operate with significantly reduced space reserved as a safety buffer. In fact, these tolerances have been reduced so dramatically that now both machines may pass side-by-side in the center of the shared maneuver space (Fig. 2.12). In a system without earned trust, these machines would not be allowed to conduct such a maneuver. Earned trust allows machines to collectively unlock unrealized efficiencies when and only when they have demonstrated the capability to do so.

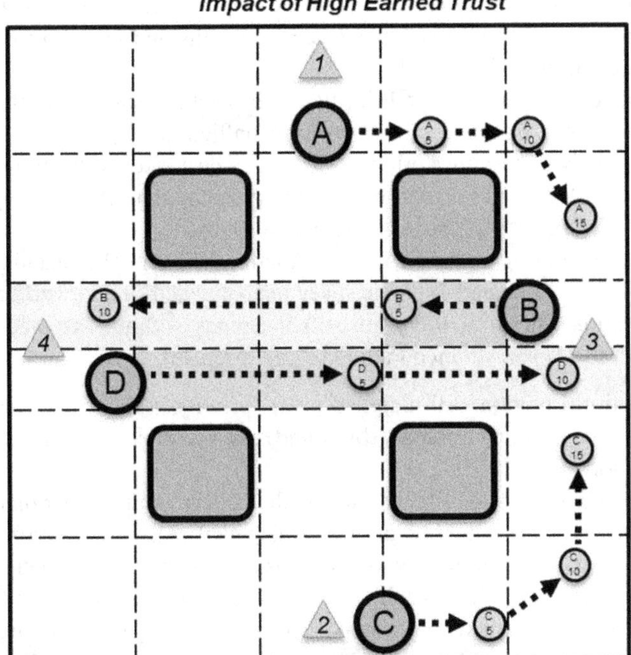

Fig. 2.12 High-trust maneuver planning

2.6 Collective Maneuver Planning: A Summary

With the introduction of the Earned Trust Ecosystem (Fig. 2.11), comprehensive collective maneuver planning may be defined at a high level as a ten-step process:

1. Ad Hoc Maneuver Group Creation. This step identifies the specific set of machines that will engage in collective maneuver planning.
2. Earned Trust Record Recovery. The maneuver group collectively requests trust reports for all machines from the Trust Consortium.
3. Collective Map Sharing. In this step, the maneuver group creates a shared world map weighted by individual machine sensor trust ratings.
4. Collective Path Planning (iterative).

   (a) Iteration Check. If all machines have assigned paths, then proceed to Transaction Creation (Step 5).
   (b) Unconstrained Path Planning. Each machine provides a desired path plan based on the current world map of obstacles and dynamic space allocated in prior rounds of path deconfliction. Note that each desired path includes the additional dynamic space required to provide maneuver tolerance based on each individual machine maneuver trust score.

(c) Conflict Identification. Plans with overlaps create conflicts. If there are no conflicts assign all machines to desired paths and proceed to Transaction Creation (Step 6).
(d) Sealed Bid Auction for Priority. Each machine submits a maximum bid for priority in this round of path deconfliction. Highest bid (ties broken randomly) determines priority with a total cost taken as the minimum of the highest bid or the second highest bid plus one unit. All yielding machines are identified for Transaction Creation (Step 5).
(e) Assignation of Dynamic Path to Auction Winner. The machine receiving priority is allocated dynamic space in an updated shared world map.
(f) Iteration Check. If there are still machines without assigned paths then return to Unconstrained Path Planning (Step 4a).

5. Transaction Creation. All assigned paths, priority assignments, payments for priority, and yielding vehicles (by round) are assembled into a multi-machine transaction.
6. Maneuver Initiation. Machines execute the collective maneuver plan.
7. Plan Verification and Disruption Contingency. Machines verify that other machines are in position or out of position with respect to the collective maneuver plan. Further, machines note clear evidence of sensor failure with respect to the world map (false-positive or false-negative). If the maneuver plan becomes untenable (say by the discovery of a new obstacle unknown to the maneuver group when the collective plan was created), then the collective maneuver plan is abandoned (all machines revert to Ad Hoc Maneuver Group creation (Step 1).
8. Transaction Finalization. Successful or disrupted, the outcome of the collective maneuver plan is finalized for recordation among the collective maneuver group. The transaction is transmitted for recordation to the Trust Consortium.
9. Transaction Recordation and Value Distribution. Trust consortium members compete to record the transaction outcome into the shared master distributed ledger system. Total value accumulated from machines receiving priority is distributed among ecosystem entities (see the following section for additional discussion).
10. Earned Trust Updating. Trust scores (by dimension) of individual machines are adjusted incrementally based on verification reports embedded in the maneuver transaction.

Researchers at Noblis (2019) have posted videos of a physical demonstration of collective maneuver planning and earned trust using small autonomous rovers.

2.7 Considerations Related to Value Distribution

How value is distributed among all the entities in the earned trust ecosystem (Fig. 2.11) can be used to ensure the alignment of operational efficiency with equitable ecosystem finance. In a fully self-sustaining ecosystem, each of these entities should be motivated and compensated. Value distribution should account for all parties facilitating aspects of the transaction, including:

- machines that yield priority
- entities that provide and maintain the maneuver space
- entities that provide maneuver and sensor verification reports
- entities providing reliable obstacle sensor data and/or more accurate machine/obstacle position and timing data and
- entities in the Trust Consortium members delivering trust reports and recording transactions.

A strawman value distribution system for initial consideration might distribute one-half of transaction value to yielding machines, and the remainder equally among the four supporting functions (maneuver space provision and maintenance, verification, world map contribution, and transaction recordation). This divides the microtransaction into elements of at least one-eighth of total transaction value.

2.8 Implications for Roadway System Operations and Finance

A long-standing issue in roadway financing is that the costs of infrastructure provision and maintenance are indirectly and increasingly unequally borne by those who benefit from the system. Fuel tax revenues, the primary source of roadway system funding, consistently fails to cover maintenance and operations costs (Kirk & Mallett, 2020). These trends are expected to continue and are likely to grow into an even larger annual shortfall. An electric vehicle, for example, makes no contribution to roadway system maintenance and operations despite having a similar impact compared to a fossil-fueled vehicle.

There is a wide range of possible actions that could be taken to correct this consistent shortfall, from raising or altering fuel tax structures, instituting new taxes related to carbon emissions, adding a supplementary fee or tax structure for electric vehicles, and introducing road user fees.

Raising fuel taxes may offer some relief for bottom-line financial considerations, but does not address powertrain equity issues (e.g., electric vehicles still do not contribute). Fuel taxes also incentivize fuel efficiency and suppress general utilization of the roadway system. This reduces revenues while simultaneously providing no incentive to the system to become more efficient. Supplementary fees for electric vehicles may address powertrain equity considerations, but do not link revenue to system utilization and efficiency in any meaningful way.

Road user fees are an increasingly popular option (Atkinson, 2019) gaining support from the public sector agencies responsible for the roadway systems (National League of Cities, 2018). These systems are primarily based on charging fixed rates for roadway miles traveled. Road user fees are directly linked to utilization, but the inherent value of travel is fixed. In other words, it assumes that all travel regardless of demand can be effectively treated equally. A dynamic version of road user fees, congestion pricing (Federal Highway Administration, 2008), varies facility-level tolls based on time of day. Such approaches are demand-responsive but are designed to influence human behavior. However, these approaches remain comparatively blunt instruments because of the limitations of human drivers to negotiate for space compared to the potential of autonomous vehicles.

A machine-centric method of collective maneuver planning based on the concepts presented in this chapter may offer another option in dealing with the persistent shortfall of operational revenues while simultaneously linking system efficiency with system revenue generation.

2.9 Conclusions

This chapter is intended to serve as a foundational primer for transaction-based ecosystems for self-organizing autonomous machines. Most critically, it presents a structured process that departs from the human-centric norms of shared behavior to improve system efficiency and safety that leverage key differences in human and machine capabilities. Machine-to-machine negotiation offers a new vista of possibilities to re-imagine how complex, shared systems might be more efficiently organized and sustainably financed.

References

Atkinson, R. D. (2019). A policymaker's guide to road user charges, information technology and innovation foundation, www.ifif.org. Retrieved 30 May 2020.

Federal Highway Administration (2008) Congestion pricing: A primer, www.ops.fhwa.dot.gov/siteindex.htm, FHWA-HOP-08-039.

Hilary, G. (2022). Blockchain and other distributed ledger technologies, a primer. In V. Babich, J. Birge, & G. Hilary (Eds.), *Innovative technology at the interface of finance and operations*. Springer Series in Supply Chain Management. Springer Nature.

Kirk, R. S. and Mallett, W. J. (2020) Funding and financing highways and public transportation, congressional research service, from https://crsreports.congress.gov, R45350. Retrieved 30 May 2020.

National League of Cities (2018). Fixing funding by the mile: A primer and analysis of road user charge systems, from www.nlc.org, Retrieved 30 May 2020

Noblis (2019). Orchestrated autonomy concept, from https://noblis.org/orchestrated-autonomy/. Retrieved 19 December 2020

Murata, S., and Kurokawa, H. (2012). Self-organizing robots, Springer Tracts in Advanced Robotics, Volume 77

Toksöz, M. A., Oguz, S., Gazi, V. (2019). Decentralized formation control of a swarm of quadrotor helicopters, 2019 IEEE 15th International Conference on Control and Automation (ICCA).

Chapter 3
Interface of Operations and Finance: A Tutorial

Volodymyr Babich and John Birge

3.1 Introduction

In many business problems it is difficult to separate operations from finance. Consider, for example, the US shale oil and gas boom, which has transformed the USA from a net importer to a net exporter of oil and oil-based products for the first time in 75 years (Blas, 2018). As a result, the USA has become the world's largest oil producer, with production exceeding those of Russia and Saudi Arabia (Egan, 2018).

The key source of shale oil is the Permian Basin of West Texas and New Mexico, whose output alone rivals those of Iran or Iraq (Sider & Olson, 2018). However, the oil production in the Permian Basin has been threatened by operational bottlenecks. Sider and Olson (2018) report that producers are encountering pipeline congestion as well as shortages of materials and workers. To relieve shortages, producers bring workers from outside, straining local resources. Hotel prices in the area spiked to $600 per night. Because pipelines take a long time to build, oil producers are relying on oil transport by trucks. However, there is a shortage of qualified truck drivers and their salaries are rising (to $140,000 per year), while the schools that are teaching how to pass the test for a commercial driver's license are packed (Wethe, 2018). In this example, to forecast future oil prices, one needs to understand how the oil production, transportation, and refinement systems operate, identify bottlenecks,

V. Babich (✉)
McDonough School of Business, Georgetown University, Washington, DC, USA
e-mail: vob2@georgetown.edu

J. Birge
University of Chicago Booth School of Business, Chicago, IL, USA
e-mail: john.birge@chicagobooth.edu

V. Babich et al. (eds.), *Innovative Technology at the Interface of Finance and Operations*, Springer Series in Supply Chain Management 11,
https://doi.org/10.1007/978-3-030-75729-8_3

predict how capacity investments will relieve them, and where new bottlenecks will arise. These are essential operational problems and questions.

Another motivating example of the link between operations and finance is the financial crisis of 2007–2008. Campello et al. (2010) conducted a survey of 1,050 CFOs in 39 countries and found that financially constrained companies planned to cut their spending on investments, technology, marketing, and employment. Garicano and Steinwender (2016) compared the spending of Spanish firms against those of multinational firms, following the financial crisis, and found that Spanish firms, being more capital constrained, had to cut investments, employment, and spending on process innovation. Again, there is clearly a link between finance and operations.

Finance and operations interface topics include Supply Chain Finance, propagation of financial information in supply chains, interactions between financial claim holders and operational claim holders of a firm, risk issues and hedging in commodity procurement.[1] Relevant for this book, many interface applications are enabled by technology, such as FinTech and OpTech.

In this chapter we offer two tutorials: (1) a finance tutorial for OM researchers and (2) an OM tutorial for finance researchers. In addition to providing a textbook treatment of key ideas, we offer examples applications of these ideas to the other discipline. This tutorial is a shorter version of Babich and Birge (2020).

The following outlines the rest of this chapter. In Sect. 3.2, we compare perspectives of finance and operations on the same object: the firm. This motivates the key questions in finance, which we present in the finance primer in Sect. 3.3 and key questions in OM, which we present in the OM primer in Sect. 3.4. We opted for depth over breadth in the discussions and, therefore, we present a few selected topics. However, we also offer suggestions on what to read next and where. Babich and Birge (2020) are a superset of this chapter. They present additional topics, in the same style as this tutorial, discuss promising research direction at the interface of operations and finance, and offer suggestions on how to write, publish, and referee interface papers.

3.2 The Blind Men and a Firm Parable

According to a well-known parable, a group of blind men encountered an elephant for the first time and tried to learn about it by touch. Naturally, they touched different parts of the animal and, therefore, their descriptions varied widely. Those who touched the elephant's trunk said that the elephant was similar to a snake. Those who touched the elephant's legs thought that the elephant was like a tree. Those who touched the tusks compared the elephant to a spear. Those who touched the elephant's sides likened the animal to a wall.

[1] This is partial list from an introductory article by Babich and Kouvelis (2018).

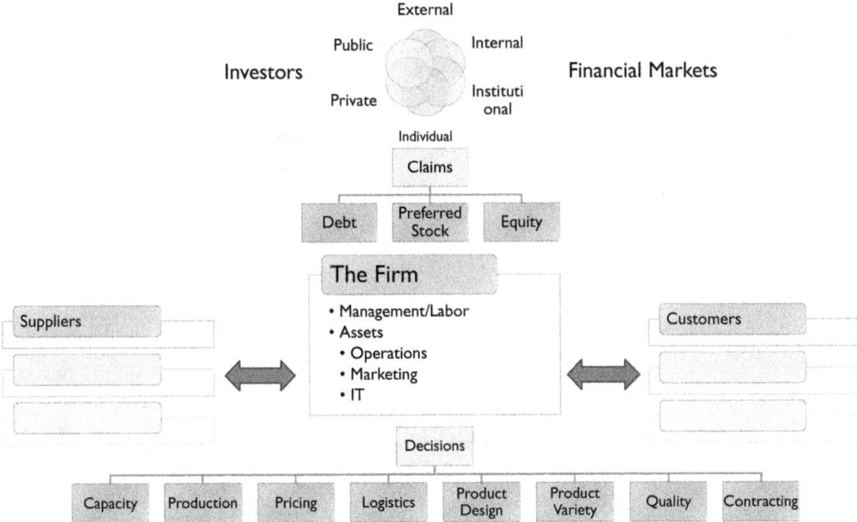

Fig. 3.1 Complex view of the firm and its environment

This parable is an apt description of how different research disciplines view a firm. With a disclaimer that we are both over-simplifying the true sophistication of research and underestimating the complexity of practice, we present Fig. 3.1, illustrating how the firm should be viewed. This is the elephant in the parable. The firm and its environment are complex and the task of understanding what it is, what it does, and what it should do is immense. The firm has human and non-human, tangible and intangible assets. Human assets are divided into management and labor. Non-human assets include operational assets (e.g., production capacity, inventory), marketing assets (brand image, information about customers), knowledge assets (intellectual property, patents, rights), and others. The firm must make many decisions: capacity, production, pricing, logistics, product design, product variety, quality, contracting, financing, etc. It faces numerous constraints. It operates in a dynamic and stochastic environment. It has to interact with customers and suppliers (who may be individuals or corporations). The firm must interact with competitors (not shown in the figure). The firm is there to serve the objectives of its stakeholders (in the broad sense). The stakeholders are either insiders or outsiders. Stakeholders or investors can be private or public, institutional or individual. The claims on the cash flows generated by the firm are governed by special types of contracts (called debt, equity, etc.). These contracts specify value distribution and control rights. They can be held privately or traded on organized exchanges, called financial markets. Trying to understand all of these details is a daunting task. But in addition, there are other entities and issues, such as governments, regulations, taxation, environmental externalities, etc. The need for simplification is apparent!

One simplification is the finance view of the firm, illustrated by Fig. 3.2. A detailed discussion of this view is in the finance primer in Sect. 3.3. Briefly, finance

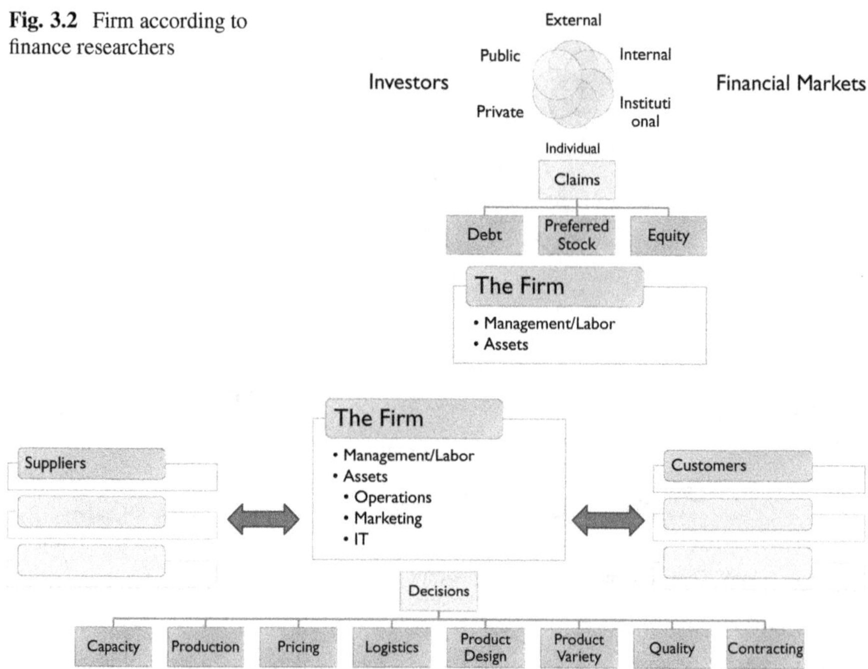

Fig. 3.2 Firm according to finance researchers

Fig. 3.3 Firm according to OM researchers

researchers focus on the upper part of the picture: investors, financial markets, claims on the firm's assets (debt, equity), interactions among different investor classes, and interactions between insiders and outsiders. Regulations and taxation are important. However, the details of how the value is generated, what interactions and decisions are involved, and supply chain relationships are typically taken as exogenous. The finance literature is, naturally, aware of the underlying complexity, but it treats these details as a black box.

Another simplification is the OM view of the firm, illustrated by Fig. 3.3. A detailed discussion of this view is in the OM primer in Sect. 3.4. Briefly, OM researchers focus on the lower part of the picture: physical assets, production, physical flows, informational flows, decisions, production and other constraints, and interactions with customers and suppliers. For the most part, the OM literature ignores the existence of investors, assumes the same objectives for all stakeholders of maximizing profit or revenues or minimizing cost, ignores the timing of cash flows (except for discounting of future cash flows), ignores financing constraints, and neglects the costs of relaxing financing constraints.

Such a stratified view of the firm is not wrong. The existence of the vast literature in each field proves that one can successfully generate practically useful insights, while ignoring the other field. Sections 3.3 and 3.4 illustrate this. However, such ignorance of the other field can be costly for a number of real problems. The detailed discussion of why joining OM and finance can reduce such costs is outside of this tutorial and can be found in Babich and Birge (2020).

3.3 A Brief Finance Primer for OM Researchers

A typical finance PhD program requires students to take a combination of courses in micro- and macro-economics, econometrics, asset pricing, corporate finance, derivatives, portfolio theory, etc. Fortunately, to do interface research, one does not need two PhDs—expertise in OM with knowledge of key ideas in finance is a sufficient starting point. The following discussion presents several key ideas from finance important for OM researchers to know. Specifically, in the following we shall discuss a few essential ideas from corporate finance (Sect. 3.3.1), and capital markets theory (Sect. 3.3.2). These are different, but related parts of the finance field's view of the firm, as illustrated in Fig. 3.2. Corporate finance tends to study the "inside" of a firm, e.g., how claims to real assets are structured, how agency conflicts between management and labor, insiders of a firm and outsiders, different claim holders on firm's assets influences firm's actions and value. Capital markets theory focuses on markets outside of a firm, where claims to firm assets are traded, and studies investors' preferences, investment decisions, and how to forecast market prices of assets.

A few words about our choice of topics and the discussion style and structure. Given space constraints, we cannot be comprehensive and we prefer depths over breadth. There are many interesting questions and topics in finance: how to value a stream of cash flows from an investment project? How do investors make decisions and how does this translate into the functioning of financial markets; what is the fair market price? Which projects should managers choose to invest in? How to value claims from different investors on the cash flows from a portfolio of projects that the firm has; can the firm's value be influenced by the CFO's decisions? How asymmetric information between investor classes affect market prices? What role do relationships play in securing financing? And many more. We chose to discuss topics that can be described as essential general knowledge and topics that have clear OM connections. Babich and Birge (2020) contain more extensive discussion, and even that manuscript is only discussing the most essential topics. Among topics that appear in Babich and Birge (2020) but not here is risk management. This topic is important for both finance and OM, and their interface, but it deserves its own tutorial. We also omit discussion of asymmetric information in corporate finance, risk-neutral pricing measures and derivative pricing in capital market theory.

In as much as applicable, we try to use unified notation throughout the discussion, thus, hopefully, making it easier for our readers to follow the connections between topics. We list new ideas and tools before each subsection, making it easier to get the gist of the following discussion. We strive to present finance ideas in their simplest, purest form. We provide references that offer more nuanced treatments of the topic. We also discuss consequences of each key finance idea for OM researchers.

3.3.1 Corporate Finance

3.3.1.1 MM World

New Ideas and Tools Introduced Here *A firm as a collection of claims; debt and equity; default on debt; terminology: principal, interest, dividend, stock repurchase; valuation function; perfect capital markets; Modigliani and Miller propositions; cash flow table; a no-arbitrage proof.*

A simple finance model of a firm is as follows. The firm exists for a single period only. At the beginning of the period an investment I is required. At the end of the period the firm generates income R, which is random. The natures of the initial investment and income are hidden in the black box of Fig. 3.2. What is important for finance is who makes and receives payments. Finance views a firm as a *collection of claims on the firm's assets*. In the simplest case, there are two types of claims: *debt and equity*. Terminology for OM readers: a distribution of the firm's value between claim types is called *capital structure* and the fraction of debt among other claims is called *leverage*.

A simple debt contract specifies (l, r). According to this contract, in return for the initial amount of capital l the holder of the contract is entitled to repayment $\min(R, r)$ at the end of the period. If the income R is not sufficient to pay amount r, then the firm is declared in *default*. Practically, the repayment amount r comprises both *the principal and the interest* $r = P+i$, but in modeling this distinction is often moot. Holders of equity are responsible for the remaining investment $I - l$ and are entitled to the residual income of the firm $(R - r)^+$. Notation: $(x)^+ = x$, if $x > 0$ and 0 otherwise. Practically, equity claims are paid either as a *dividend* or as a *stock repurchase*, but in this simple model, the two are equivalent. Table 3.1 summarizes this discussion. An important aside for OM readers: understanding the timing of cash flows is essential in finance, because finance studies questions such as: why money today is not the same as money tomorrow, whether due to time preferences of investors, or due to frictions in financial markets that may impede the investors' ability to shift wealth (and consumption) between periods. Tables like Table 3.1, spelling out the timing of cash flows, are very useful in preventing mistakes of conflating cash flows in different time periods and across different claimants.

Corresponding to each set of cash flows is the value of the claims. We discuss elements of the valuation theory in (Sect. 3.3.2). For the purposes of the current

Table 3.1 Cash flows and values to debt and equity holders

	$t = 0$		$t = 1$
Claims	Values	Cash flows	Cash flows
Debt	V_D	$-l$	$\min(R, r)$
Equity	V_E	$-(I - l)$	$(R - r)^+$
Levered firm (total)	$V_L = V_D + V_E$	$-I$	R
Unlevered firm	V_U	$-I$	R

discussion, it is sufficient that there exists a *valuation operator* $Value[\cdot]$ that maps a stream of cash flows into a number and that this operator is additive. To make this more specific, an expected discounted value $\mathbb{E}[e^{-rT}x_T]$ of random cash flows x_T occurring at time T is an example of the valuation operator.[2] Denote the time $t = 0$ value of debt claims by $V_D = Value[\min(R, r)] - l$ and equity claims by $V_E = Value[(R - r)^+] - (I - l)$. The total value of the firm at $t = 0$ is $V_L = V_D + V_E$, where index L stands for "leveraged."

We use this simple model to illustrate one of the most important results in corporate finance. The Nobel-prize-winning insights from Modigliani and Miller (1958) and Miller and Modigliani (1961) (abbreviated MM in the following) are that in perfect capital markets the choices of the capital structure and the dividend policies are irrelevant. *Perfect capital markets* are markets without transaction costs, taxes, bankruptcy costs, markets that are efficient, and where information is symmetric. Capital structure policy is the choice between using debt or equity claims. Dividend policy is the decision on how to pay the equity holders: through dividends or stock repurchases.

The proof of the MM results is based on the observation that investors can synthetically generate any capital structure and any dividend policy they desire for the firm, by trading in capital markets. For example, suppose there were two identical firms traded in the market: one unlevered (i.e., without debt claims) and one levered with debt contract (l, r). The values and cash flows for claimants for either firm are given in Table 3.1. The cash flows of the firms are identical. Therefore, to avoid *arbitrage*, the $t = 0$ values must be identical as well. *Arbitrage* is a fundamental finance concept describing trades that can never lose money and in some states of the world can make money, i.e., trades that generate risk-less profits (more in Sect. 3.3.2). The absence of arbitrage is the starting point for most finance models. Applying the no-arbitrage argument here, suppose that the firms' values differed at $t = 0$ with $V_U > V_L$. Then investors could execute the following trading strategy: short-sell all shares of the unlevered firm, generating cash amount V_U, and use this cash to buy all equity (the cost is V_E) and debt (the cost is V_D) of the levered firm. The remaining cash $V_U - V_L > 0$ represents arbitrage profit. Specifically, the net cash flow at $t = 1$ is $\min(R, D) + (R - D)^+ - R = 0$. The cash flow at $t = 0$ is $V_U - I - (V_L - I) > 0$. Thus, there is no risk for the investors and there is a strictly positive cash flow at $t = 0$. In efficient capital markets, arbitrage trading strategies should not exist. Perfect capital markets are efficient. Therefore, it cannot happen that $V_U > V_L$. A similar argument eliminates the possibility of $V_U < V_L$, leaving as the only possibility, $V_U = V_L$. This concludes the proof.

[2]Suppose that a cash flow x_T is paid at time $t = T$. The operator $Value[\cdot]$ computes the value of this cash flow at $t = 0$. As we discuss in Sect. 3.3.2, this operator comes from a general asset pricing equation $Value[x_T] = \mathbb{E}[m_T x_T]$, where m_T is a stochastic pricing kernel. Special cases of this asset pricing equation are a risk-neutral valuation ($Value[x_T] = \mathbb{E}^Q[e^{-r_f T}x_T]$, where $\mathbb{E}^Q[\cdot]$ is the expectation with respect to a risk-neutral measure), a CAPM ($Value[x_T] = \mathbb{E}[e^{-(r_f+\beta(r_M-r_f))T}x_T]$ where r_M is the return on the market and β is the beta of the asset x_T relative to the market), a Fama-French 3-factor model, or any other asset pricing model.

MM's insights generated one of the *puzzles of corporate finance*. In the MM world, corporate finance decisions are irrelevant and there is no need for different financial claims. This is in stark contrast with the real world, in which we observe a myriad of different types of financial claims. Numerous surveys show that in practice, most investments are financed by the retained earnings (i.e., internal financing), and external financing appears in various debt and equity claims with a mind-boggling array of features. For example, debt comes in multiple maturities, with fixed and floating interest, secured and unsecured by assets, having different seniorities, denominated in different currencies, with callable and putable features, convertible to equity and not, etc. Similarly, equity can be private and public, initial and seasoned, representing different classes (A, B, C), preferred and common, paying regular dividends, special dividends, and share buybacks. Moreover, there are other forms of claims that are not exactly debt, but are similar, such as accounts receivable and payable, trade credit, leases, credit lines, etc. Why does such diversity exist? The answer is that real capital markets are not perfect in the MM sense. An ocean of corporate finance research since Modigliani and Miller (1958) and Miller and Modigliani (1961) has been dedicated to exploring the consequences of market imperfections. Tirole (2005) is an excellent PhD-level discussion of this research. There are also numerous review articles, including Harris and Raviv (1991) and Parsons et al. (2009). We discuss several ideas from this literature in the following subsections.

What Is the Consequence of the MM Results for OM Researchers? Following the lead of the finance literature, we have treated income R as a black box. In reality, various investment, operational, marketing, and other decisions (denote them q) and various sources of randomness (denote them ξ) contribute to investment cost $I(q)$ and income $R = R(q, \xi)$. According to MM, in perfect capital markets decisions q are observable and contractible, and the best value maximizing strategy for a firm is to ignore financial decisions and focus on finding q that maximizes $V_U = Value[R(q, \xi)] - I(q)$. Thus, the OM traditional objectives of maximizing the expected discounted profit (or minimizing cost) are the right ones.

It is important to emphasize that the MM results describe capital markets, not investment or operational decisions. MM propositions are statements about the irrelevance of finance, not the irrelevance of operations. Therefore, it does not matter how simple or complex operational decisions are, how much a researcher "opens a black box" by adding any number of operational decisions to the model, as long as capital markets are perfect, the MM results continue to hold (see Babich & Birge, 2020).

To illustrate the last point, the following is a general and yet very simple proof that capital structure does not matter for OM's favorite model—the newsvendor model (those unfamiliar with this model may find Sect. 3.4.2 useful). Let q be a vector of various operational decisions, $\mathcal{Q}$ be the feasibility region for q, $c(q)$ be the cost function, incurred at $t = 0$, $R(\xi, q)$ be the income function, which depends on random vector ξ, realized at $t = 1$. Note that this model can capture the shortage and the excess inventory costs of the classical newsvendor setting, and many more

Table 3.2 Actions and cash flows for the newsvendor model in MM setting with unlimited internal capital

	$t = 0$		$t = 1$
	Actions	Cash flows	Cash flows
Newsvendor	q	$-c(q)$	$R(\xi, q)$

Table 3.3 Actions and cash flows for the newsvendor model in MM setting with external debt financing

	$t = 0$		$t = 1$
	Actions	Cash flows	Cash flows
Newsvendor	q	$-c(q)$	$R(\xi, q)$
	(l, r)	$+l$	$-\min(R(\xi, q), r)$
Debt investors	Finance	$-l$	$\min(R(\xi, q), r)$

features. For simplicity, and without loss of generality in this model, assume that the risk-free rate in the economy is $r_f = 0$. Then, as we discuss in Sect. 3.3.2, the valuation operator is $Value[\cdot] = \mathbb{E}[\cdot]$, under the appropriately chosen pricing measure.

To begin, consider a newsvendor with only equity in the capital structure. In perfect capital markets, there is no difference between internal and external equity. We consider the decisions that maximize the value of all equity. The actions and cash flows of this newsvendor are given in Table 3.2. Based on these cash flows, the newsvendor solves the following problem.

$$\max_{q} \quad \mathbb{E}[R(\xi, q)] - c(q) \tag{3.1a}$$

$$\text{s.t.} \quad q \in \mathcal{Q}. \tag{3.1b}$$

Next, consider the newsvendor, endowed with capital a, and able to access perfect capital markets to raise debt externally using a contract (l, r). The newsvendor's cash flows at $t = 0$ satisfy a financing constraint: $c(q) \leq a + l$. Perfect capital markets imply that actions q of the newsvendor are observable and contractible. Inventors' individual rationality condition is $l \leq \mathbb{E}[\min(r, R(\xi, q))]$. Table 3.3 presents cash flows and actions over time.

The newsvendor's problem with external debt financing is

$$\max_{(q,l,r)} \quad \mathbb{E}[R(\xi, q) - \min(R(\xi, q), r)] - c(q) + l \tag{3.2a}$$

$$\text{s.t.} \quad q \in \mathcal{Q} \tag{3.2b}$$

$$0 \leq l \leq \mathbb{E}[\min(r, R(\xi, q))] \tag{3.2c}$$

$$c(q) \leq a + l. \tag{3.2d}$$

An optimal solution of problem (3.2) possesses several intuitive properties. For $c(q) \leq a$, an optimal solution satisfies $l = 0$ and $r = 0$. In this case, problem (3.2) devolves into the financially unconstrained problem (3.1). For $c(q) > a$, an optimal solution satisfies $c(q) = a + l$, and $l = \mathbb{E}[\min(r, R(\xi, q))]$. The latter equality comes from the perfect competition among investors.

Using $\mathbb{E}[\min(r, R(\xi, q))] = l$, the objective function of problem (3.2) is transformed as follows $\mathbb{E}[R(\xi, q) - \min(R(\xi, q), r)] - c(q) + l = \mathbb{E}[R(\xi, q)] - l - c(q) + l = \mathbb{E}[R(\xi, q)] - c(q)$. Once again, problem (3.2) devolves into the financially unconstrained problem (3.1). It does not matter how complex the decision vector q, cost function c, revenue function R, and feasible set $\mathcal{Q}$ are. As long as capital markets are perfect, actions are contractible, the feasible set $\mathcal{Q}$ does not depend on what the newsvendor does in capital markets, the MM result holds and the capital structure of the newsvendor does not matter.

3.3.1.2 Static Tradeoff Theory: Interest Tax Shield vs. Bankruptcy Costs

New Ideas and Tools Introduced Here *Corporate taxes; corporate tax shield advantage of debt; bankruptcy; bankruptcy costs; static tradeoff theory between bankruptcy costs and debt tax shield.*

In practice capital markets are not perfect for a number of reasons, two of which—interest tax shield and bankruptcy costs—are at the core of the static tradeoff theory of capital structure. The US corporate tax rules make interest payments on debt tax deductible. Therefore, if the debt repayment $r = P + i$ comprises principal P and interest i amounts, and the corporate tax rate is τ, the government collects $\tau(R - i)$ in taxes (assuming $R > i$), leaving the firm's claim holders $R - \tau(R - i) = (1 - \tau)R + \tau i$. Amount τi is the *interest tax shield*. For simplicity, we assume that this value is accrued before payments to claim holders are made. The more the firm can pay as interest, the less it pays in taxes and the more it gets to keep for claim holders. This argument suggests that firms should be financed primarily by debt, to maximize the value of the interest tax shield. On the other side of the scales are bankruptcy costs. When a firm cannot pay its liabilities (i.e., $R < r$), it undergoes either private or public restructuring or liquidation. This is a complex and costly process, whose effects are approximated by adding deadweight costs BC incurred in the bankruptcy states (i.e., when $R < r$) . Table 3.4 shows the corresponding cash flows. Notation: $1_{\{bankruptcy\}}$ is the indicator of the bankruptcy state. We show aggregate values to all claim holders and do not specify the division of bankruptcy costs between debt and equity holders.

The value of a levered firm at $t = 0$ is $V_L = V_U + Value[\tau I] - Value[BC\,1_{\{bankruptcy\}}]$, which can be higher or lower than the value of an unlevered firm V_U. The tradeoff between the interest tax shield benefits and the bankruptcy costs is the basis for the *static tradeoff theory* (Myers, 1984). There are other capital structure theories, notably the *pecking order theory* based on

Table 3.4 Values from a levered and an unlevered firms at the beginning ($t = 0$) and end ($t = 1$) of the period with the corporate tax shield and bankruptcy costs

Time	Values from unlevered firm	Values from levered firm
$t = 0$	V_U	$V_L = V_D + V_E$
$t = 1$	$(1 - \tau)R$	$(1 - \tau)R + \tau I - BC\,1_{\{bankruptcy\}}$

asymmetric information (Babich & Birge, 2020 discuss pecking order theory and point to original papers).

A prediction from the static tradeoff theory is that for every firm there is an optimal debt/equity ratio, and variation in bankruptcy costs and bankruptcy probabilities leads to variation in capital structures. For example, firms that have more tangible assets have lower bankruptcy costs. Therefore, such firms have higher leverage. In contrast, firms whose main assets are intellectual capital, which can be easily lost in bankruptcy, have lower leverage. Firms differ in the riskiness of their income. According to the static tradeoff theory, less risky firms borrow more. As the market value of equity changes, managers should adjust their firm's leverage to stay close to the optimal debt/equity ratio. However, surveys of managers indicate that this does not happen in practice (Graham & Harvey, 2001).[3] Furthermore, managers are actively timing the market, asking for capital when they feel their equity or debt are over-priced. Such actions cannot be explained using the static tradeoff theory but can be described by invoking asymmetric information (see discussion in Babich & Birge, 2020).

What Are the Consequences of the Static Tradeoff Theory for OM Researchers? The bankruptcy event depends on the firm's operational policies and the sources of uncertainty. Bankruptcy costs BC themselves might depend on operational decisions, such as the amount of inventory and its type. For example, raw materials inventory could be easier to salvage than the finished goods inventory if raw materials are commodities that can be used by other firms. More generally, some investments are easier to convert to cash. To illustrate how this might be insightful, we build on the newsvendor model in Sect. 3.3.1.1. To focus on bankruptcy, we shall ignore taxes by setting $\tau = 0$.

In the rest of the discussion in this subsection, we present two versions of the analysis. First, we present a simple model with debt terms imposed exogenously. This model predicts that there can be either under- or over-investment, relative to the first-best solution. Second, we endogenize the choice of the debt contract terms. Again, there could be both under- and over-investment relative to the model without financing. The fact that both over and under-investment can happen is well-known. We should not be surprised with either observation in the iFORM field (Babich & Birge, 2020).

[3]There are no costs of adjusting leverage in the static tradeoff theory. But the pecking order theory (see discussion in Babich & Birge, 2020) recognizes that trading by insiders of the firm has costs due to signals trading sends to the market.

Table 3.5 Actions and cash flows for the newsvendor model with bankruptcy costs, with fixed debt terms

	$t = 0$		$t = 1$
	Actions	Cash flows	Cash flows
Newsvendor	q	$-c(q)$ $+l$	$R(\xi, q)$ $-\min(R(\xi, q), r)$ $-\phi 1_{\{R(\xi,q)<r\}}$
Investors	Finance	$-l$	$\min(R(\xi, q), r)$

Newsvendor Model with Exogenous Debt Contract Terms and Bankruptcy Costs Assume that the newsvendor does not raise new external financing but has the commitment to use external debt, according to contract (l, r). Any capital not invested, i.e., $a + l - c(q)$, goes into consumption by the newsvendor at $t = 0$ (i.e., the newsvendor does not save any money for a "rainy day"). There are no surprising sources of cash during the day and the newsvendor defaults at $t = 1$ if $R(\xi, q) < r$. Default fees are ϕ. An important modeling choice is whether to assume limited liability protection against these fees. After all, if the newsvendor does not have cash to repay the loan, how would the newsvendor repay the fees? We ignore this sticky point and assume that the newsvendor is responsible for the full fee amount. Table 3.5 presents the consequent actions and cash flows.

Given these cash flows, the newsvendor solves the following problem.

$$\max_q \quad \mathbb{E}[R(\xi, q) - \min(R(\xi, q), r)] - \phi\mathbb{E}[1_{\{R(\xi,q)<r\}}] - c(q) + l, \tag{3.3a}$$

$$\text{s.t.} \quad q \in \mathcal{Q}, \tag{3.3b}$$

$$c(q) \leq a + l. \tag{3.3c}$$

Three observations are in order. First, it is convenient to rewrite the objective function of problem (3.3) as follows:

$$\begin{aligned} &\mathbb{E}[R(\xi, q) - \min(R(\xi, q), r)] - \phi\mathbb{E}[1_{\{R(\xi,q)<r\}}] - c(q) + l \\ &= \mathbb{E}[R(\xi, q)] - c(q) - r + l + \mathbb{E}\left[(r - R(\xi, q) - \phi)1_{\{R(\xi,q)<r\}}\right]. \end{aligned} \tag{3.4}$$

In Eq. (3.4), terms $\mathbb{E}[R(\xi, q)] - c(q)$ are the same as in the original newsvendor problem, terms $-r + l$ are constant (thus, they do not affect the decision), and the last term represents cash flows in the bankruptcy state.

Second, the bankruptcy term $\mathbb{E}\left[(r - R(\xi, q) - \phi)1_{\{R(\xi,q)<r\}}\right]$ captures the limited liability of the newsvendor with respect to debt holders through $r - R(\xi, q)$. Limited liability increases the value of the newsvendor. The bankruptcy term also contains the fees ϕ, which reduce the newsvendor's value.

Third, under additional assumptions, the solution of the financially unconstrained newsvendor problem—the newsvendor quantity q^*—remains optimal for problem (3.3), as described in the following proposition.

Proposition 3.1 *Suppose that the income function is* $R(\xi, q) = p\min(\xi, q)$*, cost function* $c(q) = cq$*, and conditions* $cq^* \leq a + l$ *and* $r \leq pq^*$ *hold, where* q^* *is the newsvendor order quantity (Eq.* (3.42)*). Then* $\frac{d}{dq}\mathbb{E}[(r - R(\xi, q) - \phi)1_{\{R(\xi,q)<r\}}] = 0$*, the first-order condition for problem* (3.3) *is equivalent to the newsvendor's first-order condition* $p\Pr[\xi \geq q] = c$*, and the newsvendor's order quantity* q^* *is optimal for problem* (3.3).

Proof of Proposition 3.1 It must be true that $pq > r$, for otherwise the optimal solution is $q = 0$ and the firm is out of business. The bankruptcy condition $p\min(\xi, q) \leq r$ is equivalent to $(p\xi \leq r)||(pq \leq r)$, where $||$ is the logical "or" operator. By assumption, the last inequality does not hold. Therefore, the bankruptcy condition is equivalent to $p\xi \leq r$.

We can write term $R(\xi, q)$ as $R(\xi, q) = p\left(\xi 1_{\{p\xi \leq pq\}} + q1_{\{p\xi > pq\}}\right)$. Then, the bankruptcy term becomes

$$
\begin{aligned}
&E[(r - R(\xi, q) - \phi)1_{\{R(\xi,q)<r\}}] \\
&= -E[\{p\left(\xi 1_{\{p\xi \leq pq\}} + q1_{\{p\xi > pq\}}\right)\}1_{\{p\xi \leq r\}}] + (r - \phi)E[1_{\{p\xi \leq r\}}] \\
&= -E[p\xi 1_{\{p\xi \leq r\}}] + (r - \phi)E[1_{\{p\xi \leq r\}}]. \qquad (3.5)
\end{aligned}
$$

The last equality follows from assumption $pq \geq r$. Observe that bankruptcy term does not depend on q. The result follows. ■

Proposition 3.1 illustrates that financing choice can be irrelevant due to a lucky modeling choice. In Sect. 3.3.1.3, we show that adding overage and underage costs shifts the optimal order quantity away from the newsvendor's optimal value.

What if the initial financing were not sufficient for the newsvendor quantity, i.e., $cq^* > a + l$? Then, a smaller quantity than $q < q^*$ is the solution of problem (3.3). This is a simple mechanical observation that lower l or a can cause under-ordering.

What if the newsvendor quantity led to a certain bankruptcy, i.e., $pq^* < r$? The optimal solution would still satisfy $pq > r$ and, thus, will be higher than q^*. Therefore, higher debt obligation r can lead to over-ordering.

Newsvendor Model with Endogenous Debt Contract Terms, Alternative Business Lines, and Bankruptcy Costs We maintain the assumption of contractible actions, but allow debt contract terms to be determined endogenously. In addition, we introduce alternative investment opportunities for the newsvendor, where an investment of I at $t = 0$ generates payment $S(I)$ at $t = 1$. We require $I \geq 0$, for otherwise, the newsvendor can short an investment to raise initial capital, which is an interesting, but a different problem. Furthermore, the newsvendor may have cash flows Z from other lines of business, wages, or lotteries. We keep the decision to default on a loan tied to the event of a liquidity crunch, but the bankruptcy condition becomes more general: $R(\xi, q) + S(I) + Z < r$. Bankruptcy costs depend

Table 3.6 Actions and cash flows for the newsvendor model with bankruptcy costs and endogenous debt terms

	$t = 0$		$t = 1$
	Actions	Cash flows	Cash flows
Newsvendor	q	$-c(q)$	$R(\xi, q)$
	(l, r)	$+l$	$-\min(R(\xi, q), r)$
	I	$-I$	$+S(I) + Z$
Investors	Finance	$-l$	$\min(R(\xi, q), r)$
			$-\phi(\xi, q)1_{\{R(\xi,q)+S(I)+Z<r\}}$

on the operational decisions and the operational uncertainty, i.e., $\phi = \phi(\xi, q)$. In contrast to the preceding discussion, bankruptcy costs are paid by the investors and are reflected in their individual rationality constraint: $l \leq \mathbb{E}[\min(R(\xi, q), r)] - \mathbb{E}[\phi(\xi, q)1_{\{R(\xi,q)+S(I)+Z-r<0\}}]$. Table 3.6 describes cash flows and actions in this model.

Given these cash flows the newsvendor solves the following problem.

$$\max_{(q,I,l,r)} \quad \mathbb{E}[R(\xi, q) - \min(R(\xi, q), r) + S(I) + Z] - c(q) + l - I, \tag{3.6a}$$

$$\text{s.t.} \quad q \in \mathcal{Q}, I \geq 0, \tag{3.6b}$$

$$c(q) + I \leq a + l, \tag{3.6c}$$

$$l \leq \mathbb{E}[\min(R(\xi, q), r)] - \mathbb{E}[\phi(\xi, q)1_{\{R(\xi,q)+S(I)+Z-r<0\}}]. \tag{3.6d}$$

Suppose that investment I is a martingale,[4] that is, $\mathbb{E}[S(I)] = I$, which allows cancellations to happen in (3.6a). As before, for $c(q) + I \leq a$, an optimal solution satisfies $l = r = 0$ and $I = 0$ and problem (3.6) becomes problem (3.1). Consider $c(q) + I > a$ and thus $l = c(q) + I - a$. We assume that keeping cash is a part of investment I. Under perfect competition in capital markets, $l = \mathbb{E}[\min(R(\xi, q), r)] - \mathbb{E}[\phi(\xi, q)1_{\{R(\xi,q)+S(I)+Z-r<0\}}]$ and, after removing constant terms from the objective function, problem (3.6) simplifies to:

$$\max_{(q,I,r)} \quad \mathbb{E}[R(\xi, q)] - c(q) - \mathbb{E}[\phi(\xi, q)1_{\{R(\xi,q)+S(I)+Z-r<0\}}], \tag{3.7a}$$

$$\text{s.t.} \quad q \in \mathcal{Q}, I \geq 0, \tag{3.7b}$$

$$c(q) + I - a = \mathbb{E}[\min(R(\xi, q), r)] - \mathbb{E}[\phi(\xi, q)1_{\{R(\xi,q)+S(I)+Z-r<0\}}]. \tag{3.7c}$$

The solution of (3.7) is not trivial, but the analysis generates several useful observations. First, the choice of the function ϕ determines the mathematical

[4]This would be the case if the investment were market-traded. More on this in Sect. 3.3.2.

structure of the objective function. A constant fee[5] ϕ introduces an inconvenient convex term to what is otherwise a concave function. Alternatively, inspired by Li et al. (2013) and Collier and Babich (2019), we can achieve concavity in q by assuming that $\phi(\xi, q)1_{\{R(\xi,q)+S(I)+Z-r<0\}}] = \phi[r - R(\xi, q) - S(I) - Z]^+$.

Second, although bankruptcy costs are paid by investors, these costs appear in the newsvendor's objective function, due to the debt-pricing equilibrium condition. Therefore, it is no longer an issue whether the newsvendor has limited liability with respect to these costs, because investors incur the actual bankruptcy costs and they have deep pockets. Investors transfer the expected value of the bankruptcy costs onto the newsvendor during the initial debt negotiations.

Third, the alternative investment $I^* > 0$ because this investment helps to diversify the newsvendor's exposure to the bankruptcy risk. Lastly, generally, either under- or over-investment, relative to the newsvendor's first-best order quantity q^*, can happen.

3.3.1.3 Moral Hazard as Financial Frictions

New Ideas and Tools Introduced Here *Moral hazard with respect to the entrepreneur's private effort; pledgeable capital; moral hazard cost; feasibility condition for external financing; under-investment in economically viable projects problem; and debt overhang.*

Frictions in capital markets do not have to be due to taxes and bankruptcy costs, as in the proceeding subsections. Starting from the seminal works by Jensen and Meckling (1976), Myers (1977), and Myers and Majluf (1984), finance researchers have used incentives conflicts, non-contractibility of actions, and asymmetric information to motivate the relevance of financing choices. In this and the next subsections, we discuss the role of moral hazard. Babich and Birge (2020) review effects of asymmetric information, describe the pecking order theory, and give examples of applications to OM. Our discussion follows closely Holmstrom and Tirole (1997) and Tirole (2005), with notation adopted from Ning and Babich (2018) and Babich et al. (2021). For simplicity we ignore other frictions, such as taxes and bankruptcy costs.

Consider an entrepreneur who can invest in a project. At $t = 0$, the project requires an investment, whose cost is c. At $t = 1$, the project generates random revenue (income) $\tilde{R}$, which equals R with probability $p(e)$ and 0 with probability $1 - p(e)$. Probability $p(e)$ depends on the entrepreneur's effort e at $t = 0$. Effort is costly. For simplicity, assume that the effort can take one of two values, $e \in \{0, \bar{e}\}$, and these values are also costs. Assume a risk-neutral measure exists and risk-free rates are zero so that $Value[\cdot] = \mathbb{E}[\cdot]$ (see Sect. 3.3.2).

[5] Assumption that is often made in simple finance models.

Table 3.7 Actions and cash flows for the model with moral hazard if the entrepreneur's actions are contractible and the initial investment is made. Project payoff $\tilde{R} = R$ with probability $p(e)$ and 0, otherwise. Without the initial investment, all cash flows are zero

	$t = 0$		$t = 1$
	Actions	Cash flows	Cash flows
Firm	$e = 0$	$-c$	$\tilde{R}$
	$e = \bar{e}$	$-c - \bar{e}$	$\tilde{R}$

Table 3.8 Actions and cash flows for the model with moral hazard when entrepreneur has pledgeable capital $a < c$ insufficient to finance the investment. Project payoff $\tilde{R} = R$ with probability $p(e)$ and 0, otherwise

	$t = 0$		$t = 1$
	Actions	Cash flows	Cash flows
Entrepreneur	$e = 0$	$-a$	$(\tilde{R} - r)^+$
	$e = \bar{e}$	$-a - \bar{e}$	$(\tilde{R} - r)^+$
Investors	Finance	$-c + a$	$\min(\tilde{R}, r)$

We begin with the analysis of the problem without market frictions. This allows us to compute the economic value of the firm (i.e., the value in the absence of the moral hazard). Table 3.7 presents the actions and the corresponding cash flows to the entrepreneur (aka the firm) under the assumption that an investment has been made and that the entrepreneur's actions are contractible. If no investment is made, then all cash flows are zero. For simplicity, we do not include this option in the table.

From Table 3.7, the economic value of this firm at $t = 0$ is

$$V = \max_{e \in \{0, \bar{e}\}} [p(e)R - c - e]. \tag{3.8}$$

If the effort is value-enhancing, i.e., $[p(\bar{e}) - p(0)]R > \bar{e}$ and the project is economically viable with the effort, i.e., $p(\bar{e})R - c - \bar{e} \geq 0$, then the optimal actions for the entrepreneur are to invest in the project and to exert the effort. We denote by $\delta = p(\bar{e}) - p(0)$ the increase in the project's success probability due to effort.

Next, we introduce capital market frictions into the analysis. Assume that the entrepreneur does not have sufficient capital to finance the investment but has pledgeable capital whose amount $a < c$. Importantly, assume that the entrepreneur's effort is not contractible. Table 3.8 presents the actions and the corresponding cash flows of the entrepreneur and the investors. As before, no investment means that all cash flows are zero.

To raise capital to finance the investment, the entrepreneur approaches external investors with a contract according to which these investors provide the remaining capital $l = c - a$ at $t = 0$ for the promise of repayment r at $t = 1$, if the successful project payoff R is realized. If the project payoff is 0, external investors will receive 0. Given the simple structure of this example, such a financial contract can be used to model both debt and equity payments (thus, we do not need to distinguish between them). What is important is that this is a contract between the insiders of the firm (i.e., the entrepreneur) and the outsiders (i.e., the investors). Should the investors accept this contract? Assuming the entrepreneur's effort is e, the investor's expected payoff must satisfy the individual rationality condition: $p(e)r - l \geq 0$. For $e = \bar{e}$ this is equivalent to

$$r \geq (c - a)/p(\bar{e}). \tag{3.9}$$

Thus, the entrepreneur needs to offer sufficient repayment to the investors to cover their capital outlay. The entrepreneur's effort e is not contractible and its cost is private to the entrepreneur. The entrepreneur's value with effort is $p(\bar{e})(R-r)-a-\bar{e}$ and without effort is $p(0)(R - r) - a$. Having already received capital from the investors, the entrepreneur exerts the effort only if the following incentive compatibility constraint holds: $[p(\bar{e}) - p(0)](R - r) \geq \bar{e}$. Using notation $\delta = p(\bar{e}) - p(0)$, this constraint is equivalent to

$$r \leq R - \bar{e}/\delta. \tag{3.10}$$

According to this condition, the entrepreneur cannot offer more than the project maximum payoff R reduced by the amount $\bar{e}/\delta$, representing the entrepreneur's effort cost relative to the increase in the project's success probability due to effort. This amount is known as the moral hazard cost.

Analysis is simpler under an assumption that without the entrepreneur's effort the project is not economically feasible, i.e., $p(0)R - c < 0$. This implies that $p(0)r - l < 0$ and that the investors should not accept the financial contract, if they know that the entrepreneur does not exert effort. Combined, conditions (3.9) and (3.10), yield the external financing feasibility condition:

$$(c - a)/p(\bar{e}) \leq R - \bar{e}/\delta. \tag{3.11}$$

Figure 3.4 illustrates this condition using variables ($l = c-a$, $p = p(\bar{e})$). Panel 3.4a displays the region for the model where low-effort projects are not economically viable. Panel 3.4b does that for the model where low-effort projects are viable. While creating this figure, we assumed that $\delta = p(\bar{e}) - p(0)$ was constant. In Fig. 3.4a, equation $p = \frac{c+\bar{e}}{R}$ is the economic viability line under high effort. Any project with the success probability $p \geq \frac{c+\bar{e}}{R}$ is economically viable and will be undertaken if capital markets are perfect. However, in an imperfect market, because of the moral hazard, only a subset of economically viable projects will receive external financing—projects for which the entrepreneur's investment a is sufficiently high, so that condition (3.11) is satisfied (shaded region). This is the important takeaway from this analysis—moral hazard leads to under-investment (Holmstrom & Tirole, 1997).

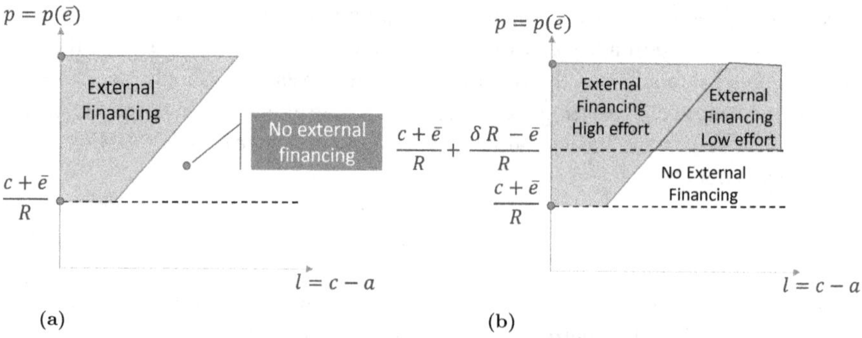

Fig. 3.4 Feasibility of external financing under moral hazard. (**a**) Low-effort projects are not viable. (**b**) Low-effort projects are viable

The analysis generates further insights. For example, consider equilibrium financing terms. If the financing feasibility condition (3.11) holds, then there exists a financial contract (l, r) that external investors will accept. If, in addition, the capital markets are perfectly competitive, the repayment amount in this contract is $r = l/p(\bar{e})$. What does the repayment $r = (1 + \rho)l$ mean in terms of the interest rate ρ charged by the investors? When condition (3.11) holds, then the implied interest rate is $\rho = r/l - 1 = 1/p(\bar{e}) - 1$. But if condition (3.11) does not hold, then the implied interest rate is $\rho = \infty$. Thus, the interest rate is (weakly) increasing and convex in the loan amount l. In other words, the greater the entrepreneur's pledgeable capital a, the lower the interest rate on the external financing. Moreover, the interest rate is (weakly) decreasing and convex in the probability of the project's success p. These observations are consistent with intuition and empirical observations.

The story of the effects of moral hazard frictions is more nuanced when the project is economically viable even without the effort, i.e., if $p(0)R - c \geq 0$, but the main insights are the same. Therefore, to move the exposition along, we do not discuss them and Fig. 3.4b in detail.

The analysis we just conducted can be easily extended to illustrate an important concept in finance, called *debt overhang* (Myers, 1977). Suppose that the entrepreneur has an existing financing contract that needs to be repaid before any payment to new investors is made. Let r_e be the repayment to existing investors. This repayment reduces the effective pledgeable capital of the entrepreneur from a to $(a - r_e)^+$ in (3.11). If r_e is high enough, then the project may be subject to credit rationing as shown in Fig. 3.4. Thus, the existing debt can preclude financing of new projects, even if those projects are economically viable.

We mentioned that for a model where project revenues take only two values 0 and R, the distinction between debt and equity is moot. A limited liability assumption would force repayment in state 0 to be $r(0) = 0$, and we only need to determine one parameter, the repayment amount in state R, i.e., $r = r(R)$. One can interpret this as coming from either debt or equity. But what about a more realistic model, e.g., where the project revenue is a continuous random variable,

R, whose probability density function $f(R|e)$ depends on the effort e? Is it better to use debt or equity to raise financing? What is the optimal contract $r(R)$? A number of papers answered the question of optimal contract design. Innes (1990) proved that a debt contract (i.e., $r(R) = \min(R, r^*)$, where r^* is a constant) is optimal for the model with a verifiable state R, increasing convex cost of effort $c(e)$, and where the probability density function satisfies $f(R|e)$ the monotone log-likelihood property, i.e., $\frac{\partial^2}{\partial R \partial e} \ln(f(R|e)) \geq 0$. Townsend (1979), Diamond (1984), and Gale and Hellwig (1985) proved that debt contracts are optimal because they reduce the costs of monitoring state R (these models are known as costly state verification models). Bolton and Scharfstein (1990), Gromb (1994), and DeMarzo and Fishman (2007) derive optimal financing contracts in dynamic settings, where the underlying state is not observable, but where the threat of terminating future financing can induce agents to exert effort.

What Are the Consequences of Moral Hazard Frictions in the Capital Market for OM Researchers? As discussed in Babich et al. (2021), many operational decisions are forms of effort that are not observable by outsiders and give rise to agency problems, e.g., the entrepreneur's decision to undertake a costly step in a product development process or test the finished product for quality. Ning and Babich (2018) consider as the effort an investment in risky R&D projects (rather than the exploitation of the existing technologies). Chod and Zhou (2014) study capacity investments and resource flexibility as sources of agency problems. The moral hazard view on frictions in capital markets dovetails nicely with the OM procurement contracting literature, especially if the latter utilizes the same methodology of information economics. It is an elegant approach for modeling financing frictions (compared with the static tradeoff discussed in Sect. 3.3.1.2).

Next, we discuss the newsvendor's ordering decisions as the source of moral hazard frictions. The key assumption is that these decisions must be non-contractible with the external investors. Such an assumption might be difficult to accept, considering the extensive OM literature on procurement contracting, but let us ignore such objections.

Let us assume that having received external financing according to the debt contract (l, r), the newsvendor can change her mind about the procurement quantity. Recall that we have analyzed a similar problem in Sect. 3.3.1.2. As we have proven in Proposition 3.1, when the newsvendor problem has a particular structure, then financial frictions do not affect the optimal order quantity. But this is due to a lucky modeling choice.

Here we shall modify the model slightly, by assuming that there are costs of inventory and backorders, i.e., $R(\xi, q) = p \min(\xi, q) - h(q - \xi)^+ - s(\xi - q)^+$.[6] It is important that all costs are either the actual financial losses or are convertible into the reduction of assets that can be used to repay debt obligations. The key to the

[6]See Sect. 3.4.2 for a discussion of these costs.

analysis is understanding the effect of the decision about q on the bankruptcy term in (3.4). This effect is described in the following lemma.

Lemma 3.1 *Suppose* $R(\xi, q) = p\min(\xi, q) - h(q-\xi)^+ - s(\xi - q)^+$ *and* $r < pq$. *Then*

$$\frac{d}{dq}\mathbb{E}\left[\{r - R(\xi, q)\}1_{\{R(\xi,q)<r\}}\right] = h\Pr\left[\xi < \frac{r+hq}{p+h}\right] - (p+s)\Pr\left[\xi > \frac{(p+s)q-r}{s}\right]. \quad (3.12)$$

Proof of Lemma 3.1 There are two cases: $\xi < q$ and $\xi \geq q$. Hence, we can rewrite the bankruptcy term as

$$E\left[\{r - R(\xi, q)\}1_{\{R(\xi,q)<r\}}\right] = E\left[\{r - R(\xi, q)\}1_{\{R(\xi,q)<r\}}1_{\{\xi<q\}}\right] + E\left[\{r - R(\xi, q)\}1_{\{R(\xi,q)<r\}}1_{\{\xi\geq q\}}\right]. \quad (3.13)$$

Conditions $\xi < q$ and $R(\xi, q) < r$ are equivalent to $\xi < q$ and $p\xi - h(q-\xi) < r$, which are equivalent to $(p+h)\xi < (p+h)q$ and $(p+h)\xi < r+hq$. From $r < pq$, condition $(p+h)\xi < r+hq$ implies $(p+h)\xi < (p+h)q$. Therefore, $\xi < q$ and $R(\xi, q) < r$ are equivalent to $(p+h)\xi < r+hq$.

Conditions $\xi \geq q$ and $R(\xi, q) < r$ are equivalent to $\xi \geq q$ and $pq - s(\xi - q) < r$, which are equivalent to $s\xi \geq sq$ and $s\xi > sq + pq - r$. From $r < pq$, condition $s\xi > sq + pq - r$ implies $s\xi \geq sq$. Therefore, $\xi \geq q$ and $R(\xi, q) < r$ are equivalent to $s\xi > sq + pq - r$.

Therefore, we can write the bankruptcy term as

$$E\left[\{r - R(\xi, q)\}1_{\{R(\xi,q)<r\}}\right] = E\left[\{r - p\xi + h(q-\xi)\}1_{\{p\xi - h(q-\xi)<r\}}\right] + E\left[\{r - pq + s(\xi - q)\}1_{\{pq-s(\xi-q)<r\}}\right]. \quad (3.14)$$

Taking the derivative with respect to q, we obtain (3.12). ■

The newsvendor solution q^* satisfies $\Pr[\xi \geq q] = \frac{c+h}{p+s+h}$. To understand the effect of moral hazard on operational decisions, consider the derivative of the objective function (3.4) evaluated at q^*. From Lemma 3.1, this derivative can be positive or negative depending on which term in (3.12) dominates. The contribution of these terms depends on the likelihoods of the demand being small. Overall, financing frictions can cause either under- or over-ordering relative to the newsvendor solution q^*. Therefore, financing choices matter for operational decisions.

As a useful check, from Lemma 3.1, when $h = s = 0$, the derivative of the bankruptcy term is zero and there is no deviation from the first-best newsvendor solution.

Importantly, we are not claiming that the order quantity will increase when the inventory cost h is high or the order quantity will decrease when the backorder cost s is high. Rather, the deviation from the newsvendor solution q^* will be higher or lower, respectively. The newsvendor solution itself is a function of h and s. The cause of the deviation from the newsvendor first-best solution is the non-contractibility of order quantities and limited liability, which is more valuable for low demand states when h is high and less valuable for high demand states when s is high.

In this analysis, we assumed financing is done using debt. We already mentioned work from finance on the optimal contract design. In an operational context, de Vericourt and Gromb (2018) applied the fundamental insight from Innes (1990) that the party exerting effort must be a residual claimant on the assets to the newsvendor problem and proved the optimality of debt financing.

3.3.2 *Capital Markets: A Few Key Results from the Asset Pricing Theory*

New Ideas and Tools Introduced Here *Absolute and relative pricing; the fundamental pricing equation; pricing kernel.*

As we discussed at the beginning of Sect. 3.3, capital market theory studies investors' preferences, investment choices, and asset pricing. There are numerous textbook treatments of the topic of asset pricing, including Ingersoll (1987), Pliska (1997), Björk (2004), Duffie (2010), Campbell (2017), and Cochrane (2001). We follow the exposition in Cochrane (2001), while highlighting OM applications.

The focus of asset pricing theory is on pricing and it uses two complementary approaches: *absolute pricing* and *relative pricing*. The absolute pricing approach establishes the fundamentals of investors' preferences, investment options, risks in the economy, markets, and firms, and determines prices using these fundamentals, usually in a general equilibrium framework. The relative pricing approach assumes some prices as given and determines prices of other assets relative to those. The approaches are complementary because often models built using the absolute pricing approach are trained on data, taking advantage of relative pricing relationships.

An example of the absolute pricing approach is the derivation of the fundamental pricing equation:

$$p = \mathbb{E}[mx], \text{ where } m = f(\text{data, parameters}). \tag{3.15}$$

We discuss the derivation of this equation is Sect. 3.3.2.1. In Eq. (3.15), p is the price of an asset with future cash flows x, and m is the *pricing kernel*. This equation is fundamental because it applies to any asset (stocks, bonds, options, money market accounts, etc.). It applies to assets that are traded and not traded. It works for investors in aggregate and for investors individually. It underlies every (or almost every) other result in asset pricing theory, although historically some of those results were not derived using this equation. The pricing kernel m is the same regardless of the asset being priced, it is the "secret sauce" in this pricing recipe, but it is not observable directly (also there could be more than one pricing kernel). The bounds on the choice of m are imposed by mathematical and economic properties of models that give rise to this equation (through absolute pricing, again) and by observed market prices (through relative pricing).

Again, due to space constraints, many important topics have been omitted. For example, transformation to a risk-neutral pricing measure, Arrow-Debreu securities, derivative pricing are discussed in Babich and Birge (2020) but not here.

3.3.2.1 The Fundamental Pricing Equation: Economic Motivation and Derivation

New Ideas and Tools Introduced Here *Consumption optimization; Law of One Price; arbitrage, absence of arbitrage; complete and incomplete markets.*

A useful economic motivation for the fundamental pricing equation (3.15) comes from a consumption optimization problem. However, the proof of the fundamental pricing equation is general and does not require this motivation. We hint to the proof after we present the motivation. The exposition follows closely asset pricing textbook by Cochrane (2001).

Consider an investor who receives endowments e_0 and e_1 at the beginning and end of a period, respectively. If the investor's consumption is c_0 and c_1 at the beginning and end of a period, respectively, the investor derives utility $U(c_0, c_1) = u(c_0) + \beta\mathbb{E}[u(c_1)]$, where β is a measure of the investor's impatience between periods, u is the interperiod consumption utility, and expectation is taken with respect to information at the beginning of a period. There is an asset that generates (possibly random) cash flows x at the end of a period and that can be bought or sold at the beginning of a period at price p (to be determined). The investor can trade any quantity q of this asset (positive, negative, fractional). The investor is a price taker, i.e., she does not believe that her trade will affect the price of the asset. We do not assume that the market is in an equilibrium. The investor's consumption optimization problem is

$$\max_{q} \quad u(c_0) + \beta\mathbb{E}[u(c_1)] \tag{3.16a}$$

$$\text{s.t.} \quad c_0 = e_0 - pq \text{ and } c_1 = e_1 + xq. \tag{3.16b}$$

The first-order condition for optimality of problem (3.16) is $-u'(c_0)p + \beta\mathbb{E}[u'(c_1)x] = 0$. Rearranging terms, we derive a pricing equation:

$$p = \mathbb{E}\left[\beta\frac{u'(c_1)}{u'(c_0)}x\right] = \mathbb{E}[mx], \text{ where } m = \beta\frac{u'(c_1)}{u'(c_0)}. \tag{3.17}$$

Observe that the pricing kernel m is random (both consumption c_1 and endowment e_1 are random) and that it measures a tradeoff between the marginal utilities of consumption between periods. Importantly the correlation between asset cash flow x and future consumption c_1 matters. Intuitively, assets that are negatively correlated with future consumption provide an opportunity for consumption smoothing and are priced higher.

The pricing equation applies to any asset. Consider a money market account with risk-free return R^f (that is, \$1 in the account at the beginning of a period grows to \$ R^f at the end, risk-free). Using pricing equation (3.15), $1 = \mathbb{E}[mR^f] = \mathbb{E}[m]R^f$. Therefore, $\mathbb{E}[m] = 1/R^f$. Consider a risk-free bond that guarantees a payment of \$1 at the end of a period. The price of this bond at the beginning of a period is $p = \mathbb{E}[m1] = \mathbb{E}[m] = 1/R^f$. Consider a stock with price p_1 and dividend d at the end of a period. Using (3.15), $p_0 = \mathbb{E}[m(p_1 + d)]$. Consider any investment with random return R (\$1 at the beginning of the period grows to R at the end of the period). Using (3.15), $1 = \mathbb{E}[mR] = \mathbb{E}\left[m\frac{R}{\mathbb{E}[R]}\right]\mathbb{E}[R] = \mathbb{E}[R]/(1+r)$, where the discount factor $1/(1+r) = \mathbb{E}\left[m\frac{R}{\mathbb{E}[R]}\right]$. The last example illustrates how the intuitive NPV pricing formula taught in MBA finance courses is a special case of the fundamental pricing equation and that the discount factor must account for risk that depends on the correlation between the pricing kernel and cash flows.

The proof of the existence of the fundamental pricing equation (3.15) does not require the machinery of consumption maximization and marginal utilities. It is a consequence of the *Law of One Price (LOOP)* and a mathematical result known as the Riesz Representation Theorem. The LOOP basically says that the security must have one price no matter through what linear combination of other securities it was created. More formally, if the set of payoffs on assets X is a Hilbert space, and payoff $x = ax_1 + bx_2$, with $x, x_1, x_2 \in X$, then under the LOOP, $p(x) = p(ax_1 + bx_2) = ap(x_1) + bp(x_2)$, where $p(\cdot) : X \to \mathbb{R}$ is the pricing function. The Riesz Representation Theorem guarantees the existence of the equivalent representation for the pricing function $p(x) = \mathbb{E}[mx]$, proving Eq. (3.15).

On the one hand, the LOOP is a weak condition to demand from financial markets. It is the least we can ask for that the price of a portfolio must equal a linear combination of prices of individual assets comprising this portfolio. On the other hand, transaction costs can cause ostensible violations of the LOOP. For example, if commodity trades require physically transporting products, prices will diverge, depending on the physical locations of products. This is the reason that oil prices are quoted for a particular location (e.g., Cushing, OK vs. North Sea). Similarly, various petroleum products are derived from the same initial component (crude oil), but because different industrial processes are required to produce heating oil and gasoline, their prices are different and are not just a linear combination of crude oil prices. Regulations, information barriers, and market structure may cause violations of the LOOP. Nevertheless, if markets are efficient in the sense that information about violations of the LOOP is available to market participants and these participants can form trades that exploit differences in prices, then the forces of supply and demand should eliminate LOOP violations.

This motivates a concept of *arbitrage*, which is stronger than the Law of One Price. An arbitrage is a trade that has non-negative cash flows at all times and has strictly positive cash flows with positive probability at some times. According to the definition of the *Absence of Arbitrage* from Cochrane (2001), for every payoff x which is non-negative almost surely and strictly positive with positive probability, the price $p(x)$ must be strictly positive. The absence of arbitrage is equivalent to a pricing kernel in Eq. (3.15) being strictly positive, $m > 0$.

To illustrate the concept of arbitrage, suppose that \$1 can be exchanged to either £0.76 or €0.84 in an FX market. Suppose that €1 can be exchanged for £0.8. There is an arbitrage opportunity because a trader can borrow £1, convert it to €$1/0.8$, convert those to \$ $1/(0.8 \times 0.84)$, and convert those to £1.13, return the borrowed £1, and keep £0.13 as a risk-free profit (noting that the FX market is very deep and these transactions can be executed almost instantly and with low transaction costs). Suppose that €1 can be exchanged for £1. Again, there is an arbitrage opportunity. A trader can borrow £1, convert it to \$ $1/0.76$, convert those to €$0.84/0.76$, and convert those to £1.11, return the borrowed £1, and keep £0.11 as the risk-free profit. One can calculate that the only exchange rate between € and £ that avoids arbitrage is €1 for £$0.76/0.84 \approx$ £0.90. In efficient markets enough traders will be aware of these opportunities and their trades will affect the relative demand for different currencies until any arbitrage opportunity disappears. The quicker the information about arbitrage opportunities is reflected in currency prices, the more efficient the markets are.

The absence of arbitrage assumption is the starting point for most asset pricing models. Just as with the LOOP, one can find examples of ostensible arbitrage opportunities. However, trading frictions usually make it impossible to act on these opportunities or turn cash flows from attempted arbitrage trades negative in at least some states of the world. Market efficiency usually justifies the absence of arbitrage assumption.

So far we have argued for the existence of a pricing kernel m and pointed out its properties ($m > 0$). Generally, a pricing kernel is not unique, except for a special case of complete markets. A market is *complete* if any payoff in any random future state can be replicated by a payoff from a portfolio of traded securities. In complete markets (and assuming the absence of arbitrage), the fundamental pricing equation (3.15) holds with unique $m > 0$. If markets are *incomplete*, there are multiple pricing kernels, some of which may violate the $m > 0$ property, but there exists at least one that satisfies it.

We motivated the fundamental pricing equation with the help of a simple one-period model. There are extensions to multi-period and continuous-time versions of this theory (see discussion in Cochrane, 2001).

What Does This Mean for Operations? Operational decisions should reflect the decision maker's objective. Firm managers are generally obligated to make decisions in the best interest of the firm owners, but managers' own objectives might conflict with those of the owners, creating agency problems. Assuming a firm-owner objective, if the owners are shareholders of a public firm, then the decisions should reflect risk preferences consistent with those of the financial market. This observation implies that uncertain cash flows affected by the operational decisions of a public firm should be viewed from a financial market perspective.

The fundamental pricing equation (3.15) is the tool to use to price payoff x from operational cash flow of the firm from a financial market perspective. Importantly, the pricing equation is linear, even if investors are risk-averse. In the following we further elaborate that when the operational payoff x is uncorrelated with the pricing kernel m, the expected value of payoff $\mathbb{E}[x]$ is the correct financial metric to use. Moreover, one can adjust the distribution of random outcomes so that even if the payoff is correlated with the pricing kernel under the original distribution, the right objective is $\mathbb{E}^Q[x]$, where expectation is taken with respect to the adjusted probability measure.

This is an important insight because operations models traditionally used expected profits, revenues, and costs and performance metrics. Operations models were correct, even if investors are risk-averse.

Of course, the operational cash flow x itself can be a result of a non-linear transformation of decision variables and random shocks. For example, for the newsvendor's revenue $x = p\min(q, \xi)$, optimization over q requires us to consider the effect of non-linearity in this function.

So, if we study the problem from the perspective of an investor who contemplates adding the newsvendor's cash flows to its portfolio, and the demand shock ξ is uncorrelated with the pricing kernel, the value of the newsvendor as a firm is the value that OM literature uses:

$$p\mathbb{E}[m\min(q, \xi)] - cq = p\mathbb{E}[m]\mathbb{E}[\min(q, \xi)] - cq = \frac{p}{R^f}\mathbb{E}[\min(q, \xi)] - cq. \tag{3.18}$$

But the above derivation assumes that the LOOP or the absence of arbitrage assumptions hold in the financial market where the newsvendor's asset is traded. If the asset is not traded or if there are significant transaction costs of trading, or if fractional positions in the newsvendor's asset are not allowed, the fundamental pricing equation predicts a range, sometimes very wide, of possible prices and the investor needs other criteria, including the investor's utility function to value this investment. Similarly, the newsvendor herself might have non-tradable attachment to this business, in which case there is a potential for agency problems to arise, such that investors use linear pricing equation (3.15) and the newsvendor, who controls the ordering decisions, uses non-linear criteria (e.g., a newsvendor's utility function).

To summarize, the choice of the optimization criteria depends on whose perspective one considers. If the perspective is that of investors and financial markets operate efficiently so that the LOOP assumption is reasonable and claims on operational cash flows are traded without significant transaction costs in financial markets, then the fundamental pricing equation (3.15) allows the use of mathematical expectation, which is a linear operator, even if investors are risk-averse, or heterogeneous in their risk preferences (see Birge, 2015 for an additional explanation).

Applying absence of arbitrage arguments as a motivation for operational assumptions and even to value operational cash flows should be done with caution. Absence of arbitrage is a statement about financial markets, and ability to form trades with certain properties in these markets. It is not an arbitrage opportunity if there is no trade possibility. An entrepreneur creating a company is not an arbitrageur if the entrepreneur has unique knowledge, insight, skills, or patents that others cannot copy without frictions. Just as with the Modigliani and Miller (1958) results, no-arbitrage pricing is a statement about why one cannot easily generate value through financial manipulations, not a statement about real assets and real economy. Clearly, firms create value every day by providing products and services to their customers.

On the other hand, relationships might exist between prices of inputs and outputs in multiple markets and a variety of intermediate holding, transportation, and transformation prices that are subject to arbitrage trades. Assuming independent processes (or constants) for prices that should depend on one another can lead to results that are far from reality. It may be possible that market participants may remain unaware of persistent arbitrage opportunities, but building such information failures into models often requires heroic assumptions that may defy credibility.

3.3.2.2 Risk-Return Trade-Off and Factor Pricing Equations: CAPM

New Ideas and Tools Introduced Here *Risk-adjustment; efficient portfolio; efficient frontier; Capital Asset Pricing Model; wealth portfolio; factor models.*

We rewrite pricing equation (3.15) to highlight a link between risk and return. Using relationships $\mathbb{E}[mx] = \mathbb{C}ov[m,x] + \mathbb{E}[m]\mathbb{E}[x]$ and $\mathbb{E}[m] = 1/R^f$, change Eq. (3.15) to

$$p = \mathbb{E}[mx] = \mathbb{C}ov[m,x] + \mathbb{E}[m]\mathbb{E}[x] = \frac{1}{R^f}\mathbb{E}[x] + \mathbb{C}ov[m,x]. \tag{3.19}$$

Equation (3.19) has an appealing structure. It says that the price of an asset equals the expected value of the payoff discounted at the risk-free rate, plus a risk-adjustment term. The value of the latter depends on the correlation between the payoff x and the pricing kernel m. If the two are uncorrelated, the variability in x does not matter for pricing and the price is based on $\mathbb{E}[x]$ only.

The fundamental pricing equation application to asset returns yields $1 = \mathbb{E}[mR]$. Applying a similar transformation to this equation, we derive the equation: $1 = \mathbb{E}[R]/R^f + \mathbb{C}ov[m,R]$. Multiplying the latter by R^f and rearranging terms to isolate $\mathbb{E}[R]$, we derive

$$\mathbb{E}[R] = R^f - R^f\mathbb{C}ov[R,m]. \tag{3.20}$$

Using definition $\mathbb{C}ov[m, R] = \rho\sigma_m\sigma_R$ in (3.20) generates

$$\mathbb{E}[R] = R^f - \rho R^f \sigma_m \sigma_R. \tag{3.21}$$

For a given amount of risk σ_R, the expected return in excess of the risk-free return depends on the correlation ρ between the return and the pricing kernel. An *efficient frontier* is a set of all securities that have the highest expected return for a given level of risk. From Eq. (3.21), the maximum return corresponds to $\rho = -1$, yielding a linear equation for the efficient frontier:

$$\mathbb{E}[R] = R^f + R^f \sigma_m \sigma_R. \tag{3.22}$$

The significance of the efficient frontier (3.22) is that it allows us to estimate pricing kernel m based on the observed prices. In particular, if we found a portfolio we believe to be efficient, with return R^*, then returns on all other efficient portfolios can be written as $R = R^f + a(R^* - R^f)$ for some a. Moreover, R^* is a linear function of the pricing kernel m and the pricing kernel m is a linear function of R^*. Therefore, if we find an efficient portfolio and can measure its returns, we can determine the pricing kernel, and apply it in the fundamental pricing equation (3.15) for all assets. To see this, let $m = a + bR^*$. After applying pricing equation (3.20) to R^* we obtain

$$\mathbb{E}[R^*] = R^f - R^f \mathbb{C}ov[a + bR^*, R^*] = R^f - R^f b\mathbb{V}ar[R^*]. \tag{3.23}$$

Therefore, $-R^f b\mathbb{V}ar[R^*] = \mathbb{E}[R^*] - R^f$. Applying the pricing equation (3.20) to an arbitrary return R, we obtain $\mathbb{E}[R] = R^f - R^f \mathbb{C}ov[a + bR^*, R] = R^f - R^f b\mathbb{V}ar[R^*]\mathbb{C}ov[R^*, R]/\mathbb{V}ar[R^*]$ and

$$\mathbb{E}[R] = R^f + \beta_{R,R^*}(\mathbb{E}[R^*] - R^f), \tag{3.24}$$

in which $\beta_{R,R^*} = \mathbb{C}ov[R^*, R]/\mathbb{V}ar[R^*]$ is the beta of return R relative to the return of the efficient portfolio. If one can observe R^*, then Eq. (3.24) offers a practical pricing formula.

The structure of Eq. (3.24) may remind some readers of the *Capital Asset Pricing Model (CAPM)*. This is not an accident. Although historically CAPM has been derived differently, it is a consequence of the fundamental pricing equation. Theoretically CAPM corresponds to $m = a + bR^W$, where R^W is the return on the total wealth portfolio. Practically, R^W is not observable but is assumed to be proxied by a stock-index return, such as the S&P500-index return. Therefore, CAPM is usually written as

$$\mathbb{E}[R] = R^f + \beta_{R,R^M}(\mathbb{E}[R^M] - R^f), \tag{3.25}$$

with market M being S&P500. The fact that the wealth portfolio is efficient should be intuitive. If we assume the existence of a representative investor and consider what assets such an investor will trade with her wealth in equilibrium, then, by definition, the only assets in the economy are the ones that the investor trades and the investor trades all of the assets in the economy. This implies $m = a + bR^W$.

One can also prove linear relationship $m = a + bR^W$ using the consumption maximization motivation of the fundamental pricing equation. Suppose that an investor has wealth W_0 at the beginning of a period. The economy comprises n assets with returns R^i, $i = 1, \ldots, n$, plus asset $n + 1$, which is a risk-free asset. A return on a portfolio with weights $\mathbf{x} = (x_1, \ldots, x_{n+1})$, such that $\sum_{i=1}^{n+1} x_i = 1$, is $R^W = \mathbf{x}^T\mathbf{R} = \sum_{i=1}^{n+1} x_i R^i$. This is the wealth portfolio because after the initial consumption c_0, the investor invests the remaining wealth into the portfolio and enjoys $W_1 = R^W(W_0 - c_0)$ by the end of the period. There is no additional endowment. Therefore, consumption at the end of the period is $c_1 = W_1$. Suppose that the interperiod utility is quadratic: $u(c) = -0.5(c - c^*)^2$. From Eq. (3.17),

$$m = \beta\frac{u'(c_1)}{u'(c)} = \beta\frac{c_1 - c^*}{c_0 - c^*} = \beta\frac{R^W(W_0 - c_0) - c^*}{c_0 - c^*}, \tag{3.26}$$

which is linear in R^W. As we already established, linearity leads to the CAPM.

It is also instructive to derive the CAPM directly following Sharpe (1964) and Lintner (1965). Assume CARA interperiod utility and normally distributed returns (if n is large and the variations in the returns correspond to sequences of additive shocks with appropriate mixing properties, then even if returns are not normal, a normal approximation works well). Let $q_i = x_i(W_0 - c_0)$ for $i = 1, \ldots, n$, be the number of shares of risky assets in the portfolio. The remainder, $(W_0 - c_0) - \sum_{i=1}^{n} q_i$, is invested in the risk-free asset. The consumption at the end of the period is $c_1 = W_1 = \mathbf{q}^T\left(\mathbf{R} - R^f\right) + R^f(W_0 - c_0)$. The utility of this consumption is

$$\mathbb{E}[u(c_1)] = -\mathbb{E}[e^{-\alpha c_1}] = -e^{-\alpha\mathbb{E}[c_1] + 1/2\alpha^2\mathbb{V}ar[c_1]}. \tag{3.27}$$

Because the exponential function is increasing, the utility optimization problem is equivalent to

$$\max_{\mathbf{q}} \mathbf{q}^T\left(\mathbb{E}[\mathbf{R}] - R^f\right) - \frac{1}{2}\alpha\mathbf{q}^T\mathbf{V}\mathbf{q}, \tag{3.28}$$

where $\mathbf{V}$ is the Variance-Covariance matrix of $\mathbf{R}$. The optimality condition for this problem is

$$\mathbb{E}[\mathbf{R}] - R^f - \alpha\mathbf{V}\mathbf{q} = 0. \tag{3.29}$$

Compute

$$\mathbf{V}\mathbf{q} = \mathbb{C}ov[\mathbf{R}, \mathbf{q}^T\mathbf{R}] = \mathbb{C}ov\left[\mathbf{R}, \mathbf{q}^T\left(\mathbf{R} - R^f\right) + R^f(W_0 - c_0)\right] = \mathbb{C}ov[\mathbf{R}, \mathbf{R}^M], \tag{3.30}$$

where R^M is the return on the market portfolio, assuming that the investor is representative. This produces the CAPM equation (although in a less familiar form):

$$\mathbb{E}[\mathbf{R}] - R^f = \alpha \mathbb{C}ov[\mathbf{R}, R^M]. \tag{3.31}$$

Applying this equation to the market portfolio itself, we derive an expression for the market price of risk and prove that it equals the risk-aversion coefficient of the CARA utility function, as follows:

$$\lambda_M = \frac{\mathbb{E}[R^M] - R^f}{\mathbb{V}ar[R^M]} = \alpha. \tag{3.32}$$

We recover the familiar CAPM equation by substituting (3.32) into (3.31) instead of α:

$$\mathbb{E}[R_i] - R^f = \beta_{i,M}(\mathbb{E}[R^M] - R^f), \tag{3.33}$$

in which $\beta_{i,M} = \mathbb{C}ov[R^i, R^M]/\mathbb{V}ar[R^M]$. In the discussion below we need a version of pricing equation (3.33), recast in terms of payoff instead of returns, as follows:

$$p = \frac{1}{R^f}\mathbb{E}[x] - \frac{1}{R^f}\beta_{x,M}(\mathbb{E}[R^M] - R^f), \tag{3.34}$$

in which $\beta_{x,M} = \mathbb{C}ov[x, R^M]/\mathbb{V}ar[R^M]$.

Applications of the fundamental pricing equation in practice require us knowing at least one efficient portfolio. CAPM uses the portfolio of the total wealth, which comprises all assets traded and non-traded. The accuracy of CAPM predictions depends on how close the observable index, like S&P500, approximates the total unobservable wealth portfolio (including non-traded assets). Finance research has shown that, although in theory CAPM is correct, in applications, it is not accurate (at least with standard proxies for the market portfolio).

Therefore, other models for estimating returns on an efficient portfolio are also used. These models argue that returns on an efficient portfolio can be written as a linear combination of well-chosen *factors*, which leads to pricing models of the form:

$$\mathbb{E}[R] = \alpha + \beta_{R,1}\lambda_1 + \beta_{R,2}\lambda_2 + \cdots + \lambda_{R,n}\lambda_n, \tag{3.35}$$

in which λ_k is the market price of risk for factor k and $\beta_{R,k}$ is the beta of return R relative to factor k. One of the factors can be the S&P500 portfolio. Other popular factors are the difference in returns between portfolios of small and big firms, and portfolios of firms with high and low book to market ratios, portfolios of past winners and losers (Fama & French, 1992, 1993; Carhart, 1997). By using multiple factors, alternative models attempt approximate an efficient portfolio better.

Theoretically, the number of factors in a model does not matter, because they are just an interpretation of the same efficient frontier in different coordinates. Practically, empirical performance of multi-factor models is superior to the classical CAPM.

Regardless of the practical implementation, the fundamental pricing equation (3.19) tells us that investors demand a price premium for systematic risks in the payoffs (i.e., payoffs that are correlated with the pricing kernel, or any of the representations of the pricing kernel). Most studies find little influence from idiosyncratic risk on asset pricing in financial markets, and perhaps because of market imperfections (such as taxes, Birge & Yang, 2007) idiosyncratic risk may even have a positive effect (Ang et al., 2006). Of course, as discussed in Babich and Birge (2020), firms may have costs that depend on the total uncertainty (including idiosyncratic risk) in their operating profits, which motivates the need for corporate risk management.

What Does This Mean in Operations? Consider the following example. We would like to price at $t = 0$ two payoffs, A and B, to be paid at $t = 1$, such that both payoffs are identically distributed with a mean \$100 and a standard deviation of \$20. To make this discussion concrete, assume both payoffs are a result of the production of trucks. The uncertainty of cash flow A is the result of a random production yield, due to the performance of an individual machine or worker, whose work performance is not affected by economic conditions. Cash flow B is the result of production of trucks with deterministic yield, but with uncertain demand that is correlated with the economy. Specifically, assume that $B = (1 + r - \bar{r})100$, where r is the sale growth, and $\bar{r} = \mathbb{E}[r]$.

Consider the valuation of payoff A by investors. Using the fundamental pricing equation (3.19), because this payoff is not correlated with the pricing kernel (and its representation though wealth portfolio return), $\mathbb{C}ov[m, A] = 0$ and the price p_A equals the expected payoff discounted at the risk-free rate. Assuming a risk-free rate of $r_f = 5\%$, a one-period money market return is $R^f = 1 + r_f$. Therefore, $p_A = \mathbb{E}[A]/R^f = 100/1.05 = \$95.24$.

Next, consider valuation of payoff B by investors. This cash flow is correlated with the economy. To apply valuation Eq. (3.34), we need to estimate β of payoffs with the market and the market risk premium. We can try to do this using historical data for similar cash flows, e.g., historical sales growth per year of the same product, and regress those against market returns. Table 3.9 presents the historical data for 10 years of North American truck sales growth and the returns on the S&P500 index over the same time period. The average return on 1-year US Treasury note (a proxy for risk-free return) over this period was $r_h^f = 1.67\%$.

To provide inputs into Eq. (3.34), we estimate the market risk premium from Table 3.9 to be $\mathbb{E}[R^M] - R_h^f = 0.0645 - 0.0167 = 0.0478$, and the regression coefficient of sales growth to market is $\beta_{r,M} = 0.3323$. Using formula $B = (1 + r - \bar{r})100$, this means that $\beta_{B,M} = 33.23$. Overall, the price of payoff B is

$$p_B = \frac{1}{R^f}\mathbb{E}[B] - \frac{1}{R^f}\beta_{B,M}\left(\mathbb{E}[R^M] - R_h^f\right)$$

Table 3.9 North American truck sales, 2007–2016 from WardsAuto Group (2018), and S&P500 index returns from Yahoo! Finance (2018)

Year	Truck sales growth (r)	S&P500 return
2016	6.4%	9.5%
2015	12.9%	−0.7%
2014	10.3%	11.4%
2013	10.1%	29.6%
2012	8.3%	13.4%
2011	13.3%	0.0%
2010	18.0%	12.8%
2009	−22.7%	23.5%
2008	−24.4%	−38.5%
2007	−4.2%	3.5%

$$= \frac{100}{1.05} - \frac{1}{1.05} \times 33.23 \times 0.0478 = \$93.73. \tag{3.36}$$

We used the historical market risk premium $\mathbb{E}[R^M] - R_h^f = 0.0478$, but the forward looking estimate of the risk-free return $R^f = 1.05$.

In this simple example, the difference in prices of cash flows A and B is about 2%. The gap $\frac{1}{R^f}\beta_{B,M}\left(\mathbb{E}[R^M] - R_h^f\right)$ depends on the beta between the cash flow and the market and on the market price premium. For example, many luxury or discretionary items have higher market sensitivity (as noted in Gaur & Seshadri, 2005). Recent results (e.g., Martin, 2013) suggest that the market risk premium can be quite volatile and may have risen to five times its long-run average during the 2008–2009 financial crisis, which would have implied substantial price differences even at short time horizons between valuations of cash flows with low and high market sensitivity.

In this example, we took the distributions of cash flows A and B as given. But the entire point of operations management is to control those cash flows. Consider a newsvendor model, as an example. Using pricing equation (3.19), the value of future revenues $x = p\min(\xi, q)$ is[7]

$$v = \frac{1}{R^f}\mathbb{E}[x] + \mathbb{C}ov[m, x] = \frac{1}{R^f}\mathbb{E}[p\min(\xi, q)] + \mathbb{C}ov[m, p\min(\xi, q)]. \tag{3.37}$$

The risk-adjustment term, $\mathbb{C}ov[m, p\min(\xi, q)]$, depends on the order quantity q. If q is low, it constrains the demand, the revenue has little correlation with the economy, and $\mathbb{C}ov[m, p\min(\xi, q)]$ is low. But if q is high, sales closely follow the unconstrained demand, and, assuming the demand is correlated with the economy, the risk-adjustment factor $\mathbb{C}ov[m, p\min(\xi, q)]$ is higher.

[7]We use variable v for value because in the newsvendor model variable p represents product sales price.

In the CAPM version of the pricing equation (3.34), the decision q affects $\beta_{x,M}$ in the risk-adjustment factor $-\frac{1}{R^f}\beta_{x,M}(\mathbb{E}[R^M] - R^f)$. Therefore, in addition to the traditional newsvendor tradeoffs (Sect. 3.4.2), we also need to analyze the effect of q on the covariance between revenues and the market. This makes the newsvendor optimization problem more challenging. One thing is certain—the risk adjustment affects the optimal order quantity.

Suppose that demand ξ is uncorrelated with market return R^M. Then, we have the classical newsvendor problem (as in Sect. 3.4.2, but with discounting of future cash flows) whose solution is q^{nv}. Suppose that demand ξ is positively correlated with market return R^M. Then the risk-adjustment factor $\beta_{x,M}$ is increasing q and one can prove that the risk-adjusted order quantity $q^{pos} < q^{nv}$, where super-index pos stands for the positive correlation between the demand and the market return. Suppose that demand ξ is negatively correlated with market return R^M. Then the risk-adjustment factor $\beta_{x,M}$ is decreasing in q and one can prove that the risk-adjusted order quantity $q^{neg} > q^{nv}$, where super-index neg stands for the negative correlation between the demand and the market return. In other words, unless product demand is uncorrelated with the market, from the perspective of investors, the solution to the classical newsvendor problem overestimates the optimal order quantity (if the demand and the market return are positively correlated) and underestimates the optimal order quantity (if the demand and the market return are negatively correlated). Intuitively, investors are risk-averse and use q to control their exposure to risk. If demand ξ is negatively correlated with the investors' portfolio, they increase exposure to ξ by increasing q. The opposite holds for positive correlation.

Finally, the risk-adjustment factor captures systematic risk (i.e., risk correlated with the entire economy). But this does not mean that idiosyncratic uncertainty in demand ξ can be ignored. Even if demand ξ is uncorrelated with the economy and the pricing formula for the newsvendor's revenue simplifies to

$$v = \frac{1}{R^f}\mathbb{E}[x] = \frac{1}{R^f}\mathbb{E}[p \min(\xi, q)], \tag{3.38}$$

the non-linear function min() exposes investors to the total variability in demand ξ and affects their valuation v. The distinction between systemic and idiosyncratic risk applies to investors' cash flows. It does not apply directly to shocks that generate those cash flows, if the transformation between shocks and investors' cash flows is non-linear.

Importantly, even if some of the operational risks are correlated with the market, there is a transformation (to a risk-neutral pricing measure) that allows us to price all (!) cash flows simply by taking the expectation with respect to that measure. This is a tremendously powerful approach, but due to space constraints we direct readers to other sources such as Babich and Birge (2020).

3.4 A Brief OM Primer for Finance Researchers

3.4.1 Overview: A Struggle to Reconcile Demand and Supply

New Ideas and Tools Introduced Here *Supply does not equal demand in real systems; approaches for managing a mismatch*

Operations management (OM) strives to design, organize, and deliver the transformational processes to an organizational system. The goal of OM practice and research is to improve the efficiency and effectiveness of these systems in meeting customer requirements, by balancing scarce resources, aligning conflicting incentives, managing difficult tradeoffs, sharing information, and increasing the system's, quality-qualified output for a given amount of input.

Increasing operational efficiency involves the optimal allocation of common and limited resources to multiple types of activities and outputs, the consideration of fixed costs and setup times for production, and understanding effects of variability in yield, quality, production time, and dimensions of consumer demand, managing complex decentralized systems, such as supply chains (see Fig. 3.3). A unifying theme of much of research in OM is the recognition that, contrary to the common financial economics assumption, most of the time *the demand does not equal supply through the power of pricing alone*. They are equal in aggregate and over long time scales or in liquid markets, in individual and short-term transactions between buyers and sellers, demand does not equal supply. Therefore, in practice, there are shortages, excess inventory, customers waiting for products and services, and customers receiving the wrong kinds of products and services. Managing the imbalance between supply and demand features in finance as well, if markets are illiquid, products are not standardized, or when studying market micro-structure (e.g., the order books management by market makers).

Fundamentally, there are four OM approaches for managing the mismatch between the demand and supply:

1. *Manage uncertainty in supply, demand, and process*: this includes forecasting, marketing, efforts to reduce variability in demand, supply, and production process, through risk pooling (Sect. 3.4.3), flexibility (Sect. 3.4.4), contracting (Babich & Birge, 2020), process improvements (Babich & Birge, 2020), and quality management (Babich & Birge, 2020);
2. *Manage capacity and inventory*: the newsvendor model (Sect. 3.4.2) exemplifies the balance between costs of supply-demand mismatch; inventory of finished products or raw materials allows response to variable demand and supply (Sect. 3.4.5);
3. *Manage customers' waiting*: instead of products waiting for customers, customers wait for products or for services; Queueing theory provides a number of useful insights about the stochastic behavior of such systems (Babich & Birge, 2020);

4. *Manage pricing*: revenue management offers insights into the optimal policy for setting prices over time to maximize the revenue from a fixed amount of inventory (Babich & Birge, 2020).

In the following sections, we describe several key ideas in OM and the relevant models that relate to these approaches. Once again, Babich and Birge (2020) discuss additional topics not included here.

3.4.2 Order Commitment and the Newsvendor Model

New Ideas and Tools Introduced Here *Overage and underage costs, newsvendor's critical fractile*

In many practical situations, production or purchase decisions are required at periodic intervals that are determined by external forces, such as the daily production of a newspaper for morning distribution. In these cases, the price of the product is often set in advance (perhaps so that consumers can plan their purchases), but the overall demand for the product is not known. The producer's decision is then to determine the optimal quantity to produce in advance of realizing the product's demand. This situation leads to the classical *newsvendor* model.

The textbook description of this model is that a newsvendor must commit to purchase quantity q at the unit cost c at time $t = 0$. The order quantity decision must be made before the demand for the product (newspapers) is known. The price of the product p is fixed.

The demand is observed by the end of the period and is modeled by a random variable ξ. For simplicity, assume that ξ is a continuous random variable with the cumulative distribution function F. Any units unsold by the end of the period incur cost h, called the holding cost. Interpretations of this cost vary, ranging from the physical cost of storing or discarding newspapers to the interest on the loan. This cost can be adjusted for the salvage value of the product (e.g., if the newsvendor sends leftovers to a recycler). For each unsatisfied unit of demand the newsvendor incurs the shortage cost s. The interpretations of this cost range from the loss of customer goodwill and future sales to monetary compensation paid to the customers. If a newsvendor can place an expedited order for additional newspapers with the publisher to meet the shortage, this is also captured through s. Assuming the newsvendor is risk-neutral, the newsvendor's goal is to determine a quantity q, which maximizes her total expected profit:

$$\pi(q) = \mathbb{E}[R(\xi, q) - cq] = \mathbb{E}\left[p \min(\xi, q) - h(q - \xi)^+ - s(\xi - q)^+ - cq\right], \tag{3.39}$$

where the expectation $\mathbb{E}$ is with respect to uncertain demand ξ. Straightforward algebraic transformations, taking advantage of the following relationships $\min(\xi, q) = \xi - (\xi - q)^+$, $cq = c(q - \xi) + c\xi$, and $(q - \xi) = (q - \xi)^+ - (\xi - q)^+$, allow us to rewrite expression (3.39) as

$$\pi(q) = (p - c)\mathbb{E}[\xi] - \mathbb{E}\left[(h + c)(q - \xi)^+ + (p + s - c)(\xi - q)^+\right]. \quad (3.40)$$

Representation (3.40) highlights the tradeoffs involved in the newsvendor's decision. If the newsvendor were able to guess the demand exactly, then the newsvendor will receive profit $(p - c)\xi$ (the expected value). Otherwise, the newsvendor suffers from two types of costs. If the newsvendor ordered too much and $q > \xi$, then the term with $(q - \xi)^+$ is activated and for every extra unit the newsvendor loses holding cost h and ordering cost c. The expression $o = h + c$ is referred to as the *overage* or *excess* cost. If the newsvendor ordered too little and $q < \xi$, then the term with $(\xi - q)^+$ is activated and for every unit short the newsvendor loses revenue p, pays shortage cost s, but avoids ordering cost c. The term $u = p+s-c$ is referred to as the *underage* cost. Thus, we see that when choosing order quantity q the newsvendor is trying to balance these two types of costs. To find q for which the optimal balance between these costs is achieved, one writes the first-order condition as follows:

$$\pi'(q) = o \Pr[q > \xi] - u \Pr[\xi > q] = 0. \quad (3.41)$$

To derive this expression we used the following property $\frac{d}{dq}\mathbb{E}[(q - \xi)^+] = \Pr[q > \xi]$, which can be proven by writing the expectation as an integral and applying the Leibnitz's rule. Using relationship $\Pr[\xi > q] = 1 - \Pr[q > \xi]$, we derive the solution of equation (3.41):

$$F(q^*) = \Pr[\xi < q^*] = \frac{u}{u + o} = \frac{p + s - c}{p + s + h}, \quad \text{or} \quad q^* = F^{-1}\left(\frac{p + s - c}{p + s + h}\right), \quad (3.42)$$

where the fraction $\frac{u}{u+o}$ is known as the *critical fractile.*

What Are the Consequences of the Newsvendor Model for Finance Researchers? The newsvendor model offers a flexible mathematical framework that fits many situations. Most economic investments require a leadtime and there are consequences of reserving too many or too few resources. Any capacity investment problem, e.g., when a firm needs to determine how many people to hire, or how many factories to build, or how much web service bandwidth to reserve, is likely to fit the newsvendor framework. Every year, the US IRS code forces American taxpayers to solve a newsvendor problem when choosing the amount to funds to put in a Flexible Spending Account.[8] Even purely financial decisions, e.g., the choice of the capital structure can be couched as the newsvendor problem. For example, suppose that the firm cannot raise debt financing frequently and must choose the level of debt with face value D that comes due at the end of the period and for which interest payments are iD. Assume that tax shield on interest payment is τiD and bankruptcy costs are s per every dollar of obligations not covered by the firm's assets. Assume the firm's assets at the end of the period are modeled as a

[8]https://operationsroom.wordpress.com/2011/12/09/the-newsvendor-and-the-tax-man-do-americans-not-put-enough-money-into-flexible-spending-accounts/.

random variable V. Then the firm chooses D so that

$$\max_D \mathbb{E}\left[V(T) - s[D(1+i) - V(T)]^+ + \tau i D\right], \tag{3.43}$$

which is a version of the newsvendor's problem.

The newsvendor model extends to many other situations in which production requires a commitment before demand is observed (see Porteus, 1990 for a discussion of generalizations of the newsvendor model and its applications).

3.4.3 Demand Risk (or Inventory) Pooling

New Ideas and Tools Introduced Here *Multi-location firm, benefits due to Jensen's inequality, benefits due to reduction in inventory, examples of demand pooling.*

An insight that received significant attention in OM since the paper by Eppen (1979) is that a single inventory pool satisfying multiple, not perfectly correlated demands, increases the firm's value, by reducing sales uncertainty. This is called *demand risk pooling* or *inventory pooling*. Intuitively, this insight is similar to the financial portfolio diversification result, but there is an additional twist because, unlike financial portfolio analysis, not only the allocation, but also the scale of the investment matters.

The following is a simple illustration of the pooling effect. Suppose a newsvendor (Sect. 3.4.2) firm operates N locations with i.i.d. demands $\{\xi_i\}_{i=1}^N$, such that $\mu = \mathbb{E}[\xi_i]$ and $\sigma^2 = \mathbb{V}ar[\xi_i]$. Assume the firm decides on the orders $\{q_i\}_{i=1}^N$ for each location independently. Then for each location i, the expected newsvendor profit (3.40) is

$$\pi_i(q) = (p-c)\mu - \sigma\mathbb{E}\left[(h+c)\left(\frac{q-\mu}{\sigma} - \frac{\xi-\mu}{\sigma}\right)^+ \right.$$
$$\left. +(p+s-c)\left(\frac{\xi-\mu}{\sigma} - \frac{q-\mu}{\sigma}\right)^+\right]. \tag{3.44}$$

If demands are normally distributed, then $z = \frac{\xi-\mu}{\sigma}$ follows the standard normal distribution. Define variable $Q = \frac{q-\mu}{\sigma}$ as the scaled version of variable q. Then the expected profit from (3.44) becomes

$$\pi_i(Q) = (p-c)\mu - \sigma\mathbb{E}\left[(h+c)(Q-z)^+ + (p+s-c)(z-Q)^+\right]. \tag{3.45}$$

Importantly, expression $K(Q) = \mathbb{E}\left[(h+c)(Q-z)^+ + (p+s-c)(z-Q)^+\right]$ does not depend on the demand parameters (μ, σ). Quantity Q^* that minimizes cost $K(Q)$ satisfies the critical fractile condition (3.42) and does not depend on (μ, σ) either. The optimal profit of the firm that operates N locations independently equals:

$$\sum_{i=1}^{N} \pi_i(Q^*) = (p-c)\mu N - \sigma N K(Q^*). \tag{3.46}$$

Next, suppose that the firm aggregates demands from all locations and fulfils aggregate demand from the inventory at one central location. Other model assumptions remain unchanged. The pooled demand is $\xi_P = \sum_{i=1}^{N} \xi_i \sim \mathcal{N}(\mu N, \sigma^2 N)$. Using Eq. (3.45),

$$\pi_P(Q) = (p-c)\mu N - \sigma\sqrt{N}\mathbb{E}\left[(h+c)(Q-z)^+ + (p+s-c)(z-Q)^+\right]. \tag{3.47}$$

The same Q^* minimizes cost $K(Q)$ and the optimal profit of the firm that pools demand and inventory at one location equals:

$$\pi_P(Q^*) = (p-c)\mu N - \sigma\sqrt{N}K(Q^*). \tag{3.48}$$

Comparing equations (3.46) with (3.48), observe that the firm that pools demand has smaller demand uncertainty cost. This benefit is accrued not just for the optimal quantity Q^* but for any Q. There is another advantage of the demand pooling in the form of reduced safety stock. In the system without pooling, $q_i = \mu + \sigma Q^*$, where part μ represents the order quantity in the absence of uncertainty and part σQ^* is the safety stock that protects against uncertainty. In the system with the pooled demand the order quantity is $q_P = \mu N + \sigma\sqrt{N}Q^*$ in total, or $q_P/N = \mu + (\sigma/\sqrt{N})Q^*$ per location, smaller than that for the non-pooling system. If the number of locations the firm operates quadruples, the safety stock in the pooled inventory system only doubles.

Using the operational performance metrics, the probability of a stock-out at a given location is the same (because it is determined by Q^*) for both systems. The total expected overage and underage costs are smaller in the system with pooled demand (they are scaled by σN in the non-pooling system and $\sigma\sqrt{N}$ in the pooling system).

We have illustrated the benefits of pooling using a simple model, but the insights transcend our modeling assumptions. For example, Eppen (1979) does not require demands to be independent. One can relax normality assumptions, consider dynamic version of the problem, introduce general dependence structures among demands (see Corbett & Rajaram, 2006, and the references therein). These insights are related to the idea that operational flexibility is valuable (Birge et al., 1998).

Many mechanisms enable demand pooling in practice. Firm can build a central physical warehouse, or adopt a computer system that pools inventory virtually. Transhipments between stores and car dealerships are an example of demand pooling (Anupindi et al., 2001; Dong & Rudi, 2004). Delayed product differentiation, where manufacturers try to postpone customization of products to a specific country or a specific customer segment, is also a form of demand pooling (Lee & Tang, 1997). Reduction in the product assortment facilitates demand pooling, as was illustrated during SARS-COV-2 pandemic panic buying, as retailers reduced the variety of brands offered to customers (Gasparro et al., 2020). Other forms of product assortment reduction are promotions and adjusting price incentives for customers to substitute from one product to another. Demand can be pooled not only geographically, but also over time, which can be particularly useful if the capacity is reusable. For example, consider Governor Cuomo's pleading with other governors to pool the ventilator capacity. New York State would use this capacity initially and once the other states become pandemic hot spots, they would get the ventilator capacity. Adelman (2020) provides detailed arguments on the benefits of sharing ventilators among states.

Inventory pooling is not without costs. Transportation times and costs can be higher and service levels lower. Concentrating inventory in one physical location increases risk that it will be lost due to a natural disaster or another supply shock. Virtual pooling of inventory requires building a more sophisticated information management system, which exposes firms to cyber risks. Designing a product that allows delayed differentiation can be more expensive. Managers must have incentives to share their inventory with other locations (e.g., a dealership that physically holds a car, receives a cut if a car is sold by another dealer).

What Are the Consequences of Demand Risk Pooling for Finance Researchers? Working capital management is one of the key problems facing firms. Demand risk pooling reduces inventory and thus working capital costs, without sacrificing customer service.

Generally, inventory pooling increases the value of the firm. However, it also changes the variability of the firm's profits, which matters for equity holders who may prefer riskier investments, and debt holders who prefer safer ones. Because equity holders control the firm, agency conflict may impede the implementation of demand pooling strategies.

Inventory is often used as loan collateral. Pooling inventory in one location allows this inventory to be diverted to satisfy the demand from other locations. While this increases the value of the firm overall, it reduces the value of inventory as a collateral for a particular location. There is an opposite effect as well. Debt covenants restricting the use of the inventory as collateral may limit the ability of the firm to enjoy inventory pooling benefits.

A number of papers studied the link between investment or operational flexibility and financing or risk management (Chod et al., 2010; Boyabatlı & Toktay, 2011; Chod & Zhou, 2014; Reinartz & Schmid, 2016; Mello et al., 1995).

3.4.4 Little Flexibility Goes a Long Way

New Ideas and Tools Introduced Here *Partial flexibility, chaining.*

Flexibility is valuable (e.g., Sect. 3.4.3), but it is costly. Setting up a factory that can produce two car models is expensive (e.g., Honda assembles its Civic and CR-V models on the same line, but the assembly line cannot be fully automated, making it less efficient, see Carey, 2018). If a factory needs to produce five or six car models, costs grow exponentially. Luckily, as shown by Jordan and Graves (1995), partial flexibility, done in a clever way, generates benefits that almost match those of a fully flexible system, but at a fraction of the cost.

To illustrate this, consider a small example, with three products and three plants. This production system can be visualized as a bi-partite graph (Fig. 3.5), with nodes representing products and plants, and arcs symbolizing that a product can be produced at a plant. Sub-figures demonstrate different levels of flexibility. Figure 3.5a shows a zero flexibility setup, in which products are produced at dedicated plants. In Fig. 3.5b, there is an extra arc allowing plant 2 to produce both products 1 and 2. In Fig. 3.5c there is another arc allowing plant 3 to produce both products 2 and 3. Figure 3.5d presents a special structure, called *a chain*. In a chain, every plant can produce two products, and every product can be produced at two plants. It is achieved by adding only three extra arcs relative to the zero flexibility system. Finally, Fig. 3.5e presents the full flexibility system, where every product can be produced at every plant, and every plant can produce every product. This system is expensive to setup because it has six extra arcs relative to the zero flexibility system, adding up to nine arcs in total. As the number of products and plants grows, the full flexibility system's cost increases polynomially (with N products and N plants, full flexibility requires N^2 arcs).

We run a simulation to measure performance of each system. In this simulation, demands for each of the three products, are independent and are drawn from a normal distribution with the mean 100 and the standard deviation 40, truncated on the interval from 20 to 180. The overage and the underage costs are 1 for all products and thus, the newsvendor solution for the zero flexibility (i.e., dedicated capacity) system is to build 100 units of capacity for each plant (see Sect. 3.4.2).

Figure 3.6a describes the performance of different systems using the expected capacity utilization (x-axis) and the expected fraction of the demand satisfied (y-

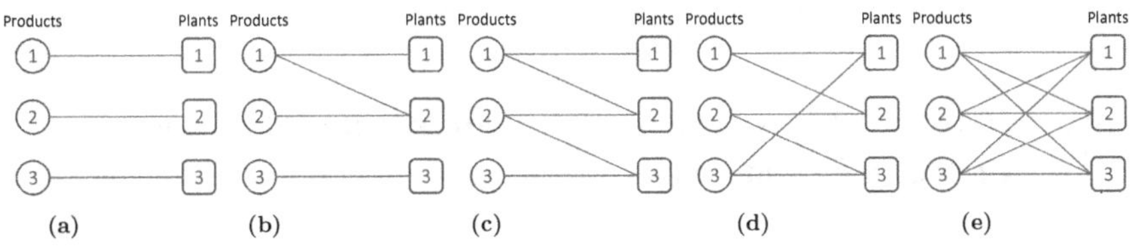

Fig. 3.5 Levels of production flexibility. (**a**) Zero flex. (**b**) One extra link. (**c**) Two extra links. (**d**) A chain. (**e**) Full flex

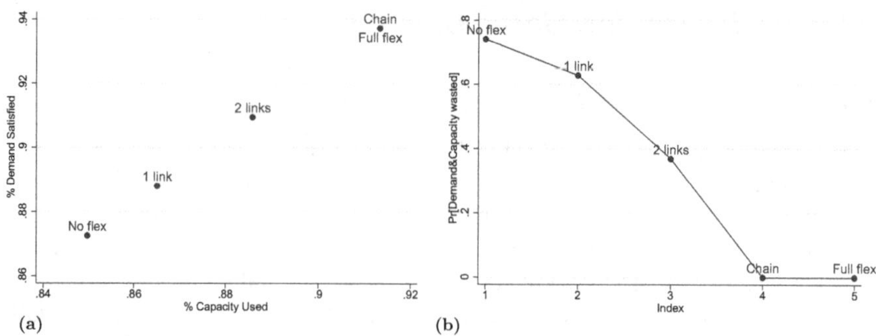

Fig. 3.6 Performance as a function of flexibility. (**a**) Customer service vs utilization. (**b**) Unsatisfied demand and idle capacity

axis). Figure 3.6b shows the probability of having both unsatisfied demand and idle capacity in the level of flexibility. The main takeaway is that a chain achieves benefits of the full flexibility system, but at smaller cost. In more realistic examples, a chain usually does not achieve full benefits, but it comes close. Perhaps most striking is the difference among systems in the probability of having both idle capacity and unsatisfied demand, shown in Fig. 3.6b. In the no-flexibility system, this probability is 0.74. In a chain, this probability drops to 0.

What Are the Takeaways from Partial Flexibility Research for Finance? First, even with full flexibility, the system does not run at 100% capacity utilization and does not satisfy 100% of the demand. Therefore, closing the gap between supply and demand is difficult.

Second, although the insights in Jordan and Graves (1995) are presented in terms of plants and products, they are more general. They apply to decisions such as where to locate factories and what position to take in the foreign exchange (FX) market. If plants are located in different currency zones from those of customer, this exposes the firm to FX risk. In a fully flexible system, a firm is required to hedge every combination of possible currencies. But with a chain, as in Jordan and Graves (1995), simpler hedging strategies among fewer pairs of currencies are sufficient.

Third, whether the flexibility of the firm's assets is value-enhancing to investors or a source of agency problems, it is essential to understand the degree of flexibility in the system.

3.4.5 Dynamic Management of Resources: Inventory and Capacity Expansion

New Ideas and Tools Introduced Here *Risk pooling over time, inventory management and capacity expansion models.*

In Sect. 3.4.3 we hinted that risk pooling can happen over time. This is accomplished by storing inventory of products to meet future demand. Imagine that a newsvendor is selling not only newspapers, but also less perishable products, e.g., SIM cards or chewing gum. Units that are not sold today are not wasted or recycled, but can be used to satisfy tomorrow's demand. What is the behavior of such a dynamic system and how is it best managed? What is the difference between a dynamic system and a simpler static one, like the newsvendor model in Sect. 3.4.2? Dynamic optimization of inventory systems is challenging. In this section, we describe the structural properties of the optimal policies for several versions of inventory models that keep complexity in check. In addition, we spotlight a number of finance applications of these ideas.

We frame the discussion in terms of inventory, using several books: Porteus (2002), Zipkin (2000), Heyman and Sobel (2004), and a book chapter: Porteus (1990). But there is a parallel story of managing a firm's capacity (production or service) over time (Freidenfelds, 1981; Luss, 1982; Van Mieghem, 2003; Birge, 2000). It turns out that the analysis of dynamic inventory systems, where the inventory is depleted over time is mathematically equivalent to the analysis of dynamic capacity expansion models, where the demand is increasing over time.

We omit or merely glance over a number of important inventory-related topics. For example, we present a DP recursion formulation of the dynamic inventory management problem, but we barely mention that under certain assumptions, solving a dynamic problem can be reduced to solving a static problem, akin to a newsvendor (Sect. 3.4.2). This powerful insight has been used in numerous papers (e.g., Sobel, 1995; Sinha et al., 2011; Sobel & Babich, 2012) including the analysis of dynamic games (Sobel, 1981). The general conditions sufficient for a dynamic problem to have an optimal myopic solution are presented in Heyman and Sobel (2004), Porteus (2002), Sobel (1990a, 1990b), Ning and Sobel (2017).

We do not discuss multi-echelon inventory models. This topic is important in its own right, because multi-echelon models describe systems where inventory is geographically distributed across several installations. In addition, multi-echelon models serve as a foundation for understanding physical flows in supply chains (one can think of multi-echelon systems as supply chains with a single decision maker). The multi-echelon literature is extensive and it originated with the breakthrough insight in Clark and Scarf (1960) that under common conditions the optimal policy at each level only needs to consider the total inventory from that level down to final finished goods (the *echelon inventory*). A significant subset of this literature studies the role and the value of local and global information (Zheng & Zipkin, 1990; Chen, 1998; Gavirneni et al., 1999).

We do not describe research on algorithmic techniques for computing optimal order quantities and parameters of inventory and production policies (e.g., Wagner & Whitin, 1958; Roundy, 1985, 1986).

We do not talk about the problem of joint inventory management and pricing (e.g., Thomas, 1974; Chen & Simchi-Levi, 2004a, 2004b).

We also focus on single-product problems. In reality, most companies manage multiple products (Veinott, 1965; Birge et al., 1998; Gilbert, 2000; Zhu & Thonemann, 2009).

3.4.5.1 Order-up-to Inventory Policies

New Ideas and Tools Introduced Here *Periodic-review model, inventory level, inventory position, order-up-to structure of the policy.*

We start with the simplest extension of the classical newsvendor model (Sect. 3.4.2) into a dynamic setting. Consider a single-product, single-location firm that would like to manage its inventory of a non-perishable product. The firm reviews its inventory periodically (e.g., at the end of every day), and it is planning for N periods. At the beginning of a given period t, previously placed orders arrive. The leadtime for orders is 1 period, i.e., orders placed one period prior to the current one arrive. After orders arrive, the firm places new orders. Demand ξ_t arrives during the period. This demand is satisfied from on-hand inventory. If demand cannot be satisfied, customers are placed in a backorder queue to be served in the future when on-hand inventory becomes positive. Demands $\{\xi_t\}_{t=1,N}$ are independent and identically distributed. Unit ordering cost is c, unit backorder (shortage) cost is s, and unit holding cost is h. After N periods, any inventory that has not been sold is disposed of and any customers in the backorder queue must be properly compensated. The terminal cost function is $v(x_{N+1})$ reflect these final transactions. The firm's objective is to minimize the expected discounted cost, where the discount factor is α.

Managing this system is challenging. The firm needs to keep track of how much inventory it has on hand, record which customers are in the backorder queue and how long they waited, count inventory that is en route from previous orders and anticipate when this inventory will be delivered (this is not an issue with one-period leadtime, but applies in extensions with longer leadtimes). Clearly, orders should depend on all this information. When placing an order the firm balances its immediate costs against costs that will be incurred in the future. A brute force approach of formulating and solving this dynamic problem, e.g., using the standard Bellman recursion proves challenging, unless we introduce several simplifying assumptions and perform variable transformations.

First, the firm does not need to know when the on-hand inventory arrived. The only information needed is the amount of on-hand inventory. Similarly, the firm does not care how long customers were in the backorder queue, just how many customers are in that queue (of course, the first-come-first-serve policy seems fair). Second, instead of keeping track of the on-hand inventory and backorders separately, we create a new variable, *inventory level*, which equals the difference between the on-hand inventory and backorders, recognizing that the two quantities cannot be positive simultaneously. Third, we aggregate information further, by combining inventory en route with the inventory level and call this new variable *inventory position*.

Given these assumptions, the following Markov Decision Problem (MDP) formulation proves tractable. The *state variable* is x_t, the inventory position at the beginning of period t. This variable can be positive or negative. The *action* is $z_t \geq 0$, the order quantity in period t. Placing an order increases the inventory position to $y_t = x_t + z_t$. Then demand ξ_t arrives, which reduces the inventory position to $y_t - \xi_t$. Therefore, the *transition equation* is $x_{t+1} = y_t - \xi_t$. The order cost is cz_t. The inventory cost is $h(y_t - \xi_t)^+$. The backorder cost is $s(\xi_t - y_t)^+$. Thus, per period cost is $cz_t + h(y_t - \xi_t)^+ + s(\xi_t - y_t)^+$. It is convenient to combine holding and backorder costs in one function $\mathcal{L}(y_t - \xi_t) = h(y_t - \xi_t)^+ + s(\xi_t - y_t)^+$ and its expectation $L(y) = \mathbb{E}[\mathcal{L}(y - \xi_t)]$. Initial inventory position is x_0. After N periods, the terminal value of the firm is a function of inventory position at that time $v_T(x_{N+1})$. The objective of the firm is to order $\{z_t\}_{t=1}^N$, where $z_t \geq 0$ is based on the information available at the beginning of period t, so as to minimize the expected value:

$$\sum_{t=1}^{N} \alpha^{t-1} [cz_t + \mathcal{L}(x_t + z_t - \xi_t)] + \alpha^N v_t(x_{N+1}), \tag{3.49a}$$

$$\text{subject to}: x_{t+1} = y_t - \xi_t. \tag{3.49b}$$

The sequential optimization problem (3.49) is equivalent to a Bellman recursion with functions f_t for $t \in \{1, 2, \ldots, N+1\}$, defined as

$$f_{N+1}(x) = v_T(x), \tag{3.50a}$$

$$f_t(x) = \min_{z \geq 0} \{cz + L(y) + \alpha\mathbb{E}[f_{t+1}(y - \xi_t)]\}, \text{for } t \in \{1, \ldots, N\}. \tag{3.50b}$$

The system of equations (3.50) has only one state variable, x, and the optimal order z^* every period is a function of this state variable. Another transformation simplifies the problem further. Replace decision variable z with y, deriving a simpler formulation:

$$f_{N+1}(x) = v_T(x), \tag{3.51a}$$

$$f_t(x) = -cx + \min_{y \geq x} \{cy + L(y) + \alpha\mathbb{E}[f_{t+1}(y - \xi_t)]\} \text{ for } t \in \{1, \ldots, N\}. \tag{3.51b}$$

In formulation (3.51), the function under min does not depend on x. Variable x affects the optimization through constraint $y \geq x$ only. Define function

$$G_t(y) = cy + L(y) + \alpha\mathbb{E}[f_{t+1}(y - \xi_t)]. \tag{3.52}$$

If we optimize function $G_t(y)$ (which does not depend on x), deriving the critical number y_t^* for a given period t, this number will characterize the optimal policy for any state x. The corresponding optimal policy is called an *order-up-to base-stock policy* and it stipulates: whenever the inventory position x_t drops below the *order-up-to level* y_t^*, the firm should increase the inventory position to the value y_t^*, and do nothing otherwise.

The formal proof proceeds in two steps. First, the following lemma describes properties of functions G_t, f_t, and the optimal policy. Second, the following proposition applies properties established by the lemma recursively.

Lemma 3.2 *For any $t \in \{1, \dots, N\}$, if function f_{t+1} is convex, then:*

(i) *function G_t is convex,*
(ii) *a base-stock policy is optimal in period t, and*
(iii) *function f_t is convex.*

The proof technique is a part of the contribution of OM research and we sketch the proof here.

Proof of Lemma 3.2 If function f_{t+1} is convex, then so is $\mathbb{E}[f_{t+1}(y-\xi_t)]$. Function $L(y)$ is convex. Therefore, function $G_t(y)$ being a sum of three convex functions is convex.

Because $G_t(y)$ is convex, the order-up-to level policy achieves a minimum for problem $\min_{y \geq x} G(y)$. This is easy to see. If $x < y^*$ then the minimum is achieved at $y = y^*$. If $x \geq y^*$, the lowest value of $G(y)$ for $y \geq x$ is at $y = x$.

From a known property of convex functions, $\min_{y \geq x} G(y)$ is convex in x. Therefore, $f_t(x)$ defined in (3.51b) as a sum of convex functions is convex. ■

Proposition 3.2 *If the terminal value function v_T is convex, then an order-up-to base-stock policy is optimal for every period t.*

Proof of Proposition 3.2 The proof is done by recursion. The first step of the recursion is to establish that f_{N+1} defined in (3.51a) is convex. Then recursively apply Lemma 3.2 for all $t \in \{1, \dots, N\}$. ■

To sum up, we have transformed a potentially intractable problem to a sequence of one-dimensional optimization problems that do not depend on a state variable. The optimal policy has a very intuitive structure: if the inventory position is short of the order-up-to level, raise the inventory position to that level, and otherwise do nothing. Figure 3.7 illustrates the inventory dynamics over 10 periods when a firm follows an order-up-to policy. We assume that the optimal order-up-to level is 100 and generate demands randomly for every period. The firm starts with 100 units in inventory at the beginning of period 1. Then demand of 83 units brings the inventory position to 17 units. The firm immediately raises the inventory position back to 100 units. The second period demand is approximately 111 units, creating a backorder of 11 units. The rest of the figure is constructed similarly.

The research on these problems originated with papers by Arrow et al. (1951, 1958), Karlin (1958), and blossomed into a vast literature. Various variations on

Fig. 3.7 Illustration of the inventory dynamics under an order-up-to policy

the problem have been considered, including those with non-stationary demands (ARMA demand), lost sales, infinite planning horizon, convex ordering costs, constraints on inventory position, and risk-aversion of the firm. Efficient algorithms for computing order-up-to level numbers have been discovered. For example, under mild additional assumptions one can prove that a solution to a static newsvendor problem is optimal for the dynamic inventory problem discussed here (Veinott, 1965). We took advantage of this in assuming that in Fig. 3.7 the order-up-to level is the same every period.

The model in this section can incorporate order lead times. Suppose that instead of one period, orders arrive l periods later (thus, $l = 1$ is the case we discussed). Inventory position x_t includes all orders placed fewer than l periods in the past. The new order z_t can satisfy demand l periods in the future at the earliest. Therefore, the new inventory position $y_t = x_t + z_t$ must balance inventory and shortage costs for the next l periods based on the cumulative demand $D[t, t + l) = \sum_{k=t}^{t+l-1} \xi_k$. Both the expected value and the variance of cumulative demand increase in l, and so do the optimal order-up-to levels y_t^*. Therefore, one mechanism for reducing inventory is reducing order lead times. This becomes even more important if demand forecasts are used because their accuracy decreases in the forecast period.

What Are the Takeaways for Finance Researchers? From Fig. 3.7, the supply does not perfectly match the demand most of the time. Either the firm carries inventory or it has backorders.

The computational techniques demonstrated here go beyond inventory models. Many resource management problems can be mapped into this framework and researchers have applied it from problems of dynamic capital management (Li et al., 2013), to modeling financial subsidies to suppliers (Babich, 2010), to understanding the effect of capital constraints on the supply of capital after natural disasters (Collier & Babich, 2019).

The textbook treatment implicitly relies on the existence of well-functioning financial markets, so that cash flows occurring at different times are combined, and attributed to the period when decisions are being made, in short, are fungible across time (possibly with discounting). There are extension that try to address that (e.g., the papers above that incorporate bankruptcy friction and studies of self-financed inventory systems, such as Chao et al., 2008; Gong et al., 2014).

The textbook treatment also ignores agency problems. With a few exceptions risk preferences of decision makers are ignored as well (although we saw how to include market risk as appropriate for public firms in Sect. 3.3.2.2). For idiosyncratic risk preferences, Bouakiz and Sobel (1992) extend the classical order-up-to result to a decision maker with CARA utility function and Chen et al. (2007) do so for combined inventory and pricing decisions. These papers can be used to understand agency problems between managers (risk-averse) and investors (risk-neutral under the appropriate transformation). But other types of agency problems, such as under-investment, failure to liquidate, and risk-seeking did not appear in conjunction with classical inventory models.

3.4.5.2 Balancing Fixed and Variable Costs: (s, S) and EOQ Inventory Policies

New Ideas and Tools Introduced Here *Fixed ordering costs, K-convexity, Economic Order Quantity.*

The convexity property, essential for order-up-to policies' being optimal (Sect. 3.4.5.1), is violated in the presence of fixed ordering costs K. In fact, if a firm were to follow the order-up-to policy, it would order every period and accumulate high fixed ordering costs over the planning horizon. What is a better policy? Should a firm order every other period, every third period? How much should it order? With less frequent orders, what is the risk of shortages? To answer these questions, we extend the analysis in Sect. 3.4.5.1, by adding fixed ordering cost K to (3.51):

$$f_{N+1}(x) = v_T(x), \tag{3.53a}$$

$$f_t(x) = -cx + \min_{y \geq x} \left\{K 1_{\{y>x\}} + cy + L(y) + \alpha E[f_{t+1}(y - \xi_t)]\right\} \quad \text{for } t \in \{1, \ldots, N\}. \tag{3.53b}$$

Using function $G_t(y) = cy + L(y) + \alpha E[f_{t+1}(y - \xi_t)]$ defined in (3.52), rewrite problem (3.53) as

$$f_{N+1}(x) = v_T(x), \tag{3.54a}$$

$$f_t(x) = -cx + \min\{G_t(x), \min_{y \geq x} G_t(y) + K\} \text{ for } t \in \{1, \ldots, N\}. \tag{3.54b}$$

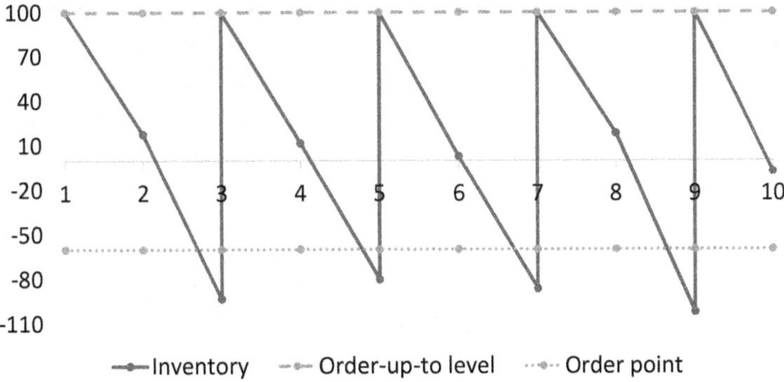

Fig. 3.8 Illustration of the inventory dynamics under an (s, S) policy

Because of fixed costs, functions f_t and G_t are not convex. But they satisfy a related property: K-convexity.[9] This property plays a similar role to convexity. We omit the formal proof, but it is similar to those of Lemma 3.2 and Proposition 3.2: One can prove recursively that functions f_t and G_t possess the K-convexity property, if the firm follows the optimal policy.

The optimal policy is called (s, S) policy and it works as follows. For some period t, define the *order level* as $S_t = \arg\min_{y \geq x} G_t(y)$. Raising the inventory position up to the order level S_t minimizes cost G_t, but the firm may forego ordering to avoid fixed cost K, if the current inventory position x is not too far from the optimal level S_t. Only when the gap $G_t(x) - G_t(S_t)$ between the cost of staying with the current inventory position and the optimal cost is greater than K, is the order placed. The highest value of $x \leq S_t$ such that $G_t(x) - G_t(S_t) \geq K$ is denoted by s_t and is called the *order point*. It can be shown that for all $x \leq s_t$, $G_t(x) \geq G_t(s_t)$. Figure 3.8 illustrates the inventory dynamics under an (s, S) policy. We used the same random demands as in Fig. 3.7 and the same order-up-to level $S = 100$. We assumed that the order point is $s = -60$ for all periods. The firm no longer replenishes the inventory immediately, but instead skips some periods avoiding fixed costs.

Unfortunately, there are no closed form expressions for (s, S) policy parameters (there are approximations). However, there is a version of the model, which captures similar tradeoffs, but whose solution is known in closed form: the Economic Order Quantity (EOQ) model.

The EOQ model is over 100 years old (Harris, 1913), and it differs from the inventory models discussed above in several ways. It is a continuous review model, that is, time is measured continuously and orders can be placed at any moment. The

[9]Function $f : \mathbb{R} \to \mathbb{R}$ is K-convex for $K \geq 0$ if and only if for any $x \leq y$, and $\theta \in [0, 1]$, $f(\theta x + (1 - \theta)y) \leq \theta f(x) + (1 - \theta)(f(y) + K)$. When $K = 0$, K-convexity is the regular convexity. For a detailed discussion of K-convexity, see Heyman and Sobel (2004) and Porteus (2002).

classic EOQ model assumes the demand is deterministic, with constant rate a. The objective is to minimize an average cost per unit of time, although extensions with discounted costs exist. The planning horizon is infinitely long. Each time an order is placed, fixed cost K is paid. The unit ordering cost is c. The order quantity Q is delivered immediately. There is inventory holding cost h. In the classical version of the model, no backorders are allowed (hence, there is no need for the backorder cost).

The analysis of this model is based on an intuitive idea (that formally comes from Renewal Theory) that minimizing an average cost per unit of time over an infinite horizon is equivalent to minimizing costs during a cycle between two orders. Orders are placed only when inventory falls to zero and the only decision is how large an order to place. If the order quantity is Q, then the cycle length is Q/a time units. During a cycle, the firm incurs unit ordering cost cQ, plus fixed cost K, plus inventory holding cost $hQ^2/(2a)$. Therefore, an average cost per unit of time is:

$$\frac{cQ + K + (hQ^2/(2a))}{Q/a} = ca + \frac{aK}{Q} + \frac{hQ}{2}. \tag{3.55}$$

The quantity Q^* that minimizes (3.55) satisfies the first-order condition: $-\frac{aK}{Q^2} + \frac{h}{2} = 0$ and equals:

$$Q^* = \sqrt{\frac{2aK}{h}}, \tag{3.56}$$

which is called the *EOQ formula*. It captures the optimal tradeoff between inventory costs and fixed costs. The corresponding optimal average cost per unit of time equals

$$ca + \sqrt{2ahK}. \tag{3.57}$$

Both the optimal order quantity and the optimal average cost feature square roots, which dampen the effects of costs. That is, if the fixed cost quadruples, the optimal order quantity only doubles. Similarly, if the holding cost quadruples, the optimal order quantity only halves. Therefore, even if those costs fluctuate over time, the optimal inventory levels stay relatively constant. Figure 3.9 shows the inventory dynamics under the EOQ formula. It looks similar to Fig. 3.8 because it captures the same tradeoff between fixed ordering and inventory holding costs.

The EOQ model allows various extensions, such as uncertainty in the demand rate and lead times (see Porteus, 1990, 2002; Zipkin, 2000). In particular, when the demand rate is uncertain and the orders are delivered with lead times, it becomes important to consider the risk of running out of inventory. This leads to the (r, Q) policy, where the reorder point r controls the risk of running out of inventory and incurring backorder costs (similar to the newsvendor tradeoffs Sect. 3.4.2) and Q balances ordering and inventory costs. The resulting inventory dynamics are similar

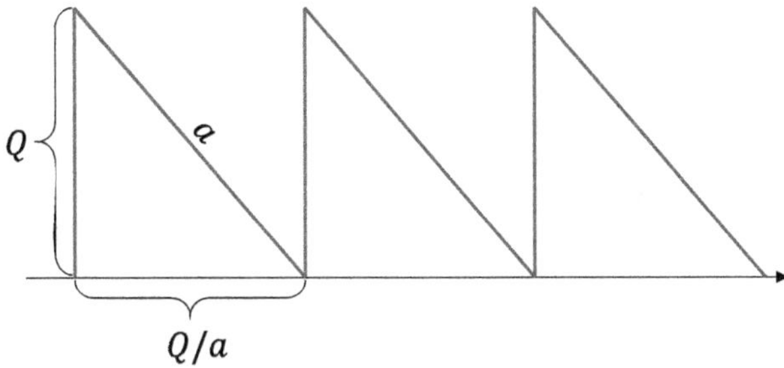

Fig. 3.9 Illustration of the inventory dynamics under the EOQ policy

to those from the (s, S) policy. Depending on the relative magnitude of various costs, it might be optimal to set the reorder point to be negative.

What Does This Mean for Finance? Even if demand is deterministic, there could be a gap between supply and demand due to fixed costs. Therefore, firms will always carry inventory. When the demand is random, firms may have both inventory and backorders.

This insight applies not just to traditional production settings. Cloud computing investments, such as how much server capacity to order (e.g., from Amazon) are subject to the same forces. Order-book management by market makers can be modeled using inventory models. Most financial trades have fixed costs (typically ignored for analytical convenience). In fact, Baumol (1952), Miller and Orr (1966) relied on EOQ and the (s, S) optimal policies to solve cash management problems by individuals and firms in the presence of fixed cash withdrawal costs and interest carrying costs.

If the inventory and backorders proxy for market imperfections, then inventory theory brings bad news. As we have seen for the EOQ formula (3.56), there is a square root relationship between the inventory and fixed ordering costs. Therefore, to reduce inventory by one-half, we need to reduce the fixed cost by one-fourth.

On the other hand, again from the EOQ formula, the optimal inventory and the corresponding costs are not sensitive to fluctuations in holding costs. A significant component of holding costs is the cost of capital. Therefore, even as the cost of capital fluctuates, the optimal order quantities and the optimal average cost to the firm should remain stable.

Although the average inventory does not change much, there are significant fluctuations in inventory levels and costs on a daily basis, even if model inputs remain the same. The higher the fixed cost, the greater the fluctuations in daily inventory levels, even if there are no other sources of variability in the system.

These are important considerations for understanding the role of inventory in corporate finance, earnings manipulation, and managerial incentives. For example, inventory values below average can indicate an attempt to manipulate financial metrics, or represent normal inventory dynamics, as in Fig. 3.9. Lai (2008) presents

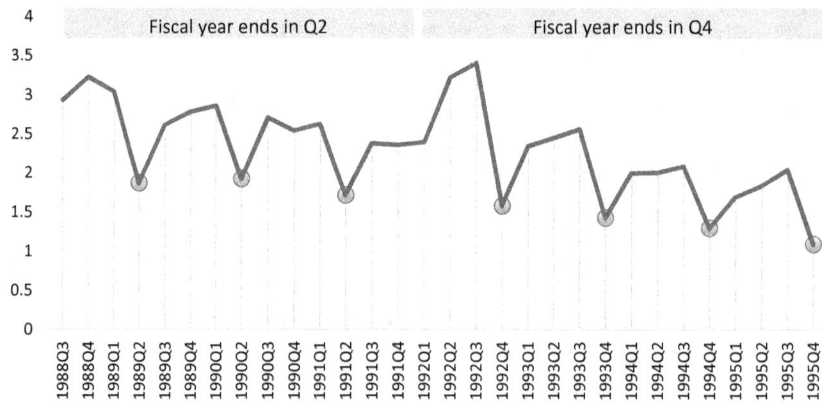

Fig. 3.10 RadioShack's quarterly inventory/COGS

a figure (reproduced in Fig. 3.10) showing that RadioShack's inventory drops by the end of a fiscal year consistently, even if the fiscal year definition moves the end from Q2 to Q4 (the end-of-year observations are marked by disks on Fig. 3.10). Is this evidence for earnings manipulations or does RadioShack always place orders at the end of a fiscal year, regardless of when it is?

3.4.6 Endogenous Sources of Variability in Supply Chain Procurement: Bullwhip Effect

New Ideas and Tools Introduced Here *A Beer Game, bullwhip effect: causes and consequences.*

Variability in supply chains stems not only from exogenous supply, demand, and price shocks, but also from endogenous structural causes. Students taking OM courses learn about those endogenous causes when they play the *Beer Game*, in which they assume the responsibility for managing inventory at one of the four companies comprising a beer supply chain: a Retailer, a Wholesaler, a Warehouse, and a Factory. Students fulfill orders received from downstream and place orders upstream, while lacking information about the demand and inventory position beyond their own firm. Orders arrive with fixed lead times and the game score is kept based on the amounts of inventory and backorders.[10] At the end of a game session, when the performance of teams representing different supply chains is tallied, students usually arrive to the main "Aha!" moment: a remarkable pattern arises in

[10]This game was invented in 1960 by Jay Wright Forrester, who studied system dynamics in his research, and used this game to illustrate the dynamics of supply chains, as well as the importance of information and collaboration (Dizikes, 2015).

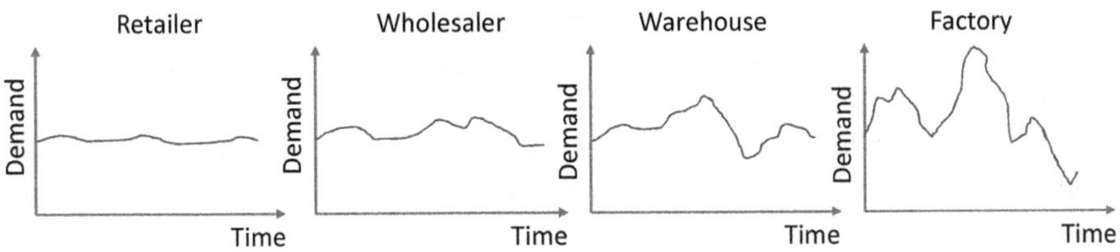

Fig. 3.11 Bullwhip demand patterns in the Beer Game

the demand that each company observes—even though the demand variability at the retailer is small, it is higher at the wholesaler, and higher still as we look upstream.[11] This pattern is illustrated in Fig. 3.11.

The interest in the order-variability magnification phenomenon has exploded since the publication of the seminal paper by Lee et al. (1997). In their paper, Lee et al. (1997) identify four causes of the bullwhip effect: (1) demand signal processing, (2) rationing game, (3) batching of orders, and (4) price variation.

To illustrate the demand signal processing effect, Lee et al. (1997) study an inventory model in Sect. 3.4.5.1, but with the demand following an AR(1) process. They prove that when demand is positively auto-correlated, the optimal inventory policy produces higher order variance than variance of the demand. Moreover, the longer the replenishment lead time, the greater the order variance. Therefore, mitigation strategies include reducing replenishment lead times, and sharing actual demand information, instead of just placing orders or sharing forecasts.

The rationing game arises when multiple retailers place orders for limited manufacturer capacity. In the event of shortage, the manufacturer allocates capacity proportionally to orders received. An equilibrium strategy of the retailers is to inflate their orders to claim a higher proportion of limited capacity. Mitigation strategies for this capacity-rationing cause of the bullwhip effect include changing the allocation policy (e.g., allocate capacity based on past sales instead), sharing capacity information (so that panic buying does not occur), limiting flexibility of the retailers to renege on order quantities, and centralizing procurement decisions with a single decision maker, who aggregates demand information from retailers and distributes capacity, according to the observed demands. Interestingly, the COVID-19 pandemic presented numerous illustrations of rationing-game bullwhip effects. The panic buying by consumers of excessive amounts of toilet paper, pasta, and cleaning supplies was partly due to lack of information about the availability of these products in supply chains. In the US, there were shortages of N95 masks, surgical gloves, and ventilators, but instead of centralizing the procurement at the federal level, the US federal government shifted the procurement responsibility to individual states, where this responsibility was further fragmented to a county, city,

[11] The demand variability gets magnified akin to the increasing amplitude of the sinusoidal pattern of a bullwhip, as we get further away from the source of the initial variation, hence the name—the *bullwhip effect*.

and hospital level. The result was a chaotic system with massive over-ordering, numerous cancelled orders, and grossly inefficient allocation of limited resources (Slotkin, 2020; WHO, 2020).

Order batching is caused by firms aggregating orders to justify fixed costs (see Sect. 3.4.5.2). These aggregate orders are larger than daily demands. The mitigation strategies for order batching are various fixed costs reductions (e.g., using third-party logistics providers, who by serving several clients in the same geographic area, can spread the fixed costs among them).

The last cause of the bullwhip effect discussed in Lee et al. (1997) is the variation of prices charged by the manufacturer to the retailers. The optimal retailer's ordering policy is to order more during low price periods and less during high price periods. This creates additional variation in orders beyond the variation due to the consumer demand. The mitigation strategy is to keep the manufacturer's prices constant.

Literature on the bullwhip effect, both theoretical and empirical, is extensive. Within the empirical literature, Bray and Mendelson (2012) find that two thirds of the firms in their sample inflate orders, creating a bullwhip effect, but the bullwhip effect declines from the period 1974–1994 to the period 1995–2008.

What Does the Bullwhip Effect Mean for Finance? Increasing order variability raises costs of managing this variability (e.g., if firms carry more inventory), and increases cash flow variability, which is important for financial risk management. To illustrate ramifications of the bullwhip effect on cash position of a firm, Shang (2019) augments the classical Beer Game to allow students to learn about cash management. Chen et al. (2013) demonstrate how liquidity shocks propagate along supply chains following the bullwhip effect patterns.

It is important to recognize endogenous causes of variability. Otherwise, by looking exclusively at the external shocks, one can underestimate risks in supply chains. Because supply chains are at the core of value creation, it behooves us to understand dynamics of these systems better, including which risks they generate, how these risks are correlated with macro-economic variables (Osadchiy et al., 2016), and how these risks are priced in financial markets (Agca et al., 2017).

Classical OM insights about the bullwhip effect were derived without considering agency problems prominent in the finance literature. Additional distortions due to conflicts between debt and equity holders or between insiders and outsiders can interact with the bullwhip effect inefficiencies in interesting ways.

References

Adelman, D. (2020). Thousands of lives could be saved in the us during the COVID-19 pandemic if states exchanged ventilators: Study examines how lives could be saved by allowing us states to exchange ventilators during the COVID-19 pandemic. *Health Affairs, 39*(7), 1247–1252.

Agca, S., Babich, V., Birge, J., & Wu, J. (2017). Credit risk propagation along supply chains: Evidence from the CDS market. Working paper.

Ang, A., Hodrick, R., Xing, Y., & Zhang, X. (2006). The cross-section of volatility and expected returns. *Journal of Finance, 61*, 259–299.

Anupindi, R., Bassok, Y., & Zemel, E. (2001). A general framework for the study of decentralized distribution systems. *Manufacturing & Service Operations Management, 3*(4), 349–368.

Arrow, K. J., Harris, T., & Marschak, J. (1951). Optimal inventory policy. *Econometrica: Journal of the Econometric Society, 19*, 250–272.

Arrow, K. J., Karlin, S., Scarf, H. E., et al. (1958). *Studies in the mathematical theory of inventory and production*. Stanford University Press.

Babich, V. (2010). Independence of capacity ordering and financial subsidies to risky suppliers. *M&SOM, 12*(4), 583–607.

Babich, V., & Birge, J. (2021). Foundations and Trends in Research at the Interface of Finance, Operations, and Risk Management. *Foundations and Trends: Technology, Information and Operations Management, 15*(1-2), 1–203.

Babich, V., & Kouvelis, P. (2018). Introduction to the special issue on research at the interface of finance, operations, and risk management (iFORM): Recent contributions and future directions. *M&SOM, 20*(1), 1–18.

Babich, V., Marinesi, S., & Tsoukalas, G. (2021). Does crowdfunding benefit entrepreneurs and venture capital investors? *M&SOM, 23*(2), 508–524.

Baumol, W. J. (1952). The transactions demand for cash: An inventory theoretic approach. *The Quarterly Journal of Economics, 66*(4), 545–556.

Birge, J. R. (2000). Option methods for incorporating risk into linear capacity planning models. *Manufacturing & Service Operations Management, 2*, 19–31.

Birge, J. R. (2015). Operations and finance interactions. *Manufacturing & Service Operations Management, 17*, 4–15.

Birge, J. R., Drogosz, J., & Duenyas, I. (1998). Setting singe-period optimal capacity levels and prices for substitutable products. *International Journal of Flexible Manufacturing Systems, 10*, 407–430.

Birge, J. R., & Yang, S. A. (2007). A model for tax advantages of portfolios with many assets. *Journal of Banking and Finance, 31*, 3269–3290.

Björk, T. (2004). *Arbitrage theory in continuous time* (2nd ed.). Oxford, NY: Oxford University Press.

Blas, J. (2018). The U.S. just became a net oil exporter for the first time in 75 years. *Bloomberg*. Accessed on May 29, 2019 from https://www.bloomberg.com/news/articles/2018-12-06/u-s-becomes-a-net-oil-exporter-for-the-first-time-in-75-years

Bolton, P., & Scharfstein, D. S. (1990). A theory of predation based on agency problems in financial contracting. *The American Economic Review, 80*, 93–106.

Bouakiz, M., & Sobel, M. J. (1992). Inventory control with an exponential utility criterion. *Operations Research, 40*(3), 603–608.

Boyabatlı, O., & Toktay, L. (2011). Stochastic capacity investment and flexible vs. dedicated technology choice in imperfect capital markets. *Management Science, 57*(12), 2163–2179.

Bray, R., & Mendelson, H. (2012). Information transmission and the bullwhip effect: An empirical investigation. *Management Science, 58*(5), 860–875.

Campbell, J. Y. (2017). *Financial decisions and markets: A course in asset pricing*. Princeton University Press.

Campello, M., Graham, J. R., & Harvey, C. R. (2010). The real effects of financial constraints: Evidence from a financial crisis. *Journal of Financial Economics, 97*(3), 470–487.

Carey, N. (2018). Japanese carmakers' weapon of choice in trump trade war: Flexible factories. *Automotive News*. Accessed on May 25, 2020 from https://www.autonews.com/article/20181101/OEM01/181109993/japanese-carmakers-weapon-of-choice-in-trump-trade-war-flexible-factories

Carhart, M. M. (1997). On persistence in mutual fund performance. *The Journal of Finance, 52*(1), 57–82.

Chao, X., Chen, J., & Wang, S. (2008). Dynamic inventory management with cash flow constraints. *Naval Research Logistics, 55*(8), 758–768.

Chen, F. (1998). Echelon reorder points, installation reorder points, and the value of centralized demand information. *Management Science, 44*(12-part-2), S221–S234.

Chen, T.-K., Liao, H.-H., & Kuo, H.-J. (2013). Internal liquidity risk, financial bullwhip effects, and corporate bond yield spreads: Supply chain perspectives. *Journal of Banking & Finance, 37*(7), 2434–2456.

Chen, X., Sim, M., Simchi-Levi, D., & Sun, P. (2007). Risk aversion in inventory management. *Operations Research, 55*(5), 828–842.

Chen, X., & Simchi-Levi, D. (2004a). Coordinating inventory control and pricing strategies with random demand and fixed ordering cost: The finite horizon case. *Operations Research, 52*, 887–896.

Chen, X., & Simchi-Levi, D. (2004b). Coordinating inventory control and pricing strategies with random demand and fixed ordering cost: The infinite horizon case. *Mathematics of Operations Research, 29*(3), 698–723.

Chod, J., Rudi, N., & Van Mieghem, J. A. (2010). Operational flexibility and financial hedging: Complements or substitutes? *Management Science, 56*(6), 1030–1045.

Chod, J., & Zhou, J. (2014). Resource flexibility and capital structure. *Management Science, 60*(3), 708–729.

Clark, A. J., & Scarf, H. (1960). Optimal policies for a multi-echelon inventory problem. *Management Science, 6*(4), 475–490.

Cochrane, J. H. (2001). *Asset pricing*. Princeton University Press.

Collier, B. L., & Babich, V. O. (2019). Financing recovery after disasters: Explaining community credit market responses to severe events. *Journal of Risk and Insurance, 86*(2), 479–520.

Corbett, C. J., & Rajaram, K. (2006). A generalization of the inventory pooling effect to nonnormal dependent demand. *M&SOM, 8*(4), 351–358.

de Vericourt, F., & Gromb, D. (2018). Financing capacity investment under demand uncertainty: An optimal contracting approach. *M&SOM, 20*(1), 85–96.

DeMarzo, P. M., & Fishman, M. J. (2007). Optimal long-term financial contracting. *The Review of Financial Studies, 20*(6), 2079–2128.

Diamond, D. W. (1984). Financial intermediation and delegated monitoring. *The Review of Economic Studies, 51*(3), 393–414.

Dizikes, P. (2015). The many careers of Jay Forrester. *MIT Technology Review, 6*, 23.

Dong, L., & Rudi, N. (2004). Who benefits from transshipment? Exogenous vs. endogenous wholesale prices. *Management Science, 50*(5), 645–657.

Duffie, D. (2010). *Dynamic asset pricing theory*. Princeton University Press.

Egan, M. (2018). America is now the world's largest oil producer. *CNN*. Accessed on May 29, 2019 from https://money.cnn.com/2018/09/12/investing/us-oil-production-russia-saudi-arabia/index.html

Eppen, G. D. (1979). Note—effects of centralization on expected costs in a multi-location newsboy problem. *Management Science, 25*(5), 498–501.

Fama, E. F., & French, K. R. (1992). The cross-section of expected stock returns. *The Journal of Finance, 47*, 427–465.

Fama, E. F., & French, K. R. (1993). Common risk factors in the returns on stocks and bonds. *Journal of Financial Economics, 33*, 3–56.

Freidenfelds, J. (1981). *Capacity expansion: Analysis of simple models with applications*. Amsterdam: Elsevier North Holland, Inc.

Gale, D., & Hellwig, M. (1985). Incentive-compatible debt contracts: The one-period problem. *Review of Economic Studies, 52*(4), 647–663.

Garicano, L., & Steinwender, C. (2016). Survive another day: Using changes in the composition of investments to measure the cost of credit constraints. *Review of Economics and Statistics, 98*(5), 913–924.

Gasparro, A., Bunge, J., & Haddon, H. (2020). Why the American consumer has fewer choices—maybe for good. *WSJ*. Accessed on August 17, 2020 from https://www.wsj.com/articles/why-the-american-consumer-has-fewer-choicesmaybe-for-good-11593230443?st=tfdng2hsjzcxviy

Gaur, V., & Seshadri, S. (2005). Hedging inventory risk through market instruments. *M&SOM, 7*(2), 103–120.

Gavirneni, S., Kapuscinski, R., & Tayur, S. (1999). Value of information in capacitated supply chains. *Management Science, 45*(1), 16–24.

Gilbert, S. (2000). Coordination of pricing and multiple-period production across multiple constant priced goods. *Management Science, 46*, 1602–1616.

Gong, X., Chao, X., & Simchi-Levi, D. (2014). Dynamic inventory control with limited capital and short-term financing. *Naval Research Logistics (NRL), 61*(3), 184–201.

Graham, J. R., & Harvey, C. R. (2001). The theory and practice of corporate finance: Evidence from the field. *Journal of Financial Economics, 60*(2–3), 187–243.

Gromb, D. (1994). Renegotiation in debt contracts. Work. Pap., INSEAD.

Harris, F. W. (1913). How many parts to make at once. *Factory. The Magazine of Management, 10*(2), 135–136.

Harris, M., & Raviv, A. (1991). The theory of capital structure. *The Journal of Finance, 46*(1), 297–355.

Heyman, D., & Sobel, M. J. (2004). *Stochastic models in operations research. Stochastic optimization* (Vol. 2). Dover.

Holmstrom, B., & Tirole, J. (1997). Financial intermediation, loanable funds, and the real sector. *The Quarterly Journal of Economics, 112*(3), 663–691.

Ingersoll, J. E. (1987). *Theory of financial decision making* (Vol. 3). Rowman & Littlefield.

Innes, R. D. (1990). Limited liability and incentive contracting with ex-ante action choices. *Journal of Economic Theory, 52*(1), 45–67.

Jensen, M. C., & Meckling, W. H. (1976). Theory of the firm: Managerial behavior, agency costs and ownership structure. *Journal of Financial Economics, 3*(4), 305–360.

Jordan, W. C., & Graves, S. C. (1995). Principles on the benefits of manufacturing process flexibility. *Management Science, 41*(4), 577–594.

Karlin, S. (1958). Optimal inventory policy for the Arrow-Harris-Marschak dynamic model. In K. Arrow, S. Karlin, & H. Scarf (Eds.), *Studies in the mathematical theory of inventory and production* (pp. 135–154). Stanford, CA: Stanford University Press.

Lai, R. K. (2008). Is inventory's fiscal year end effect caused by sales timing? a test using a natural experiment from germany. Harvard Business School Technology & Operations Mgt. Unit Research Paper. Available at SSRN: https://ssrn.com/abstract=1016892

Lee, H. L., Padmanabhan, V., & Whang, S. (1997). Information distortion in a supply chain: The bullwhip effect. *Management Science, 43*(4), 546–558.

Lee, H. L., & Tang, C. S. (1997). Modelling the costs and benefits of delayed product differentiation. *Management Science, 43*(1), 40–53.

Li, L., Shubik, M., & Sobel, M. J. (2013). Control of dividends, capital subscriptions, and physical inventories. *Management Science, 59*(5), 1107–1124.

Lintner, J. (1965). The valuation of risk assets and the selection of risky investments in stock portfolios and capital budgets. *Review of Economics and Statistics, 47*, 13–37.

Luss, H. (1982). Operations research and capacity expansion problems: A survey. *Operations Research, 30*(5), 907–947.

Martin, I. (2013). Simple variance swaps. Working paper, Stanford University, Stanford, CA. http://web.stanford.edu/~iwrm/simple%20variance%20swaps%20latest.pdf

Mello, A. S., Parsons, J. E., & Triantis, A. J. (1995). An integrated model of multinational flexibility and financial hedging. *Journal of International Economics, 39*(1–2), 27–51.

Miller, M. H., & Modigliani, F. (1961). Dividend policy, growth, and the valuation of shares. *the Journal of Business, 34*(4), 411–433.

Miller, M. H., & Orr, D. (1966). A model of the demand for money by firms. *The Quarterly Journal of Economics, 80*(3), 413–435.

Modigliani, F., & Miller, M. (1958). The cost of capital, corporation finance, and the theory of investment. *The American Economic Review, 48*, 261–297.

Myers, S. C. (1977). Determinants of corporate borrowing. *Journal of Financial Economics, 5*(2), 147–175.

Myers, S. C. (1984). The capital structure puzzle. *The Journal of Finance, 39*(3), 574–592.
Myers, S. C., & Majluf, N. S. (1984). Corporate financing and investment decisions when firms have information that investors do not have. *Journal of Financial Economics, 13*(2), 187–221.
Ning, J., & Babich, V. (2018). R&D investments in the presence of knowledge spillover and debt financing: can risk-shifting cure free-riding? *M&SOM, 20*(1), 97–112.
Ning, J., & Sobel, M. (2017). Easy affine Markov decision processes: Theory. Working paper, Weatherhead School of Management, Available at SSRN: https://ssrn.com/abstract=2998786
Osadchiy, N., Gaur, V., & Seshadri, S. (2016). Systematic risk in supply chain networks. *Management Science, 62*(6), 1755–1777.
Parsons, C., Titman, S., et al. (2009). Empirical capital structure: A review. *Foundations and Trends® in Finance, 3*(1), 1–93.
Pliska, S. R. (1997). *Introduction to mathematical finance: Discrete time models*. Oxford: Blackwell Publishers, Ltd.
Porteus, E. L. (1990). Stochastic inventory theory. In D. P. Heyman & M. J. Sobel (Eds.), *Handbooks in OR & MS* (Vol. 2, Chap. 12, pp. 605–652). North-Holland: Elsevier.
Porteus, E. L. (2002). *Foundations of stochastic inventory theory*. Stanford, CA: Stanford University Press.
Reinartz, S. J., & Schmid, T. (2016). Production flexibility, product markets, and capital structure decisions. *The Review of Financial Studies, 29*(6), 1501–1548.
Roundy, R. (1985). 98%-effective integer-ratio lot-sizing for one-warehouse multi-retailer systems. *Management Science, 31*(11), 1416–1430.
Roundy, R. (1986). A 98%-effective lot-sizing rule for a multi-product, multi-stage production/inventory system. *Mathematics of Operations Research, 11*(4), 699–727.
Shang, K. (2019). Cash beer game. *Foundations and Trends® in Technology, Information and Operations Management, 12*(2–3), 173–188.
Sharpe, W. F. (1964). Capital asset prices: A theory of market equilibrium under conditions of risk. *Journal of Finance, 19*, 425–442.
Sider, A., & Olson, B. (2018). Is the U.S. shale boom hitting a bottleneck? *The Wall Street Journal (U.S. Edition)*. Accessed on May 29, 2019 from https://www.wsj.com/articles/is-the-u-s-shale-boom-choking-on-growth-1524056400
Sinha, C. S., Sobel, M. J., & Babich, V. (2011). Computationally simple and unified approach to finite and infinite horizon Clark-Scarf inventory model. *IIE Transactions, 43*(3), 207–219.
Slotkin, E. (2020). Five ways the federal government can help health-care professionals get critical gear. *The Washington Post*. Accessed on August 17, 2020 from https://www.washingtonpost.com/opinions/2020/03/30/five-ways-federal-government-can-help-health-care-professionals-get-critical-gear/
Sobel, M. J. (1981). Myopic solutions of markov decision processes and stochastic games. *Operations Research, 29*(5), 995–1009.
Sobel, M. J. (1990a). Higher-order and average reward myopic-affine dynamic models. *Mathematics of Operations Research, 15*(2), 299–310.
Sobel, M. J. (1990b). Myopic solutions of affine dynamic models. *Operations Research, 38*(5), 847–853.
Sobel, M. J. (1995). Lot sizes in serial manufacturing with random yields. *Probability in the Engineering and Information Sciences, 9*, 151–157.
Sobel, M. J., & Babich, V. (2012). Optimality of myopic policies for dynamic lot-sizing problems in serial production lines with random yields and autoregressive demand. *Operations Research, 60*(6), 1520–1536.
Thomas, L. (1974). Price and production decisions with random demand. *Operations Research, 22*, 513–518.
Tirole, J. (2005). *The theory of corporate finance*. Princeton University Press.
Townsend, R. (1979). Optimal contracts and competitive markets with costly state verification. *Journal of Economic Theory, 21*(2), 265–293.
Van Mieghem, J. A. (2003). Capacity management, investment, and hedging: Review and recent developments. *M&SOM, 5*(4), 269–302.

Veinott, A. F. Jr. (1965). Optimal policy for a multi-product, dynamic, nonstationary inventory problem. *Management Science, 12*, 206–222.

Wagner, H., & Whitin, T. (1958). Dynamic problems in the theory of the firm. *Naval Research Logistics Quarterly, 5*, 53–74.

WardsAuto Group. (2018). U.S. vehicle sales, 1931-2016. Accessed December 28, 2018. http://wardsauto.com/keydata/historical/UsaSa01summary

Wethe, D. (2018). Shale country is out of workers. that means $140,000 for a truck driver and 100% pay hikes. *Los Angeles Times*. Accessed on May 29, 2019 from https://www.latimes.com/business/la-fi-shale-oil-boom-20180608-story.html

WHO. (2020). How WHO is re-imagining and fixing the links in the supply chains during COVID-19. https://www.who.int/news-room/feature-stories/detail/how-who-is-re-imagining-and-fixing-the-links-in-the-supply-chains-during-covid-19

Yahoo! Finance. (2018). ^ GSPC historical prices. Accessed December 28, 2018. http://finance.yahoo.com/q?s=^GSPC

Zheng, Y.-S., & Zipkin, P. (1990). A queueing model to analyze the value of centralized inventory information. *Operations Research, 38*(2), 296–307.

Zhu, K., & Thonemann, U. (2009). Coordination of pricing and inventory control across products. *Naval Research Logistics, 56*, 175–190.

Zipkin, P. H. (2000). *Foundations of inventory management*. New York: McGraw Hill.

Chapter 4
The Past, Present, and Future of the Payment System as Trusted Broker and the Implications for Banking

Joseph Byrum

Abbreviations

ACH	Automated clearing house
AI	Artificial intelligence
AML	Anti money laundering
API	Application programming interface
ATM	Automated teller machine
BIS	Bank for International Settlements
CBDC	Central bank digital currency
CPMI	Committee on Payments and Market Infrastructures (BIS)
CSD	Central securities depository
DLT	Distributed ledge technology
DNS	Deferred net settlement
ECB	European Central Bank
FI	Financial institution
FPS	Fast (retail) payment system
FPTF	Faster Payments Task Force
FSB	Financial Stability Board
GTB	Global transactions banking
KYC	Know your customer
NFC	Near-Field Communications
OCC	Office of the Comptroller of the Currency (U.S. Treasury)
P2P	Peer to peer
POS	Point of sale

J. Byrum (✉)
Principal Financial Group, Des Moines, IA, USA
e-mail: jrbyrum@umich.edu

V. Babich et al. (eds.), *Innovative Technology at the Interface of Finance and Operations*, Springer Series in Supply Chain Management 11,
https://doi.org/10.1007/978-3-030-75729-8_4

PSP Payment service provider
RTGS Real-time gross settlement

4.1 Introduction

4.1.1 Background and Context

For decades, the majority of payment services have been provided by traditional financial institutions (FIs). But the payments industry is currently going through a major transformation, part of the digital revolution that is sweeping the world, including banking. There is increased standardization, and instant payments are becoming the expectation, if not the norm. The payments market is being entered by nonbanks such as big technology enterprises and small fintechs. The base rate for payments is declining as new entrants cherry-pick the more lucrative payment services. Banks are being squeezed because they still need to fund the current payment infrastructure with declining revenues from payments.

A key advantage that incumbent banks still have is their security credentials, which offer them the opportunity to incrementally innovate and come up with new services still close to their core, such as payment-overlay services integrated with invoicing. However, if a more radical disruption occurs, the locus of trust may be wrested away from banks. This is a potentially existential threat to the conventional finance industry. If banks are no longer the trusted brokers for payments, their ability to cross-sell other traditional banking services such as lending will be severely impacted.

The payment system we use is closely related to the means of payment in use, which is our money or currency. Payment in cattle has to be processed entirely differently than payment in digital currency, and different rules will apply to specify how each respective payment is settled. Thus, whenever the means of payment change, so will the payment system itself and particularly the rules for processing payments. The aspect of trust has been an ever-present consideration. Even when using specie currency such as precious-metal coins, the buyer needs to be reassured that those coins are what they are represented to be and that they weren't debased by using a lesser alloy, or clipped to make them contain less precious metal, or weighed on biased scales. Such tricks were used, rediscovered, and used again by crooked merchants and cash-poor kings throughout the centuries. (And these concerns have usually been solved by the combined use of trusted intermediaries and government regulation.)

It is, therefore, useful to start with a brief refresher on money and its relationship to payments. Money has three basic functions: a medium of exchange, a unit of account, and a store of value. All of these functions are relevant to the payment process. In a payment transaction, the recipient has to trust in the value of the money used as the means of payment and be willing to accept it as final payment for the obligation being discharged. That acceptance also depends on the belief (trust) by the recipient that the next person the recipient will pass the money to, will also trust in its value and hence accept it. Money that cannot be successfully passed on is useless as a medium of exchange. Money that doesn't have a stable value is also unsuitable as a means of payment. Therefore, any discussion of trust in payments has to start by considering the trustworthiness of the currency used as payment. As the Bank for International Settlements (BIS) states in its most recent annual report:

> The foundation of a safe and efficient payment system is trust in money. In a fiat money system, where money is not backed by a physical asset, such as gold, trust ultimately depends on the general acceptance of pieces of paper that cannot be redeemed in anything but themselves. General acceptance is what ultimately makes them valuable, alongside confidence that payments made with them can irrevocably extinguish obligations ("finality"). In countries around the world, central banks have become the designated institution to pursue this public interest. (BIS, 2020a, 2020b)

A trusted payment thus requires two essential elements: A trusted payment currency (i.e., money or form of money), and a trusted payment mechanism. Whoever operates the payment system is essentially in a position of a trusted broker. In the status quo, the trusted currency is the responsibility of central banks, while the payment mechanisms (i.e., payment systems) are largely left to the private sector to develop, with a central-bank-supplied foundation and regulations. However, even this part of the status quo is under assault with the introduction of private digital currencies, which are accompanied by their integrated payment systems. Likewise, the introduction of new currencies and the popularization of new payment methods will give rise to new payment systems. As a consequence, the locus of trust in the payment process may also shift. The changing locus of trust is the focus of this paper. But to understand the future and interpret new developments, we will first need to understand the past and present of this crucial property of the payment system.

4.1.2 *Payment System Basics*

4.1.2.1 Types of Payments

The World Bank's Global Findex survey (World Bank, 2017) collects responses to questions about nine types of payments that can be grouped into five major categories:

1. *Payments from government to people*, that is, public sector wages, public sector pensions, and government transfers.
2. *Payments from businesses to people,* that is, private sector wages.
3. *Other payments for work,* that is, payments for the sale of agricultural products and payments from self-employment.
4. *Payments from people to businesses,* that is, utility payments.
5. *Payments between people,* that is, domestic remittances, both those sent and those received.

4.1.2.2 Definitions and Terms

The latest BIS definitions of a payment system and related concepts are as follows (BIS, 2020a, 2020b):

A **payment system** is a set of instruments, procedures, and rules among participating institutions, including the operator of the system, used for the purposes of clearing and settling payment transactions. Its infrastructure usually involves payments flowing through a "front end" that interacts with end users and a number of "back end" arrangements that process, clear and settle payments.

The **front-end** arrangements initiate the payment. They encompass the following elements:

- Underlying transaction account (e.g., deposit transaction) represents the source of the funds.
- Payment instrument (e.g., cash, cheque, card), which can vary across payment service providers (PSPs) and use cases.
- Service channel (e.g., bank branch, automated teller machine (ATM), point-of-sale (POS) terminal, payment application) connects the payer/payee and PSP.

The **back-end arrangements** generally focus on specific stages of the payment chain:

- Processing encompasses authentication, authorization, fraud and compliance monitoring, fee calculation, and so on.
- Clearing is the process of transmitting, reconciling, and in some cases, confirming transactions prior to settlement.
- Settlement is the process of transferring funds to discharge monetary obligations between parties.

Overlay systems provide front-end services by using existing infrastructure to process and settle payments (e.g., Apple Pay, Google Pay, PayPal). These systems link the front-end application to a user's credit card or bank account.

Closed-loop systems (e.g., Alipay, M-Pesa, WeChat Pay) provide front-end to back-end services, have back-end arrangements largely proprietary to their respective firms, and do not interact with or depend much on the existing payment infrastructure.

4.1.2.3 System Architecture

The major system elements and the high-level payment process are depicted in Fig. 4.1.

4.1.3 Scope of this Paper

The future evolution and ownership of payment systems will be examined within the context of the trust-based payment relationship, and what shifts in this relationship might mean for the future ownership of the payment system. The paper will start by examining how high-trust facilitation of payments led to the development of the modern banking system, and what lessons this holds for the future. It will cover major trends driving the present transformation of payment services, the types of new payment platforms emerging, and which developments to watch for an indication of what the future state of the payment system might be. We will consider the changing locus of trust under various future payment scenarios, and how control of the payment relationship and infrastructure will determine who wins the future of banking.

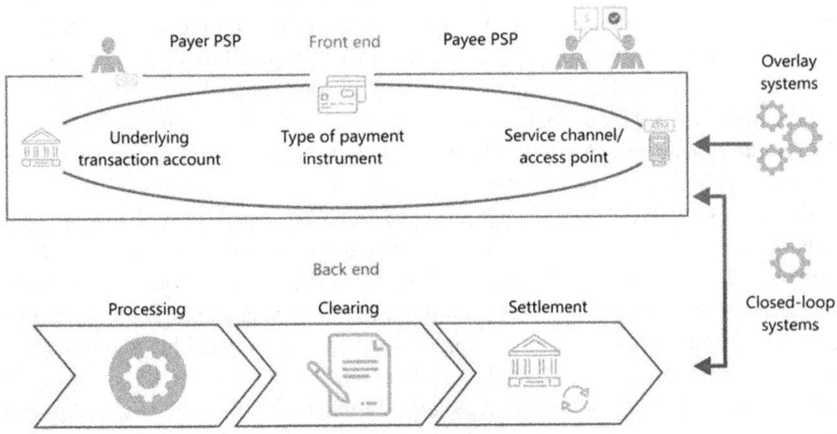

Fig. 4.1 Payment system infrastructure and elements (Source: BIS)

4.2 A Short History of Payments to the Present Day

4.2.1 Money and Payments in the Ancient World

The histories of money, payments, and banking are closely intertwined. Perhaps not so obvious is that the history of recordkeeping is also closely related to the history of payment and banking. Writing was invented for the recordkeeping of transactions.

With banking and potential disputes about payments also comes regulation. The Code of Hammurabi, the well-preserved code of law of ancient Mesopotamia dated between 1700 and 1800 BC, contains several laws on trading and money. Ancient Mesopotamia was a feudal agrarian society that used commodity money, but the principles are clearly recognizable, as is the fact that a trusted third party, the "agent" was involved in the transaction and that the agent was required to keep careful records. For example, Law 104 states:

> If a merchant gives to an agent grain, wool, oil or goods of any kind with which to trade, the agent shall write down the value and return (the money) to the merchant. The agent shall take a sealed receipt for the money which he gives to the merchant.

In ancient Egypt, banks mostly stored grain and other produce, handled deposits, granted loans, collected taxes, and processed payments. Coin money was first put into widespread use by the ancient Greeks. During the Roman empire, money in the forms of imperial coins was widely circulated across the ancient world. The expansion of trade between the second-century BC and the third-century AD fostered the development of a banking system to support this commerce. Money was often held in the basements of thousands of temples that were secure as they were always manned by devout workers and priests, and often patrolled by soldiers. The temple priests were trusted to keep accounts of deposits and loans. The temple of Saturn in Rome even housed the public treasury.

The *argentarii*, private Roman citizens who belonged to a guild, initially exchanged foreign for Roman currency. Their role expanded to include functions associated with modern banks like holding deposits, lending money, determining the value of coins, and putting newly minted coins into circulation. The most highly-respected argentarii came from the upper class, served the wealthy, and conducted large-scale banking business. Smaller scale argentarii came from the lower classes and were looked down upon. They typically charged higher rates like today's payday lenders. Most interesting is the role the argentarii played in bills of exchange. They would, for example, receive a sum of money to be paid in Athens and would then draw a bill payable in Athens by a *correspondent banker*. Payments were facilitated when owners of money instructed the argentarius to make them. The argentarii kept meticulous books called codices to document the transfer of money from one party to the other. These codices were trusted to have high authority and relied on as evidence by courts of justice (Labate, 2016).

After the fall of the Roman empire, trade collapsed as trade routes became hazardous, and money in the form of coin fell into disuse in many areas in favor of payment in kind or barter, although there was a brief resurgence in monetary society under Charlemagne in the eighth century. Lending was continually suppressed by the Catholic Church's prohibition against usury.

4.2.2 Payment History from the Medicis to Modern Banks

Modern banking has its origins in Renaissance Italy. During the Renaissance, trade revived and the grip of religious doctrines on the secular world including banking eased just enough for loopholes to be found in the usury laws. This created the space for banking to be reinvented. The great banking houses of major cities such as Venice, Genoa, and Florence are the predecessors of all modern banks. Double-entry bookkeeping, bills of exchange, letters of credit, and deposit accounts were all pioneered (if not necessarily invented) by the Italian bankers. It gave them a virtual monopoly over European finance at the time.

A Victorian-era study of the origins of banking in the Republic of Venice connects the evolution of the Bank of Venice to acts and regulations of the Venetian Senate passed between 1270 and 1530 (Dunbar, 1892). Private banking in Venice had its origin in the business conducted by *campsores*, dealers in foreign money, since merchants in the city conducted trade with many countries. The dealers had an important role in managing the stream of payments resulting from this activity. As early as 1270 they were required to give security to the government as a condition of carrying on with their business. Between 1270 and 1318, the moneychangers of Venice became bankers in the proper sense of the word, known by the Italian terms *bancus scriptae* and *bancherius scriptae*, indicating that a banker is one who keeps written records of transferable deposits. By 1584 the transfer of credit was an important means of paying because it saved the bank the trouble of counting the coin and manually delivering it. Coin was deposited at the bank for credit from which coin could be withdrawn on demand. The banker was a trusted intermediary, and both buyers and sellers were satisfied that the moment when "pen moves over page" the transfer was made and the debt settled, without having to count and transfer a "great number of coins." A 1467 regulation required banks to exhibit their books to any interested person who wished to inspect his accounts and balances. Loans to individuals were routinely offered by the late fifteenth century at least.

Many Venetian banks failed during the early sixteenth century, leading to regulatory reform which established what was essentially a public bank, a *banco de scritta* under a governor appointed by the Senate for a term. This public bank received all cash deposits and kept them subject to call, with transfers allowed only in the presence of the depositor and with his written consent. It was specifically required that credit be given to the transferee *at the same time* that the transfer is debited. The bank's operating costs were paid by duties levied on imported goods.

The monopoly of the single public bank, the *banco de scritta*, was eventually eroded with private-sector banks rising to compete in payment services. In the late fifteenth-century Venice, many banks classified as *banci di scritta* performed essential payment services. The core of their business was literally writing transfers of deposits from one account to another. Where one merchant wanted to pay another, both parties appeared before the banker and personally ordered the necessary transfer to be made in the banker's books. This was a great convenience as it eliminated the slow counting of coins and the common problem of dealing with imperfect coins. Furthermore, the banker's book entry became the legal and official record of the entire transaction, obviating the need for other legal documents. (This is analogous to how using PayPal for an online payment today can save the consumer from having to create an account with that online vendor.) It is estimated that one out of every 30 Venetian citizens at the time had bank accounts, some with quite small balances, signifying significant banking penetration among the population. Some deposits were earmarked by the bankers as "conditioned deposits," meaning that they were meant to be used for a specific purpose and already assigned to a specific beneficiary, akin to today's escrow accounts. Dowries and taxes owed to the state were examples of such accounts (Lane, 1937).

Late-medieval Italy was in a state of political and economic flux, with the fortunes of cities and families waxing and waning. Being able to borrow money was essential for entrepreneurs who wanted to grow their businesses and thereby increase their social standing; it also financed the frequent wars that the princes of the city-states waged against one another, and it financed cross-border trade. However, the roads were not safe to travel with cash payments in the form of gold coins. The solution was a *bill of exchange* granted in one city and drawn on in the other. Bankers made money on the spread—by posting different exchange rates in different cities. Most theologians signed off on this banking practice as non-usurious. The *letter of credit* was another Italian banking innovation.

To better understand how trust was maintained in this prototypical banking system, we can follow a transaction from a Medici bank in Florence to London:

- A credit-worthy merchant approaches the bank in Florence requesting to enter into the following contract: 1000 florens in cash in return for the merchant's promise to pay back the equivalent amount at 40 pence to the florin "as is the custom" to the bank's appointed representative in London, England.
- The note is written by an authorized Medici manager and signed by the merchant. The note is authenticated by the handwriting of the Medici manager since all Medici banks and their correspondents have handwriting samples of all authorized managers.
- The Medici's correspondent in London will visit the merchant's agent in London, likely a bank, which is also Italian and therefore known, to demand payment on the appointed day.
- The phrase "as is the custom" governed several important contract terms that were set by the Exchangers' Guild, the trade organization of the bankers. This included specifying the maximum time to journey from one financial center to the other, 90 days in the case of Florence to London. These 90 days become the repayment period from the date the florins are received to the date the pounds need to be paid in London.

- The bank ran its courier system and all the individuals in the chain knew each other by name. The bank's correspondent in London who received the funds, and the client's agent who paid it, respectively received commissions (i.e., transaction fees).
- Included in "as is the custom" was the exchange rate. Exchange rates were set daily by brokers meeting on open streets, taking into consideration the relative debasement of currencies and fluctuations in value. The bank makes money on the exchange rate spread, for example, it would sell florens in London at 36 pennies to the floren. The principle was that the base currency quoted was always worth a little more in the country of the currency's issue (Parks, 2013).

The similarities with how modern payments work are apparent, even if the technology was more primitive. A key ingredient of trust was located in the people employed in the Italian banks and their branches abroad. At the time, only your countrymen could be fully trusted: "Where there is an Italian community, there is a chance of a bank. Where there is no Italian community, there is no bank." (Parks, 2013) Aside from being Italian, these bankers had to be of sober habits. For example, Medici employees had to sign a pledge that they would not gamble. The historian Niall Ferguson points out another important reason why the Florentine banks were so well trusted: The Medicis and a few other rich families also controlled the city's government and finances (Ferguson, 2008).

In the late sixteenth century, the center of gravity shifted to northern Europe, following shifting patterns of international trade (toward the New World and the Far East) that favored seaports in Flanders and the Netherlands. Banking follows trade activity, and so do bankers. Many Venetians moved to northern European cities to lend their expertise to the new banks, which essentially copied the Italian banking and payment methods described above. Eventually, Amsterdam became the major financial center, with the Bank of Amsterdam dominant in the seventeenth century, largely due to the business brought in by the Dutch East India Company. The Bank of Amsterdam was originally established to value the coins—of many kinds, and often of dubious quality–received by Dutch merchants. The Bank, as a trusted broker, then converted coins deposited with it into book credits, which could be reliably used for payments.

The Bank of England was given a royal charter by King William III in 1694. It was established with private shareholders contributing capital for the initial purpose of financing William's wars. Gradually English merchant shipping value overtook that of the Dutch. By the end of the eighteenth century, Dutch banking had become vulnerable due to several financial and political crises. During the Napoleonic era, London took over the mantle as the financial center of Europe (Coispeau, 2017). In the City of London, Lombard Street (reflecting the Italian heritage of banking) became the financial center of the modern banking system during the nineteenth century.

4.2.3 Essential Linkages between Payment and Credit Services

Trade credit is essential to grease the wheels of commerce. Merchants need access to working capital to finance their voyages or production or tide them over until payment finally arrives. The trusted relationship they have with the bankers who are processing their payments, and the bankers' knowledge of their business and income, create a natural opportunity for the extension of credit by the banker against the security of future payments to be received by the merchant.

Bankers like the Medicis understood this well, but they were still subject to the Church's usury laws. Their ingenious solution for customers who needed more time to pay their bills of exchange when they came due, was to sell them a new bill of exchange with a later due date at a higher rate. In this way, a loan was essentially disguised as a currency transaction, which the theologians were willing to approve as long as geographical distance was maintained, and an exchange rate was present. On the other side of the ledger, depositors were given "gifts" for their patronage when they withdrew their money (Parks, 2013).

4.2.4 Brief Overview of the Current Payment Architecture

According to the BIS, a *payment system* is "a set of instruments, procedures, and rules for the transfer of funds between or among participants. The system encompasses both the participants and the entity operating the arrangement." The two main types of payment are retail payments and wholesale payments. *Retail payments* relate to purchases of goods and services by consumers and businesses and are typically low in volume but high in volume. Retail payments include person-to-person (transfer of funds between people who know each other), person-to-business (e.g., purchases or bill payments) business-to-person (e.g., salaries), and business-to-business payments. Wholesale payments are settlements between financial institutions, which are lower in volume or frequency, but much higher in value (transaction amount). Wholesale payments are made to settle securities and foreign exchange trades or transfer between financial institutions and central banks, or as part of interbank funding arrangements (Bech et al., 2020).

Payment systems today are built upon a two-tier structure: The central bank ensures trust in the money, supplying the ultimate safe medium to settle both wholesale and retail transactions, while commercial banks supply the bulk of retail payment instruments (BIS, 2020a, 2020b).

Payments flow through a *front end* where the payer initiates the payment through a *back-end* where the payment is cleared and settled. The front end is comprised of the funding source, the service channel, and the payment instrument. The back end is comprised of all the arrangements needed for the clearing and settlements of the payments. *Clearing* entails transmitting, confirming, and reconciling transactions prior to final settlement. Payment service providers (PSPs), usually banks, may clear transactions bilaterally, but more often this is facilitated by automated clearing houses (ACHs). ACHs are multilateral institutional arrangements that facilitate the exchange of payments between PSPs. *Settlement* is the process of transferring funds to discharge the pecuniary obligations between parties (Bech et al., 2020).

Global transaction banking (GTB) is big business for banks. Annual GTB revenues are around 1 trillion dollars. Trade finance, domestic, and cross-border payments make up about half of this revenue, with domestic payments having the lion's share, followed by cross-border payments. The other half of the GTB revenue pool comes mostly from current accounts and savings deposits. Banks are well aware of the need to protect this huge revenue pool from disruptive new entrants while catering to the higher demands of their customers for easier, faster payment processing. A McKinsey survey of banking executives reveals that the top three current priorities for investing in innovation are first, mobile channels; second, domestic real-time payments; and third, cross-border real-time payments (Botta et al., 2020).

4.2.4.1 Domestic

The United States is the largest payment market in the world and its domestic payment system is comprised of a conglomerate of public and private payment systems. Payment systems can be categorized by payment type (wholesale or retail), operator (private sector or central bank, and settlement mode (real-time or deferred). Refer to Fig. 4.2 for a simple taxonomy along these dimensions.

In the United States, the core payments system infrastructure is privately owned and operated by the Payments Company, which belongs to the Clearing House, a bank association and payments company. The Payments Company is the only private-sector ACH and wire operator in the United States. It clears and settles almost $2 trillion of payments a day, which is estimated to be about half of all ACH and wire volume.

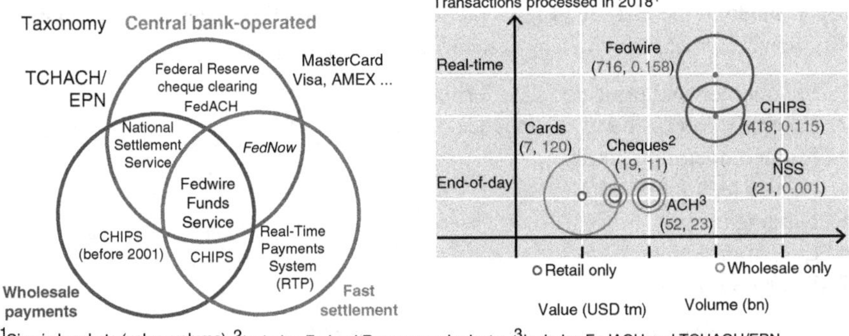

Fig. 4.2 U.S. payment systems (Source: BIS)

4.2.4.2 International/Cross-Border

Cross-border payments are those sent by individuals, businesses, or government agencies in one jurisdiction to recipients in another. A recent CPMI report describes this market as "complex, involving many different parties, use cases and underlying arrangements." (BIS, 2018) The payer and payee are typically located in different jurisdictions and therefore require intermediaries operating in multiple jurisdictions. PSPs such as banks typically provide the interface for end users and are mostly seen in the "first and last mile" of the payment. Payment instruments can be cash but are increasingly electronic payments. At the bank end, various service providers such as transaction banks and payment infrastructure operators are present. Arrangements include correspondent banking. Processes include messaging, clearing, settlement, and foreign exchange and liquidity management.

Most international payments today are done by means of messages sent over the SWIFT network. SWIFT is a member-owned cooperative that transmits the financial messages, which enable the payments to be made and the funds to be transferred.

A *correspondent bank* provides local account and payment services for banks based abroad. Together these correspondent banks form a *correspondent banking network*. The mechanism whereby payments are made by correspondent banks is to send SWIFT messages to one another. These SWIFT messages include instructions to debit and credit accounts.

Business customers have long been unhappy with cross-border payment services. In a 2020 survey of European SMEs who sell online, only 15% of respondents said that they have not experienced problems when trying to arrange cross-border payments through their banking partners. High fees, slow responses, poor FX rates, a poor digital experience, and poor customer service were the most common complaints (Banking Circle, 2020). Cross-border payments are indeed an area where everyone acknowledges that many challenges still remain. The key challenges are high cost, low speed, limited access, and limited transparency. These are mostly due to the low rate of straight-through-processing in payments and include delays in clearing and settlements of cross-border payments and the complexities driven by anti-money laundering and terrorism financing laws (Valladares, 2020). In a recent report made to the G20, the Financial Stability Board (FSB) identified seven major "frictions" causing the challenges to cross-border payments:

1. Fragmented and truncated data formats
2. Complex processing of compliance checks
3. Limited operating hours
4. Legacy technology platforms
5. Funding costs
6. Long transaction chains
7. Weak competition

There are ongoing initiatives to address this problem:

- SWIFT has launched the global payment innovation (GPI) initiative to establish a new standard for fast, digital cross-border payments. SWIFT claims that nearly two-thirds of its traffic is now over GPI and that $77 trillion was moved over GPI last year.
- The Committee on Payments and Market Infrastructures (CPMI) of the BIS is working on setting new standards to achieve faster, cheaper, more transparent, and also more inclusive cross-border services. A report just published by the CPMI—covering both retail and wholesale payments—identifies 19 building blocks that directly address the challenges and frictions listed, thereby offering "a comprehensive set of measures to enhance cross-border payments."

Thanks to the EU Directive on Payment Services in The Internal Market, payments between countries within the European Union have been greatly streamlined and sped up over the last number of years. The directive's main purpose was to increase competition across the EU, increase participation in the payments industry also from nonbanks, and provide for a level playing field by harmonizing consumer protection and the rights and obligations for payment providers and users. The stated key objectives of the updated directive (called PSD2) are creating a more integrated European payments market, making payments safer and more secure, and protecting consumers.

4.2.5 Locus of Trust in the Current Payments System

A modification to the data in a trusted ledger is required to settle any payment. The modification of the ledger is what effects the payment operation and completes it, resulting in *finality*. While there is a diversity of cross-border payment arrangements, they may be categorized in terms of the characteristics of the ledger used to affect the settlement, and the *trust relationships* needed among the participants that will enable the ledger to fulfill the payment settlement. According to a recent report by the FSB (Financial Stability Board, 2020), the payment arrangements may be classified based on the types of structures:

1. **One-sided trusted ledger** in which the settlement ledger is managed by one of the PSP on which the other PSP has an account. This is the simplest and most basic structure. One PSP has to trust another PSP, and individuals need to each trust their respective PSP. *Examples are simple correspondent banking and closed-loop transactions of global bank branches.*
2. **Multi-sided trusted ledger** managed by a third party. The third party will have an account on the other participant (usually another third party in a different jurisdiction) and will have to trust that third party. PSPs must trust their respective third parties, and individuals must trust their PSPs. Examples are *complex correspondent banking relationships* and arrangements *interlinking payment infrastructures*, on either a bilateral or regional basis.

3. **Directly accessible shared ledger** in which both the payer and payee trust and can directly instruct their payments. The ledger serves as the bridge that connects different jurisdictions. In this structure, individuals only need to trust the unique ledger. No trust of unknown PSPs is required. This structure is found where financial intermediation has been eliminated such as when using *stable-tokens*, or where the payer and payee share the same PSP, obviating the need of third parties, such as *internal transactions with a global bank.*
4. **Shared ledger** through the intermediation of multiple PSPs. PSPs must trust the centralized ledger, but not necessarily each other. Individuals must trust their PSPs. Examples are *cross-border card payments* for retail transactions, as well as *crypto-assets* that are operated only through trusted and validated intermediaries.

4.2.6 Lessons and Opportunities for the Future

Up to recently, exchanging cold hard cash has been the only way to make a payment absent a trusted broker or intermediary.

According to the Federal Reserve, the number of core noncash payments, comprising debit cards, credit cards, ACH, and check payments, reached 174.2 billion in 2018, an increase of 30.6 billion from 2015. The value of these payments was $97.04 trillion in 2018, an increase of $10.25 trillion from 2015. Almost two-thirds of these payments by value, $64 trillion in 2018, were ACH payments, which have been growing by 6% a year in recent years. On the other hand, check payments have been declining (Federal Reserve, 2019).

A recent BIS paper emphasizes how much technological innovation is transforming payments. For those with access, domestic payments are convenient, virtually instantaneous, and available 24/7. The two big gaps in payments are first the lack of access, primarily but not exclusively in emerging markets and developing countries; and second cross-border payments, which are slow, expensive, and not transparent (Bech et al., 2020).

Worldwide there are still 1.7 billion adults who do not have transaction accounts and rely solely on cash as their means of payment (Powell, 2017). The lack of banking access in emerging markets, and the problems with cross-border payments combine to cause big problems for senders and recipients of remittances from expatriate workers, which can make a substantial portion of some developing country GDPs. This situation is begging for a solution. If it is not solved by the traditional financial system, it may well be solved by disruptive challengers to the status quo such as fintechs or cryptocurrency players.

4.3 Trends Driving the Present Transformation of the Payment System

4.3.1 Changes in User Needs and Preferences

The major trends in consumer payments are the move away from cash payments and paper checks, the fast growth of mobile payments, and the increasing popularity of peer-to-peer (P2P) payments on any internet platform, but particularly mobile. The retail point-of-sale (POS) is becoming anywhere, any time. On the payment-overlay side, the biggest trend is the accelerating adoption of digital and mobile wallets. Digital payments have already become indispensable in the new economy powered by Uber and AirBnB.

Underlying these trends is the consumer's ever-increasing demands for speed and ease of use. In an important 2017 speech on payment innovation made as Fed governor, the now current Fed chair, Jerome Powell predicted this:

> Mobile devices, high-speed data communication, and online commerce are creating expectations that convenient, secure, real-time payment and banking capabilities should be available whenever and wherever they are needed (Powell, 2017).

The Federal Reserve's latest *2019 Survey of Consumer Payment Choice* (Federal Reserve Bank of Atlanta, 2019) provides a snapshot into the current payment activity and preferences of U.S. consumers, who made on average 69 payments each month during 2019.

- Forty-two payments per month were done using debit, credit, or prepaid cards; 18 using cash or paper checks, and 8 using electronic or other means.
- Mobile banking services were used by 59% and online banking services by 75%.
- Half of the consumers surveyed had used or signed up for at least one online payment method, such as PayPal, Venmo, or Zelle.
- Half of the consumers made at least one P2P payment.
- About four in ten of P2P payments were made with a card or electronically, for example, via a payment app.
- Between 2015 and 2019 cash payments declined from 18.65% to 14.70%.
- Even for the lower-income group, cash has declined from 21.06% to 16.64%.
- Cash usage is the lowest in the 25–34 age group at only 10.8% in 2019.

Perhaps the most consequential trend in consumer payment preferences is the shift to digital and mobile wallets. Consumers like them because they make both online and in-person shopping easier. As e-commerce payment preferences, digital and mobile wallets have increased from 36% of spending to 42% between 2018 and 2019. In China, the leader, digital and mobile wallet use now stands at 71% of e-commerce spend. In India, it is at 32%, in Germany 25%, and the United States 24%. It is also estimated that one billion consumers will make a digital or mobile wallet payment in 2020. POS payment adoption has risen from 16% in 2018 to 22% in 2019 (Worldpay, 2020). The smartphone is effectively becoming the new wallet, with especially younger consumers leaving their physical payment cards at home.

4.3.2 Technological Developments

An *application programming interface (API)* allows two software applications to interact with each other and provides a structured layer on which this interaction may be arranged. APIs have been around for a long time, but their increased availability in payments enables open banking (see below) models. For example, in the United Kingdom, the open banking mandate requires banks to provide open access to a comprehensive set of APIs to registered financial services providers to enable standardized sharing of data and payments initiation processes (Dietz et al., 2018)."

Big data analytics are heavily used by FIs including in payments where they are useful to authenticate customers and detect fraud patterns.

Biometric technologies such as fingerprint, iris, and facial scans can augment and sometimes replace traditional identity verification measures. In payments, they can reduce the reliance on personal identification numbers (PINs), passwords, or social security numbers, and can help to extend access to illiterate customers.

Contactless technologies at the point of sale (POS) such as near-field communications (NFC), now also built into all smartphones, already enable payment cards to be waived instead of inserted into POS terminals. Most importantly, they enable mobile phone-based smart wallets. Such payments are also called *proximity mobile payments.*

Tokenization is when sensitive data such as an account or card number is replaced by a surrogate number that is not visible in transmission or to third parties, including vendors. It does not change the payment process itself but is a useful security measure.

Digital identity, or *digital ID*, is the electronic capture of attributes and credentials that uniquely identify an individual or a company for use in transactions. A natural person's digital ID may be comprised of biographic as well as biometric data. Digital ID is particularly useful in the absence of government-issued ID.

Smart contracts are computer programs that automatically execute obligations between parties when certain inputs (typically from electronic sensors) are received. This includes the triggering of payments, based on established protocols. Smart contracts eliminate the need for trusted intermediaries and drastically lower transaction costs.

The *Internet of Things (IoT)* collectively comprises the billions of sensors embedded in physical devices which can communicate with one another and with servers over the internet. IoT enables the creation of smart contracts and automatic electronic payments, for example, based on consumption data. The IoT is responsible for the generation of most big data.

Open banking is when FIs allow third-party providers access to their customers' financial data. The sharing of customer data enables an easier transfer of funds and making of payments. While open banking is driven by requirements set by regulators, the intention is that it will spur innovation in the private sector. In the European Union and the United Kingdom, it is currently mandatory, but in the

United States it is not, leaving the field open entirely to private-sector innovation and for private-sector companies to form their partnerships.

Distributed ledger technology (DLT) comprises the processes and related technologies that enable nodes in a computer network to propose, validate, and record state changes (or updates) to a synchronized ledger that is distributed and copied across the network's nodes. In the context of payment, clearing, and settlement, DLT can enable payment transactions without necessarily relying on a central authority to maintain a single "golden copy" of the ledger. DLT, and its major implications for payments, is covered in more detail in Sect. 4.4.4.

Banking-as-a-Service refers to off-the-shelf, cloud-based solutions that lower the entry barrier to newcomers, thereby encouraging innovation and driving down margins. One example is Treezor, a fintech that provides platform-based payments processing services, which was acquired by Société Générale 2 years ago.

4.3.3 Increasingly Cashless Societies

Governments have an economic incentive to promote electronic payments, because informal cash payments enable shadow economies in which taxes are not paid, and money can be more easily laundered. In the European Union, the shadow economy was recently estimated as 17% of official GDP (Medina & Schneider, 2018).

Cash-handling costs (sorting, transportation, insurance) have been estimated at 5–10% of bank costs, and 5–15% of retail costs. Consumers may be charged to withdraw cash at some ATMs. Yet, more than $1.6 trillion of cash circulates in the U.S. economy, and consumers still rate cash highly for convenience and acceptance as a payment medium. India's disastrous and ultimately futile attempt in 2016 to withdraw higher value banknotes from circulation to squeeze the shadow economy, stands as a recent lesson of the endurance of cash. During power and network outages, cash is still good while electronic money is inaccessible. There is also a fear that going cash-free will disproportionately hurt low-income people who transact more in cash, often because they are unbanked. Therefore, multiple cities have started to ban, or are considering banning, retailers from not accepting cash. Cash is also still preferred for small in-person payments like buying an item at a garage sale or paying a babysitter, though mobile P2P payment apps are eroding this preference. Some stores maintain minimum amounts for credit card transactions (van Biljon & Lajoux, 2020).

But we may be at a new inflection point. Cash is literally dirty and unhygienic to handle. Not surprisingly, cashless payments have significantly increased since the start of the COVID-19 pandemic. During the COVID-19 crisis, cash payments have decreased worldwide in favor of remote payment methods (Botta et al., 2020). According to Square, only 8% of its sellers were effectively cashless (defined as accepting 95% or more of transactions via credit or debit card) on March 1, 2020. A mere 54 days later on April 23, the number of cashless sellers had risen to 31%. The corresponding before and after numbers for Canada are 9% and 48%; and for

Great Britain, 10% and 50%. Of U.S. small-business owners surveyed on behalf of Square, 69% said that it is likely that COVID-19 will accelerate the adoption of cashless transactions. However, 85% said they will never stop accepting cash.

4.3.4 Peer-to-Peer (P2P) Payments

Consumers like the ease of use of P2P apps. Users do not need to exchange financial account information to make or receive real-time payments. The payment is instead made via the email or phone number associated with an account. There are two different types of P2P apps, those that piggyback off existing bank accounts and relationships, and those that create their accounting relationships.

P2P payments have several economic advantages over traditional payments such as mailing checks. The first is lowering transaction costs, not just in terms of fees but in terms of time spent on payments, and the second is lowering opportunity costs because the time is better spent on more productive activities. A third advantage is an increase in economic activity because it supports the work of contractors and freelancers, who can be paid more quickly and easily (Caceres-Santamaria, 2020).

The number of P2P payment users in the United States has increased from 64 million (28% of adult mobile phone users) in 2017 to 96 million (40% of adult mobile phone users) in 2019 (Cakebread, 2018).

PayPal was the first popular P2P system. Its continuing close relationship with eBay has been a big driver of its growth, especially in the early years. eBay sellers and buyers need a P2P payment service to make the online marketplace work. PayPal accounts are linked to a user's checking, debit, or credit card account. It replaces paying by check or money order. PayPal is also a useful intermediary for users who prefer not to share their credit card details with online merchants they may not trust.

4.3.5 Growth in Value-Added Payment-Overlay Services

Digital wallets, also sometimes called *mobile wallets* when existing in a smartphone app, facilitate payments for purchase and money transfers without the physical use of cash, checks, or credit or debit cards. Digital wallets secure personal and payment information through authentication, data encryption, and monitoring as well as other security features like tokenization where sensitive data is replaced by randomly generated numbers that can then be securely transmitted over existing card networks (Stackhouse, 2019).

There are two main types of mobile wallets, *single purpose,* which are branded apps like store apps or credit card apps or that only offer one choice of payment, and *multipurpose,* which allow users to access a number of credit cards, debit cards, gift cards, and loyalty cards in one wallet. The adoption of digital wallets has been delayed by a lack of consumer awareness, but this is changing fast. One Mastercard study tracked 3.5 million social media conversations and found that over 75% concerned digital wallets (AlliedWallet, 2020).

The most popular digital wallets are Apple Pay, Google Pay, and Samsung Pay, with Amazon Pay being a fast-rising challenger. (Early in 2018, Google unified all its payments technologies under a single brand, Google Pay.) Amazon reported 59% active merchant growth and 103% overall revenue growth for Amazon between 2017 and 2018, and it is growing at double-digit rates in all global markets (Worldpay from FIS, 2020).

In China, the two largest incumbents together hold 92% of a $46 trillion mobile payment market, Tencent-owned We-Chat Pay is dominant in P2P while Ant Financial-owned Alipay is dominant in payments to firms. Payment users load their digital wallets from their bank accounts after which they can pay for almost anything. These digital wallets have an interesting customer-retention model where they only charge users fees when they move money out of the wallets. (Merchants are charged transaction fees.) Alipay is now accepted in more than 50 countries outside of China, although it is still primarily used by Chinese travelers. However, observers think that these two firms harbor ambitions to eventually build an international cross-border wallet platform (The Economist, 2020a, 2020b, 2020c).

According to McKinsey's latest *Digital Payments Consumer Survey* of U.S. consumers taken in 2019, over three-quarters of U.S. consumers made a mobile payment of some kind in the 12 months ending August 2019. The largest increase is in the use of digital wallets. Close to half of consumers are now using in-app digital wallets. While the digital transition is led by the Millennial cohort with 93% making mobile payments, all age groups are showing significant uptake with 80% of Generation X and 64% of Baby Boomers using mobile payments. With the growth of digital wallets, traditional banks have tried to get their cards to be "top of wallet" (the default payment option), and even offering incentives to do so, under the assumption that once that choice was made it would be sticky. However, the payments card preference is not nearly as sticky as banks have hoped, with consumers switching to non-default cards frequently (defined as every couple of weeks or more in the survey): 64% for online purchases, 73% for in-store purchases, and 67% for in-app purchases. The card switching is facilitated by app functionality from market leaders like Amazon and Uber. This suggests that digital wallets are becoming more like leather wallets, with consumers deciding to pull out which card for a particular payment occasion (Anan et al., 2020).

PayPal is the most popular payment method at 58% penetration for in-app purchases by U.S. consumers, followed by Visa Checkout at 20%, and Apple Pay at 16%. For in-store purchases, Apple Pay is the most popular at 40%, followed by Google Pay (20%), and Samsung Pay (16%). For online purchases, PayPal is first (41%), followed by Amazon Pay (13%), and Visa Checkout (9%). PayPal rules the P2P payment space with 72%, followed by Venmo (29%) and Zelle (28%) essentially tied for second place.

Shopify, a Canadian e-commerce provider, had the second largest share of online retail sales in the United States in 2019. It processes most online payments not made on Amazon.com. Globally it powers more than one million online merchants in 275 countries, processing payments for over $60 billion in 2019. Its value-added services beyond payments include virtual store set-up including inventory management and shipping all on a single platform (Pearson, 2020).

4.3.6 Instant Payments

Instant payments are payments in which the transmission of the payment message and final availability of funds occur within seconds of each other, with 24/7 service availability. Instant payments, therefore, resemble cash with the added benefit that they can be done over a distance.

Fast (retail) payment systems (FPSs) are defined by the CPMI as a system in which the transmission of the payment message and the availability of the final funds to the payee occur in real-time or near real-time on as near to a 24/7 basis as possible. FPSs facilitate payments between account holders at multiple PSPs rather than just between the customers of the same PSP. Currently, 56 jurisdictions have FPSs, and this number is projected to rise to 64 in the near future (BIS, 2020a, 2020b).

Retailers currently pay fees for accepting cards. Instant payments at the POS will not only provide faster responses than credit or debit cards but eliminate the card fees paid by the vendor. Instant payments are more easily integrated with loyalty programs that the retailer may run, thereby also giving the retailer access to the transaction data. Banks can still profit if they provide the overlay services that enable this (CGI, 2019).

The end vision is for true *zero-touch payments* enabled by face or other biometric recognition technology. This will allow customers to simply walk into a store, pick up an item, and walk out without even going past a pay point. That will mean that payment, as an activity, will become an invisible part of commerce, not even be noticed by customers.

There are currently multiple initiatives worldwide to revamp domestic payment systems in pursuit of near-instant bank transfers. Authorities also view this as an opportunity to reassert their control over the payment structure. The United Kingdom has had instant payments for over a decade. Europe is far along, after successfully connecting payment networks that serve a block of 35 countries and over 500 million people. The European instant payment initiative is closely related to its regulatory push for open banking, something that is currently absent from the United States and Canada.

In South-East Asia India and Singapore connected their networks this past March. It is anticipated that China will eventually use the system that Malaysia is in the process of developing (The Economist, 2020a, 2020b, 2020c).

In the United States, the Federal Reserve convened the Faster Payments Task Force (FPTF 2015) in 2015. Comprised of over 300 payment experts, the Fed had tasked it to come up with an ambitious plan for implementing faster, safe, and ubiquitous payments by 2020. In its final report delivered in 2017, it envisioned a faster payments system that would allow competing solutions to interoperate. The FPTF specified desired outcomes in terms of speed, security, efficiency, international choices, and collaboration, and it set 36 effectiveness criteria spread across six major categories: ubiquity, efficiency, safety and security, speed, legal, and governance. The Federal Reserve's instant payment solution was named FedNow^{SM}, but the original implementation year of 2020 turned out to be overly ambitious. It has now slipped to 2023 or 2024 according to recent statements by the Fed executive in charge (Federal Reserve, 2020). The Fed continues to operate a community dedicated to payments improvement, called the FedPayments Improvement Community to communicate with and involve stakeholders in the payment ecosystem.

In Canada, Payments Canada is entrusted by the Canadian parliament with running the payments system. It has been at the center of a payment modernization program for the last few years. The latest modernization roadmap reflects the reality that cash payments have declined 40% over the last five years and seeks to modernize the payment systems and rules at the heart of Canada's payment ecosystem. A major goal is to have a real-time payment rail implemented by 2022.

4.3.7 Convergence between Instant Payments and Lending

Before the Covid-19 crisis, unsecured lending volumes in the United States were already at an all-time high. A major growth driver has been the increased offerings and uptake of point-of-sale (POS) financing. An estimate from McKinsey puts the total U.S. outstanding balances which originated from POS installment lending offering at $94 billion in 2018, expected to grow to $110 billion in 2019, which is about 10% of all unsecured lending (Dikshit et al., 2020).

As digital and mobile payments gain market share in North America, *pay-later* solutions such Affirm, Afterpay, and Klarnare piggyback on them to expand their e-commerce market share. The pay-later solutions are expected to triple from 1% to 3% over the next three years (Worldpay from FIS). While North American consumers were long thought to be content with their credit and debit cards, and resistant to payment innovation, the well-connected Generation Z is quick to adopt all types of seamless mobile technologies. This is a major long-term threat to established payment methods like credit cards, and ultimately to the associated banking relationships.

Square has been expanding its credit offerings, leveraging its payment relationships to cross-sell credit. Lately, Square's market capitalization has doubled between May and July 2020, to stand at $55 billion at the beginning of July. This is below only four banks in the KBW Bank Index and just $20 billion shy of

Goldman Sachs Group Inc.'s market valuation. The reason for the rally in Square's shares is increasing optimism over digital-payments growth during the coronavirus pandemic and its deft handling of government stimulus payments during the pandemic. But Square has also been drawing away deposits from traditional banks without comprehensive digital offerings. The latest rally was set off when an analyst suggested that Square could win up to 20% of U.S. direct deposits (Wittenstein, 2020).

POS financing is an area where traditional banks are lagging digital disrupters such as Afterpay, Klarna, and Sezzle. These fintechs have figured out how to seamlessly integrate their financing offerings into the purchase process to provide financing for purchases lower than $500 and as low as $200–$300. These small purchase loans are estimated to have totaled between $8 billion to $10 billion in 2019 and are growing at rates exceeding 40–50%. Some premium merchants are offering 0% APRs from POS providers, which are now attracting prime customers. In 2019 about 55% of origination volume is expected to be from the prime segment (credit scores above 680). For the financing of large purchases, about three-quarters of consumers decide to do so early in their purchase journey, well before the actual transaction. If the loan offerings can be embedded earlier in the purchase journey by making consumers aware of the offer throughout a merchant's website, the conversion rate is increased by two to three times versus only offering the loan at checkout. But marketing the offer only on the lender's website—something traditional banks tend to do—has very poor conversion rates.

Instant payment providers are also directly taking on banks in the area of small business lending. Swift Financial was recently acquired by PayPal for this purpose. PayPal already offers LoanBuilder an online small-business loan offering that is configurable in terms of terms and fees charged. PayPal's loans are provided as a service by PayPal but issued by WebBank, a member of the FDIC.

4.3.8 Funding Needs and Liquidity Risks

Settlement may be either done immediately on a gross basis for each transaction, *real-time gross settlement (RTGS)*; or on a delayed net basis by netting out obligations between parties and processing them as a batch), *deferred net settlement (DNS)*. RTGC requires more funding to operate and has a higher *liquidity risk*. On the other hand, DNS has a higher *settlement risk* because of the delayed, periodic settlements. Settlement risk comprises both credit risk—a PSP defaulting prior to final settlement—and liquidity risk due to a potential delay in receipt of payments. (Because of the batch structure of DNS, one default can affect all surviving PSPS in a batch as the failed PSP is unwound and all net obligations recalculated.) *Final settlement* is a legal term for when funds have been irrevocably transferred (Bech et al., 2020).

Instant or real-time payments hold the promise to greatly reduce the need for liquidity in the world's payment systems. Large amounts of funds are held up every day especially in slow-mowing, high-value cross-border payments. New providers such as the RippleNet aim to use blockchain technology to move money instantaneously among 300+ providers worldwide. The consortium currently includes American Express, PNC, Santander, and MoneyGram.

4.3.9 Changes in Financial Intermediation

Historically, payment systems in most jurisdictions have been legally and operationally intertwined with the traditional banking system and subject to regulation by central authorities. The central authorities (usually the central bank) would also ensure system stability by standing ready to provide emergency liquidity assistance, guarantee deposits, and act as a lender of last resort. In addition, special bankruptcy mechanisms would provide resolutions in case of bank failure. In recent years, we have seen the development of an alternate payment system, also called a *shadow payment system*, which is characterized by a proliferation of P2P systems such as PayPal, mobile platforms such as M-Pesa, and crypto-currency exchanges such as Coinbase. This shadow payment system performs the same functions as bank-owned payment systems but outside of the current regulatory structure and its accompanying safety net. This has led to the emergence of substantial risks to financial and economic stability (Awrey & van Zwieten, 2018).

Banks are still at the apex of a complex global system of financial intermediation yielding massive revenues to banks that were estimated by McKinsey to be $5 trillion in 2017 at approximately 190 basis points (down from an average of 220 bps in 2011). Payments-related revenue constitutes over $700 billion of this revenue (14% of the total), and is the second biggest growth area, just behind wealth and asset management. This lucrative position is under threat from both technological (incl. data) innovation and changes in the regulatory and socio-political environment, which are opening the financial system to new entrants (Dietz et al., 2018).

Correspondent banks, integral to cross-border payments since the earliest days of banking, have seen their role diminished across the last decade. Over this period, cross-border correspondent bank relationships declined by about 20% as banks withdrew from countries with poor governance and AML controls. The BIS is concerned about the loss of payment channels as well as the rising costs of cross-border payments due to lessened competition (Rice et al., 2020).

The intense brand loyalty that smartphone users have to their iOS (Apple) or Android handsets are influencing whom they trust to be their payment providers. Android users (the majority of U.S. smartphone users) trust PayPal more (56%) than their banks (50%) followed by Google (43%). iOS users have essentially the same level of trust in their banks (53%) versus Apple (52%), and PayPal (51%). Apple's new credit card, launched with Goldman Sachs, makes use of this trend. It offers more rewards for using Apple Pay for in-store payments, which is intended to boost digital wallet use (Anan et al., 2020).

PayPal, Apple Pay, and Google Pay have added layers on top of the current payment infrastructure that changes the customer experience and expectations. New technologies are putting the middle (the domain of the banks), which traditionally collects most of the fees, under tremendous pressure. As technologies evolve, the value of costly intermediaries to the payments process is coming increasingly into question. When half of U.S. deposits are held at only five large banks, bankers have to answer why *direct connections* between merchants, customers, and banks cannot process payments instead of expensive intermediaries.

In China, half of the domestic payments already flow through nonbank third-party platforms. Soaring internet and e-commerce penetration has enabled tech giants such as Alibaba, Tencent, Ping An, and Baidu to muscle in on this attractive market, particularly in retail payments. Technology firms grew their market share in Chinese retail payments to almost 50% in 2017, up from just 5% in 2012 (Dietz et al., 2018).

M-Pesa, the Kenyan-based mobile payment service which is also used in neighboring African countries, processes over 11 billion transactions a year (The Economist, 2020a, 2020b, 2020c).

The technology giants are already competing with banks in the West too. For example, Amazon is disrupting traditional credit card models: its card, offered in partnership with JPMorgan Chase, has no annual fee, no foreign transaction fees, and no earning cap or expiration for loyalty points. In 2017, it launched Amazon Cash, which allows customers to add money to their Amazon account via cash payments at partner retailers. Back in 2018, Amazon partnered with Bank of America to issue loans up to $750,000 (Dietz et al., 2018).

4.3.10 The Ongoing Impact of COVID-19

The social distancing measures introduced by governments to fight the COVID-19 coronavirus pandemic, and the fears of consumers and workers of getting infected, are accelerating payment trends that were already well underway, particularly in further digitization and the desire of consumers for contactless payments, accompanied by an increased aversion to paying with and receiving cash. For example, in Germany, many merchants have for long accepted only cash payments, and many consumers have preferred cash because of concerns about tracking. But after COVID-19 came along, retailers are seeing jumps in over 30% in card payments, while merchants who previously only accepted cash now accept cards (Syed, 2020).

However, not all digital forms of payments are contactless, with POS terminals often requiring buttons to be pushed on touch screens. This may push consumers to pay with their mobile devices. A U.S. study found that 30% of consumers reported using contactless methods like cards and smartphones for the first time after the pandemic hit. A full 70% of these first-time users expect to continue after the pandemic is over (PYMENTS, 2020). The future of retail checkouts is predicted to be frictionless, with no shopper–staff interaction or queuing (Clement, 2020).

Banking consumers across all age groups are getting comfortable with services such as Apply Pay and P2P payments that started out with younger consumers. One FI reports that their mobile deposits have risen 82% since the start of the COVID-19 outbreak, as customers who previously resisted that feature have adopted it (BAI, 2020).

While B2B cross-border payments have understandably plummeted during the pandemic as trade and economies contracted, they are expected to rise 30% from the current COVID low by 2022 (Payments Next, 2020). Global e-commerce sales in 2020 are still expected to grow but at a reduced rate of 16.5% compared to 20.2% in 2019. Retail e-commerce sales for 2020 are projected to be $2.45 trillion in Asia-Pacific, $749 billion in North America, and $498 billion in Western Europe (Cramer-Flood, 2020).

The switch to digital payments is happening everywhere. An analysis of M-Pesa's P2P transfers in Rwanda in the first 4 months of 2020 shows a rapid rise in transaction volume and value—five times more in April than in February (taken as the pre-pandemic norm). It is thought that Rwandans switched to digital payments because restrictions on the movement made it hard for them to transact in cash, and they may have also sent money to loved ones in need. Some of the growth in transactions may also have been the result of government policy. The central bank ordered telecom companies to eliminate charges on mobile transfers and raised the transaction limits.

Telecom firm MTN has reported a rise in payments across the 15 African markets it serves (The Economist, 2020a, 2020b, 2020c). A countervailing force is the drying up of remittances as the virus depresses economic activity and wages across the world. For example, payments companies have reported large declines in transfers from the United Kingdom to East Africa and from Italy to Africa after the start of the crisis (The Economist, 2020a, 2020b, 2020c). Migrants are often low-wage workers who have been hit hardest by the pandemic.

4.4 The Emergence of New Payment Platforms

4.4.1 Mobile Payments

In a matter of just a few years, North American consumers have gone from providing a signature that matches the back of their credit card, to entering a PIN, to tapping their cards. Using a smartphone seems like another shift in payment behavior that will come naturally to consumers.

Mobile phone payments at the POS are facilitated by near-field communications (NFC) technology, which requires close *proximity* (but not touching) between the device and the payment terminal. While the United States has been lagging behind

Asia and Northern Europe in mobile and P2P payment adoption, both volumes and average transaction sizes have been growing rapidly. About 30% of U.S. smartphone users (nearly 70 million people) are now making proximity mobile payments. Apply Pay is currently the top proximity payment provider (Wurmser, 2019).

In the P2P space, PayPal is leading, with Venmo (a PayPal subsidiary) in the second position, demonstrating how different functionality and branding cater to different segments. Zelle, the bank-owned alternative, is in third place, reflecting that most demographic cohorts still (for now) like banks to be their provider of digital payment services. Zelle has a significantly higher transaction size than the former two, reflecting a different user and use case. Zelle has expanded into business-to-consumer (B2C) payment such as rebates or rewards, while PayPal-owned Venmo has expanded the other way, offering consumer-to-business (C2B) payments on millions of websites using the PayPal infrastructure. This could be the same evolution that MobilePay in the Nordics went through, starting as a P2P solution and transforming into a general-purpose wallet (Anan et al., 2020).

While Venmo is most popular with the younger demographic, particularly millennials, their parents prefer Zelle, because it is closely associated with their existing bank accounts. Zelle, a person-to-person (P2P) payment app that directly competes with Venmo, was launched in 2017 by traditional banks. Zelle is intended for the direct exchange of funds between persons who already know and trust each other, and the money moves from the sender's bank account to the recipient's in minutes. It is currently supported by a comprehensive list of 837 large and small U.S. banks and credit unions. MasterCard and Visa are also involved as payment network partners. Zelle claims a 2019 network volume of $187 billion in payments and 743 million transactions. Consumers can access Zelle via the mobile banking apps of one of the banking partners, or use the Zelle app. To send money with Zelle, only the email address or mobile number of the recipient is needed. Zelle stresses that it should be *a trusted recipient*. On its homepage, it says: "Zelle is a fast, safe, easy and contact-free way to send and receive money with friends, family, and others *you trust*. You can receive money directly into your bank account in minute" (italics added).

Clearly, the Zelle payment system requires *preexisting trust* between the payment parties, and it makes no claim to have any mechanism to ensure or establish such trust. In that sense, Zelle operates like a real-time debit order against the payer's account. The only difference is that the recipient does not need to have the bank account and branch number of the payer, but can rely on the email address or cell phone number that is directly linked to that information in the Zelle database. Interac is a Canadian equivalent of Zelle, operating in much the same way.

4.4.2 Invisible Payments and IoT Technology

The willingness of consumers to accept automated payments was tested in a recent U.K. survey by asking whether they would accept pulling up to a gas station and have a built-in computer in their care to automatically make the payment to the gas station. A full 84% said that they would be comfortable with that, with 76% saying that would be a more convenient way to pay for gasoline, and 62 would trust the payment method (Worldpay from FIS, 2019).

But there are lingering privacy concerns with IoT technology and concerns about its abuse. In the United Kingdom, Mercedes-Benz has acknowledged that it is using location-tracking technology built into its vehicles to find and repossess financed cars when customers default on their loans (Weber, 2019). And while consumers may be happy to have a cup of coffee or a tank of gas automatically charged, they still want to deliberately authenticate big-ticket purchases in the more traditional way (Rolfe, 2020).

4.4.3 Digital Currencies

The advent of the cryptocurrency revolution was in 2008 when the concept for bitcoin was published in an online paper titled "Bitcoin: A Peer-to-Peer Electronic Cash System" by a mysterious author, Satoshi Nakamoto (likely a pseudonym—Nakamoto, 2008). Coming in the wake of the financial crisis, bitcoin gave form to a simmering rebellion against central banks and the financial ecosystem. A core principle is that no single entity can be entrusted with the safekeeping and the management of the currency. Accordingly, a block of transactions can only be added to a chain (hence "blockchain") when all the nodes in a distributed network can achieve consensus on the addition through a cryptographic process. The ledger is not kept in a single place by a trusted central party (there is none) but distributed to all nodes, who together ensure the integrity of the ledger. In the case of a pure public blockchain, such as bitcoin, all transactions (the entire blockchain) are visible to all nodes.

Interestingly, the word "trust" appears 14 times in Satoshi's seminal paper, and the word "honest" 16 times, introducing bitcoin as a "*system for electronic transactions without relying on trust.*" The whole point of the bitcoin system is to do away with a single trusted intermediary, such as a financial institution, which has the discretion to reverse transactions. In the paper's introduction, Satoshi directly connected the need for trust to the inherent *reversibility* of transactions in the current payment system:

> While the system works well enough for most transactions, it still suffers from the inherent weaknesses of the trust based model. Completely non-reversible transactions are not really possible, since financial institutions cannot avoid mediating disputes. The cost of mediation increases transaction costs, limiting the minimum practical transaction size and cutting off the possibility for small casual transactions, and there is a broader cost in the loss of ability to make non-reversible payments for nonreversible services. With the possibility of reversal, the need for trust spreads. Merchants must be wary of their customers, hassling them for more information than they would otherwise need. A certain percentage of fraud is accepted as unavoidable. These costs and payment uncertainties can be avoided in person by

> using physical currency, but no mechanism exists to make payments over a communications channel without a trusted party.
>
> What is needed is an electronic payment system based on cryptographic proof instead of trust, allowing any two willing parties to transact directly with each other without the need for a trusted third party. Transactions that are computationally impractical to reverse would protect sellers from fraud, and routine escrow mechanisms could easily be implemented to protect buyers. In this paper, we propose a solution to the double-spending problem using a peer-to-peer distributed timestamp server to generate computational proof of the chronological order of transactions. The system is secure as long as honest nodes collectively control more CPU power than any cooperating group of attacker nodes.

The bitcoin system relies on a multitude of independent *miners* to provide *proof of work* (solving a complex and time-consuming cryptographic puzzle) for a block to be added to the chain to complete each transaction. The miner who solves a particular puzzle first gets a commission on the transaction, but the other miners see the solution and first have to validate it before it gets added. The purpose of this elaborate process is to prevent the obvious problem with any form of digital money—that it can be copied and recreated, and thus be spent twice. This problem is solved by the mechanisms inherent in bitcoin and other cryptocurrencies. A more generic term is the *consensus algorithm*—proof of work is only one type of consensus algorithm and bitcoin's is the most expensive in terms of computing power and hence energy expended.

However, bitcoin has a built-in flaw related to its democratic nature. It is known as the 51% problem because if anyone or any coordinated group can control more than 51% of the computer mining power in the network at any time, they would theoretically be free to manipulate the currency. Therefore, the locus of trust in bitcoin is a diverse crowd of miners of which most presumably have the enlightened economic self-interest not to do anything to jeopardize the currency in which they have a stake.

Bitcoin's price in U.S. dollars has been highly volatile: It started at around $100 in 2013, first reached $1,000, and sharply rose to nearly $19,000 all in 2017. Then it sharply declined to bottom out at about $3,200 at the end of 2018. It has risen again subsequently and is currently trading just above $11,000. While this makes for an exciting speculative investment for some, a trusted means of payment cannot be this volatile in value. The attempted solution to the volatility problem is to create a cryptocurrency called a *stablecoin*, which value is tied to a basket of bank securities and deposits held in hard currencies. There are several *stablecoins* in operation, and Facebook's Libra was also proposed as a type of *stablecoin* (See Sect. 4.4.5).

Another issue with cryptocurrencies is that in the beginning, their blockchain-based networks were not as scalable as conventional payment networks in terms of speed and volume. The global benchmark, Visa, claims an ability to handle over 65,000 transaction messages on its global network, handling over $11 trillion in annual payment volume (Visa Fact Sheet, 2020). However, much effort has been put into addressing this problem by cryptocurrency developers through several modifications (known as "forks") to cryptocurrency protocols. The latest Ethereum update in late 2019 claims to enable network processing of 9,000 cryptocurrency transactions per second, which now puts it within the competitive range of Visa,

Mastercard, and PayPal (Reynaldo, 2020). And Ripple's XRP—which moves conventional money, not cryptocurrency, across a worldwide blockchain—claims the ability to handle 50,000 transactions per second (Ripple, 2019). The scale and speed advantage of traditional payment networks can no longer be taken for granted.

Central banks see the threat of cryptocurrencies and are determined to maintain control of the coin of the realm. If central banks are disintermediated because private digital currencies are used in trade, it would undermine financial stability and their ability to execute monetary policy. However, digital currencies that central banks may issue will likely be different from a private currency such as bitcoin and this is also why the generic term digital currency is preferred over cryptocurrency. In an article for the Federal Bank of St. Louis, Berentsen and Schär presented a three-dimensional model for how to think about digital currency as a payment medium, and why it is so different from what we are used to (Berentsen & Schar, 2018). Their model characterizes money based on its control structure. It has the following three elements:

- *Representation*—whether the money is physical or virtual.
- *Money creation*—whether there is a monopoly on creation or if it's competitive.
- *Transaction handling*—whether it is centralized or decentralized.

Since cash is money represented by a physical object like a bill or a coin, the ownership rights of the currency are clear: Cash belongs to the holder. This facilitates decentralized payment as cash changes hands between the payer and payee without the need for involvement by a third party. No recordkeeping is required to enable the transaction. In modern economies, central banks are the monopoly issuers of cash. Commodity gold has similar characteristics except that there is not a monopoly on mining it. However, commercial bank deposits are virtual money, which only exists as a record in an accounting system. Payments are made by deducting the amount from the buyer's account and crediting it to the seller. In this case, a third party, a bank, is responsible for keeping records, which are essential for the transaction. This is why commercial bank deposits are transacted in a centralized payment system. Since commercial banks compete for deposits, the creation of money as bank deposits is competitive. Central bank money is, of course, also virtual money, which is issued monopolistically and transactions are recorded in a centralized payment system.

The pattern is clear: before cryptocurrencies came along, virtual money and payments made with it were managed in a centralized system. Bitcoin was the first virtual money for which ownership rights are managed in a completely decentralized network. Another way that cryptocurrencies are different is in their creation, which is competitive as anyone can mine cryptocurrencies like bitcoin, which is a characteristic similar to gold. However, similar to the gold-mining industry, the rising cost of mining has been squeezing the small players out of cryptocurrency mining.

4.4.4 Distributed-Ledger Technology

Since the inception of bitcoin and other blockchain-based digital currencies, several industries including the financial industry have been exploring ways in which the underlying technology may be used for other applications needing secure record management.

Blockchain-based technology, more generally referred to as distributed ledger technology (DLT), has the potential to disrupt payment and settlement activities. (Blockchain is the most well-known type of DLT, but not all DLTs are structured as blockchains.) In short, a DLT entails a set of synchronized ledgers managed by one or multiple entities. In finance, DLTs have the potential to totally change the traditional model of relying on a *central ledger* managed by a *trusted entity* for recording the transfer of funds. In an important 2017 paper that provides a detailed analytical framework for considering the use of DLT in payment, clearing, and settlement, the BIS more precisely defines DLT as follows:

> DLT refers to the processes and related technologies that enable nodes in a network (or arrangement) to securely propose, validate and record state changes (or updates) to a synchronized ledger that is distributed across the network's nodes (BIS, 2017).

DLTs could completely change payment processes and have attracted a lot of interest from central banks. Cryptocurrency is a type of digital currency, but distinct from conventional digital currency which makes use of conventional payment technology. The main difference between DLTs and conventional payment systems is that in DLT the payment clearing and settlement (the final two steps) are combined into a single validation step as the nodes of the network achieve consensus on accepting the transaction. In other words, sending the financial transaction information and moving the money is one step. This removes the risk that funds may not be settled after payment financialization. The number of agents required for the end-to-end payment process is also reduced—most importantly, the DLT removes the need for participants to trust a centralized payment authority. There are four important design choices to be made for each DLT. These can be seen in Table 4.1 (Wadsworth, 2018a, 2018b).

Bitcoin is based on a blockchain that is permissionless, public, non-hierarchical, and open-source. Anyone can download the blockchain to start validating transactions. Bitcoin needs its *proof of work* mechanism to avoid the double-spend problem of digital money in a situation where no trust between nodes exists. The proof of work is hard to compute but easy to verify, which is how bitcoin ensures transaction security. However, regulated financial institutions are forced by know-your-customer (KYC), anti-money-laundering (AML), and privacy laws to make the opposite DLT design choices. The DLTs that have been developed in the conventional banking world where a trusted third party already exists and regulations apply are typically permissioned, private, hierarchical, and closed source.

A *public blockchain* is an open platform that anyone can join without restrictions—it is therefore permissionless. A *private blockchain* is dedicated only

Table 4.1 Key elements of distributed ledger technology (Source: Wadsworth, Bank of New Zealand Bulletin, May 2018)

1	Permissionless	Any node (computer) can download the ledger and validate transactions.
	Permissioned	Permission is required to download the ledger and validate transactions.
2	Public	Any node can read and initiate transactions on the ledger.
	Private	Only a selected group of nodes can read and initiate transactions.
3	Nonhierarchical	Each node has a full copy of the ledger.
	Hierarchical	Only designated nodes have a full copy of the ledger.
4	Open source	Anyone can suggest improvements to the code underpinning the ledger platform.
	Closed source	Only trusted entities can see and add improvements to the code underpinning the ledger platform.

to the private sharing and exchange of data among individuals in one organization or across multiple organizations, which is why it is always permissioned and involves some form of centralized control. It is neither immutable nor irreversible because the central authority can make any changes it wants. A *consortium blockchain* is a hybrid between public and private blockchain. It is partially private and permissioned, but without any one organization or gatekeeper deciding on who may join. Instead, a predetermined set of validator nodes make that decision, and these nodes also sign off on block creation. It is neither immutable nor irreversible because a majority of the consortium can make changes (van Biljon & Lajoux, 2020).

An evaluation of the bitcoin-type blockchain as a payment system shows that it holds distinct advantages in cross-border payments because it is as borderless as the internet and the location of payer and payee does not matter (Wadsworth, 2018a, 2018b). It also uses a private currency not tied to any country. Blockchain payments are processed every 10 min, which is much slower than existing payment systems. That is because the payment is not certain before it is validated. However, validation brings immediate payment, which is superior to existing payment systems and helpful to liquidity management. Validation also occurs 24/7 due to the global network of blockchain. On the other hand, blockchain's transaction validation is much costlier than conventional systems because of the enormous amount of computing power that the proof-of-work process consumes. It also means that a blockchain based on these design choices is not scalable. There is no reconciliation needed with blockchain—each block contains all its transaction information, which means the blockchain is the complete, global transaction history. It can be viewed by anyone, which means it is fully transparent. On the downside, there is no payment netting in blockchain with each transaction requiring full payment in real time. While this is not an issue at the consumer level, it does create a liquidity challenge at the wholesale or institutional level. The blockchain has the advantage of not having any single point of failure, although it still is vulnerable to code bugs or 51% attacks. Conversions between bitcoin and other cryptocurrencies can actually reintroduce a single point of failure which is what happened in the Mt. Gox crypto-exchange hack where nearly half a billion dollars were stolen.

A recent study of blockchain adoption in the global banking industry identified the main supporting factors of adoption as improving the KYC process and transaction speed, and enabling smart contracts (Kawasmi et al., 2019). The main barriers were found to be governance, legislation and regulation, and currency stability. Scalability of platforms was also a main concern. The authors concluded that legislators and regulators need to step up their role to adapt regulations to enable further adoption.

4.4.5 Social Networks that Become Payment Networks

The most notable development in the last year was Facebook's June 2019 announcement of Libra, a cryptocurrency consortium (the Libra Association) comprising 20+ partners including Mastercard, Visa, and PayPal. The original plan was to create a digital *stablecoin* called Calibra that would be backed by real financial assets such as a basket of national currencies and U.S. Treasury securities. However, Libra quickly faced heavy political and regulatory pushback. A week after its announcement, French Finance Minister Bruno Le Mair said that Libra threatens the monetary sovereignty of governments, had the potential for abuse of market dominance, and systemic financial risks. "This eventual privatization of money contains risks of abuse of dominant position, risks to sovereignty, and risks for consumers and for companies" Le Mair said, which meant that "Libra is not welcome on European soil" and that France would block it (Thomas, 2019).

With these regulatory headwinds, October 2019 saw a mass desertion of founding members with PayPal, eBay, Mastercard, Stripe, Visa, Mercado Pago, and Booking Holdings leaving the Libra Association. Vodaphone Group PLC left shortly afterward. By January 2020, Libra dropped the idea of a mixed currency basket. Libra would instead be a collection of *stablecoins* with each pegged to a particular currency. By March 2020, Facebook had scaled back its ambitions for Libra to offering users a digital version of government-backed currencies that would include the U.S. dollar and euro, in addition, the Libra token. In April 2020, global payment service provider Checkout.com announced that it would join the Libra Association. In May 2020, Libra announced a new CEO: Stuart Levey, a former undersecretary of the U.S. Treasury who spent the last 8 years as HSBC's chief legal officer. The hiring of a Libra CEO with this strong compliance background indicates what the Libra Association sees as its most exigent challenge. Levey promised that "he would closely scrutinize the currency project to ensure that it lived up to regulatory expectations regarding money laundering, privacy and the handling of financial reserves backing its token" (Horwitz, 2020).

Social media is an increasingly powerful force of consumer behavior with 89% of Generation Z following companies and brands on social media, nearly half making purchases. Those of Generation Z who buy on social media, do so very frequently—

26% of this subgroup make purchases on social media every day (Worldpay from FIS, 2019).

While most—71% according to a 2019 U.K. survey—consumers still prefer to use credit or debit cards when buying online, a rising number prefer to use digital wallets such as Apple Pay, Google Pay, Amazon Pay, or PayPal. Twenty-one percent of all respondents use mobile phones to make contactless payments in-store between one and three times a week. Digital-wallet use is particularly prevalent among Generation Z where a third prefer mobile wallets, and a full 87% have used them for online purposes. The speed aspect of mobile wallets is what appeals most to Gen Z consumers, while the older users are most attracted to the perceived safety of mobile wallets. Yet, there is significant consumer resistance to biometric verification of identity—60% dislike it because it "doesn't feel right." The unpopularity of biometrics varies with the method, with fingerprints being more acceptable facial or voice recognition (Worldpay from FIS, 2019).

The privacy concerns about a payment platform like Libra which is fully integrated with a social media network like Facebook are significant. The connection of the payment and social platforms will generate data that connects purchases with locations, behaviors, relations, employment, purchasing, and eating habits, and more. With powerful AI mining this data, Libra (and thus Facebook) would have unprecedented predictive powers about customers. Concerns have been expressed that this will imply the lack of privacy that already prevails in China where digital privacy is not as highly valued as in the Western world. Top Chinese payment platforms WeChat Pay operated by Tencent and Alipay, which is part of the Alibaba empire, are pioneering ever easier new ways to pay including authentication by facial recognition (Webb, 2019). The questions are where will the big data generated by Libra be housed, and who will have what levels of access to it?

4.4.6 Major Banking and Technology Consortia

There are three leading technology consortia for the advancement of DLT generally: The Enterprise Ethereum Alliance (EEA); HyperLedger from the Linux Foundation which includes IBM, Microsoft, and Salesforce.com; and R3 (the Corda platform) which includes several large FIs. These consortia provide companies across industries with a vehicle to pool their resources and jointly figure out how to benefit from DLT.

A number of multibank consortia, some of which use DLT technology, are active in the payments or adjacent spaces, typically in trade finance which does not require high-volume processing like retail payments but can benefit from the security offered by blockchain-type transfers. These consortia include:

- Contour (formerly Voltron), a collation of over 50 banks and corporates including HSBC, Citi, Standard Chartered, and ING, is having a trade-finance network built on R3's Corda blockchain platform. It will issue and exchange digitized letters of credit.

- P27, a joint company owned by six Nordic banks, aims to provide a payment infrastructure for both domestic and cross-border payments across the Nordic countries.
- Batavia, a global trade finance platform developed by a consortium of five banks, UBS, BMO, CaixaBank, Commerzbank, and Erste Group together with IBM. It is built on the IBM Blockchain Platform and aims to "support the creation of multi-party, cross-border trading networks by establishing Batavia as an open ecosystem that can be accessed by organizations big and small around the world."
- We.trade, a joint-venture company owned by 16 European banks, has developed a digital platform to simplify trade finance.
- eTradeConnect is a DLT platform being built by an Asia-Pacific banking consortium managed by the Hong Kong Monetary Authority. It will facilitate trade financing and settlement.
- Marco Polo, a global network of over 20 banks, facilitates cross-border trade and working-capital finance solutions.

Progress is generally slower than expected as building these new DLT-based solutions is taking longer than expected in the majority of cases. Most of these networks have not yet progressed beyond the pilot stage (Golden, 2020).

Several proofs of the concept of using DLTs to facilitate payment and settlement have been run in recent years. For example, the South African Reserve Bank (SARB), in a consortium with seven commercial banks, used Quorum, an enterprise-grade implementation of Ethereum, to create a blockchain-based interbank system. The pilot was considered a big success. It processed the typical daily volume of payments with full confidentiality and finality in record time, exceeding the transaction performance target of 70,000 transactions in less than 2 hours, while achieving privacy objectives (Khoka 2019).

4.4.7 Why DLTs May Not Solve the Trust Problem

A critic of blockchain, the author Bruce Schneier, points out that while bitcoin's blockchain eliminates trusted intermediaries, the user still needs to trust bitcoin itself (Schneier, 2019). As we have seen, public blockchains are comprised of three elements: A distributed ledger that anyone can read, but which is immutable (the past cannot be changed); a consensus algorithm (also called the mining process); and the currency, which is some kind of digital token that is publicly traded and transactions stored on the ledger.

Tech-loving blockchain users often err in conflating algorithmic verification with trust, but trust is a much broader concept. Schneier posits that humans use four systems to promote trustworthy behaviors. These are *morals, reputation, institutions*, and *security systems*. The first two scale only to a certain population size. (The Renaissance Italian bankers only worked with people who were well known to them.) Institutions address the scalability problem through rules and laws that push people to conform and sanction them if they don't. Banking is a highly regulated industry for a reason. Lastly, security systems such as locks, alarm systems, and safes are part of modern banking, as are anti-counterfeiting features on the currency. But even more important today are the IT security systems, which include anti-fraud and anti-money-laundering mechanisms.

The problem with blockchain is that it shifts all trust entirely to the technology—the cryptography, the protocols, the computers, and the network. These are often single points of failure and when the trust is broken, there is no recourse. If the cryptocurrency exchange gets hacked, all your money is gone. If you forget your login details, all the coin in your account is lost to you forever. There is no human who can help you retrieve it.

In real life, there will always be a need to override rules, due to circumstances that computer programs cannot foresee. In modern banking, transactions can be reversed and overridden upon appeal. With blockchain, there is no such possibility.

4.5 Developments to Watch

4.5.1 Standardization and Interoperability

A concern with the advent of new private payment systems is that they can become walled gardens, where transactions are easily conducted within, but interconnectivity to the outside is a problem. Designers of new payment systems need to anticipate the need for interconnectivity. BIS general manager Agustin Carstens sees the continuing value of central banks to new payment systems as providing a big platform for such payment systems to be built on. The BIS welcomes innovation but needs early engagement with the private sector to set standards. The Silicon Valley mentality of "disrupt and move on" is incompatible with maintaining a secure and reliable payment system, according to Carstens. BIS has started its Innovation Hub trying to avoid being surprised again like they were with Libra (Carstens, 2019).

Three years ago, a major payments technology vendor described the vision that the industry was working toward for 2027:

> All payments will be easy to make, fast, low cost, interconnected, interoperable and work the same way in most countries. There will be no difference between sending a payment as a consumer or as a business, and all beneficiaries will be reachable and addressable via a proxy such as their phone number or email address. It will be just as simple to send a payment to someone in another country as it is domestically. (CGI, 2017)

The infrastructure needed to achieve this vision will comprise domestic instant payment platforms that are interconnected to that all payments, with rare exceptions, will flow through these platforms. It is expected that the current card payment systems will be either cannibalized or will at least see their back-end infrastructure replaced with newer instant payment schemes. Instant domestic payment schemes will need to be ubiquitous across countries, and a global interconnection mechanism must for settlement be created. While it is a possibility, a digital currency is not a prerequisite for this solution. Money already exists mostly in its digital form and the system technology to move it exists today. What will be replaced is the current proliferation of payment types and systems. The lack of interoperability between DLTs is also a major challenge and holding back the consolidation of DLT-based markets.

While the technology is feasible today, setting up such a solution requires coordination between many jurisdictions that will result in a common set of governance, rules, and liability models. There will need to be a global rule setter or adjudicator, which will probably require a global regulator.

4.5.2 The Changing Economics of Payments

The current paradigm for settling accounts is under increasing pressure, perhaps more than it has been in decades. Regulators are increasingly taking the side of consumers in challenging fee levels and complexity, merchants long resentful over paying 1.5–3% on accepting card payments are very open to every opportunity to lower such fees. Banks are growing fearful of a squeeze on margins and revenues, and worse still, disintermediation. Fast-evolving digital technologies seem to make anything possible, if not today, then by tomorrow. Digital disruptors are everywhere, happy to start small and to pick up fees and interest payments where traditional banks are not active, but ultimately looking to usurp banks. In today's card payment model, the greatest share of profits goes to the middlemen, but as the complexity of the model is peeled away by new technologies, the value will move away from operating the piping of the payment system toward those who have better insights into the needs of customers and can meet them. As a recent report by ACI, a payment provider, states:

> Changing payment systems means deep changes to what banks and merchants fundamentally are to consumers, how and why these consumers shop and what they expect, and what brands and revenue streams will be—or can be—to banks and merchants in the future (ACI Universal Payments, 2017).

Today, because it is so hard, cross-border payments are done in large, bundled amounts requiring complex management. But when more consumers can send cross-border payments, these payments are expected to become smaller and much lower in value, and much faster. This "atomization" of cross-border payments will be done by standardizing the movement of money (KPMG, 2019).

An important property of payment structures is that they display strong *network effects*, meaning that the more users a payment system has, the more valuable it is to each user. For example, when credit cards started, consumers were reluctant to use the new form of payment if merchants would not accept it, and merchants were reluctant to adopt card payment if sufficient numbers of consumers would not use it. But once a payment network is entrenched it is hard to dislodge it (Angel & McCabe, 2014).

4.5.3 Fintech Partnerships and Other Ecosystem Developments

In a January 2020 survey of over 200 financial services leaders focusing on their digital journey, two-thirds reported that they feel the pressure from fintechs and their disruptive impact on the industry. However, 60% reported that they are either currently collaborating with a fintech or planning to do so in the near future. The most popular areas for such partnerships are payments and funds transfer, as these are at the center of the customer digital experience. Of those who partner with fintechs, 65% are doing so for payments, and 59% for funds transfer (BAI, 2020). According to a McKinsey survey, 79% of leading banks have partnered with a fintech to collaborate on innovation in various areas including payments (McKinsey, 2019).

Big tech companies are making deep inroads into payments, presenting a real threat to incumbents because they bring massive scale in infrastructure and big data, deep pockets, and the ability to cross-subsidize new offerings from existing product portfolios. Big techs are also nimble and happy to use partnerships with FIs to temporarily complete their offerings until they are ready to offer those financial services themselves. In the United States, Amazon has partnered with JP Morgan and Bank of America to offer financial services. Google Pay has partnerships with more than a dozen banks across Asia, Europe, and Australia.

While fintechs have enabled banks to enhance their capabilities, they are increasingly evolving their business models to become more equal partners or even competitors. Segment-focused value propositions developed by fintechs, like the Dutch payment company Adyen, are seen by banks as the biggest threat according to a recent survey. Another threat is that some fintechs such as Square, Stripe, and Robinhood use tier-two and tier-three banks for their infrastructure (and licensing) needs. In Europe, AliPay has partnered with Norway's DNB and Vipps and Finland's ePassi (Capgemini Research Institute, 2019).

However, there is a distinction between big tech and fintechs: Fintechs need banks to provide core financial services and access to customers. They are accordingly more likely to partner. Big techs on the other hand bring their own customer base of millions of users and can cross-subsidize. The latter is the bigger threat to incumbent FIs.

4.5.4 Changes in Regulatory Climate and Philosophies

According to a BIS white paper, technology is driving the transformation of payment systems, pushing it to the top of policymakers' agenda (Carstens, 2020). The BIS along with central banks acknowledge the role regulators must take in shaping the next evolution of the payment system.

In a recent lecture at Princeton University, Agustin Carstens, general manager of the BIS, said that three big recent developments have been a wake-up call to central banks and elevated payments to the top of the regulatory agenda: The introduction of bitcoin and other cryptocurrencies, the entry of big tech in financial services, and the announcement of Libra, Facebook's proposed digital currency (Carstens, 2019). Central bankers acknowledge these challenges to the conventional wisdom and the current money and payment system. But Carstens also asserts that the strengths of the current payment system must be appreciated. First, central banks have been very successful in preserving the value of money. Second, payment transactions are financially assured by book entry at the central bank. Third, central banks provide *intraday liquidity* to make the payment system work and avoid gridlock. In extreme situations, the central bank acts as a *lender of last resort*. And lastly, central banks set the standards for payments and regulate the payment process. Carstens sees two ways forward for central banks. One is to develop a central bank digital currency (CBDC) accessible to retail. (It already exists for wholesale.) The other is for central bank digital tokens to be issued. The first option would essentially place central banks in direct competition with private sector banks (Carstens, 2019).

In its 2020 annual report, the BIS emphasizes the role that central banks play to maintain trust in the payment system by acting as guarantors of the stability of money and payments:

> Payment systems today build upon a two-tier structure provided by the central bank together with commercial banks. The central bank plays a pivotal role by ensuring trust in money, a core public good for the economy at large, while the private sector leads on innovation in serving the public. The central bank supplies the ultimate safe medium to settle both wholesale and retail transactions, while commercial banks supply the bulk of retail payment instruments (BIS, 2020a, 2020b).

The current Wirecard AG scandal has highlighted the risks of private-sector payment innovation when unchecked by adequate regulation. The formerly high-flying Germany-based digital payments provider had to file for insolvency after $2 billion of assets on its balance sheets could not be found by auditors. According to reports, the missing funds are not believed to exist. The $2 billion amount is roughly equal to Wirecard's entire net income for a period of over a decade (Davies, 2020). In the wake of this scandal, Germany is changing its oversight mechanisms and going so far as to cancel the existing regulator's contract beyond 2021 (Trentmann, 2020).

The instant messaging app, WhatsApp (owned by Facebook) has been attempting to launch its payment solution, WhatsApp Pay. However, it has encountered regulatory headwinds in the emerging economies it has been focusing on. China banned it outright, and it had to close down in Brazil within a week after launching in June 2020 when Brazil's Central Bank ordered it to cease operations. (Even the fact that it had partnered with Cielo, Brazil's largest card credit and debit card operator did not help.) India is WhatsApp's largest market followed by Brazil. In both countries, the app is heavily used by private individuals and small businesses. And in both countries, regulators are reluctant to allow Facebook to dominate the payments sector. But Brazilian authorities have recently suggested that they may allow WhatsApp Pay under certain conditions, which may include a commitment by Facebook for stricter privacy (Kapronasia, 2020).

A major question is when a technology company becomes a financial intermediary. Central banks will not allow companies to take advantage of the payment infrastructure without also taking on obligations such as offering lending services. The line between the payment facilitator and the financial intermediary is an important and consequential one. Payment facilitators are required to hold 100% of payment amounts in reserve, while intermediaries are not required to hold 100% but are subject to regulation as financial institutions (Carstens, 2019).

4.5.5 Central Bank Digital Currencies

The decentralized nature of cryptocurrency transactions enables users to remain anonymous and allows permissionless access. The problem with creating a central bank cryptocurrency that is anonymous like cash is that banks who process payments in such a currency would fall foul of KYC (know your customer) and AML (anti-money laundering) procedures, and be exposed to great regulatory and reputational risks. That is one reason why a pure central-bank cryptocurrency that behaves like bitcoin is not feasible. What is more feasible is some form of central-bank electronic money that is controlled centrally and can still subject payers and payees to KYC and AML procedures (Berentsen & Schar, 2018).

Several central banks are therefore considering introducing their digital currencies that they can control, called central bank digital currency (CBDC). At the end of 2019, 18 central banks had already publicly announced the development or launch of their own CBDC, including four that had already launched a CBDC: the central banks of Senegal, Tunisia, Uruguay, and Venezuela (Zheng, 2020).

Earlier this year, a group of central banks comprised of the Bank of Canada, the Bank of England (BoE), the Bank of Japan, the Sveriges Riksbank (Sweden), and the Swiss National Bank, together with the European Central Bank (ECB) and the Bank for International Settlements (BIS) announced that they would be collaborating as they assess the potential for introducing CBDCs in their respective jurisdictions (Hall, 2020a, 2020b). Bank of England governor, Andrew Bailey, said recently that they are looking at whether it should create a digital currency, and that such a move would have "huge implications on the nature of payments and society" (Ward, 2020).

The European Central Bank (ECB) is looking at developing a digital currency out of a major concern that Euro region will be left behind Asia and the United States in the global payments market. Benoît Cœuré, then an ECB board member, was quoted late in 2019 as saying that "a central bank digital currency could ensure that citizens remain able to use central bank money even if cash is eventually no longer used" (Marin 2019). Policymakers were jarred into action by Facebook's plan to launch its digital currency, Libra, not because they were worried that it would fail, but that it would succeed since it would fulfill currently unmet consumer needs. Most recently, in June 2020, Cœuré, now a member of the BIS executive committee, said "COVID-19 will be remembered by economic historians as the event that pushed CBDC development into top gear" (Hall, 2020a, 2020b).

An early 2020 BIS-CPMI survey found that about 40% of central banks are moving from conceptual research to CBDC experiments. The emerging market motivation for CBDCs is even stronger, given the unmet needs for, payments safety, domestic payments efficiency, and financial inclusion.

The Chinese government has recently started a pilot program for a digital version of its currency, the yuan. This digital cash is essentially an all-electronic version of cash, a banknote or coin, but it will reside in a digital wallet on a person's smartphone. Individuals would be able to exchange it using digital wallets, and would not need bank accounts. That could make it accessible to the 225 million Chinese who currently do not have bank accounts. There are a number of concerns with the program, not least that it would provide Chinese government authorities a level of control not possible when citizens are carrying cash. The digital wallets could, for example, be linked to China's social credit system which would enable some individuals to be whitelisted or blacklisted based on their earned-credit status, and whether they have been associated with crimes or smaller infractions. Another concern is that the digital yuan could cannibalize the market share of privately-owned Alipay and WeChat. A major U.S. concern with a digital yuan would be that it would undermine U.S. global financial dominance, and could eventually be used in international trade to evade U.S. sanctions against countries like Iran, or U.S. AML mechanisms (Bloomberg Businessweek, 2020).

4.5.6 Payment System Features

4.5.6.1 Real-Time Anti-Money Laundering (AML) and Fraud Control

With new types of payments like P2P, come new kinds of fraud such as selling products that do not exist to pocket instant payments. Other types of fraud involve stealing passwords that many users do not properly guard and carelessly manage. The use of continuous identity proofing is seen as one effective measure against this. This also entails analyzing as many data sources as possible to validate the identity and payment (GIACT, 2020). Another fraud and AML measure is to use machine-learning-based artificial intelligence to check the digital identity and perform credit scoring at each POS.

4.5.6.2 The Erosion of User Dependence on Bank Security Credentials

To prevent fraud and promote financial inclusion, the development of internationally agreed digital-identity standards that will include biometrics is seen as essential. Such a digital identity would be the "golden key" that can access banking services from multiple providers (KPMG, 2019). While this is a robust mechanism, it will weaken the user's unique security dependence on any one FI.

4.5.6.3 Tokens and New Settlement Arrangements

Distributed ledger technology (DLT) supports the use of *digital tokens*, which are digital representations of value not recorded in accounts. A major application of digital tokens is to lower the billions of dollars spent annually on processing securities trades. We have already done away with paper certificates for securities and the need for physical transfers. Today securities are electronically kept (as book entries) in central securities depositories (CSDs). But in the future, securities such as equities and bonds could reside in distributed ledgers held across a network of traders, where each trader will have an identical synchronized copy of the ledger.

Many countries have a CSD with an indirect holding system, where trusted intermediaries such as custodians or brokers hold securities on behalf of their clients. The settlement cycle is the time between trade execution—on a stock exchange or over-the-counter (OTC) market. After trade execution follows *clearing*, the process during which details are transmitted to third parties who reconcile and confirm what needs to be settled, taking into account offsets and netting. *Securities settlement* is the transfer of ownership in accordance with the terms of the agreement. There are two legs entailing two transfers: one is the delivery leg entailing the transfer of security ownership to the buyer. The other is the payment leg entailing a transfer of cash from the buyer to the seller. By tokenizing securities and transferring ownership on a distributed ledger, these processes will be made more efficient (Bech et al., 2020).

More generally, the tokenization of financial assets could allow for the peer-to-peer transfer of ownership on new DLT-based settlement platforms without the use of a trusted third party to affect the settlement. For settlement of wholesale transactions, safety is paramount, which is why it is currently being done using central-bank funds, instead of commercial-bank funds, which can still carry credit risk. But a well-designed token transfer system can eliminate this risk without the need for a third party such as a settlement against or payment system operator. Digital tokens can therefore support P2P settlement of wholesale transactions between private sector parties (BIS, 2019).

4.5.6.4 The Persistence of Legacy Products and Systems

A useful way to look at new payment technologies is to consider their relationship with the established payment infrastructure and systems. Many seemingly novel technologies run on top of existing payment services that are operated by banks and credit card companies. Such new technologies leverage established payment systems but in a way that makes them faster, more convenient, and often replace the cash portion of the transaction. This makes the providers partners to incumbent payment providers, instead of direct competition.

Then there are the truly novel technologies that aim to replace current payment systems with entirely new ones, making them direct competitors to the incumbent payment providers. The latter technologies have been making much more rapid progress in developing countries, where traditional payment infrastructures are poor or nonexistent and cash is still king than in developed countries such as the United States or Canada, where payment infrastructures are well developed and penetration is high among consumers and merchants. This leapfrogging process is analogous to what happened with telecommunications where, for example, countries in Africa were never able to roll out copper-wire based landline service to every village and house, but mobile phone technology was rapidly adopted, solving the coverage problem. The mobile phone of course also plays a central role in the new payment platforms (e.g., M-Pesa).

4.5.7 The Rise of New Bank Archetypes

Ant Financial Services, the owner of AliPay, may well be the type of new technology-based bank, which traditional banks have most to fear from. It already runs the biggest business-orientated blockchain platform in China, and it processes payments for as many as a billion users a day, where mobile payments are ubiquitous. Ant Group is currently planning an initial public offering (IPO) on the Hong Kong and Shanghai stock exchanges, shunning New York amid the current tensions between the United States and China. The IPO is aiming for a market valuation in excess of $200 billion. By comparison, Goldman Sachs has a market cap of about $70 billion (Xie, 2020).

According to a McKinsey analysis, big technology companies and fintech players are focusing on the banking segments where the return on equity (ROE) is the highest and where the intensity of customer engagement accompanied with data availability is also high. The banking areas where both these factors are highest are retail deposits and payments, and these are indeed the areas we have seen being cherry-picked by digital competitors (McKinsey, 2019).

In one plausible outcome, pure banking will become invisible as transactions such as payments are seamlessly embedded into customers' digital lives. In this world, banks could still own or be partners in digital platforms. But banks will have to add new services to payments and transactions if they want to fight commoditization. Banks' advantages include the ability to construct virtual currencies and leverage their merchant relationships and small business lending portfolios. As neutral parties, banks may be positioned to build marketplaces to compete with global tech giants (Dietz et al., 2018).

Accenture has defined four banking archetypes that could succeed in the new digital world (Accenture, 2017):

- Digital relationship manager. This is suitable for large banks that provide a full range of services but requires a big transformation to achieve true integration between physical and digital channels, and an ecosystem approach to leverage the platforms of digital natives like Amazon and Google.
- Digital category killer. This requires a bank to choose a niche and execute well in it, like PayPal in payments or Quicken Loans in mortgages.
- Open platform player. This means offering customers a flexible, trusted platform where other best-of-breed providers can interact with them and sell them products and services. It effectively allows customers to build their bank. The danger of this archetype is that it could be assimilated by the larger digital natives.
- Utility provider. This entails providing end-to-end solutions requiring specialist talent and technology at a low overhead cost to other banks and corporates to use. But the model entails letting go of the bank's customer relationships.

4.5.8 Lessons from Emerging Markets for Developed Markets

Emerging markets are leapfrogging the developed world in payment innovation. China has essentially skipped checks and payment cards to go straight to all-digital payment. And in China, platform firms increasingly dominate the payments business. Subject to local regulation, data owned by platform companies will enable ever-greater levels of personalized marketing to consumers (Dietz et al., 2018).

Merchants used to have their primary financial relationships with their banks, but payments companies have increasingly intruded on that relationship, leveraging their role in online, mobile, and next-generation point-of-sale solutions into developing a broader banking relationship that includes loans, payroll management, and customer loyalty rewards. In reaction, established FIs have been buying up payment fintech start-ups in recent years. For example, payments startup WePay was bought by JP Morgan Chase in 2017 in the hope that it would expand the reach of its Chase Pay mobile wallet (Rudegeair, 2017). WePay primarily serves online businesses like marketplaces and crowdfunding sites. Its API solution supports payment processing, fraud detection, and complex payouts.

4.6 Synthesis: The Changing Locus of Trust

4.6.1 Transformative Trends in Financial Disintermediation

The role of a trusted intermediary or broker is as old as commerce itself. Through the centuries, banks have been the trusted intermediaries for moving money, and they owned the trusted networks to do so. These networks range from intrabank to interbank, from domestic to international. The role of correspondent, a trusted bank agent in a different locale, goes back at least as far as Roman times. Bills of exchange and letters of credit in the modern sense originated in Renaissance Italy, as did the concept of making payments through the simple transfer of book credits, without the need for cash to move.

Today we are living in the waning days of cash, with digital electronic ledger entries already having replaced physical book entries. We are close to a world of all-digital money. We are asking questions such as: What will the future all-digital payment industry look like? What type of institution will dominate it, and how will it be regulated?

The first question that looms over this entire debate—one that only gets revisited every generation or more—is "What is sound money?" More specifically, what currency would be generally accepted as payment? And what currency would best facilitate fast and secure payment?

The second question concerns the payment system. However, the choice of payment system and the choice of payment vendor are both closely related to the first, the choice of payment currency.

And lastly, it is possible that different choices will be made for different types of payment, whether person to business, government to person, person to person, and so on.

There are radical answers to these questions, such as bitcoin or other private cryptocurrencies, although their applications will likely continue to appeal only to a niche market at least as long as they have scalability problems and central banks restrict the use of such alternative private currencies.

The vast majority of consumers and businesses are not looking for a revolution. They are simply looking for speed, low transaction costs, and security. The two-tier financial system governed by central banks, and serviced by financial institutions can transform itself by moving fully to digital payments in national currencies. But even in this evolutionary model, traditional banks risk being disintermediated by digital natives who are not held back by legacy infrastructures, know how to leverage their strengths in the handling and moving of data, and are willing to make big, bold bets.

If central banks go ahead with CBDCs and allow each citizen an account with the central bank, commercial banks could be disintermediated in the provision of core payment services. But fortunately for banks, central bankers realize the consequences and are hesitant to make this jump, at least not just yet.

4.6.2 The Competitive Threat from Large Digital Enterprises

The primary financial relationships that bank customers form are often initiated by their need for deposit and payment services. All other services usually follow, including lucrative services such as lending and wealth management.

In their desire to cut staffing costs, and by pushing customers online or to call centers, banks have weakened the once-strong bonds between bank customers and their local branches. The imposing Greek-inspired branch architecture that signals permanence, seriousness, and trustworthiness, and which impressed and reassured customers on their regular bank visits have faded into the past. In its place are call-center experiences that are at best tolerated, and at worst loathed, and online portals and mobile apps that attempt to be state of the art, but are usually a step or two behind those of the digital natives.

Unfortunately for banks, payment provision is one of the easiest financial services for digital challengers to enter. It has high volume, high, profitability, and large numbers of retail customers, as well as many SME merchants. Payment is a sweet spot as far as digital competitors are concerned, with its high ROE and intensity of customer engagement that also generates big data which can easily be mined by AI.

While startup fintechs seem to be the hotbeds of innovation, they rarely go on to become large digital enterprises. Of those with viable business models and technology, the vast majority are acquired by either banks or tech giants.

Large digital enterprises have not only the scale and the technological know-how but also the big data and existing customer relationships to compete and win in this area. They are good at improving services, particularly those that consumers have long been frustrated with. For example, PayPal's Zoom service offers easier and cheaper cross-border transfers worldwide, including currency conversion, than any bank in North America. Digital enterprises are also masters at "stickiness". Once you have an Amazon Prime account, you will keep returning to buy a variety of products, even from non-Amazon vendors. Once you have set up PayPal and connected it to your bank accounts, it is easy to keep using it for local P2P as well as cross-border payments.

Banks still rely on their regulatory licensing to shield them from some types of competition, but digital enterprises find it quite easy to partner with second or third-tier FIs to satisfy such requirements when they need to.

4.6.3 The Importance (or Not) of Infrastructure Ownership

Today's banks are already mostly IT companies with banking licenses and a diminishing façade of bricks-and-mortar branches. The IT infrastructure they operate, however, is creaking because of the prevalence of a multitude of often-siloed legacy systems of different vintages. This has slowed down digital initiatives generally and is also a hindrance to payment innovation. Modern-looking apps can be quickly developed, but these apps always have to interface with the legacy systems in the back end.

Challengers and new entrants not encumbered by legacy systems can not only move faster to offer innovative new payment services but can scale fast by leveraging virtually unlimited cloud-based infrastructure that is for rent. Consumers do not ask anymore whose computers and networks their money moves over; they only need to be assured that their assets and data are safe.

Established banks and payment networks do, however, still have an advantage in security, since ensuring trust has always been at the core of the banking and payment business. However, it is unlikely that this will protect them in case of major disruption such as a complete shift to payments in cryptocurrencies.

4.6.4 How Losing the Payment-Broker Role Could Disrupt Credit and Other Banking Services

Transactional POS financing offerings are picking up rapidly and may surpass similar bank offerings which come later in the buying process.

Today, the large digital enterprises know their customers so much better than the banks know the same individuals, which enable them to offer novel credit offerings based on data-rich credit-scoring models that banks cannot easily compete with because they don't have such data.

Banks could lose much of their ability to cross-sell lending and other bank services if they are no longer fully present in the payment process. The core of their problem is not necessarily a relationship problem, but that they are too late to the consumer decision-making process and not in the position to anticipate their customers' needs.

4.6.5 The Changing Nature of High-Trust Customer Relationships

We seem to be living in the middle of a secular trend toward the *decentralization* of consumer trust, manifested by an erosion of trust in traditional, centralized institutions such as governments and corporations, including FIs. Consumers want more control over, and transparency into, how their data are being used. As a consequence, society is exploring new tools that enable decentralized and distributed power, and consumers are increasingly finding what they are looking for in the technologies themselves, rather than in trusted, centralized third parties. Examples of such technologies are by now well known, they are DLTs, smart contracts, and crypto wallets. The decentralization trend is driven by the desire for freedom and protection from entities, whether private or public, which hold too much power over individuals. Satoshi's bitcoin white paper was a seminal event in this journey. Most significantly, these new technologies also enable alternate payment methods.

Ultimately the value of any broker or intermediary is in its value added to the process, in the eyes of the customer. Up to now, banks have relied on trust as the foundation stone of their value-add. If trust in the operation of the payments process becomes less important, because it becomes fully standardized and universalized through universal digitized networks, a continued reliance by banks on being the trusted brokers will have to rely on a completely updated notion of trust.

Banks still have a key advantage in the area of privacy, which is that they are much more trusted than digital enterprises to not abuse their customer knowledge. The updated concept of trust will have to emphasize financial and personal privacy, which is part of a larger concept today called data agency. If banks can deliver on this new need for trust, they can reestablish themselves as trust brokers in the provision of payments.

4.6.6 Plausible Scenarios for Future Disruptions and Transformations of Payment Systems

Despite the hype, the slow development of DLTs and the paucity of successful large-scale DLT applications give banks some time to prepare and react for a future that will be quite different than the past.

A common element of all future payment scenarios is that payments will go fully digital, will be real-time or close to real-time, and will move over seamless networks, not only domestically but also cross-border. Aside from that, the range of future scenarios will be defined by the answers to the following questions:

What will be the dominant payments technology? Will it be a fully digital national currency such as a digital dollar or euro, or will private cryptocurrencies such as Ethereum or Calibra capture a large part of the payments market?

What will be the degree of centralization? On one extreme (full decentralization and disintermediation), payments could go totally P2P. On the other extreme (full centralization), central banks could allow citizens to keep electronic money accounts and facilitate all payments directly. Or it could be something in between like we have today.

Where will the competitive commercial advantage in payments reside? Will control of essential payments networks, whether cross-border, wholesale/retail or the last mile to the consumer hold any commercial advantage? Or will these become highly regulated, large-scale monopolies or state-owned infrastructure like the public-roads network? To what extent will the competitive advantage shift to payment overlay and other value-added consumer and business services? What level of digital ability and data ownership will be needed to compete on this terrain?

What will be the future locus of trust in payments? To what extent will it shift from the current trust in the safe-keeping of funds and secure handling of payments, to the safekeeping of personal data? And how can banks differentiate themselves from large tech companies to be the most trusted brokers of both payments and related consumer data?

4.7 Conclusion

Several scenarios for the future of payments can be constructed, but they all entail a new basis of competition and a new locus of trust. Competition for the trusted broker role is likely to be most intense between the incumbent banks and the digital behemoths. The technology itself is important, but will not be determinative of the future of payments. Regulators and legislators will still have a big say on the ultimate architecture of the new payment system, and there are several consequential choices to be made.

While trust will be just as important in the future as in the past, the meaning of trust is changing fast. In a world of instant payments, universal connectivity between payment networks, and perhaps even central-bank accounts for ordinary citizens to keep their digital funds, the role of banks could be quite different than it has been for the last centuries. Banks will be able to succeed in this new world by honoring the age-old values of dependability and trustworthiness, but interpreting them anew for a world where data is king, and privacy and individual freedoms are still valued by most.

References

Accenture. Banking business models fit for the path ahead. May 15, 2017.

ACI Universal Payments. The future of payments: Who is positioned for advantage, 2017.

AlliedWallet. Why digital wallets are gaining popularity. (Retrieved August 5, 2020).

Anan, L. et al. (2020). Are convenience and rewards leading to a digital flashpoint? McKinsey on Payments, Volume 12, Issue 30, January 2020, McKinsey & Company Global Payments Practice, McKinsey & Company.

Angel, J. J. and McCabe, D. M. The ethics of payments: Paper, plastic, or bitcoin?," Jan.14, 2014.

Horwitz, J. Facebook-Backed Libra Project Gets New CEO, The Wall Street Journal, May 6, 2020.

Arnold, M. ECB seeks to develop own digital currency: Global payments. Financial Times, Nov 27, 2019.

Awrey, D., & van Zwieten, K. (2018). The shadow payment system. *Journal of Corporation Law, 43*(4), 775–816.

BAI. (2020). BAI banking outlook special report: Digital banking

Bank for International Settlements. Chapter III. Central banks and payments in the digital era. BIS Annual Economic Report, June 24, 2020a.

BIS. Bank for International Settlements. "Cross-border retail payments," Committee on Payments and Market Infrastructures, Feb. 2018.

BIS Bank for International Settlements. "Payment aspects of financial inclusion in the fintech era," Committee on Payments and Market Infrastructures, April 2020b.

BIS Bank of International Settlements. "Wholesale digital tokens," Committee on Payments and Market Infrastructures, Dec. 2019.

Banking Circle (2020). Mind the Gap—How payment providers can fill a banking gap for online merchants

Bech, M. L., Hancock, J., Rice, T.; and Wadsworth, A.. On the future of securities settlement. BIS Quarterly Review, March 2020.

Beck, Morton and Hancock, Jenny. Innovations in payments. BIS Quarterly Review, March 2020.

Berentsen, Aleksander and Schar, Fabian. The case for central bank electronic money and the non-case for central bank cryptocurrencies. Federal Reserve Bank of St. Louis Review, Second Quarter 2018, pp. 97–106.

BIS Annual Economic Report. Central banks and payments in the digital era. June 24, 2020.

Bloomberg Businessweek. Who's afraid of a digital Yuan. June 8, 2020.

Federal Reserve (2019). The 2019 federal reserve payments study.

Botta, A., et al. (n.d.). *A global view of financial life during COVID-19*. McKinsey & Company.

Botta, A., et al. Global transaction banking: The $1 trillion question. McKinsey on Payments, Volume 12, Issue 30, January 2020, McKinsey & Company Global Payments Practice, McKinsey & Company, 2020.

Caceres-Santamaria, A. J. Peer-to-Peer (P2P) payment services. Page One Economics, Federal Reserve Bank of St. Louis, April 2020.

Cakebread, C.. Who's Using P2P Payments in the US?. eMarketer, Dec. 2018.

Capgemini Research Institute (2019). World payments report 2019.

Carstens, Agustín. Shaping the future of payments. BIS Quarterly Review, March 2020.

Carstens, Agustín. The future of money and the payment system: what role for central banks? Lecture at Princeton University, Dec. 5, 2019.

CGI (2017). A vision of payments in 2027

CGI (2019). Banking transformed. Exploring payment overlay services

Clement, L.. Re-inventing the retail experience after COVID-19. Retail, Aug. 11, 2020

Coispeau, O. (2017). *Finance masters: A brief history of international financial Centers in the last millennium*. World Scientific.

Consensys. Project Khokha: Blockchain case study for central banking in South Africa," June 2019

Cramer-Flood, Ethan. Global Ecommerce 2020—Ecommerce Decelerates amid Global Retail Contraction but Remains a Bright Spot. eMarketer, Jun. 22, 2020.

Davies, P. J. Wirecard Says Missing $2 Billion Probably Doesn't Exist. The Wall Street Journal, June 22, 2020.

Dietz, M. (2018) et al. New rules for an old game: Banks in the changing world of financial intermediation, McKinsey McKinsey & Company. Global Banking Annual Review 2018

Dikshit, P. et al. (2020). US lending at point-of-sale: The next frontier of growth. McKinsey on Payments, Volume 12, Issue 30, January 2020, McKinsey & Company Global Payments Practice, McKinsey & Company.

Distributed ledger technology in payment, clearing and settlement—An analytical framework, Committee on, Bank for International Settlements (BIS). Payments and Market Infrastructures, Feb. 2017

Dunbar, C. F. (1892). The Bank of Venice. *The Quarterly Journal of Economics, 6*(3), 308–335.

Faster Payments Task Force. The U.S. path to faster payments, Final Report Part Two: A Call to Action, 2017.

Federal Reserve Bank of Atlanta (2019). Survey of consumer payment choice, 2019.

Federal Reserve (2020). Progress and Next Steps with FedNowSM Service. FedPayments Improvement blogs.

Ferguson, N. (2008). *The ascent of money* (pp. 72–73). Penguin.

Financial Stability Board. Annex—Trusted ledger arrangements for payment arrangements. Enhancing Cross-border Payments, Stage 1 report to the G20: Technical background report, Apr. 9, 2020.

GIACT (2020). The changing landscape of identity fraud: Fraudsters strike back

Golden, P. Blockchain platforms see Covid-19 trade finance opportunity, EuroMoney, July 30, 2020,

Hall, I. Central bank digital currency developments hit "top gear" amid coronavirus. Global Government Forum, June 18, 2020a.

Hall, I. Central banks pool brainpower on digital currencies. Global Government Forum, Feb. 2, 2020b

International Monetary Fund (2018). Learn Over the Last 20 Years? IMF Working Papers

Kapronasia. Will Brazil greenlight WhatsApp Pay? July 29, 2020.

Kawasmi, Z., Gyasi, E. A., & Dadd, D. (2019). Blockchain adoption model for the global banking industry. *Journal of International Technology and Information Management, 28*(4), 112–154.

KPMG. (2019). *10 predictions for the future of payments*. KPMG.

Labate, V.. Banking in the Roman World. Ancient History Encyclopedia, Nov. 17, 2016.

Lane, F. C. (1937). Venetian bankers, 1496-1533: A study in the early stages of deposit banking. *Journal of Political Economy, 45*(2), 187–206.

McKinsey & Company (2019). The last pit stop? Time for bold late-cycle moves, McKinsey Global Banking Annual Review 2019

Medina, L. and Schneider, F. (2018). Shadow economies around the world: What did we.

Nakamoto, S.. Bitcoin: a peer-to-peer electronic cash system. Oct. 2008.

Parks, T. (2013). *Medici money: Banking, metaphysics and art in fifteenth-century Florence*. Profile Books.

Payments Next (2020). B2B cross-border payments may recover 30% by 2022.

Pearson, N. O. The Little Canadian Company Powering Online Shopping. Bloomberg Businessweek, June 15, 2020, pp. 22–23.

Powell, J. Innovation, technology, and the payments system. Speech made at Blockchain: The Future of Finance and Capital Markets?, The Yale Law School Center for the Study of Corporate Law, New Haven, Connecticut, March 3, 2017

PYMENTS. "Deep dive: Why contactless card-not-present transactions are gaining new momentum," July 6, 2020.

Reynaldo, "Improved scalability: Ethereum can reach 9.000 transactions per second," Crypto Flash News, Jan 7., 2020., https://www.crypto-news-flash.com/scalability-of-the-ethereum-can-reach-9k-tops-due-to-istanbul/

Rice, T., von Peter, G., & Boar, C. (2020). *On the global retreat of correspondent banks*. BIS Quarterly Review.

Ripple. "Speed and Cost of Payments Don't Need to Be at Odds," Sep. 4, 2019.

Rolfe, A.. What's blocking the future of invisible payments and why? Payments Cards and Mobile, Jul. 14, 2020.

Rudegeair, P. J.P. Morgan to buy payments Firm WePay in first major fintech acquisition. The Wall Street Journal, Oct. 17, 2017.

Schneier, B.. There's No Good Reason to Trust Blockchain Technology. WIRED, Feb. 6, 2019.

Squareup (n.d.). Making Change – Payments and the Pandemic. https://squareup.com/us/en/making-change/covid

Stackhouse, Julie. Fintech: How digital wallets work. On the Economy Blog, Federal Reserve Bank of St. Louis, June 25, 2019.

Syed, Sarah. Mein Liebling Credit Card. Bloomberg Businessweek, May 4, 2020, pp. 22–23.

The Economist. Covid dries up a cash cow. Apr. 18, 2020a, p. 34

The Economist. Dial it up. May 30, 2020b

The Economist. Piping Up. Special report on international banking, May 9, 2020c

Thomas, L. France: We can't allow Facebook's Libra in Europe. Reuters, Sept. 12, 2019.

Trentmann, N. Germany moves to overhaul accounting oversight amid Wirecard Scandal. The Wall Street Journal, June 29, 2020.

Valladares, M. R. Improving Cross-Border Payments Is Critical to Support Global Economic Growth, Trade And Financial Inclusion. Forbes, Jul. 13, 2020 van Biljon, P., & Lajoux, A. (2020). *Making money – The history and future of society's most important technology* (pp. 213–231). De Gruyter.

Visa Fact Sheet (2020). https://usa.visa.com/dam/VCOM/download/corporate/media/visanet-technology/aboutvisafactsheet.pdf (Retrieved August 13, 2020).

Wadsworth, A. (2018a). Decrypting the role of distributed ledger technology in payments processes. *The Reserve Bank of New Zealand Bulletin, 81*, 5.

Wadsworth, A. Decrypting the role of distributed ledger technology in payments processes. The Reserve Bank of New Zealand Bulletin, Vol. 81, No. 5, May 2018b.

Ward, J. Bank of England debating digital currency creation, Bailey Says. Bloomberg, July 13, 2020.

Webb, A.. Facebook's Libra cryptocurrency sounds a lot like what China's doing. Here's why that should scare you. Inc., Oct. 2019

Weber, H. Mercedes-Benz might track your car's location if you don't make your payments. Fast Company, Aug. 20, 2019.

Wittenstein, J.. Square rally sends valuation into ranks of biggest U.S. Banks. Bloomberg, July 6, 2020

World Bank (2017). Global Findex Database

Worldpay from FIS. Consumer behavior & payments report 2019, 2019.

Worldpay from FIS. Global payments report—The pathways of people and payments, Jan 2020.

Wurmser, Y. US Mobile Payment Users 2019. eMarketer, Oct. 14, 2019.

Xie, S. Y.. How Jack Ma's Ant Group went from business disrupter to Chinese Tech Champion. The Wall Street Journal, Jul. 21, 2020.

Zheng, S.. At least 18 central banks are developing sovereign digital currencies, The Block, Dec. 26, 2020.

Chapter 5
Machine Learning in Healthcare: Operational and Financial Impact

David Anderson, Margret V. Bjarnadottir, and Zlatana Nenova

5.1 Introduction

Machine learning is revolutionizing every organization, business, and even our private lives, and healthcare is no exception (Bastani et al., 2022). Machine learning applications include managing healthcare systems, predicting no-shows at outpatient offices and everything in between. Within hospitals, predictive analytics are being used in multiple applications across different departments to accelerate workflow and to monitor patients. As a result, the literature on machine learning used in healthcare applications is vast. Studies range from risk prediction (Baechle et al., 2020) and understanding patient flows to automation of imaging (Esteva et al., 2017) and robo assistants (Jack et al., 2008). A simple keyword search on PubMed [1] for "readmission" and "machine learning" returns over 100 academic papers. In this chapter we therefore do not attempt to survey the extensive literature on machine

[1] PubMed is a free resource supporting the search and retrieval of peer-reviewed biomedical and life sciences literature with the aim of improving health, both globally and personally. PubMed was developed and is maintained by the National Center for Biotechnology Information (NCBI), at the U.S. National Library of Medicine (NLM), located at the National Institutes of Health (NIH).

D. Anderson (✉)
Villanova University, Villanova, PA, USA
e-mail: david.anderson@villanova.edu

M. V. Bjarnadottir
University of Maryland, College Park, MD, USA
e-mail: mbjarnad@umd.edu

Z. Nenova
University of Denver, Denver, CO, USA
e-mail: zlatana.nenova@du.edu

V. Babich et al. (eds.), *Innovative Technology at the Interface of Finance and Operations*, Springer Series in Supply Chain Management 11,
https://doi.org/10.1007/978-3-030-75729-8_5

learning in healthcare. Rather, we aim to highlight some of the many applications of machine learning with direct impact on operations and/or financial outcomes within hospital settings and also to address the important topics of fairness and transparency in this context.

The examples in this chapter, as well as those in the broader literature, use an array of machine learning methods, from simple logistic regression (Barnes et al., 2016) and classification trees (Bertsimas et al., 2008) to ensemble methods (Min et al., 2019) and deep learning models (Xie et al., 2018), and everything in between. For instance, we discuss the application of topic modeling to identify groups of patients at risk of readmission (Baechle et al., 2020), using distribution fitting to estimate the range of potential bed demand and comparing prediction accuracy to a theoretical minimum (Davis & Fard, 2020), and using neural networks to train machine vision models that perform as well as dermatologists in diagnosing skin cancer (Esteva et al., 2017). As in any field that applies machine learning, the sophistication and complexity of the models have increased over time. Yet in contrast to some other fields where models probably do not inform life or death decisions, the healthcare field often prioritizes transparent models over black boxes. As a result, many of the applications we discuss use "explainable" models.

5.1.1 Short, Simplified Overview of Hospital Operations

Hospitals are highly complex systems that operate under conditions of high uncertainty and numerous constraints. Furthermore, departments are interlinked, so decisions in one department may affect another.

Patients typically arrive at a hospital either as scheduled patients (e.g., a patient coming in for a scheduled heart surgery) or unscheduled patients who come in through the emergency department. Patient arrivals to emergency departments are highly variable and uncertain. As a result, inpatient units and ICUs have noisy patient demand with both seasonality and varying trends. This ED arrival uncertainty can impact operating rooms because surgeons must accommodate emergency surgeries into their schedules. Such uncertainty in the system is intensified by the variability in healthcare "service times," the time an operation takes or the time a patient takes to improve enough to be discharged. Figure 5.1 shows a simplified overview of patient flows in and out of the hospital.

Hospitals operate under both budget and capacity constraints. As a result, they are challenged to provide the best possible care for their patients under resource restrictions and in a context where a decision about one patient's treatment can have both down- and upstream impacts. For example, if a new critically ill patient arrives in the ICU and there is no bed available, another patient needs to be discharged from the ICU to a step-down unit in order to accommodate the new arrival. The (early) discharged patient may then be at increased risk of deteriorating health and as a result at risk of readmission to the ICU, which would in turn impact the system and its patients (Anderson et al., 2012, 2011). The entire hospital is therefore

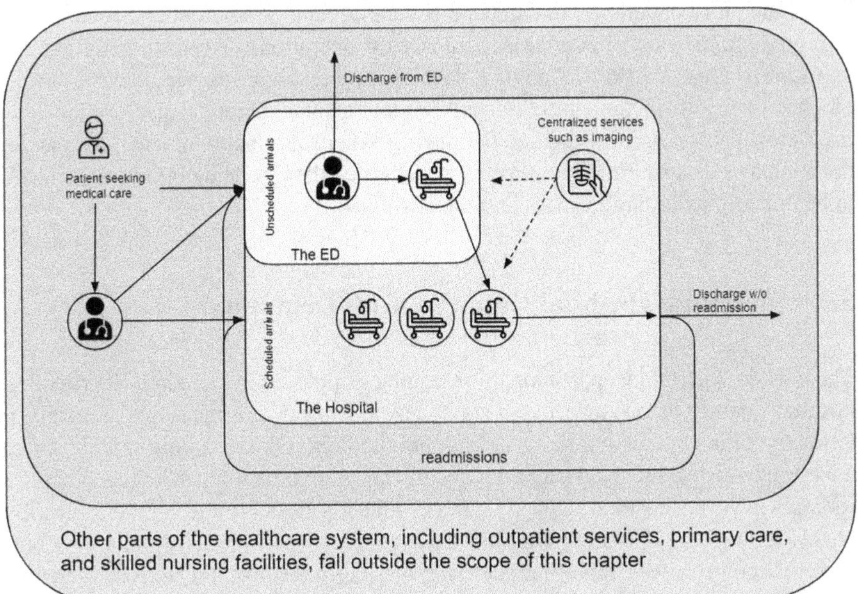

Fig. 5.1 Stylized overview of patient flow within the hospital, highlighting some of the applications included in this chapter

interdependent: decisions made on the hospital floors impact the emergency room, decisions in the ICU impact step-down units, and so on.

Given this impact that one decision focused on a single patient can have on the overall system and given the importance of bed management, there is increased focus on real-time demand and capacity predictions (Cai et al., 2016). Larger hospitals now have centralized bed control (Reuille, 2004), and some hospital departments now focus their morning huddle, which traditionally focused on the most critical patients, on identifying the patients most likely to be discharged (Barnes et al., 2016).

Against this backdrop, machine learning is applied to aid in operational and clinical decision-making. Machine learning models have been introduced to help with patient flow decisions and in concert with prescriptive analytics to maximize the overall patient benefit. Hospital executives are optimistic that machine learning will lead to dramatic reductions in cost and improvement in the quality of care (Lagasse, 2019). Over half of executives expect to see cost reductions over 15% of medical costs over the next 5 years due to better health outcomes, fewer medical errors, and reduced utilization (Society of Actuaries, 2018). However, the academic literature contains mixed findings on the economic and financial impacts of machine learning in healthcare (Wolff et al., 2020).

To provide a better picture of the emerging landscape of machine learning in healthcare, we review some of its many applications in the hospital setting. We first focus on two well studied areas, resource demand prediction and readmission risk prediction, which have a clear impact on operations. We next highlight two application areas that are changing hospital processes. First, we discuss the use of chatbots, both in the literature and in documented practical use. Second, we examine machine learning applied to imaging, where automatic imaging is replacing traditional processes. Finally, we discuss current challenges and opportunities for AI in healthcare, including fairness and transparency.

5.2 Matching Hospital Capacity with Demand

The classic operations problem of matching supply with demand is critical in hospital operations because the costs of any mismatch are measured not only in terms of dollars but also in terms of patient outcomes. On the supply side, hospitals have relatively stable physical capacity in terms of inpatient beds and operating rooms. However, hospital capacity can be adjusted through altering variables like nurse staffing and operating room scheduling ahead of time. Hospitals also have marginal control over some demand streams like inter-hospital transfers, elective surgeries, and ED diversion. But, as discussed in the introduction, hospitals operate in an environment of high demand uncertainty. In hospital settings it is therefore particularly hard to match supply with demand due to limited flexibility in capacity, uncertainty in demand and supply, and lack of control over demand. Accurate demand forecasts and available capacity predictions are therefore critical in this context, as they allow hospitals to make capacity adjustments to the best of their ability.

Such accurate predictive models of demand for medical resources can be generated through two main machine learning approaches: macro or micro. The difference between these two approaches lies in whether the unit of analysis is a patient (micro) or a hospital unit (ED/OR/inpatient ward) (macro). For each modeling approach, many different predictive models can be used, including regression-based time series forecasting methods (Channouf et al., 2007; Jones et al., 2002), neural networks (Menke et al., 2014), and distribution fitting (Davis & Fard, 2020). The simpler models are easier to fit, require fewer variables, and have less complex data architecture, but they do not give as accurate or specific predictions as more complex models (Mackay & Lee, 2005). The appropriateness of a model depends on the decision it needs to support: a simple occupancy prediction (macro) can help staff decide whether to bring in an on-call nurse, whereas patient-specific predictions (micro) are necessary for discharge planning.

Papers that use this approach include (Channouf et al., 2007; Jones et al., 2002; Davis & Fard, 2020). For instance, Channouf et al. (2007) has shown that simple auto-regressive time series models, updated hourly, can predict emergency department loads with enough accuracy to make flex-staffing decisions (Channouf et al., 2007). It is widely accepted that a method that uses simple time series approaches and adjusts for a small number of covariates generates reasonably accurate, operationally useful predictions of future bed demand and patient load.

The micro approach attempts to model individual patients' predicted duration or length of stay and uses individual predictions to forecast overall demand. Individual predictions are aggregated either by adding up probabilities or by taking the average of discrete event simulations that use individual patient characteristics as inputs. Examples of the micro approach include (Littig & Isken, 2007; Kayış et al., 2015; Stepaniak et al., 2010; Alaeddini et al., 2011). These papers show that consideration of individual patient status (diagnosis, current length of stay, vital signs, etc.) can improve these prediction models, but at the cost of more model complexity and higher data collection requirements. Additionally, individual patient-level predictions do not just give better overall demand estimates: they give information that can be used for discharge planning and prioritization (Barnes et al., 2016).

One example of micro-level forecasting was developed by Littig & Isken (2007), who use patient-level predictions of inflows and outflows to make short-term occupancy predictions. The predictions are made using data in a predictive occupancy database (POD), which stores historical and real-time data including patient clinical and demographics data; bed allocation and occupancy data; and financial and scheduling information. The POD is used to train a suite of multinomial logistic regression models forecasting patient inflow (arrivals), throughput (transfer to another unit), outflow (length of stay (LOS), and discharge from the hospital. Specifically, the researchers trained multiple models to predict the number of elective and emergency surgical patients, the number of admissions from the ED, the number of direct admissions, and the number of transfers into the unit from other units. Arrival numbers are predicted through time series modeling, while the probability of movement (transfer or discharge) for each patient is fit through a multinomial regression. The expected locations for each patient are then summed up for each day in the planning horizon and added to the expected number of arrivals. Thus, unit-level forecasts can be generated for each location in the facility. Based on this model and compared to the baseline staffing method previously used, the hospital was able to staff the correct (optimal) number of nurses for an additional 119 days of a 351-day follow-up period. The model was also able to identify more situations where post-operative beds were either at a critical level (and surgeries would be delayed) or at a low enough utilization level where a ward could be closed and staffing reduced. Specifically, the model allowed for week-ahead predictions of "open" or "critical" post-operative bed state at 70% accuracy, compared to 21% for the baseline method.

Another useful micro-level forecasting application supports hospitals' increasing focus on discharging patients early in the day so that the bed can be turned over and hold a new patient for the following night (Wertheimer et al., 2014). Predictions that indicate which patients are most likely to be discharged in the next day or two can help hospital staff prioritize patients for rounding and discharge planning. Staff can then review and coordinate discharges early in the day for those patients who are ready, the bed can be turned over more quickly, and the effective capacity of the hospital will increase. As another example, the authors of Barnes et al. (2016) build logistic regression models and random forest models and compare the results to predictions made by clinicians. The models focus on real-time, short-term predictions, so the researchers build on readily available data to ease the integration of these models into operational processes. They found that elapsed LOS and whether the patient is under observation were the most important predictive factors for the population of their inpatient medical unit. Further, day of the week (Sunday or weekday), chest pain, disposition, age, and syncope[2] were all found to influence the predictions. The authors conclude that the models outperform clinician judgement in terms of both predicting the number of discharges and ranking patients on their likelihood of discharge.

In a recent paper by Shi et al. (2019), the authors took a decision-oriented approach to support capacity planning. Rather than predicting LOS, the authors aimed to identify patients who would not benefit (or who would benefit the least) from additional time in the hospital. For each patient, the authors predict the readmission survival curve if the patient is discharged either today or on each of the following k days. This generates a risk trajectory for the current day and any future day. In contrast to many purely predictive models, this paper attempts to estimate, for each individual patient on each day, the causal relationship between longer LOS and readmission risk. To estimate the causal relationship, the authors build a three-stage estimation model, using a logistic regression to estimate the probability of ever being readmitted, then instrumenting for LOS by using day of week of admission. Finally, for those patients predicted to be readmitted, a mixture model is estimated using an expectation-maximization algorithm. These risk curves are then used to inform a Markov decision process optimization model that accounts for hospital occupancy levels to decide when to discharge each patient. The algorithm has been implemented as a webtool at a partner hospital and in conjunction with a healthcare analytics startup, and the authors find that post-discharge identification of readmission risk has increased from 44 to 51% accuracy. The pilot is ongoing, but simulations show an expected prevention of over a hundred readmissions per year.

In summary, the multiple papers on demand and utilization prediction highlight the importance of timely and accurate predictions for operational decision-making in healthcare. In order to make effective staffing decisions and to optimize schedules, advance knowledge of future demand is critical. Knowing when demand is expected to be high or low allows hospitals to adjust staffing levels, increase or decrease scheduled caseloads, accept or reject patient transfers, or set diversion status for the emergency department. Each of these actions helps keep resource utilization high while minimizing overtime and congestion, improving patient care and financial outcomes for the provider.

Table 5.1 summarizes selected papers that use machine learning to improve the match between capacity and demand, including the outcome of interest, data, methods used, and financial impact of the resulting models. Many of these papers

---

[2]Syncope is a medical term for fainting that is caused by a temporary drop in the amount of blood that flows to the brain.

do not give direct financial impacts, but many estimate amounts of cost savings or revenue increase. The main areas that offer cost savings are lowered staffing costs and decreased unplanned overtime. The increases in revenue come from increased throughput by decreasing idle capacity, particularly through improvements in overbooking policies and surgical scheduling.

5.3 Readmission

Hospitals have always been under pressure to maintain costs and improve the quality of care delivered. The readmission rate is the fraction of discharged patients admitted back to a hospital within a certain time period, typically 28–30 days. A provider's readmission rate signals its ability to maintain cost and quality of care, which is why it is used to evaluate hospital performance in the USA, a number of European countries (Kristensen et al., 2015), Australia, and New Zealand (Project health, 2019).

The readmission literature dates back to the 1970s. An overview highlights that most readmission research published in that decade focused on individuals with mental conditions and paralysis (Burgess Jr & Hockenberry, 2014). In the 1980s, the research focus shifted to Medicare patients, examining the quality rather than the cost of care. This research concluded that readmission rates differed across diseases. This finding motivated a careful examination and identification of the risk of readmission across individuals with specific comorbidities—heart failure, ischemic heart disease and acute myocardial infarction, COPD, and pneumonia (Stanton et al., 1985). Despite the diversity in statistical models and patient characteristics utilized in publications, Ross et al. concluded that "none found that patient characteristics strongly predict readmission" (pp. 1381) in individuals with heart failure (Ross et al., 2008). Similar conclusions were reached in Kansagara et al. (2011), still the authors argued that models could improve the cost effectiveness of readmission-reduction interventions.

To overcome the limitations of standard modeling techniques, the Institute of Medicine began highlighting the predictive capabilities of machine learning methods (National Research Council, 2003), which can account for non-linear and highly dimensional relationships between model predictors. A recent review of the literature on predictive models for readmissions (Artetxe et al., 2018) highlighted the significant increase in publications on the topic since 2007, corresponding with machine learning methods' increased presence in the last decade. The authors indicate that among machine learning models, the three most commonly utilized are tree-based, neural-network-based, and support-vector-machine-based.

To examine the quality of these new machine learning models, researchers compared the performance of standard models (e.g., logistic regression) against that of machine learning models (e.g., random forest, support vector machines, a weighted combination of gradient-boosting regression trees and convolutional

Table 5.1 Summary of operational and financial impact of selected papers related to matching capacity with demand

Domain	Paper	Methods	Results	Impact or Value
ER	Xu & Chan (2016)	Queueing theory and stochastic modeling	Using predictions to set optimal diversion policies can reduce wait times by up to 15% while seeing increased patient volume.	Reduced waits and increased throughput lead to higher revenue and patient satisfaction
	Channouf et al. (2007)	Auto-regressive time series models	Average prediction error of less than 3 cases over 2-h prediction windows	Simple models, updated hourly, can be used for flex staffing and ED diversion decisions
	Jones et al. (2002)	Time Series ARIMA models	Average error under 3% up to 32 days in advance	Demand volatility drives waiting times and patient outcomes
		Self-organizing maps are used to identify patient types and resource demands	Patient profiles and clusters discovered that can predict resource demands	Knowing future inpatient resource demands helps with bed allocation and staff scheduling.
	Zaerpour et al. (2000)	Regression models to predict volume and wait time	Volume predicts wait time, case mix predicts quality of care	Operational planning requires knowledge of future patient volume but also patient acuity.
ER Summary	Predicting demand can lead to better staffing decisions, better resource utilization, and smarter day of operational decisions, leading to shorter waits, higher volumes, and better profit.			
Inpatient	Davis & Fard (2020)	Estimates bed occupancy probability distribution, using Poisson arrival assumption	Average prediction error of 7.8 patients (5.1) 14 days (1 day) out—compared to theoretical minimum errors of 7.3 (3.7)	Fewer diversions, better transfer acceptance decisions, and less wasted capacity
	Littig & Isken (2007)	Aggregates individual predictions using multinomial regressions	Accurate predictions 70% accurate week-ahead predictions of staffing requirements	119/351 days with improved staffing levels

(continued)

Table 5.1 (continued)

Domain	Paper	Methods	Results	Impact or Value
	Mackay & Lee (2005)	Overview—more complex models have better prediction accuracy, but are harder to train and implement		
Inpatient summary	Predicting future demand can lead to better staffing and operational decisions—diversions and surgery cancellations.			
Surgery	Kayış et al. (2015)	Elastic Net—surgeon, team, time, case data	70% R-squared, average prediction error of 40 min	Increased operating room flow by more intelligent scheduling
	Tiwari et al. (2014)	Linear regression from booking data	Average error of 8.27 cases 14 days in advance	Ability to schedule more surgeries or reduce staffing—5% increase in volume with no increase in staffing or facility space
	Stepaniak et al. (2010)	ANOVA and long-duration regression	Decrease in mean absolute prediction error from 17.6 to 9.3 min	Better OR and staff scheduling—fewer delays and reduced overtime costs
Surgery summary	Predicting surgery duration and daily caseload, as well as post-operative recovery time allows for more surgeries to be done, and more hospital revenue.			
Outpatient	Alaeddini et al. (2011)	Gaussian Mixture Models using demographic data and past appointment information	80% accuracy—compared to 50% baseline	Improved overbooking policies incorporating predictions into optimization, lowering waiting times, overtime, and idle resource capacity
	Harris et al. (2016)	Markov Model on individual patient histories	Can identify 32% of no-shows by addressing 10% of cases	Improved inputs into scheduling optimization
Outpatient summary	Understanding no-shows allows for better scheduling and reduced overtime and spoilage costs.			

neural network models) (Mortazavi et al., 2016; Morgan et al., 2019). They concluded that machine learning models performed substantially better. Contrary to this finding, Christodoulou et al. concluded in their paper, that based on previously published studies, there is no significant performance benefit of using machine learning models over traditional logistic regression models (Christodoulou et al., 2019). Additional paper similarly showed that machine learning models are not always better, which suggests the need for careful data procurement and model development for the proper use of these complex modeling tools (Frizzell et al., 2017). This highlights the challenge in applying machine learning models in healthcare: model performance is dependent on both the population and the data, and therefore the results are not consistent across providers.

Despite the lack of consistently reported benefits, machine learning models have become popular in the medical community. This is evidenced by multiple recent publications, including a recent paper which compared a variety of machine learning models when predicting readmission risk for COPD patients (Min et al., 2019). The authors made five major observations. First, clinical knowledge was crucial when building prediction models. Second, data-driven features were helpful but not as useful as the clinical knowledge features. Third, models' prediction performance did not improve substantially when the observation time window (prior to discharge) was more than a year. Fourth, among the logistic regression and machine learning models tested (random forests, support vector machines, gradient boosting decision trees (GBDT), multi-level perceptions), the most powerful was the GBDT model. Finally, the authors found that deep learning methods (convolutional and recurrent neural networks) were not significantly better than the simpler GBDT model. Following these results, the authors concluded that "incorporating domain knowledge into the model building process is of vital importance" as the "medical knowledge people accumulate from clinical practice are invaluable and powerful" (pp. 9).

Acknowledging the invaluable knowledge of doctors, Baechle et al. proposed a novel method that uses unstructured notes data when identifying patients at high risk of readmission (Baechle et al., 2020). In their work, the authors attempted to address two common model shortcomings: localized modeling and limited misclassification cost consideration. Localized modeling is problematic because building disease- and/or hospital-specific models can result in discarding potentially useful and available data. Limited misclassification cost considerations assume that false positives and false negatives are equally costly, so they are undesirable in readmission models. The authors used data from multiple hospitals and Latent Dirichlet Allocation(LDA)[3] unsupervised machine learning algorithm to identify

[3]LDA is a machine learning method that is among the most popular topic models algorithm (Jelodar et al., 2019). The goal of a topic model is to identify the topics a document discusses. In the case of patient data, a topic model can help identify the health complication group/s (i.e., topic/s) a patient (i.e., document) belongs to.

(i) topics (i.e., groups) a patient could belong to. The model assigns a weight (w_i) to each topic. The authors then built topic-specific models, their results ($p_{i,k}$, which is the probability of readmission given topic-specific model i for patient k) are aggregated using the LDA weights ($\sum_i w_i p_{k,i} \geq 0.5$) and a soft majority voting rule is applied. As the authors noted, the weighting approach allows for proper (1) aggregation of heterogeneous patient and provider data across hospitals and (2) clinical analysis of patients with multiple comorbidities. The model performed better than most baseline methods when evaluated on the data from a hospital of primary interest. Its suboptimal performance in some settings was attributed to the discrepancy in patient populations between the primary and auxiliary hospitals. Still, the results suggest that this new method may be better at aggregating multiple sources of unstructured data than popular transfer learning methods (i.e., TrAdaBoost), which translates into more accurate predictive models for readmission.

Researchers have worked not only on evaluating (Min et al., 2019) and improving models through examining rich data sources (Baechle et al., 2020) but also on enhancing models already available in the machine learning literature. In a 2018 paper (Xie et al., 2018), the authors designed a model with two components: (1) a trajectory-based representation and (2) a Trajectory-BAsed DEep Learning (TADEL) unit, which is based on a long short-term memory (LSTM) deep learning model unit. In this approach, the trajectory representation accounts for the dynamic nature of a patient's health progression, while the TADEL unit learns the diverse patient states and hospitalization trajectories. Unlike the LSTM unit, the TADEL unit can account for the recency of past hospitalization and can thus utilize information from past readmission records better. The authors showed the superior performance of their new method when compared against logistic regression, support vector machine, naive Bayes, hidden Markov model, Cox, LSTM, and two recent trajectory-based deep learning models (Pham et al., 2017; Baytas et al., 2017). The model achieved an AUC measure of 88.4%, which was higher than the result achieved by all other models (which ranged from 48.4 to 84.2%). The authors noted that in recall, the model outperforms all standard methods by 29%, which could translate into substantial savings for the healthcare system. They verified the robustness of their results across different (1) chronic conditions (e.g., heart failure, pneumonia), (2) readmission complexities, (3) readmission periods (e.g., 30 days, 3 months, 6 months), and (4) historical data time windows. The authors showed (similarly to Min et al. (2019)) that using more than 1 year of historical data did not improve the predictive capabilities of their model.

In addition to enhancing previously designed machine learning models (Xie et al., 2018), researchers have utilized multi-methodological machine learning-based approaches to improve post-discharge monitoring and staff allocation. In Helm et al. (2016) the authors created personalized monitoring policies with the help of machine learning and prediction models. They predicted patients' readmission in three steps: (1) produce a population-based time-to-readmission model, (2) use Bayesian inference and MCMC methods to personalize the prediction, and (3) improve prediction accuracy for those with limited data. This novel approach outperformed standard data mining models (e.g., decision trees, support vector machine). Through numerical analysis, the authors found that their monitoring policy identifies between 40 and 70% of patient readmissions.

In summary, there is a long tradition of applying machine learning to the estimation of readmission risk. Advances in machine learning such as topic modeling and deep learning models have recently been applied to this problem, with some success. However, as highlighted above, even with more advanced models, medical insights and guidance in the modeling phase can significantly improve modeling outcomes. Readmission research has increased in recent years, and both multiple-hospital-level (Baechle et al., 2020) and single-hospital-level (Helm et al., 2016) data are utilized. However, to the best of our knowledge, readmissions studies primarily use US data, and there is no machine learning-based multinational research that employs data from countries with active readmission-based reimbursement laws (Kristensen et al., 2015). Such analysis could be very informative for policymakers as it would help quantify the impact of different reimbursement incentives on both patients and hospitals.

5.4 New and Emerging Machine Learning and AI Technologies

We have discussed two areas in which machine learning is already being widely deployed in hospital management: patient flow and readmission prevention. In this section, we discuss two emerging areas where machine learning and artificial intelligence have the potential to revolutionize healthcare delivery and operations. In both of these areas, machine learning and AI are able to move beyond using structured data to predict or classify one quantified outcome; rather, they use unstructured data like text and images and can provide more complex information about outcomes. As machine learning and AI techniques improve, the breadth of application areas will continue to grow.

5.4.1 Chatbots

Automated conversational agents, or chatbots, are becoming increasingly common in healthcare. They are used to interact with patients with the aim of improving healthcare outcomes, reducing readmissions, increasing medication and treatment adherence, and helping to remotely triage and diagnose patients, among other uses. A large body of literature exists on their design and implementation. For example, a 2019 survey summarized over 4000 studies of conversational agents in healthcare, finding they have been deployed across a wide range of medical domains (Montenegro et al., 2019). Further, a number of clinical trials have been run to estimate their effectiveness and drivers of adoption. However, few studies have measured the financial and operational impact of chatbots on medical processes.

One exception to this norm is also a particular success story. Louise is the chatbot at the heart of the Re-Engineered Discharge (RED) program at Boston University (Jack et al., 2009; Greenwald et al., 2007; Jack et al., 2008; Bickmore et al., 2009). This chatbot simulates face-to-face discharge instruction using an animated face and synthesized speech, and it delivers personalized discharge information. Throughout the discharge process, Louise ensures that patients can correctly answer questions about their medications, discharge instructions, and other key facts about their condition. Patients generally had positive impressions of the process, and 74% of patients actually preferred Louise to a human—the most common reason being that the chatbot was never in a hurry and was able to review information multiple times to ensure understanding.

Beyond patient satisfaction, Louise was also found to provide a 30% reduced risk of 30-day all-cause readmission in a randomized control trial of 749 patients, which was part of a 2008 pilot study. This corresponded to a 34% lower average cost in the group that received discharge instructions from Louise. The chatbot also allowed the hospital to increase insurance billing for the discharge process by an average of $50 added revenue per discharged patient. In addition, Louise resulted in decreased ED usage following discharge by 33%, potentially helping to reduce ambulance diversion rates and saving capacity for higher value patients.

While the implementation of Louise was promising, there are still challenges to the widespread implementation of chatbots for discharge or other medical applications. Each specific use case must be individually programmed, tested, and validated. Additionally, as patient populations change, medical practice changes, and new procedures and medications become available, chatbots need to be updated and recalibrated. Such programming is an onerous task: in many settings, especially diagnostic and triage settings, the scope of inputs is incredibly large, and it is hard to elicit accurate and pertinent information for diagnosis. Symptoms and diseases do not match up perfectly one-to-one, and translating medical knowledge and intuition into a deterministic question tree is difficult. Further, while Louise was well received in its implementation, patients might generally prefer talking to a human being rather than being screened by a computer. If chatbots are to succeed, it will be important to make them seem real and human and react to patient concerns.

5.4.2 Automation in Imaging

One of the biggest areas of impact that machine learning will have in healthcare in the near future is in computer vision. Computer vision as a field broadly focuses on understanding images and video. In the healthcare context, this translates to identifying tumors on an X-ray or MRI (Esteva et al., 2019), for example. By applying computer vision techniques, typically deep convolutional neural networks, to medical images, machine learning algorithms are beginning to reach human-like levels of performance in diagnostic testing in a wide range of applications. A few examples include breast cancer detection from mammograms (Samala et al., 2016), liver tumor detection in MRIs (Wang et al., 2019), segmenting brain lesions from strokes (Xue et al., 2020), and identifying brain tumors (Sharma et al., 2018). While it is unlikely machine learning algorithms will completely replace human physicians in radiology, the technology has the potential to vastly augment radiologists' accuracy and speed. Below, we discuss in further detail two interesting cases of machine learning which combined with increased hardware capabilities will change how healthcare operates. As a result, this technology has changed medical business models in dermatology and cardiology.

A major function of dermatologists is the detection and monitoring of skin cancer. Skin cancer is a serious issue in the USA: between 2007 and 2011, an average of 4.9 million cases of skin cancer were treated at a cost of over $8 billion annually (Guy Jr et al., 2015). While skin cancers are typically non-fatal, they are the cause of death for roughly 20,000 Americans annually (Skin Cancer Foundation, 2020). Melanoma (a common type of skin cancer that kills 60,000 people per year worldwide) is most commonly diagnosed using dermoscopy, or magnified pictures of skin lesions. This requires an in-person visit to a dermatologist and expensive machinery. The diagnosis of skin lesions is typically done visually by a dermatologist and then confirmed by biopsy.

The visual classification of cancer cells has been a target of computer vision research, with recent results reaching or exceeding human accuracy (Esteva et al., 2017; Rajab et al., 2004; Nasr-Esfahani et al., 2016; Jaleel et al., 2013). As high-quality smartphone cameras become ubiquitous, companies have started to develop smartphone apps that help perform the screening and diagnosis of skin lesions (Galan, 2019). Other apps, released by both academic medical centers and for-profit companies, can classify users' photos of moles and lesions as high risk or not high risk. Still, other apps monitor lesion appearance and growth over time by comparing photos of large areas of skin. These apps replace expensive, infrequent in-person dermatologist visits, instead selling subscriptions or one-off access to what is essentially software-based cancer monitoring at essentially zero marginal cost. This new business model is enabled by advances in machine learning software and in computer and optical hardware.

Cardiology is another domain where machine learning and advances in hardware are combining to change medical care and financial models. Cardiologists use electrocardiogram (ECG) output as one of their main screening tests to detect anomalies like arrhythmias. Recent research has shown that well-designed neural networks can be as good as, if not better than, cardiologists at detecting arrhythmias on ECGs (Martis et al., 2013; Rajpurkar et al., 2017; Jambukia et al., 2015; Hannun et al., 2019). Replacing human analysis of ECG output with machine learning allows for longer monitoring time and better detection at lower cost. At the same time, ECG machines have been miniaturized and their cost has decreased, so they are now affordable consumer electronics. Again, the combination of more portable, high-quality hardware, and highly accurate machine learning models allows screening and other diagnostic tests to be done at home, rather than in person during an office or hospital visit.

5.5 Fairness and Transparency

Almost daily, headlines warn that machine learning has the potential to perpetuate social inequity. Even big technology companies, which are familiar with the challenge of maintaining fairness in machine learning, have struggled to develop unbiased models. For example, Amazon had to abandon a machine learning recruitment tool because it ranked male job candidates higher than females (Dastin, 2018). Similarly, Google Photo was surrounded by controversy after it labeled dark-skinned people as gorillas (Pachal, 2015). The same types of problems arise when machine learning is applied in healthcare—however, the potential for physical harm is far more serious. To begin to offset this risk, researchers must emphasize fairness, equity, and transparency in any machine learning research and implementation.

Data bias in healthcare studies can lead to significant inequities because in the case of an unbalanced dataset, trained machine learning models perform better on the majority class. Recently, bias in the training samples of medical studies has raised serious concerns about the equity of these models. For instance, Google Brain's highly touted acute kidney injury prediction effort was trained on a dataset that was 94% male. In another case, a machine learning algorithm studying the diagnosis of melanoma was trained on a dataset of photographs of skin lesions—and over 95% of those photos were of light-skinned individuals. Risk calculators based on longitudinal data such as data from the Framingham study (Mahmood et al., 2014) are applied indiscriminately across the population, even though the study population is almost entirely of European descent.

As a first step towards equitable machine learning models in healthcare, a standard should be created for their presentation and evaluation. Such a standard could facilitate research fairness and equity through the inclusion of (1) a model evaluation broken down by demographic variables such as age, sex, race, and insurance status and (2) a thorough discussion of how inclusion/exclusion criteria affect the generalizability of the results. These practices would make the variables driving predictive decisions more transparent and help expose potential biases. They could also facilitate the objective evaluation of highly touted but potentially biased models like those discussed above. In a push for increased transparency, the Institute for Clinical and Economic Research argues in a published paper (Carlson et al., 2019) that transparent research requires the careful design of pathways where researchers are properly incentivized to create models that are accessible even during their developmental stages. While this approach would always be challenging, if only due to data privacy concerns and the additional work associated with annotating and preparing a model for third-party use and review, it highlights the gravity of these equity and transparency considerations.

Transparency, whether achieved through a publishing standard or other means, is inextricably linked with machine learning fairness. In a call for increased transparency, the European Union introduced a new restriction in 2018 (Sect. 5.4, Article 22 of the GDPR), which requires all implemented AI models to be interpretable so that the end user understands how models make or support decisions. This will at least temporarily restrict the use of whole classes of more complex learning algorithms due to their opaque prediction methods. When it comes to algorithmic selection, the healthcare field is traditionally conservative because practitioners prefer to rely on more transparent models. Regardless, this new EU regulation will inevitably incentivize the development of novel methods for interpreting complex deep learning models (e.g., neural networks), which will benefit the field in the long run.

With machine learning fueling much of the decision modeling in healthcare operations, we expect model presentation to undergo a large shift towards transparency, and we anticipate a growing emphasis on equity. For example, a recent paper (Samorani et al., 2019) on predictive appointment overbooking highlights that in some cases not only are the predictive models biased, but they can result in systematically longer waiting times for black patients. Through reformulation of the appointment optimization problem, the authors show that scheduling decisions can achieve near-perfect balance between races in terms of average waiting time while losing nearly nothing in terms of performance. We expect numerous topics in the healthcare literature and practice to be revisited in a similar manner over the next couple of years.

5.6 Conclusions

Successful implementation of real-time predictive models requires overcoming multiple practical and computational challenges. Even if the models are quite simple, computing something like a risk score on the fly requires coordination with multiple data sources, along with appropriate interfaces and/or embedding into other software. Further, as clinical practice evolves, so does the data available for training the machine learning algorithms, and as a result, the models require periodic retraining. For example: when a model includes the results of a lab value or clinical test that is the standard of care, if that standard changes, the resulting algorithm may misinterpret the lab value for new patients. Similarly, if coding or billing procedures change, algorithms with billing codes as inputs may become outdated.

Even if these implementation challenges are overcome in specific contexts, machine learning in healthcare in general still faces some barriers to realizing its potentially significant, lasting, and widespread impacts on the finances and operations of healthcare systems. Perhaps the biggest obstacle is its lack of broad-scale replicability. Machine learning models are built and validated on specific datasets, stored in unique formats, and use idiosyncratic variable names. There are multiple major EHR systems, all of which have different data types, variable definitions, and underlying data ontologies. An algorithm developed using one provider's data will not be immediately portable to a new institution that has an entirely different IT infrastructure and data architecture.

The second obstacle lies in the fact that clinical practice and vocabularies, testing and treatment procedures, and coding vary widely across geographic regions, hospital types, and even across individual providers. A test or treatment that may help predict a negative outcome in the dataset where a model was trained may be part of the routine standard of care in another hospital. A model trained in one setting is likely to perform worse, possibly significantly worse, in a different clinical setting, even in the unlikely case where the exact model inputs are all easily accessible.

Even in the face of all these challenges, machine learning is becoming central to the broader efforts that are also the focus of healthcare research. Healthcare research aims to help improve patient care by highlighting challenges (Miotto et al., 2018) and improving patient treatments (Meyer et al., 2018) or hospital processes, which would facilitate patient care through improvements like better provider availability (Delen et al., 2009) or shorter wait times (Curtis et al., 2018). Despite a vast body of literature and the fact that machine learning is helping to bring about these desirable outcomes, few papers study the performance, operational or financial implications of actual implemented models.

This scarcity is not new and in fact goes back to discussions in the 1970s about why published academic research is not utilized by practitioners (Watt, 1977; Wilson, 1981). More contemporary research has identified five main barriers that keep methods such as simulation, which is accepted as the gold standard in other fields, from being frequently used in hospitals (Brailsford, 2005). These are (1) practitioners' psychological resistance to models, (2) the cost of developing models and the competitive nature of the healthcare business, which incentivizes hospitals to avoid sharing, (3) the difficulty of obtaining quality data, (4) the mismatch in incentives among model-developers (academicians) and model-users (hospitals), and (5) management's perception that the unique context of their hospital necessitates creating a model totally from scratch, which in case of machine learning is true, as an algorithm developed using one provider's data needs to be adapted for use in another institution.

However, there is hope that the practical effects of machine learning on healthcare systems will receive more attention in the future. There is a growing anecdotal, if not quantitative, support for its benefits and impact in the form of multiple news stories and conference presentations by chief healthcare executives. For example, at the mHealth and Telehealth World Congress conference, William Morris, the Associate CIO of Cleveland Clinic, spoke about the implementation of a remote telemetry monitor program. He cited a dramatic decrease in unplanned ICU transfers as well as a decrease in length of ICU stay. Such reports may prompt more rigorous investigation.

Lastly, the fact that the broad application of machine learning continues to cause ground-level changes in hospital systems may also lead to a rich pathway of future research and implementation in practice with tangible operational and financial impacts. Machine learning is decisively altering processes such as imaging, as computer vision continues to be adopted in radiology. Other growing applications capitalize on increasing computational power and analytical techniques and cheaper, higher quality hardware: for example, smartphone apps and cameras are able to accurately screen for skin cancer, and at-home ECGs are cheaper and higher quality (longer duration) than traditional in-office ECGs or long-term monitoring solutions like Holter monitors. Such shifts may, as they have been shown to do in research studies, be leading to extended diagnostic and hospital operations capability, and cost savings, as machine learning continues to inform some hospital processes and transform others.

References

Alaeddini, A., Yang, K., Reddy, C., Yu, S. (2011). A probabilistic model for predicting the probability of no-show in hospital appointments. *Health Care Management Science, 14*(2), 146–157.

Anderson, D., Price, C., Golden, B., Jank, W., & Wasil, E. (2011). Examining the discharge practices of surgeons at a large medical center. *Health Care Management Science, 14*(4), 338–347.

Anderson, D., Golden, B., Jank, W., & Wasil, E. (2012). The impact of hospital utilization on patient readmission rate. *Health Care Management Science, 15*(1), 29–36.

Artetxe, A., Beristain, A., & Grana, M. (2018). Predictive models for hospital readmission risk: A systematic review of methods. *Computer Methods and Programs in Biomedicine, 164*, 49–64.

Baechle, C., Huang, C. D., Agarwal, A., Behara, R. S., & Goo, J. (2020). Latent topic ensemble learning for hospital readmission cost optimization. *European Journal of Operational Research, 281*(3), 517–531.

Barnes, S., Hamrock, E., Toerper, M., Siddiqui, S., & Levin, S. (2016). Real-time prediction of inpatient length of stay for discharge prioritization. *Journal of the American Medical Informatics Association, 23*(e1), e2–e10.

Bastani, H., Zhang, D. J., & Zhang, H. (2022). Applied machine learning in operations management. In Babich, V., Birge, J., & Hilary, G. (Eds.), *Innovative technology at the interface of finance and operations*. Springer Series in Supply Chain Management. Springer Nature.

Baytas, I. M., Xiao, C., Zhang, X., Wang, F., Jain, A. K., & Zhou, J. (2017). Patient subtyping via time-aware LSTM networks. In *Proceedings of the 23rd ACM SIGKDD International Conference on Knowledge Discovery and Data Mining* (pp. 5–74).

Bertsimas, D., Bjarnadóttir, M. V., Kane, M. A., Kryder, J. C., Pandey, R., Vempala, S., Wang, G. (2008). Algorithmic prediction of health-care costs. *Operations Research, 56*(6), 1382–1392.

Bickmore, T. W., Pfeifer, L. M., & Jack, B. W. (2009). Taking the time to care: empowering low health literacy hospital patients with virtual nurse agents. In *Proceedings of the SIGCHI Conference on Human Factors in Computing Systems* (pp. 1265–1274).

Brailsford, S. (2005). Overcoming the barriers to implementation of operations research simulation models in healthcare. *Clinical and Investigative Medicine, 28*(6), 312.

Burgess Jr, J. F., & Hockenberry, J. M. (2014). Can all cause readmission policy improve quality or lower expenditures: A historical perspective on current initiatives. *Health Economics, Policy & Law, 9*, 193.

Cai, X., Perez-Concha, O., Coiera, E., Martin-Sanchez, F., Day, R., Roffe, D., & Gallego, B. (2016) Real-time prediction of mortality, readmission, and length of stay using electronic health record data. *Journal of the American Medical Informatics Association, 23*(3), 553–561.

Carlson, J. J., Walton, S. M., Basu, A., Chapman, R. H., Campbell, J. D., McQueen, R. B., Pearson, S. D., Touchette, D. R., Veenstra, D., Whittington, M. D., & Ollendorf, D. A. (2019). Achieving appropriate model transparency: Challenges and potential solutions for making value-based decisions in the united states. *PharmacoEconomics, 37*(11), 1321–1327.

Channouf, N., L'Ecuyer, P., Ingolfsson, A., & Avramidis, A. N. (2007). The application of forecasting techniques to modeling emergency medical system calls in Calgary, Alberta. *Health Care Management Science, 10*(1), 25–45.

Christodoulou, E., Ma, J., Collins, G. S., Steyerberg, E. W., Verbakel, J. Y., & Van Calster, B. (2019) A systematic review shows no performance benefit of machine learning over logistic regression for clinical prediction models. *Journal of Clinical Epidemiology, 110*, 12–22.

Curtis, C., Liu, C., Bollerman, T. J., & Pianykh, O. S. (2018). Machine learning for predicting patient wait times and appointment delays. *Journal of the American College of Radiology, 15*(9), 1310–1316.

Dastin, J. (2018). *Amazon scraps secret AI recruiting tool that showed bias against women.* Reuters, World Wide Web, https://www.reuters.com/article/us-amazon-com-jobs-automation-insight/amazon-scraps-secret-ai-recruiting-tool-that-showed-bias-against-women-idUSKCN1MK08G. Accessed on 29 Feb 2020.

Davis, S., & Fard, N. (2020). Theoretical bounds and approximation of the probability mass function of future hospital bed demand. *Health Care Management Science, 23*(1), 20–33.

Delen, D., Fuller, C., McCann, C., & Ray, D. (2009). Analysis of healthcare coverage: A data mining approach. *Expert Systems with Applications, 36*(2), 995–1003.

Esteva, A., Kuprel, B., Novoa, R. A., Ko, J., Swetter, S. M., Blau, H. M., & Thrun, S. (2017). Dermatologist-level classification of skin cancer with deep neural networks. *Nature, 542*(7639), 115–118.

Esteva, A., Robicquet, A., Ramsundar, B., Kuleshov, V., DePristo, M., Chou, K., Cui, C., Corrado, G., Thrun, S., & Dean, J. (2019). A guide to deep learning in healthcare. *Nature Medicine, 25*(1), 24–29.

Frizzell, J. D., Liang, L., Schulte, P. J., Yancy, C. W., Heidenreich, P. A., Hernandez, A. F., Bhatt D. L., Fonarow, G. C., & Laskey, W. K. (2017). Prediction of 30-day all-cause readmissions in patients hospitalized for heart failure: Comparison of machine learning and other statistical approaches. *JAMA Cardiology, 2*(2), 204–209.

Galan, N. (2019). *How effective are skin cancer apps for early detection?* https://www.medicalnewstoday.com/articles/285751. Accessed on 13 July 2020.

Greenwald, J., Denham, C., & Jack, B. (2007). The hospital discharge: A care transition with a high potential for errors. *Journal of Patient Safety, 3*(2), 97–106.

Guy Jr, G. P., Machlin, S. R., Ekwueme, D. U., & Yabroff, K. R. (2015). Prevalence and costs of skin cancer treatment in the us, 2002–2006 and 2007–2011. *American Journal of Preventive Medicine, 48*(2), 183–187.

Hannun, A. Y., Rajpurkar, P., Haghpanahi, M., Tison, G. H., Bourn, C., Turakhia, M. P., & Ng, A. Y. (2019). Cardiologist-level arrhythmia detection and classification in ambulatory electrocardiograms using a deep neural network. *Nature Medicine, 25*(1), 65.

Harris, S. L., May, J. H., & Vargas, L. G. (2016). Predictive analytics model for healthcare planning and scheduling. *European Journal of Operational Research, 253*(1), 121–131.

Helm, J. E., Alaeddini, A., Stauffer, J. M., Bretthauer, K. M., & Skolarus, T. A. (2016). Reducing hospital readmissions by integrating empirical prediction with resource optimization. *Production and Operations Management, 25*(2), 233–257.

Jack, B., Greenwald, J., Forsythe, S., O'Donnell, J., Johnson, A., Schipelliti, L., Goodwin, M., Burniske, G. M., Hesko, C., Paasche-Orlow, M., Manasseh, C., Anthony, D., Martin, S., Hollister, L., Jack, M., Jhaveri, V., Casey, K., & Chetty, V. K. (2008). Developing the tools to administer a comprehensive hospital discharge program: The reengineered discharge (RED) program. In *Advances in patient safety: new directions and alternative approaches* (Vol. 3: Performance and Tools), Agency for Healthcare Research and Quality (US).

Jack, B., Chetty, V., Anthony, D., Greenwald, J., Sanchez, G., Johnson, A., Forsythe, S. R., O'Donnell, J. K., Paasche-Orlow, M. K., Manasseh, C., Martin, S., & Culpepper, L. (2009).

The re-engineered discharge: A RCT of a comprehensive hospital discharge program. *Annals of Internal Medicine, 150*(178), e188.

Jaleel, J. A., Salim, S., & Aswin, R. (2013). Computer aided detection of skin cancer. In *2013 International Conference on, Circuits., Power and Computing Technologies (ICCPCT)* (pp. 1137–1142). IEEE.

Jambukia, S. H., Dabhi, V. K., & Prajapati, H. B. (2015). Classification of ECG signals using machine learning techniques: A survey. In *2015 International Conference on Advances in Computer Engineering and Applications* (pp. 714–721). IEEE.

Jelodar, H., Wang, Y., Yuan, C., Feng, X., Jiang, X., Li, Y., & Zhao, L. (2019). Latent Dirichlet allocation (LDA) and topic modeling: models, applications, a survey. *Multimedia Tools and Applications, 78*(11), 15169–15211.

Jones, S. A., Joy, M. P., & Pearson, J. (2002). Forecasting demand of emergency care. *Health Care Management Science, 5*(4), 297–305.

Kansagara, D., Englander, H., Salanitro, A., Kagen, D., Theobald, C., Freeman, M., & Kripalani, S. (2011). Risk prediction models for hospital readmission: A systematic review. *Jama, 306*(15), 1688–1698.

Kayış, E., Khaniyev, T. T., Suermondt, J., & Sylvester, K. (2015). A robust estimation model for surgery durations with temporal, operational, and surgery team effects. *Health Care Management Science, 18*(3), 222–233.

Kristensen, S. R., Bech, M., & Quentin, W. (2015). A roadmap for comparing readmission policies with application to Denmark, England, Germany and the United States. *Health Policy, 119*(3), 264–273.

Lagasse, J. (2019). *Healthcare business and financial analytics market to hit $50b by 2024*. https://www.healthcarefinancenews.com/news/healthcare-business-and-financial-analytics-market-hit-50b-2024

Littig, S. J., & Isken, M. W. (2007). Short term hospital occupancy prediction. *Health Care Management Science, 10*(1), 47–66.

Mackay, M., & Lee, M. (2005). Choice of models for the analysis and forecasting of hospital beds. *Health Care Management Science, 8*(3), 221–230.

Mahmood, S. S., Levy, D., Vasan, R. S., & Wang, T. J. (2014). The Framingham heart study and the epidemiology of cardiovascular disease: a historical perspective. *The Lancet, 383*(9921), 999–1008.

Martis, R. J., Acharya, U. R., Lim, C. M., & Suri, J. S. (2013). Characterization of ECG beats from cardiac arrhythmia using discrete cosine transform in PCA framework. *Knowledge-Based Systems, 45*, 76–82.

Menke, N. B., Caputo, N., Fraser, R., Haber, J., Shields, C., & Menke, M. N. (2014). A retrospective analysis of the utility of an artificial neural network to predict ed volume. *The American Journal of Emergency Medicine, 32*(6), 614–617.

Meyer, P., Noblet, V., Mazzara, C., & Lallement, A. (2018). Survey on deep learning for radiotherapy. *Computers in Biology and Medicine, 98*, 126–146.

Min, X., Yu, B., & Wang, F. (2019). Predictive modeling of the hospital readmission risk from patients' claims data using machine learning: a case study on COPD. *Scientific Reports, 9*(1), 1–10.

Miotto, R., Wang, F., Wang, S., Jiang, X., & Dudley, J. T. (2018). Deep learning for healthcare: review, opportunities and challenges. *Briefings in Bioinformatics, 19*(6), 1236–1246.

Montenegro, J. L. Z., da Costa, C. A., & da Rosa Righi, R. (2019). Survey of conversational agents in health. *Expert Systems with Applications, 129*, 56–67.

Morgan, D. J., Bame, B., Zimand, P., Dooley, P., Thom, K. A., Harris, A. D., Bentzen, S., Ettinger, W., Garrett-Ray, S. D., Tracy, J. K., & Liang, Y. (2019). Assessment of machine learning vs standard prediction rules for predicting hospital readmissions. *JAMA Network Open, 2*(3), e190348–e190348.

Mortazavi, B. J., Downing, N. S., Bucholz, E. M., Dharmarajan, K., Manhapra, A., Li, S. X., Negahban, S. N., & Krumholz, H. M. (2016). Analysis of machine learning techniques for heart failure readmissions. *Circulation: Cardiovascular Quality and Outcomes, 9*(6), 629–640.

Nasr-Esfahani, E., Samavi, S., Karimi, N., Soroushmehr, S. M. R., Jafari, M. H., Ward, K., & Najarian, K. (2016). Melanoma detection by analysis of clinical images using convolutional neural network. In *2016 38th Annual International Conference of the IEEE Engineering in Medicine and Biology Society (EMBC)* (pp. 1373–1376). IEEE

National Research Council (2003) New opportunities, new challenges: The changing nature of biomedical science. In *Enhancing the vitality of the national institutes of health: organizational change to meet new challenges*. National Academies Press (US). https://www.ncbi.nlm.nih.gov/books/NBK43496/

Pachal, P. (2015). *Google Photos identified two black people as 'gorillas'*. Mashable.com, World Wide Web, https://mashable.com/2015/07/01/google-photos-black-people-gorillas/#N1nR3mgs1uqf. Accessed on 29 Feb 2020.

Pham, T., Tran, T., Phung, D., & Venkatesh, S. (2017). Predicting healthcare trajectories from medical records: A deep learning approach. *Journal of Biomedical informatics, 69*, 218–229.

Project Health (2019). *Avoidable hospital readmissions. report on Australian and international indicators, their use and the efficacy of interventions to reduce readmissions*. Technical Report, Sydney Australia, https://www.safetyandquality.gov.au/sites/default/files/2019-08/d19-8961_acsqhc_avoidable_hospital_readmissions_literature_review_on_australian_and_international_indicators_july_2019.pdf. Accessed on 13 July 2020.

Rajab, M., Woolfson, M., & Morgan, S. (2004). Application of region-based segmentation and neural network edge detection to skin lesions. *Computerized Medical Imaging and Graphics, 28*(1–2), 61–68.

Rajpurkar, P., Hannun, A. Y., Haghpanahi, M., Bourn, C., & Ng, A. Y. (2017). *Cardiologist-level arrhythmia detection with convolutional neural networks*. Preprint arXiv:170701836.

Reuille, R. (2004). Bed control report: a computer-based system to track patient admissions delayed or rescheduled due to a bed shortage. *JONA: The Journal of Nursing Administration, 34*(12), 539–542.

Ross, J. S., Mulvey, G. K., Stauffer, B., Patlolla, V., Bernheim, S. M., Keenan, P. S., & Krumholz H. M. (2008). Statistical models and patient predictors of readmission for heart failure: a systematic review. *Archives of Internal Medicine, 168*(13), 1371–1386.

Samala, R. K., Chan, H. P., Hadjiiski, L., Helvie, M. A., Wei, J., & Cha, K. (2016). Mass detection in digital breast tomosynthesis: Deep convolutional neural network with transfer learning from mammography. *Medical Physics, 43*(12), 6654–6666.

Samorani, M., Harris, S., Blount, L. G., Lu, H., & Santoro, M. A. (2019). *Overbooked and overlooked: machine learning and racial bias in medical appointment scheduling*. Available at SSRN 3467047.

Sharma, M., Purohit, G., & Mukherjee, S. (2018). Information retrieves from brain MRI images for tumor detection using hybrid technique k-means and artificial neural network (KMANN). In *Networking communication and data knowledge engineering* (pp. 145–157). Springer.

Shi, P., Helm, J., Deglise-Hawkinson, J., & Pan, J. (2019). *Timing it right: Balancing inpatient congestion versus readmission risk at discharge*. Available at SSRN 3202975.

Skin Cancer Foundation (2020). *Skin cancer facts and statistics*. https://www.skincancer.org/skin-cancer-information/skin-cancer-facts/. Accessed on 13 July 2020.

Society of Actuaries (2018). *2018 predictive analytics in healthcare trend forecast*.

Stanton, B. A., Jenkins, C. D., Goldstein, R. L., Vander Salm, T. J., Klein, M. D., & Aucoin R. A. (1985). Hospital readmissions among survivors six months after myocardial revascularization. *JAMA, 253*(24), 3568–3573.

Stepaniak, P. S., Heij, C., & De Vries, G. (2010). Modeling and prediction of surgical procedure times. *Statistica Neerlandica, 64*(1), 1–18.

Tiwari, V., Furman, W. R., & Sandberg, W. S. (2014). Predicting case volume from the accumulating elective operating room schedule facilitates staffing improvements. *Anesthesiology, 121*(1), 171–183.

Wang, C. J., Hamm, C. A., Savic, L. J., Ferrante, M., Schobert, I., Schlachter, T., Lin, M., Weinreb, J. C., Duncan, J. S., Chapiro, J., & Letzen, B. (2019). Deep learning for liver tumor diagnosis part ii: convolutional neural network interpretation using radiologic imaging features. *European Radiology, 29*(7), 3348–3357.

Watt, K. F. (1977). Why won't anyone believe us? *Simulation* 28 (1), 1–3.

Wertheimer, B., Jacobs, R. E., Bailey, M., Holstein, S., Chatfield, S., Ohta, B., Horrocks, A., & Hochman, K. (2014). Discharge before noon: an achievable hospital goal. *Journal of Hospital Medicine, 9*(4), 210–214.

Wilson, J. T. (1981). Implementation of computer simulation projects in health care. *Journal of the Operational Research Society, 32*(9), 825–832.

Wolff, J., Pauling, J., Keck, A., & Baumbach, J. (2020). Systematic review of economic impact studies of artificial intelligence in health care. *Journal of Medical Internet Research, 22*(2). https://doi.org/10.2196/16866.

Xie, J., Zhang, B., Ma, J., Zeng, D. D., & Lo Ciganic, J. (2018). *Readmission prediction for patients with heterogeneous medical history: A trajectory-based deep learning approach*. Available at SSRN 3144798.

Xu, K., & Chan, C. W. (2016). Using future information to reduce waiting times in the emergency department via diversion. *Manufacturing & Service Operations Management, 18*(3), 314–331.

Xue, Y., Farhat, F. G., Boukrina, O., Barrett, A., Binder, J. R., Roshan, U. W., & Graves, W. W. (2020). A multi-path 2.5 dimensional convolutional neural network system for segmenting stroke lesions in brain MRI images. *NeuroImage: Clinical, 25*, 102118.

Zaerpour, F., Bischak, D. P., Menezes, M. B. C., McRae, A., Lang, E. S. (2000). Patient classification based on volume and case-mix in the emergency department and their association with performance. *Health Care Management Science, 23*(3), 387–400.

Chapter 6
Digital Lean Operations: Smart Automation and Artificial Intelligence in Financial Services

Robert N. Boute, Joren Gijsbrechts, and Jan A. Van Mieghem

6.1 Introduction

Financial services firms focus on originating and facilitating financial transactions, including the creation, liquidation, and management of financial assets as well as the execution of transfers of ownership (Pinedo & Xu, 2017). We will focus on trade finance processing, involving all tasks that banks take to ensure correct execution of financial transactions. Accenture estimates that revenues related to these transactions will amount to up to 48 billion US dollars by 2021 (Bemmann et al., 2020). Yet many transactions are still executed manually and paper-based. The risk-averse nature of banks has resulted in few banks running their operations in a digital way. The labor-intensity of these processes has put operational efficiency improvements, in particular, with regards to cost, productivity, and risk management, high on the agenda.

Not surprisingly, concepts of lean operations have found their way to the financial services industry during the past decade(s). Lean offers the potential to lower costs and reduce errors through the elimination of waste. Lean for manufacturing and lean for finance are not that different: the paper-driven operations of financial services are

R. N. Boute
KU Leuven and Vlerick Business School, Ghent, Belgium
e-mail: robert.boute@kuleuven.be

J. Gijsbrechts
Católica Lisbon School of Business and Economics, Lisbon, Portugal
e-mail: jgijsbrechts@ucp.pt

J. A. Van Mieghem (✉)
Kellogg School of Management, Northwestern University, Evanston, IL, USA
e-mail: vanmieghem@northwestern.edu

V. Babich et al. (eds.), *Innovative Technology at the Interface of Finance and Operations*, Springer Series in Supply Chain Management 11,
https://doi.org/10.1007/978-3-030-75729-8_6

characterized by lots of waste and a need to mitigate operational risks and errors in their highly secured business environment.

The fourth industrial revolution or Industry 4.0 promises a new wave of operational efficiency improvements beyond Lean: a shift towards digital operations. A digital operation is defined as a process with digital workflow, meaning that all needed information for execution (work instructions and data) is digitized. Through digital operations, visibility to information or data can be easily shared among the various actors or "processing resources," including the customer. Hence a digital transformation can change information flow and thus lead to changes in who performs activities or how activities are performed.

Digital operations enable smarter decision-making by employing artificial intelligence, robotics, the Internet-of-Things, and cloud computing. In a nod to the fourth industrial revolution, Deutsche Bank calls their smart automation program "Operations 4.0" or "Banking 4.0." The digitization and smart automation of back-office operations may revolutionize the entire financial services industry. Large investment banks, for instance, employ thousands of people in back-office functions performing repetitive tasks manually, including settlement and clearing of trades. When these banks turn to technology to automate these processes, it may result not only in dramatic productivity improvements but also in thousands of job cuts (Clarke, 2019).

The digital transformation is further accelerated by recent events such as the Covid-19 pandemic (Baig et al., 2020). The Belgian KBC Bank, for instance, is moving from an omni-channel to a *digital-first* strategy, as clients increasingly make use of the bank's digital services during the 2020 lockdowns. More than half of its clients seldomly or no longer visits their branches. In November 2020, it introduces its digital assistant Kate to provide customized service based on data analytics and artificial intelligence (Claerhout, 2020).

A prerequisite for the benefits of automation or the application of artificial intelligence is the digitization of the process flow. Digitizing the workflow is required to automate its execution, allowing the work to be performed by a machine instead of a human. In services this is referred to as *Robotic Process Automation (RPA)*. RPA is a software application that performs automated tasks, simply known as a bot. By interacting with applications just as a human would, software bots can open email attachments, complete e-forms, record and re-key data, and perform other tasks that mimic human action. Robots and automation are well-integrated in manufacturing. Today software bots increasingly appear in the service industry as their capabilities are expanding while their development and licensing costs are falling. The economics are hard to ignore: while labor costs have been steadily rising, robot prices continue to fall. A recent McKinsey report projects that by 2030 more than a fifth of current work activities may be automated in Europe (Smit et al., 2020).

[1]Byrum (2022a) highlights *operational efficiency* as one of the three key goals of Artificial Intelligence—the highest level of smart automation we discuss in this chapter.

The digitization and automation of operations also create new opportunities for smarter decision-making. Just like self-driving vehicles rely on sensors and the state-of-the-art algorithms for autonomous driving, operations may become more autonomous and smart. The integration of cognitive capabilities, driven by artificial intelligence, into RPA platforms has led to the development of cognitive robotic process automation (CRPA) software bots. Cognitive RPA is much smarter than ordinary RPA. Whereas ordinary RPA software automates repetitive, rules-based processes usually performed by people sitting in front of computers, CRPA platforms can automate perceptual and judgment-based tasks through the integration of multiple cognitive capabilities including natural language processing, machine learning, and speech recognition.

Adopting more digital operations seems promising, but the collection of buzzwords surrounding Industry 4.0 urges the need for a holistic framework. Boute and Van Mieghem (2021) propose a diagnostic tool to map each process in terms of its current, as well as desired future state of digital, automated, and smart execution. We apply their framework to financial services. We report in a case study how a financial services firm digitizes and automates its back-office processes. Our objective is not to showcase it as the only, let alone the best, example of automation in financial service operations. Rather, the case study allows us to reflect on what service firms can learn to plan their own digitization journey. We also use the case study to give guidance to the opportunities that could emerge when employing smart intelligence applications and cognitive data-driven solutions. The solutions range from descriptive models that analyze historical data, to predictive analytics that predict what will happen, and prescriptive analytics that support the actual operational decision-making.

6.2 Diagnostic to Assess the Opportunities of Digital Operations

The emergence of data-driven technologies encourages financial services firms to digitize their operations to reap the benefits of (smart) automation. Digitization also can provide a strategic response to, and easy interaction with, agile fin tech start-ups that thrive on these technologies. While digitization may spur automation and autonomy, it may also open the door to transition towards smarter data-driven decision-making.

The digitization of financial service operations seems a promising avenue to drive efficiency gains, as many processes in financial services remain paper-driven and high-volume and repetitive tasks comprise a significant portion of the industry. Accenture estimates that approximately 60% of the processes in financial services are repetitive and profitable to be automated; the remaining 40% require too many complex tasks such as handling exceptions or checking information from third-parties on the Internet (Bemmann et al., 2020). Many processes also suffer from country-dependent regulations at both sides of the transaction creating a tangled web of rules and requirements. They come with several controls to validate whether all documents are complete and correct. These checks are so complex that they can only be automated by a machine (bot) that is sufficiently intelligent or "smart."

To identify how financial firms can benefit from digitization we leverage the framework of Boute and Van Mieghem (2021) that captures the levels of *Digitization*, *Automation*, and *Smart execution* (DAS) of a process. The DAS framework, depicted in Fig. 6.1, evaluates the depth of each process across each of its three dimensions.

While there is no prescribed sequence to implement digitization, automation, and smart controls, in service operations digitization often is the first step prior to automating operations and using data to add intelligence. The automation of simple repetitive tasks through RPA bots requires the digitization of the workflows, as well as the existence of the data in digital format. While simple tasks are performed by executing straightforward instructions or scripts, more advanced processes generally require more intelligence and smart control algorithms. Automation and smart

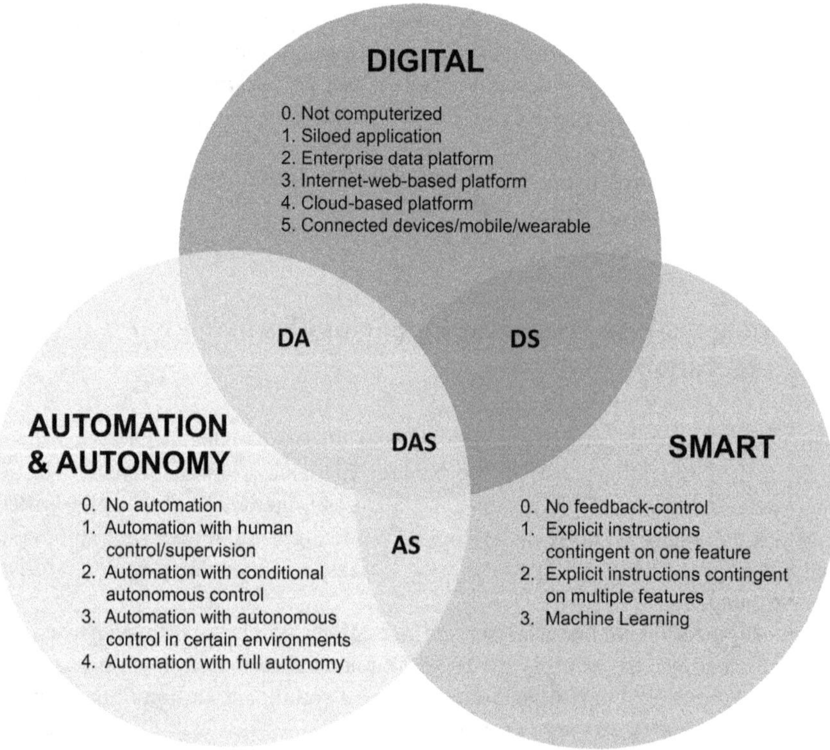

Fig. 6.1 The DAS framework of Boute and Van Mieghem (2021) evaluates the levels and reach of a process' digitization, automation, and smart control

control are thus intertwined for complex processes. In Sect. 6.4 we explore how data science can support the transition towards smart automation.

Consider, for example, the clearance of a simple payment. Its process consists of four sequential steps (Bemmann et al., 2020). First, a staff member receives the information of the transaction, either on paper or in a digital format, and transfers the information into the system. Subsequently, reviews and checks (e.g., credit checks) are performed. Then, anti-money laundering and anti-financial crime compliance checks are completed before the decision is made to proceed. Finally, all required inputs related to the transaction are approved and sent to an external SWIFT company that executes all transactions.

The evaluation of the levels and reach of digitization, automation, and smart control of this payment process provides a diagnostic tool that can guide future directions. Adopting the DAS framework, we assess five levels of digitization (see red circle of Fig. 6.1). A Level 0 digital process is a non-digital paper-driven process. Upgrading our payment process to a level 1 digital process would entail that the documents are sent in a digital format, but the process is siloed such that the obtained data cannot be easily shared across departments. For instance, papers are received digitally as a scan, but information needs to be copied manually to a different system to perform the credit checks and maybe even a different system to interact with the external SWIFT supplier. Upgrading to a level 2 digital process integrates silos through the development of an enterprise platform. This way, once information has been entered into the system different checks no longer require a manual transfer of information. When the company-wide system is connected to the Internet, the process reaches digital level 3, such that the firm may easily share data across companies or integrate with various partners. For instance, when data is missing a digital message can be sent back to the customer or the process can be integrated with the SWIFT supplier. The shift towards cloud-based solutions, in which hardware is no longer on-premise but shared, results in digital level 4, allowing to easily scale up or down. When the number of transactions fluctuates significantly between periods cloud solutions allow the bank to rent additional capacity only on high-volume months. Evolving to digital level 5 would allow for full connectivity between systems and connected physical devices within the Internet-of-Things. For instance, customer apps may gather information from customers and the data may be used to perform credit checks.

Once the workflows are digitized, one can consider the automation of their execution (see yellow circle in Fig. 6.1). Level 0 automation implies that payments may be digitized but all steps are still manual, i.e., performed by a human. A level 1 automated process would entail automation but always under full supervision of a person who would verify every step. For instance, the checks could be performed by a bot, but a human would always validate before proceeding to the next task. When checks run autonomously if certain conditions are satisfied (e.g., payment amount is below a certain threshold and no data entries are missing), the process is at (autonomous) automation level 2. The level of autonomy can be further increased when the execution runs fully automated for several restricted environments, in which case it is denoted automation level 3. For instance, several countries may allow for full automation of payments while others may not. Only in automation level 4 does the process run automatically with full autonomy and no longer requires any human checks.

The mere digitization and automation of the workflow do not imply intelligence in its execution. Yet, a digital foundation enables companies to utilize advanced algorithms, including artificial intelligence, for real-time analysis and optimization. Significant advancements have been made in that respect. We can again distinguish different levels of smart control (see blue circle in Fig. 6.1). Smart level 0 implies there is no intelligence or feedback-control in the execution of the work. In smart level 1 explicit instructions are followed, either by a human or by the machine, based on one variable or "feature." For instance, a payment check is only processed if and only if all data entries are completed. A smart level 2 control check would include multiple features and multiple if-then statements to steer a process. This corresponds to a rigorously defined decision-tree that leaves no room for interpretation. When the number of features is very large, hard-coding explicit instructions become impractical, if not impossible, such that more advanced algorithms become desirable. Smart level 3 features machine learning algorithms that may use an exceedingly large number of input variables to suggest or make a decision.[2]An algorithm may, for instance, screen all inputs related to the background of customers to decide whether an additional check of the form is needed. While artificial intelligence consists of all algorithms that broadly mimic human abilities, machine learning is a subset of AI in which machines no longer receive specific instructions on how to perform a task but learn based on a reward function. Especially deep learning, a subgroup of ML in which large neural nets mimic the human brain, has gained significant attention recently due to significant performance improvements.

In the next section we apply the DAS framework to Euroclear, a global provider of financial market infrastructure services that settles domestic and international securities transactions, covering bonds, equities, derivatives, and investment funds.

6.3 Digital Operations at Euroclear

Euroclear provides securities services to financial institutions located in more than 90 countries. In 2020 they have about 1400 FTEs working in Operations. The bank launched an ambitious lean transformation program in 2007. They adopted a structured and standardized approach where the different organizational units were transformed in different "waves." Their lean journey was mainly focused on standardization, reduction of variability and process efficiency improvements.[3]

---

[2]See Bao et al. (2022) for a more in-depth discussion on the use of AI for fraud detection.

[3]The lean program mainly focused on Euroclear's back-end operations, similarly to those defined in Byrum (2022b).

Ten years after the start of their lean journey, Euroclear initiated a digital operations program as the next continuous improvement program after lean. The bank did not abandon their lean principles; on the contrary, they continue with the same efforts as before. Nonetheless, as the cost of software robots continued to fall, the time was ripe to start with the next stage of operational excellence, call it Lean 2.0.

Euroclear follows the Eliminate-Optimize-Automate (EOA) approach. Similar to the introduction of lean in their different organizational units, they digitize their operations in waves, where each wave comprises the following steps per workflow:

- First analyze the process and simplify the workflow, which means identifying and eliminating unnecessary redundancies and waste;
- Next optimize and standardize the workflow as much as possible;
- Finally, automate the standard optimized workflow by developing a software bot. Euroclear outsources bot development to a third party.

This EOA approach shows that digital operations do not replace lean. In fact, just the opposite is true. For every wave, Euroclear first goes back to the core lean principles: eliminate waste, optimize, and standardize the workflow. Only then is a bot developed to automate the workflow (see also Fig. 6.2). Once the bot is developed, the workflow is again reconsidered in function of the bot to further eliminate waste and re-optimize the workflow. If it turns out that a bot cannot automate the work, it is analyzed whether the workflow can be adapted to make the bot work. Each wave takes about 2–3 months for the process analysis and about 2–4 months for the development of the bot. Euroclear targets about 6–8 waves per year, so that all operations are digitized in 3 years' time.

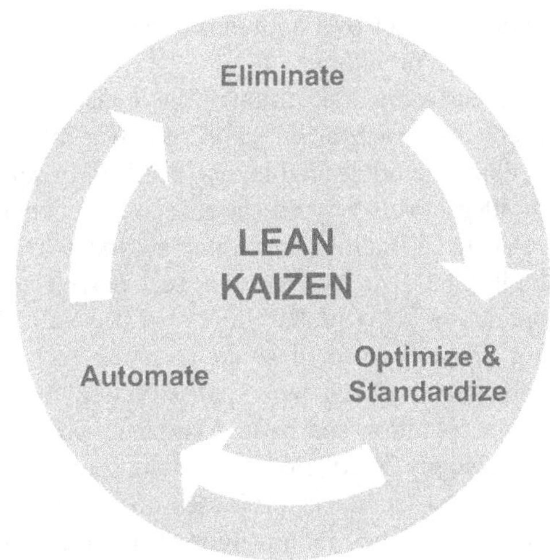

Fig. 6.2 The Eliminate-Optimize-Automate (EOA) approach adopts the traditional lean methods of waste elimination, process optimization, and standardization prior to automating the workflow. Once automated, a continuous improvement (kaizen) loop reconsiders the workflow in function of the bot to further eliminate waste and re-optimize the workflow

One example is the current digitization of tax certificates, where a team previously had to manually process thousands of tax certificates based on input received in paper forms or in pdf format. In the former case, smart scanning technologies are required. Even if data are received from a digital pdf format, the challenge remains that these tax forms are country-dependent. That means that as long as these forms are not standardized, significant programming work is required to cope with exceptions. Every automation for which an exception has to be accommodated, is costly. Therefore, prior to automation, the structure of these input forms is revised to facilitate further automation of the workflow, as also prescribed by the EOA approach.

Interestingly, the organizational units that were not successful during the lean transformation, are also not successful with automation. The potential of automation to a large extent depends on how much waste was removed; otherwise one "automates waste." Lean also led to standardization, which is a key enabler for automation: without standardization, it is difficult and expensive to automate the workflow.

During each wave the most repetitive tasks are tackled first, and it is those tasks where most time and workload is spent. This thought process, in combination with the available technologies (as not everything can be automated), gives guidance on what to automate first. Complex tasks with moderate uncertainty, such as workflows in marketing or human resources are much harder to automate.

Euroclear started with attended or supervised automation, where a digital application on the desktop supports the human operator. This is equivalent to Automation level 1 in Fig. 6.1. Euroclear gradually transitions to autonomous automation, where the bots execute the workflow autonomously in the background. For simple standardized processes, Euroclear has implemented autonomous automation level 2 (i.e., provided certain conditions are met), and level 3 (for certain restricted countries with standardized inputs). The regular execution of the process requires no human intervention or oversight during the normal course of operations. This provides the true value of automation.

Clearly, the digitization of the input data is a prerequisite for further automation. Many data points are already digitally available, either in pdf files or in spreadsheets. If those are not available, one needs to manually enter these fields into the system, or alternatively rely on smart scanning technologies. The latter require some form of artificial intelligence, which are today available in off-the-shelf text recognition tools (and also discussed in Sect. 6.4). The output of these AI applications is a prediction or a "probability" of the specific data. At this moment Euroclear does not yet make use of smart scanning technologies, yet they are exploring their application. Given the rapid evolution in prediction accuracy improvements of text recognition and natural language processing techniques, we believe they will increasingly be adopted in practice, spurring digitization to higher levels.

Several Euroclear processes do not yet run full autonomous due to the complexity, and they require (conditional) human control or supervision (automation levels 1 or 2)—which aligns with their inherent risk-aversion. Yet, as the cognitive performance of machine learning algorithms continues to reach higher levels, this form of attended automation may in the future gradually be replaced by more autonomy (automation levels 3 or 4). Evolving towards more autonomy typically requires an increase in the level of smart control. For instance, cognitive intelligence embedded in the so-called smart algorithms may support the development of customized FAQs or chat bots[4]to support and/or fully replace the human operator. Or, an algorithm may perform a credit check and decide autonomously to contact the customer for additional information before independently approving or rejecting a transaction. Enhancing the level of smart control within financial operations, however, requires an investment in new skills and technologies to reap the full benefits of smart automation. We elaborate on the promise of smart automation in the next section.

6.4 The Promise of Smart Automation

The Euroclear case demonstrates how digitization enables the automation of standardized processes. In addition to removing waste from processes, digital operations also open up new opportunities to embed intelligence in the form of smarter control algorithms. We believe this is a plausible, natural path in financial services: first digitize and automate simple tasks using the EOA approach, then reap the benefits of adding intelligence, which in its turn can enable further automation of more complex processes. Intelligence by machines comes from their ability to learn based on data. It is thus no surprise that these self-learning algorithms are thriving on the tremendous increase in data generation, further fueled by companies continuing to digitize their operations. Not only is the data collection exploding, affordable computational power is now easily accessible through cloud solutions while data-driven algorithms become increasingly powerful, largely driven by advancements in machine learning. The flourishing *data science* field allows adding more intelligence into processes and further enhance autonomous automation.

Embracing artificial intelligence and incorporating data science is vital for transitioning towards *smart* automation of complex processes. Companies excelling in the adoption of data science have thrived, with Apple, Amazon, and Alibaba as lead examples approaching or exceeding dazzling trillion-dollar valuations. Tesla's market cap quadrupled in the first half of 2020 as investors continue to bet on its disruptive technologies such as its autonomous driving software. In the wake of these successes more traditional firms—such as the trade finance processing industry we study—increasingly incorporate data-driven strategies resulting in a raging war for data science talent (Smit et al., 2020). In what follows we highlight some important recent advancements at the intersection of data science and operations. While the former usually aims at extracting insights from data, the latter

[4]See also Anderson et al. (2022) for an additional example of autonomous operations and chat bots in healthcare operations.

typically focuses on enhancing the actual decision-making. Increasingly, however, we observe a convergence and merger of both fields—especially in the most advanced methods. Embracing data-driven technologies may push the operations of traditional firms into the era of analytics, in which data is used to gain insights as well as support decision-making.

When adding intelligence from data, it is useful to distinguish among descriptive, predictive, and prescriptive analytics.[5] *Descriptive analytics* shed light on what is hidden in big data pools. They focus on describing what happened, for instance, through the development of business intelligence tools or dashboards that closely monitor the process and spot anomalies. Typical tools include querying languages such as SQL, often combined with visualization applications such as Power BI, Tableau, or Excel. Descriptive analytics are essential to steer managers towards the right decisions. In financial services, for instance, identifying which tasks of the payment process consumed most time provides valuable information on how the end-to-end payment clearing processing time can be most effectively reduced. In addition to the mere visualization of data, a deeper analysis may come from unsupervised machine learning algorithms, such as k-means or hierarchical clustering. These algorithms effectively reduce the dimension of data by clustering large sets of elements within a data set into smaller clusters. This is useful to segment customers or financial assets to take more tailored actions. In financial services, for instance, this could support the segmentation of customers into smaller subgroups and have better targeted credit checks. A higher prediction accuracy of anomalies may enable higher levels of automation and autonomy in deciding which customers to check, effectively reducing the need for humans to intervene.

Predictive analytics elevate data analysis to a higher level by not only describing the past but also predicting future process behavior. For instance, we may forecast future sales, customer needs, or processing times based on actual performance. Traditionally, mathematical and statistical tools were used to predict the future. In its simplest form a simple linear regression model may translate historical data into a forecast. Nowadays, more advanced algorithms have come into play. Supervised machine learning methods rely on labeled data to train an algorithm to predict the labels. Recent breakthroughs have made these techniques more powerful than ever. In particular, the performance of deep learning has soared during the past decade, also raising the bar of predictive analytics technologies. Deep learning relies on a neural network with multiple layers between input and output, mirroring how the human brain processes information. In 2010 a deep neural net beat the best benchmark in the ImageNet competition (Russakovsky et al., 2014) where algorithms must recognize (or predict) the content of a picture. Neural nets are now embedded in many devices and applications such as face recognition, self-driving vehicles screening their environment or speech, and text recognition supporting virtual chat bot assistants.

[5]Our discussion is complementary to Bastani et al. (2022). An excellent example of using predictive and prescriptive analytics in retail is provided in Li et al. (2022).

Predictive analytics offer great potential in financial services, for instance, through their integration in smart bots (Claerhout, 2020) or text recognition facilitating the digitization of paper documents. Programming a neural network is more advanced compared to traditional if-then-else coding. Yet, major technology firms such as Google and Facebook have developed high-level libraries such as TensorFlow, Keras, or PyTorch that interface well with popular coding languages of data scientists such as Python or R. With limited coding knowledge data scientists now have these powerful tools at their disposal. While predictive analytics are useful to support decision-making, the actual decision is still made by a human. In order to eliminate the need for human supervision, corresponding to automation levels 3 and 4 of the DAS framework, more advanced methods are desirable.

This is where *prescriptive analytics*, the most advanced type of analytics, come into play. In addition to predicting future behavior, prescriptive analytics also devise explicit instructions (prescriptions). In machine learning, for instance, we observe remarkable breakthroughs in reinforcement learning where an agent (a bot) trains itself through trial and error to take the (near-optimal) actions in each specific state of the process. The combination of deep learning and reinforcement learning resulted in algorithms to outperform human behavior, initially in simple Atari computer games (Mnih et al., 2013) and later in very complex settings where the number of states is exceedingly large. A milestone was reached in 2016 when the deep reinforcement learning algorithm named AlphaGo beat the best human player Lee Sedol in the ancient game of Go (Mnih et al., 2015). The ancient game of Go has about 10^{172} possible states, more than the number of atoms in the universe. Enumerating explicit instructions (prescriptions) for how to play in each state is impossible. The same prescriptive deep learning algorithms can be used to make decisions in complex environments in financial services. For instance, the decision to perform a credit check could be made autonomously based on all information available (representing the state of the system) in order to minimize the risk (i.e., the reward function).

Adopting the most advanced analytics and smart autonomous algorithms not only requires a mental mind shift, it also requires a new type of programming. The sequential if-then-else decision logic is replaced by more advanced methods such as deep learning to support and even make decisions autonomously. A downside of deep learning methods is that their excellent ability to approximate very complex functions comes at the cost of a lack of interpretability. Despite research efforts focusing on their interpretability (Molnar, 2020), the output of deep learning algorithms remains a *black box*, leaving managers puzzled about the behavior of the models. In contrast, alternatives such as decision trees are easier to interpret and may perform well dependent on the application and the amount of data available (Bertsimas & Dunn, 2019). Random forests (Breiman, 2001) combine multiple trees and have been widely adopted in research and practice, despite being less interpretable than simple decision trees. As understanding of the output of a model is essential in some business settings, new research streams such as safe learning focus on the interpretation of results and policies. The developments of these research streams are necessary to make machines more autonomous. Explaining machine behavior also is essential from a regulatory and legal perspective for implementing autonomous automation.

6.5 Discussion

After years of implementing lean programs, digital operations have the potential to further improve operational efficiency. In financial services, digitization can facilitate automating the workflow of back-office operations. Digitizing alone, however, is not a magic bullet. Digitizing and automating a process teeming with waste would simply automate waste. Digital operations are thus not a replacement for the traditional lean implementation. Rather, in certain industries including financial services, the combination of lean and digital operations amplifies the impact of each individually and can yield greater benefit than the sum of its parts.

Some tasks and processes are more amenable to autonomous automation than others. A useful start is segmenting operational activities into standardized repetitive operations versus customized processes with more complexity and uncertainty. Digitizing and automating standardized and controlled processes are more likely to result in efficiency improvements. More complex processes require smart control, possibly including artificial intelligence tools, before automation is considered.

Similar to the continuous improvement (kaizen) cycle in traditional lean operations and the EOA approach (Fig. 6.2), continuous improvement should also be pursued with automated complex processes: During operation, more data is generated that can further improve the algorithmic prescription (i.e., "continuing machine learning"). The generation of additional data may also require investment in more advanced levels of digitization. For example, the installation of remote sensors and/or additional computation power may lead to digitization levels 4 and 5 in the DAS framework. This in turn may improve the level of intelligence and smart control, and the resulting higher prediction accuracy of the smart algorithms can then lead to higher levels of autonomy. Figure 6.3 graphically summarizes this symbiosis of the digital DAS framework with traditional lean operations, which is our view of lean 2.0.

The symbiosis between human and machine also presents novel questions about our embrace of automation and artificial intelligence on the work floor. Will office clerks need to be able to work with software bots, just like many can work with spreadsheets? And how will we learn to work with AI? At the end of the day, smart algorithms relying on artificial intelligence are seldom perfect; most work with confidence intervals. Will we trust a bot that returns a result with confidence level of 90%, and is such bot economical? Clearly, if a manual check is required to eliminate the 10% uncertainty, the automation has less value. A higher degree of automation can only be obtained when we can increase the level of confidence in the algorithms. And yes, bots make mistakes just like humans do. But the former is harder to accept.

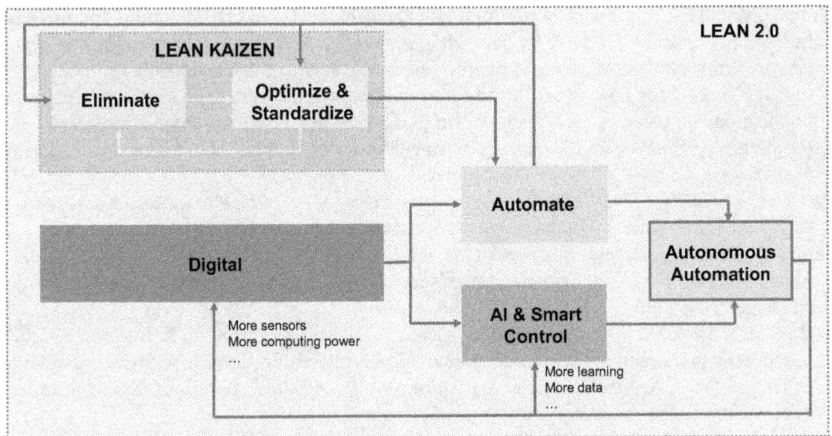

Fig. 6.3 Lean 2.0 aims for operational excellence by combining traditional lean operations and digitization. Automation of simple financial services back-office processes requires both. Autonomous automation of complex processes additionally requires artificial intelligence and smart control.

Acknowledgments We are grateful to Yvan Vangeneugden for his input on Euroclear's digital operations journey.

References

Anderson, D., Bjarnadottir, M. V., & Nenova, Z. (2022). Machine learning in healthcare: Operational and financial impact. In Babich, V., Birge, J., & Hilary, G. (Eds.), *Innovative technology at the interface of finance and operations*. Springer Series in Supply Chain Management. Springer Nature.

Baig, A., Hall, B., Jenkins, P., Lamarre, E., & McCarthy, B. (2020). The covid-19 recovery will be digital: A plan for the first 90 days. *McKinsey Digital*. https://www.mckinsey.com/business-functions/mckinsey-digital/our-insights/the-covid-19-recovery-will-be-digital-a-plan-for-the-first-90-days

Bao, Y., Hilary, G., & Ke, B. (2022). Artificial intelligence and fraud detection. In Babich, V., Birge, J., & Hilary, G. (Eds.), *Innovative technology at the interface of finance and operations*. Springer Series in Supply Chain Management. Springer Nature.

Bastani, H., Zhang, D. J., & Zhang, H. (2022). Applied machine learning in operations management. In Babich, V., Birge, J., & Hilary, G. (Eds.), *Innovative technology at the interface of finance and operations*. Springer Series in Supply Chain Management. Springer Nature.

Bemmann, R., Ranjan, R., & Ramaswamy, V. (2020). *Automation in trade finance processing*. https://www.accenture.com/_acnmedia/PDF-117/Accenture-Trade-Finance-Processing-Automation

Bertsimas, D., & Dunn, J. (2019). *Machine Learning Under a Modern Optimization Lens*. Dynamic-Ideas.

Boute, R. L., & Van Mieghem, J. A. (2021). Digital operations: Autonomous automation and the smart execution of work. *Management and Business Review, 1*(1), 177–186.

Breiman, L. (2001). Random forests. *Machine Learning, 45*, 5–32.

Byrum, J. (2022a). Ai in financial portfolio management: Practical considerations and use cases. In Babich, V., Birge, J., & Hilary, G. (Eds.), *Innovative technology at the interface of finance and operations*. Springer Series in Supply Chain Management. Springer Nature.

Byrum, J. (2022b). The past, present, and future of the payment system as trusted broker and the implications for banking. In Babich, V., Birge, J., & Hilary, G. (Eds.), *Innovative technology at the interface of finance and operations*. Springer Series in Supply Chain Management. Springer Nature.

Claerhout, P. (2020). *KBC lanceert digitale assistente kate*. https://trends.knack.be/economie/bedrijven/kbc-lanceert-digitale-assistente-kate/article-analyse-1612181.html

Clarke, P. (2019). *Deutsche bank turns to robots to meet 18,000 job cut target. Financial News*. https://www.fnlondon.com/articles/deutsche-bank-turns-to-robots-to-meet-18000-job-cut-target-20191118

Li, H., Simchi-Levi, D., Sun, R., Wu, M. X., Fux, V., Gellert, T., Greiner, T., & Taverna, A. (2022). Large-scale price optimization for an online fashion retailer. In Babich, V., Birge, J., & Hilary, G. (Eds.), *Innovative technology at the interface of finance and operations*. Springer Series in Supply Chain Management, Forthcoming. Springer Nature.

Mnih, V., Kavukcuoglu, K., Silver, D., Graves, A., Antonoglou, I., Wierstra, D., & Riedmiller, M. (2013). *Playing Atari with deep reinforcement learning*. Preprint arXiv:13125602

Mnih, V., Kavukcuoglu, K., Silver, D., Rusu, A. A., Veness, J., Bellemare, M. G., Graves, A., Riedmiller, M., Fidjeland, A. K., Ostrovski, G., Petersen, S., Beattie, C., Sadik, A., Antonoglou, I., King, H., Kumaran, D., Wierstra, D., Legg, S., & Hassabis, D. (2015) Human-level control through deep reinforcement learning. *Nature, 518*, 529–533.

Molnar, C. (2020). *Interpretable machine learning*. Leanpub.

Pinedo, M., & Xu, Y. (2017). Operations in financial services: Processes, technologies, and risks. *Foundations and Trends in Technology, Information and Operations Management, 11*(3), 223–342.

Russakovsky, O., Deng, J., Su, H., Krause, J., Satheesh, S., Ma, S., Huang, Z., Karpathy, A., Khosla, A., Bernstein, M., Berg, A. C., Fei-Fei, L. (2014). *ImageNet large scale visual recognition challenge*. PreprintarXiv:1409.0575

Smit, S., Tacke, T., Lund, S., Manyika, J., Thiel, L. (2020). *The future of work in Europe*. https://www.mckinsey.com/featured-insights/future-of-work/the-future-of-work-in-europe

Chapter 7
Applied Machine Learning in Operations Management

Hamsa Bastani, Dennis J. Zhang, and Heng Zhang

7.1 Introduction

In recent years, the abundance of data being collected and stored, together with more affordable and faster computing power, has driven algorithms' rapid development to find trends or patterns in data. This has given rise to the field of machine learning (ML). Born as a sub-field of computer science, it uses light modeling assumptions and relies on data, statistics, and computational theory to build scalable algorithms capable of dealing with large data sets to discover useful decision rules. As more algorithms are discovered to cover a wide range of applications from business to engineering, ML is helping most academic fields substantially improve their use of data sets, and the field of operations management (OM) is no exception. On the one hand, ML has helped OM researchers to better solve estimation problems in operations design and optimization. On the other hand, it has triggered OM researchers to rethink OM problems—besides using mathematical models to derive insights, one can also combine ML algorithms and data to facilitate accurate predictions, discover diagnoses, and directly find solutions for the problem at hand.

In this chapter, we aim to provide a preliminary introduction to the modern ML literature (for a more in-depth discussion of ML literature, readers can refer to

H. Bastani
Wharton Business School, University of Pennsylvania, Philadelphia, PA, USA
e-mail: hamsab@wharton.upenn.edu

D. J. Zhang
Olin Business School, Washington University in St. Louis, St. Louis, MO, USA
e-mail: denniszhang@wustl.edu

H. Zhang (✉)
W. P. Carey School of Business, Arizona State University, Tempe, AZ, USA
e-mail: hengzhang24@asu.edu

V. Babich et al. (eds.), *Innovative Technology at the Interface of Finance and Operations*, Springer Series in Supply Chain Management 11,
https://doi.org/10.1007/978-3-030-75729-8_7

Bishop, 2006; Friedman et al., 2001; Goodfellow et al., 2016) and to shed light on how the ML literature has helped to reshape the OM literature in recent years. The ML literature can be classified into *supervised learning*, *unsupervised learning*, and *reinforcement learning*. In *supervised learning*, ML models are trained with labeled data to learn a function mapping from inputs, often referred to as features, and outputs (i.e., labels) based on example input-output pairs. In *unsupervised learning*, the ML algorithm tries to look for data patterns in a data set with no pre-existing labels. For example, one may consider the day-to-day operations of an online advertising platform that helps manage the advertisers' campaigns. The platform collects a huge number of data records of users visiting websites and clicking on ads. Supervised learning helps the platform to predict whether a given user will click on a given advertisement. In this case, the focal user's historical behaviors, as well as demographics and the characteristics of ads, are features, and the label is the focal user's action towards an ad, such as a click or conversion. In this same setting, one can also utilize unsupervised learning to identify patterns of previous consumer behaviors, classify consumers into different categories, and adjust ad exposure accordingly. This example falls into unsupervised learning since the customer categories are learned from the features rather than the labels.

The third type of ML problem, related to the extensive dynamic optimization literature in OM, is *reinforcement learning*. It applies to settings in which an agent interacts with the environment, takes different actions, and learns from the resulting reward. Unlike supervised learning, where rewards are immediately defined (based on whether the label is correct), the rewards in reinforcement learning are more long-term since the state can be dynamically altered by actions. The *multi-arm bandit* (MAB) problem is an essential and special case of reinforcement learning, where there is only one state. As an example, in online advertising platforms, firms may use reinforcement learning to continuously update advertising strategies during consumer interactions to maximize long-term cumulative revenue and minimize the long-term impact of ads on consumer experience.

On the OM side, one can divide ML models' application in OM settings into two types, *descriptive analysis* and *prescriptive analysis*, depending on the desired research goals. In the former, ML models' results either carry important managerial insights by themselves or can be directly used in operational decision-making. In the latter, ML models are embedded as part of an optimization problem to solve typical operations problems. Nowadays, all three ML models discussed above are applied in descriptive and prescriptive analyses in OM. For example, one may also refer to Boute et al. (2022) for an in-depth discussion about the potential of using ML for both descriptive and prescriptive analytics in financial service industry operations.

We organize the remainder of this chapter as follows. In Sect. 7.2, we provide a parsimonious introduction to the history of the ML literature. We discuss supervised learning in Sect. 7.3, unsupervised learning in Sect. 7.4, and reinforcement learning in Sect. 7.5. In each section, we provide a brief introduction of the background knowledge and an overview of how one can use these tools in the OM literature. In Sect. 7.6, we conclude the chapter and discuss future possible research directions at the intersection of ML and OM.

7.2 A Brief History of ML

Early ML techniques emerged from ideas in the statistical modeling literature. Two prominent examples in this literature are linear regression, whose creation is often attributed to Adrien-Marie Legendre and Carl Gauss in the nineteenth century, and Bayesian inference, which Thomas Bayes and Pierre-Simon Laplace founded in the eighteenth-century (Angrist & Pischke, 2008; Berger, 2013). In both examples, statistical models were utilized to extract patterns from data that were useful for decision-making. The real interest in using machines to solve statistical models and find patterns—or in other words, "learn"—did not occur until the 1950s and 1960s. Arthur Samuel, an American pioneer who worked for IBM, created the first computer learning programs designed to play checkers in 1952 and coined the term "machine learning" in 1959 (McCarthy & Feigenbaum, 1990). In 1957, Frank Rosenblatt created the very first neural network for computers. In 1963, Donald Michie started using reinforcement learning to play Tic-tac-toe (Wylie, 2018). 1967 saw the invention of nearest neighbor algorithms, which is often regarded as the start of modern pattern recognition (Marr, 2016). During this period, the ML community also showed renewed interest in Bayesian methods. Then in the 1970s, the ML community was relatively silent, perhaps due to the first "AI winter" caused by pessimism about the ability of ML to solve real-world problems.

Researchers' interest in ML began to pick up again in the 1980s. In 1982, John Hopfield popularized Hopfield networks, a type of recurrent neural network that can serve as content-addressable memory systems (Hopfield, 1982). The critical step of using backpropagation in neural networks came in 1986, when David Rumelhart, Geoffrey Hinton, and Ronald J. Williams extended an earlier algorithm created in 1962 (Rumelhart et al., 1986). This allowed multiple layers to be used in a neural network and dramatically increased neural networks' power in approximating complex functions. Simultaneously, the seminal work Breiman et al. (1984) on decision trees, published in 1984, marked the start of tree-based learning methods. In 1989, Christopher Watkins developed Q-learning, which significantly improved the performance of reinforcement learning (Watkins, 1989).

The popularity of ML kept increasing in the research community in the 1990s, and many important discoveries were made. A fundamental shift in ML, triggered by the rapid growth of computing power and data availability, was from a knowledge-driven approach to a data-driven approach. The concept of boosting was first presented in a paper by Rober Schapire (Schapire, 1990). In 1995, Tin Kam Ho published a paper discussing random decision forests (Ho, 1995), and the influential work on support vector machines (SVM) by Corinna Cortes and Vladimir Vapnik was published (Cortes & Vapnik, 1995). Sepp Hochreiter and Jürgen Schmidhuber invented long short-term memory (LSTM) recurrent neural networks in 1997, greatly improving the efficiency and practicality of recurrent neural networks (Hochreiter & Schmidhuber, 1997). In that same year, a remarkable event marked the first super-human behavior of machines in human games—the IBM computer

Deep Blue, which utilized decision rules and statistical models to play chess, beat the world chess champion.

Named by Geoffrey Hinton in 2006, deep learning is a type of supervised learning built on large neural networks (Hinton et al., 2006), and it has played an essential role in ML development in the twenty-first century. ImageNet was created by Fei-Fei Li in 2009 (Deng et al., 2009). It is a large visual database, often deemed the catalyst for the deep learning boom of the twenty-first century, since many deep learning researchers test their work using this database. The influential paper Glorot et al. (2011) was published in 2011, showing that neurons based on the rectified linear unit (ReLU) can result in better training and better performance of deep neural networks. The generative adversarial network (GAN) was proposed in 2014 (Goodfellow et al., 2014). These developments immensely helped popularize the application of deep learning in both academia and industry. Many leading information technology firms realized the importance of ML and its enormous potential for their business growth and decided to join the field. Several large projects, such as GoogleBrain by Google (2012), DeepFace by Facebook (2014), and DeepMind by Google (2014), led the development of ML in this new era in the industry. In particular, in 2014, Facebook researchers published their work on DeepFace, which could identify faces with 97.35% accuracy, rivaling human performance (Taigman et al., 2014). In 2016, the AlphaGo algorithm developed by DeepMind defeated a professional player at the Chinese board game Go, which is considered the most complex board game in human history. Later, AlphaZero, which extended the techniques from AlphaGo and combined them with reinforcement learning to train itself from zero bases, was able to surpass the ability of AlphaGo with only 3 days' training.

In the OM literature, the practice of applying an ML-related approach may have started with the early applications of time series methods in demand forecasting for inventory problems, such as the well-known Box-Jenkins method (Box et al., 1970) and other subsequent extensions (Croston, 1972; Gardner Jr, 1985). Regression models, often regarded as one of the fundamental techniques in ML, usually serve as the building blocks in such applications. The last decade has witnessed a growing trend of data analytics in OM research, owing to the increasing availability of data and computing power. This has led to the fast-growing literature in this area, which we discuss in detail in the next three sections.

7.3 Supervised Learning

In this section, we focus on supervised learning. After a brief introduction, we will review applications in both descriptive and prescriptive problems in OM.

7.3.1 General Introduction to Supervised Learning

Supervised learning algorithms are designed to "learn by example"—i.e., to infer a function from a set of labeled training examples. These training examples serve as "supervisors" to ensure that the algorithm generates a model that can produce a high-quality forecast of these labels. More formally, one may write each training example in the form of $(\mathbf{x}_i, y_i)$, with $\mathbf{x}_i$ as the observed feature vector and y_i as the observed label, which can be either discrete or continuous. We usually assume that $(\mathbf{x}_i, y_i)$ are i.i.d. realizations from certain unknown distribution. For example, $\mathbf{x}_i$ may describe the characteristics of a customer visiting a website, such as gender, age, location, and even the brand of the mobile device being used; and $y_i = 1$ if the consumer clicks an advertisement and 0 otherwise. A supervised learning algorithm would choose a function f from a class of functions, say $\mathcal{F}$, such that $y_i \approx f(\mathbf{x}_i)$. The quality of learning is usually measured by the difference between the predicted labels and the correct label in the data (commonly referred to as a loss function), such as the widely used mean squared error (MSE). In this case, one can describe the training loss of any function $f \in \mathcal{F}$ as

$$\sum_i (y_i - f(\mathbf{x}_i))^2.$$

Then, in the training process, we aim to find $\hat{f} \in \mathcal{F}$ that minimizes or approximately minimizes the chosen error metric. Once the function $\hat{f}$ is trained, it is usually straightforward to apply it in a new testing example with feature vector $\mathbf{x}$ and to predict its label as $f(\mathbf{x})$.

It is not always desirable to specify a very complex function class $\mathcal{F}$, so that one can drive the training loss as small as possible or even achieve zero training loss. A function class of higher complexity usually has a lower bias, meaning that it entails a function that can better mimic the true underlying relationship between $\mathbf{x}_i$ and y_i. However, with high complexity, the training process's output, $\hat{f}(\cdot)$, is usually more sensitive to small fluctuations in the training data and, therefore, exhibits a more considerable variance. This usually leads to a model with inadequate generalizability that over-fits the training data's noise and performs poorly on the new testing data. This well-known phenomenon is called *bias-variance tradeoff*.

In fact, one can show that the mean squared error on the true underlying distribution, which arguably represents what a modeler is genuinely interested in, can be exactly decomposed as the sum of the error due to bias and variance. Therefore, a key element to the discovery of high-performance models lies in balancing bias and variance to obtain models with high generalizability. Different techniques to address this issue and control model complexity are designed for different supervised learning models, as reviewed in detail in Friedman et al. (2001). A typical method that is core to many such techniques is the data-driven procedure of *cross-validation*. In a typical cross-validation process, one partitions the training data into complementary subsets—training models with different complexity parameters on one subset and validating these models on the other. To reduce the variability, one usually performs multiple rounds of cross-validation using different partitions and then combines (e.g., by averaging) the validation results over the rounds to estimate the predictive performance of these models. An appropriate model complexity parameter is then chosen to train the final output model on the entire training data set.

Supervised learning has been the most widely applied method in ML. In the business world, it has become the workhorse of many modern industries. For instance, recall the running example of online advertising we discussed in Sect. 7.1: supervised learning algorithms are used to make predictions of consumer clicking behaviors, enabling large platforms to run auctions selling display advertisement opportunities. This has evolved into an industry that generated about $130 billion across the USA in 2019 (PwC, 2020). It is also worth mentioning that optimizing advertising auctions in a large-scale internet market is a complex operations problem beyond just making predictions with ML models. For an excellent discussion of this from a market equilibrium perspective, please refer to (Kroer & Stier-Moses, 2022).

Supervised learning has also been one of the most active research areas in the past few decades. This realm is so large that most algorithms go beyond the scope of our review. We now briefly introduce several important classes of supervised learning models that have recently received attention in OM applications. For a more comprehensive list of well-known supervised learning models and relevant work in the computer science literature, please refer to Table 7.1.

One may consider *linear-regression-based models* the most straightforward class of supervised learning models. In its most basic form, $f(\mathbf{x})$ is modeled as a linear function of $\mathbf{x}$, namely $\boldsymbol{\beta} \cdot \mathbf{x}$, for some $\boldsymbol{\beta}$ to be estimated from data by minimizing the training error. There are several variations of linear regression models, such as logistic regression models suitable for classification tasks or regression models with regularization (e.g., LASSO or ridge regressions) that are designed to control model complexity and perform better for high-dimensional problems. Another popular class of models is *nonparametric local learning models*, in which one uses local information of training examples to model the relationship between $\mathbf{x}$ and y. A brute force implementation of such models is the k-nearest-neighbor model (KNN), in which, given any testing data, we find a few training examples that are the most similar to it in terms of the feature vectors. This model has significant memory and computational requirements to find neighbors, so more efficient models are more prevalent in practice. Specifically, tree-based models extend these local models by using a tree-like structure to store local information effectively. They are easy to implement with good empirical performance and are amenable to visualization and interpretation. Therefore, they are often viewed as an "off-the-shelf ML method." However, a disadvantage of decision tree models is that they often over-fit the data, as trees can be arbitrarily complex. Ensemble methods, such as random forests or gradient boost trees, effectively overcome this challenge.

It is widely recognized that the most powerful method for supervised learning developed so far is probably deep learning. It uses artificial neural networks, a model

Table 7.1 Some well-known supervised learning models and seminal papers

Class	Model	Papers
Regression-based methods	LASSO regression	Tibshirani (1996)
	Ridge regression	Hoerl and Kennard (1970)
	Generalized linear models	Nelder and Wedderburn (1972)
	Generalized additive models	Hastie and Tibshirani (1990)
Local methods	k-nearest neighbors (KNN)	Fix (1951)
	Local linear regression	Cleveland (1979), Cleveland and Devlin (1988)
	Classification and regression trees	Breiman et al. (1984)
Ensemble methods	Bagging	Breiman (1996a,b), Ho (1995)
	Random forest	Breiman (2001)
	Boosting	Freund (1995)
Other methods	Naive Bayes and Bayesian networks	Friedman et al. (1997), Lewis and Ringuette (1994), Sahami et al. (1998)
	Support vector machine (SVM)	Cortes and Vapnik (1995)
Deep neural networks	Deep FeedForward neural network (D-FFNN)	Fukushima (2013), Lu et al. (2017)
	Convolutional neural network (CNN)	LeCun et al. (1989), Scherer et al. (2010)
	Residual network	He et al. (2016)
	Long short-term memory (LSTM) network	Hochreiter and Schmidhuber (1997)
	Radial basis function (RBF) network	Buhmann (2003)

ensemble architecture inspired by the human brain, to simulate complex functional forms. The term "deep" comes from the fact that a network with deep layers usually works well for complex ML problems. Recently, deep learning has taken off as the most popular ML method because of its capability to model complex functional forms, its superior ability to process large numbers of features, and its insuperable prediction accuracy when supported with enough training data. For a comprehensive discussion of deep learning, please refer to Goodfellow et al. (2016).

7.3.2 Supervised Learning for Descriptive Analysis in OM

In the OM literature, the goal of descriptive analysis typically is either *prediction* or *inference*. In prediction settings, researchers use ML models to forecast an outcome variable that can be used later in operational decisions; here, the accuracy of prediction is the foremost quality measure. In contrast, in inference problems, we are interested in understanding how an outcome variable is generated as a function of the input data. Typically, this function is specified by a model, and our goal is to learn the underlying model parameters. Causal inference—i.e., evaluating the effect of different treatments or policies on subjects—is central to this literature.

7.3.2.1 Prediction with Supervised Learning

Many authors in OM develop supervised learning-based prediction models for operational problems. Often, ML models have to be customized for operational settings to achieve higher accuracy. One typical application is demand forecasting in inventory management. For example, to predict the demand for new products (for which demand data are scarce), Baardman et al. (2017) develop an ML model that pools comparable products together to "borrow" information to forecast with higher precision. The innovation lies in the simultaneous determination of the product clusters and demand forecast, which the authors implement through an iterative algorithm that alternates between learning and optimal cluster assignment. The authors demonstrate, both theoretically and empirically, through real data that the model outperforms traditional ML models in terms of prediction accuracy. Another example in supply chains is Cui et al. (2018), which uses different ML models to forecast the demand of fashion products utilizing social media information. The authors specifically adapt the forecasting model to the context and estimate the value of social media information in demand forecasting. One can also incorporate data from auxiliary sources to improve prediction, otherwise known as *transfer learning* in the ML literature (Pan & Yang, 2009). Along these lines, Farias and Li (2019) use tensor completion to improve product recommendations from multiple customer responses, while Bastani (2021) uses high-dimensional techniques to improve prediction from proxy data sources.

In healthcare, Ang et al. (2016) propose the Q-LASSO method for hospital emergency department wait-time forecasting by mixing the celebrated LASSO approach with queuing theory. Using real data, the authors show that Q-LASSO outperforms known forecasting methods in predicting waiting times by a large margin. Queenan et al. (2019) empirically study the relationship between technology-enabled continuity of care, patient activation measures (which describes patients' skills, knowledge, and motivation to actively engage in their health care), and patient readmission. In this study, they use the SVM model to predict patient activation measures for individual patients and show that technology-enabled continuity of care is a significant predictor.

An interesting discussion regarding machine-learning-based predictions versus experience-based human forecasts in healthcare settings is provided in Ibrahim and Kim (2019). It shows that a combined predictor that integrates physicians' forecast of surgery duration with that from data-based models performs better than either forecast. The follow-up study Ibrahim et al. (2021) discusses this phenomenon in more general settings with a theoretical model. It is proven that, rather than directly merging a human forecast with that from data-driven algorithms, more accurate predictions can be obtained by carefully leveraging private human information about how the algorithm should adjust its forecast to account for the information that only the human has access to.

In revenue management, one can use ML techniques to obtain more predictive models. For example, Chen and Mišić (2019) propose a nonparametric choice model that relaxes the rationality assumption of consumer choice behavior. It assumes that each customer type can be represented by a binary decision tree—which describes a decision process for making a purchase based on checking for the existence of specific products in the assortment—and that there is a distribution over different customer types. Morales and Wang (2010) discuss cancellation rate forecasting, which plays a vital role in revenue management with selling perishable service products with fixed capacity through a fixed booking horizon. They show that different relevant variables in different booking horizon stages can be fed into supervised learning algorithms—for example, kernel logistic regression, SVM, and random forest—to achieve improved forecasting of cancellation rates.

7.3.2.2 Causal Inference with Supervised Learning

One is often interested in evaluating the *causal* effect of different treatments or policies on subjects. A typical use case of ML methods is to precisely estimate *heterogeneous* treatment effects across different subjects and target treatments to subjects that will generate the highest reward. For example, in healthcare, an important question is: what are the effects of different medical treatments on a given patient, and how can we develop personalized treatment policies to cater to different patients' needs? As an example, Bertsimas et al. (2017) study personalization for patients with diabetes. The authors use the KNN method to determine the most similar patients to a focal patient in terms of their medical attributes. Then, these "neighbors" are used to estimate the impact of a drug on the patient's HbA1C (a measure of a patient's baseline blood glucose level) under different drug choices with regression-based methods. Data from Boston Medical Center validates their approach.

Recent work in economics, operations, and statistics has moved beyond KNN to focus on developing more flexible algorithms adapted from decision trees to analyze heterogeneous treatment effects (Athey and Imbens, 2016; Chipman et al., 2010; Wager & Athey, 2018). The basic idea is to use trees to recursively divide subjects based on their attributes and observed heterogeneity in their response. The implementation of this idea requires solving several challenges. First, the treatment effect is never simultaneously observed on the same individual, and, therefore, it is not obvious how to construct a loss function for tree splitting. Second, treatments on subjects are often endogenous or subject to selection bias. Athey and Imbens (2016) and Wager and Athey (2018) overcome these challenges—under the conditional independence assumption—by modifying the loss function used for tree splitting in CART. Wang et al. (2017) and Wang et al. (2018) extend this literature by incorporating instrumental variables into the causal tree framework proposed in Athey and Imbens (2016) to correct for potential endogeneity bias. They validate their approach by examining heterogeneous health care outcomes of cardiovascular surgical procedures.

Another important application of ML in causal inference is to generate variables that researchers may use as dependent or independent variables. This is especially valuable if the researchers are using unstructured data, such as image, text, audio, and video, or when labeling is costly. For example, in Zhang et al. (2016), the authors assess the impact of having an Airbnb room listing's photo verified by a professional photographer. Using a difference-in-differences approach, they find that the effect of photo verification is positive and significant on room demand. To separate the effect of photo quality from the effect of verification, the authors build a supervised learning algorithm that can predict an image's aesthetic quality for a large number of images. This allows the authors to show that improving photo quality in listings alone can significantly increase revenue. As another example, in Cui et al. (2018), the authors use natural language processing techniques to label the sentiment of Facebook posts and comments in order to forecast demand. Similarly, Loughran and McDonald (2011) use textual information from financial documents to estimate the impact of sentiment on stock returns.

Researchers also utilize ML models to directly estimate average treatment effects when units in the control conditions are rare (Varian, 2016) or the response function is highly nonlinear (Burlig et al., 2020). For example, Varian (2016) proposed a method of constructing synthetic control units based on supervised learning. In particular, when there are only treated unit observations in a time period, one can instead *predict* the counterfactual under the control arm using the treated units' covariates. Comparing the results allows estimation of the treatment effect. In a similar spirit, Burlig et al. (2020) apply ML on high-frequency panel data to forecast the counterfactual energy consumption paths of schools in the absence of any energy-efficiency investments. This enables the authors to study the treatment effect of energy-efficiency investments. The authors compare their method with standard panel fixed-effect approaches and find that the latter's estimates are sensitive to the set of observations included as controls and the fixed effects included in the specification, while ML methods are substantially more stable.

7.3.3 *Supervised Learning for Prescriptive Analysis*

One salient characteristic of data analytic work in OM is its focus on transforming raw data into *prescriptive* operational decisions, which we discuss in detail in this section.

7.3.3.1 Prediction, Then Prescription

Some work uses a "prediction, then prescription" approach. Here, an ML model is trained in the first stage, and then, its predictions are utilized in an optimization problem for decision-making in the second stage.

A classic example is the assortment optimization problem under the multinomial logit (MNL) model, in which we want to determine the optimal assortment of products to be offered to a consumer to maximize total revenue. Under the MNL model, one can describe a product's purchase probability given the assortment by a multi-class logistic regression model. While one can train the model in a standard way—i.e., a gradient descent algorithm on the logit loss function—an operational lens is required to determine how to optimize the resulting assortment. Rusmevichientong et al. (2010) and Talluri and Van Ryzin (2004) utilize the particular structure of the problem and show that it can be solved very efficiently.

However, would this approach offer advantages over other ML models in practice where the optimization model is more straightforward and less structured? Jacob et al. (2018) provide an affirmative answer by conducting a large-scale field experiment on Alibaba for finding the optimal set of products to display to customers landing on Alibaba's online marketplaces. Alibaba uses a sophisticated ML algorithm to estimate the purchase probabilities of each product for each consumer, trained with thousands of product and customer features. Jacob et al. (2018) show that, despite the lower prediction power of the MNL-based approach, it, in fact, generates significantly higher revenue per consumer visit, primarily due to the closer integration of MNL with the downstream optimization problem.

In a similar vein, Ferreira et al. (2016) use ML to estimate the demand of new products for online fashion retailers in promotion events. They use an interpretable regression tree model trained with many features (e.g., product price, relative prices of competing products) to perform demand forecasting and use the resulting model to optimize prices. Due to the nonparametric nature of the regression tree model and the cross-dependence of products' demand and price, a naive formulation of the pricing problem would require an exponentially large decision variable space. Nevertheless, leveraging the tree model structure, the authors transform the problem into an integer optimization problem with a much smaller variable space and develop an efficient algorithm to solve the problem. For optimization under generic tree ensemble models, if decision variables in the optimization problem are also used as independent variables, Mišić (2020) shows that one can design optimization algorithms based on a mixed-integer linear program and perform well even for large-scale instances. Biggs and Hariss (2018) study a similar problem under the random forest model.

Glaeser et al. (2019) describe how a tree-based prediction together with optimization can be used in the study of optimizing spatio-temporal location optimization. Liu et al. (2018) minimize the delay in last-mile delivery services, using delivery data and ML models to predict uncertain driver travel times, which affect optimal order assignments. The authors identify several predictors for travel time, which unfortunately are influenced by the order assignment decision; this makes the multi-period order assignment problem particularly challenging. The authors discuss classes of tractable prediction models as well as optimization reformulations that can be efficiently solved.

Alley et al. (2019) go a step further and combine ML, causal inference, and optimization towards improved operational decision-making in a revenue management application. The goal is to estimate price sensitivity when pricing tickets in a secondary market. Because of the heterogeneous nature of tickets, the unique market conditions at the time each ticket is listed, and the sparsity of available tickets, demand estimation needs to be done at the individual ticket level. The paper introduces a double/orthogonalized ML method for classification that isolates the causal effects of pricing on the outcome by removing the conditional effects of the ticket and market features. Furthermore, the paper embeds this price sensitivity estimation procedure into an optimization model for selling tickets in a secondary market.

7.3.3.2 Better Prescriptiveness

Instead of taking a predict-then-optimize approach, an essential facet of some recent work is directly incorporating ML models into optimization, leading to superior prescriptions. This is because ML tools are typically designed to reduce prediction error without considering how the predictions will be used, i.e., a small out-of-sample prediction error does not necessarily coincide with a favorable out-of-sample decision.

Bertsimas and Kallus (2020) demonstrate this point by studying a stochastic optimization problem with historical data $\{x_i, y_i\}_{i=1}^N$. After observing a new feature vector $X = x$, the decision-maker makes a choice z to minimize $\mathbb{E}[c(z; Y)|X = x]$, where $c(\cdot)$ is some known function. A typical example under this framework is the classical inventory ordering problem. To illustrate, let Y denote the uncertain demand, X denote some auxiliary observable that can be used for demand forecasting, and z denote the order quantity. Also, $c(\cdot)$ describes the total inventory cost.

A traditional approach would be to first use $\{x_i, y_i\}_{i=1}^N$ to build a point forecast of $\hat{Y}$ and then minimize $c(z; \hat{Y})$. As pointed out in Bertsimas and Kallus (2020), this approach ignores the uncertainty around $\hat{Y}$ and can lead to sub-optimal decisions. Instead, the authors propose to choose a decision

$$\hat{z}_N^{\text{local}}(x) \in \arg\min \sum_{i=1}^{N} w_{N,i}(x) c(z; y_i),$$

in which $w_{N,i}(x)$ is a weight assigned to observed instance i (the weights are larger for x_i's that are closer to x). Within this framework, several well-known supervised learning models can be used to find the weights, such as KNN (Friedman et al., 2001), local linear regression (Cleveland & Devlin, 1988), CART (Breiman et al., 1984), or random forest (Breiman, 2001). The authors show that the proposed approach improves the quality of the decision significantly.

Elmachtoub and Grigas (2017) propose a general framework called Smart "Predict, then Optimize" (SPO) to integrate prediction and prescription better. In SPO, the loss function in the ML training process takes into account the decision error in the downstream optimization problem induced by ML prediction. To handle the computational challenge in training with the SPO loss, the paper proposes a surrogate loss that is tractable and is statistically consistent with the SPO loss. The authors show that this new estimation approach leads to decisions that exhibit significant improvement over those derived from traditional methods in several classical optimization problems. Mandi et al. (2019) extend SPO to solve large-scale combinatorial optimization problems, such as the weighted knapsack and scheduling problems. Elmachtoub et al. (2020) focus on training decision trees under the SPO framework and proposes a tractable and interpretable methodology. Relatedly, Ciocan and Mišić (2020) adapt decision tree models for optimal stopping problems.

7.4 Unsupervised Learning

Unlike supervised learning, unsupervised ML algorithms deal with data sets without reference to known or labeled, outcomes. A common theme in unsupervised learning algorithms is to detect the underlying structure of the data that are previously unknown. In this section, we first introduce the general concepts in unsupervised learning and then discuss the important use cases of unsupervised learning in the OM literature.

7.4.1 General Introduction to Unsupervised Learning

A widely applied class of unsupervised learning algorithms is the *clustering analysis*. Such analyses' goal is to group a set of data points, $\{\mathbf{x}_i\}_{i=1}^n$, such that those data points in the same cluster are more similar to each other than to those in other clusters. Similarity between two data points i and j is measured by some notion of distance, for example, the Euclidean distance $\|\mathbf{x}_i - \mathbf{x}_j\|_2$. Often, such clusters represent data groups with distinctive characteristics and, therefore, form a logical structure on which deeper nuts-and-bolts analysis and operational policies are based.

Classic examples of clustering include hierarchical clustering methods, which date back to the 1960s. For example, one may initialize each data point as a cluster and build a tree in a bottom-up fashion by merging similar clusters. This leads to the well-known hierarchical agglomerative clustering (HAC) algorithm (Ward Jr, 1963). Another widely used algorithm of clustering analysis is the k-means clustering algorithm. Taking k as an input to the algorithm, it divides the data into k clusters by iterating between two steps until convergence. In the first step, given the data points' assignments to the k clusters, we calculate the center of each cluster. In the second, given the center of each cluster, we assign each data point to the cluster whose center is the closest to that data point. The choice of parameter k is usually subjective, but the overarching principle is to strike a balance between the in-cluster-similarity and model complexity. The k-means clustering falls into the categories of centroid-based clustering, in which a center defines a cluster. Other well-known algorithms within this family include the k-medroids algorithm (Kaufman & PJ, 1987), the k-Harmonic means algorithms (Zhang et al., 1999), and the fuzzy c-means algorithm (Bezdek, 1973). The key difference among these algorithms lies in defining the centers and how to determine cluster assignments. A criticism of these methods is that they tend to favor sphere-like clusters and have great difficulty with anything else. This criticism motivates other algorithms, such as the density-based spatial clustering of applications with noise (DBSCAN) algorithm, which can give arbitrary-shaped clusters and requires no prior knowledge of the number of clusters (Ester et al., 1996).

Another broad class of unsupervised learning algorithms is *latent variable models*, which assume that some underlying latent variables generate the observable data. Local independence is often assumed, meaning that once these latent variables are controlled for, the variables manifested in the data are purely randomly generated with noise. Depending on the purpose of the analysis, the goal is either to uncover the data-generating process or to pinpoint the latent variables. One important example in latent variable models is the mixture of models. In such models, we assume that each data point $\mathbf{x}_i$ is generated by one of the several underlying distributions without knowing the actual distributions and the membership of data points. The membership of data points to these distributions are the latent variables we do not observe. We are usually interested in these latent variables, as well as in the parameters of the distributions. The starting point to estimate such a model is to note that different specifications of the underlying distributions lead to a different likelihood of the observed data. Therefore, one may resort to the maximum log-likelihood estimation (MLE) method in the statistics literature. The central difficulty, however, is that since the latent variables are not observed, the MLE on marginal distributions is usually hard to optimize. The famous expectation–maximization (EM) algorithm solves this issue by alternating between performing an expectation (E) step, which creates a function for the expectation of the full log-likelihood function using the current estimate for the parameters and the posterior distribution of latent variables, and a maximization (M) step, which computes parameters maximizing the expected log-likelihood found in the E step (Dempster et al., 1977; Moon, 1996). One can show that EM necessarily leads to a (local) maximum likelihood. Alternatively, one can also estimate such models with moment matching (Day, 1969). Another well-known model in this class is the hidden Markov chain model (HMM): one observes sequential data that are assumed to be governed by an unobservable Markov chain (Baum & Petrie, 1966). The parameters of the HMM can also be recovered by the EM algorithm.

Using the concept of latent variable models, we often want to infer a latent but much simpler or structured representation of the complex, unstructured, or high-dimensional data we observe. Such a task is referred to as *representation learning*, which can serve as the basis for building classifiers or other predictors. For instance, this can be particularly useful when dealing with the curse of dimensionality. In predicting whether a consumer will click on an advertisement, we may have more features than the data set's size. Therefore, one would wish to work with low-dimensional data while keeping the primary information in the original data, and this is where such learning techniques come in handy. A canonical analysis for representation learning is principal component analysis (PCA), in which we assume that a linear combination of low-dimensional latent variables that are orthogonal to each other generates the high-dimensional data. Based on the eigenvalue decomposition of the covariance matrix, one can approximately recover these low-dimensional components. Alternatively, one can use singular value decomposition or matrix factorization with Markov Chain Monte Carlo. Recent developments in representation learning for applications such as speech recognition, signal processing, and natural language processing highlight the role of deep neural networks. For example, Bengio et al. (2003) use deep neural networks to learn a distributed representation for each word, called a word embedding. For a review of representation learning, please refer to Bengio et al. (2013).

Other applications of unsupervised ML techniques include *anomaly detection* and *association mining*. Anomaly detection can automatically discover unusual data points to pinpoint fraudulent transactions, discover faulty hardware pieces, or identify an outlier caused by a human error. Association mining identifies patterns that frequently occur together in the data and is frequently used by retailers for basket analysis to discover goods often purchased simultaneously. A recent milestone of using deep learning methods for unsupervised learning is the generative adversarial network (GAN), which, given a training set, learns to generate new data statistically similar to data in the training set (Goodfellow et al., 2016). For example, a GAN can be used for voice impersonation, mimicking the pitch and other perceivable signal qualities, as well as the style of the target speaker. It is proven very useful for strengthening the performance of both supervised learning and reinforcement learning algorithms. These unsupervised ML techniques are not directly relevant to the OM literature (so far), so we will not review their details (please refer to Table 7.2).

Table 7.2 Some well-known unsupervised learning models and seminal papers

Class	Model	Papers
Clustering	Hierarchical agglomerative clustering (HAC)	Ward Jr (1963)
	k-means clustering	MacQueen et al. (1967)
	k-medoids	Kaufman and PJ (1987)
	k-Harmonic means	Zhang et al. (1999)
	Fuzzy c-means	Bezdek (1973)
	Density-based spatial clustering of applications with noise (DBSCAN)	Ester et al. (1996)
Latent variable models	Mixture of models	Day (1969)
	Expectation maximization (EM) algorithm	Dempster et al. (1977), Moon (1996)
	Hidden Markov chain model (HMM)	Baum and Petrie (1966)
Representation learning	Principal component analysis (PCA)	Pearson (1901)
	Word embedding	Bengio et al. (2003)
Other unsupervised models	Anomaly detection	Breunig et al. (2000), Knorr et al. (2000)
	Association ruling learning	Agrawal et al. (1993)
	Autoencoder	Kramer (1991)
	Generative adversarial network (GAN)	Goodfellow et al. (2014)
	Deep belief network	Hinton et al. (2006)

7.4.2 Unsupervised Learning for Descriptive Analysis

7.4.2.1 Unsupervised Learning for Prediction

Unsupervised learning techniques often play an essential role in structuring the data to aid predictions. For example, clustering analysis allows the analyst to "divide and conquer" in prediction tasks—once data are appropriately grouped, one can customize the prediction model for each group to achieve higher accuracy. Predictions based on clustering often outperform the naive implementation of predictions. Li et al. (2011) adopt this research strategy. The authors consider the forecast of product returns based on return merchandise authorization (RMA) information. They first conduct a clustering analysis to segment customers based on their historical RMA records and then use counting regression models to generate a forecast for each customer cluster. In this process, the clustering analysis allows the authors to fully exploit customer heterogeneity and leads to improved forecast accuracy in comparison with two benchmark models. This point is further illustrated by a paper Hu et al. (2019) in the setting of demand forecasts for electronic retailers. The authors present a cluster-then-predict approach to forecast customer orders of new products similar to past products, which leads to mean absolute errors approximately 2–3% below the partner firm's existing forecasts. The same clustering method is adopted by Sun et al. (2020) for exploratory analysis, which investigates the impact of different cross-border fulfillment options, such as the fulfillment by Amazon (FBA) option and in-house fulfillment on the sales and bottom line of e-retailers. In a similar vein, Cohen et al. (2019) also utilize clustering to predict customer demand. More specifically, Cohen et al. (2019) study the demand forecasting problem for retailers in a scenario in which certain products have a large amount of historical data, while others are newly introduced and have scarce demand-related data. The authors propose a procedure that first applies the maximum likelihood estimation approach to estimate a different coefficient vector for each product and then combines hypothesis testing and k-means clustering to identify the correct aggregation level for each coefficient.

One often uses latent variable models in prediction problems in the OM literature. For example, in Shen and Huang (2008), the authors develop dimension-reduction methods for forecasting incoming call volumes. Their approach is to treat the intra-day call volume profiles as a high-dimensional vector time series. They propose, first, to reduce the dimensionality by singular value decomposition of the matrix of historical intra-day profiles and, then, to apply time series and regression techniques. The authors show that their method is very competitive in out-of-sample forecast comparisons using two real data sets. The hidden Markov model (HMM) is used in Montoya and Gonzalez (2019) to identify unobserved on-shelf out-of-stock (OOS) by detecting changes in sales patterns resulting from unobserved states of the shelf. They identify three latent states, one of which characterizes an OOS state, specify the model using a hierarchical Bayes approach, and use a Monte Carlo–Markov chain methodology to estimate the model parameters. Their HMM approach performs well in predicting out-of-stocks, combining high detection power (63.48%) and low false alerts (15.52%). A recent paper Chen et al. (2020) introduces Product2Vec, a method based on the representation learning technique Word2Vec, as discussed in Mikolov et al. (2013), to study product-level competition when the number of products is extensive. Their model takes consumer shopping baskets as inputs and generates a low-dimensional vector for every product that preserves essential product information.

Some exciting research work that combines latent variable models and clustering analysis for prediction is presented in Jagabathula et al. (2018). The authors study the problem of segmenting a large population of customers into diverse clusters based on customer preferences, using preference observations such as purchases, ratings, and clicks. In real applications, the universe of items can be vast and unstructured, while individual customer data are highly sparse, which prevents the applicability of existing techniques in marketing and ML. Their proposed method proceeds in two steps: *embed* and *cluster*. In the *embed* step, they squeeze individual customer data into the low-dimensional space by calculating the likelihoods of each customer's observed behavioral data regarding each of a small number of product categories under a representative probabilistic behavior model. In the *cluster* step, the clustering analysis is applied to low-dimensional embedding. The authors derive the necessary and sufficient conditions to guarantee asymptotic recovery of the true segments under a standard latent class setup, and they show empirically that their method outperforms standard latent variable methods.

7.4.2.2 Using EM Algorithms in Choice Model Estimation

As we reviewed in Sect. 7.4.1, the EM algorithm is a useful technique to deal with latent variable models. While this algorithm is derived from solving unsupervised learning problems, it has been widely used in OM choice modeling literature. In choice modeling, while customer purchases are often observed through transactional or point-of-sales data, customers who enter the store but do not purchase are often not observable to researchers, especially in brick-and-mortar retailing. Such one can view such missing data as latent variables, and there is a large stream of OM literature that builds different EM algorithms to estimate customers' arrival process.

This literature started with the seminal work (Vulcano et al., 2012). The paper proposes a method for estimating substitute and lost demand when only sales and product availability data are observable, and only a selected subset of items is offered to the consumer in each period. The model considers an MNL choice model with a non-homogeneous Poisson model of consumer arrivals and applies the EM algorithm to estimate the model parameters; it does so by treating the observed demand as an incomplete observation of the demand that would have been observed if all products had been available in all periods. It shows that all limit points of the procedure are stationary points of the incomplete data log-likelihood function.

Subsequently, the EM algorithm is used to estimate the parameters of various choice models. In Şimşek and Topaloglu (2018), the authors adapt the EM algorithm to estimate the Markov chain choice model. The parameters of the Markov chain choice model are the probability that the customer arrives in the system to purchase each one of the products and the transition probabilities. The authors treat the path that a customer follows in the Markov chain as the latent variables. For the E step, they show how to compute the probability of consumer purchase and the expected number of transitions from a particular product to another, conditional on the final purchase decision of a customer. For the M step, they show how to efficiently solve the optimization problem that appears in the M step. Numerical experiments demonstrate that their algorithm, together with the Markov chain choice model, leads to better predictions of customer choice behavior compared with other commonly used choice models. Several other authors consider the estimation of the rank-based model in which each customer has a ranked list of products in mind, and purchases the most preferred available product with the EM algorithm (Farias et al., 2013; Jagabathula & Rusmevichientong, 2017; Jagabathula & Vulcano, 2018; van Ryzin & Vulcano, 2015, 2017).

In summary, EM algorithms have proven to be effective in the estimation of many choice models. In fact, they have become an off-the-shelf method that one may consider for dealing with choice model parameter estimation.

7.4.3 Unsupervised Learning for Prescriptive Analysis

In this section, we will review several recent works on applying unsupervised learning for prescriptive analysis. This literature is still relatively young and sparse, but we expect it to quickly grow in the near future, in view of the wide application of unsupervised learning in other fields.

Bernstein et al. (2019) investigate the personal assortment optimization when there are heterogeneous customers with unknown product preferences and known features. The authors consider a dynamic clustering policy embedded into an exploration-exploitation framework with MNL as the assumed choice model. The clustering policy aims to learn both the underlying mapping of profiles to clusters and the preferences of each cluster with the Dirichlet process mixture model, which can be estimated by a Markov Chain Monte Carlo (MCMC) sampling scheme. The case study presented in Bernstein et al. (2019) suggests that the benefits of such a strategy are substantial. Compared with a data-driven policy that treats customers independently and a linear-utility policy that assumes that products' mean utilities are linear functions of available customer attributes, it generates over 37 and 27% more transactions, respectively.

Another recent work Govindarajan et al. (2021) studies a multi-location newsvendor network when only first- and second-moment information of demand are known by using a distribution-robust model to find inventory levels that minimize the worst-case expected cost among the distributions consistent with this information. The authors show that the problem is NP-hard, but they develop a computationally tractable upper bound on the worst-case expected cost if the costs of fulfilling demands follow a nested structure. They propose an algorithm that can approximate general fulfillment cost structures by nested cost structures, which gives a computationally tractable heuristic for the optimization problem. To show that nested structures offer sufficient modeling flexibility, they develop a simple algorithm that stems from the HAC algorithm to approximate any general distance-based fulfillment cost structure as a nested cost structure.

7.5 Bandits and Reinforcement Learning

In both supervised and unsupervised learning, the training data set is assumed to be provided through an exogenous process. However, in general, the decision-maker's actions can *affect* the data that we observe, thereby affecting the quality of the downstream predictive model. For instance, let us return to our earlier example on supervised learning for advertising: $\mathbf{x}_i$ describes the characteristics of a customer who is offered an advertisement, and $y_i = 1$ if the consumer clicks on this advertisement. Yet, we observe that this data set is available *only if* the platform shows some customers this specific advertisement. If not, the platform does not observe the resulting customer response and, consequently, cannot make predictions for new customers. In other words, the platform's current decisions directly affect the data it observes, and thereby its ability to make good decisions in the future. Multi-armed bandits (MAB) and reinforcement learning (RL) provide a general framework and near-optimal algorithms for making these types of sequential decisions in the face of uncertainty.

7.5.1 Multi-Armed Bandits

The term "multi-armed bandits" comes from a stylized gambling scenario in which a gambler faces several slot machines that yield different payoffs. In the classical multi-armed bandit, the decision-maker has access to K actions (referred to as "arms"). As a running example, let each arm be a new treatment for a disease. Each arm i is associated with an expected reward μ_i—i.e., the expected improvement in patient outcomes from this treatment. We sequentially observe T homogeneous new patients, and the decision-maker chooses one arm for each patient. Upon assigning a patient treatment, she immediately observes a noisy signal of the treatment's reward μ_i—thus, if she assigns this arm to a sufficient number of patients, she can obtain a good estimate $\hat{\mu}_i$ of the arm's expected reward. This is termed *exploration*—i.e., a good policy must try each arm in order to learn if it is promising. However, to maximize long-term performance across all patients, a good policy must also *exploit* the data it has accumulated thus far and offer the estimated best arm to patients. This *exploration-exploitation tradeoff* underlies the design of all bandit algorithms.

Table 7.3 provides some typical applications of bandits, as well as their corresponding actions (arms) and the reward (feedback).

The celebrated Gittins indices (Gittins, 1979) show that the optimal solution to an infinite-horizon Bayesian multi-armed bandit satisfies an index-based policy. However, this solution is generally computationally intractable, and thus, the near-optimal and computationally simpler Upper Confidence Bound (UCB) algorithm (Auer and Ortner, 2010) became the workhorse bandit algorithm. UCB leverages the "principle of optimism" to trade off exploration and exploitation: when uncertain about an arm's reward, act assuming that it has the highest possible reward based on its confidence set. This approach naturally induces exploration since arms that have few observations will have large confidence sets, and at the same time, it avoids wasteful exploration since only arms that have some reasonable probability of being the best will be played. Recently, Thompson Sampling has risen to prominence, demonstrating superior empirical performance as well as similar near-optimality guarantees (Russo et al., 2018; Thompson, 1933)

Table 7.3 Some common applications for multi-armed bandits, adapted from Slivkins (2019)

Application	Action	Reward
Clinical trials	Which drug to prescribe	Patient outcome
Web design	Font color, page layout, etc.	#clicks, engagement time, etc.
Content optimization	Featured items/articles	#clicks, engagement time, etc.
Web search	Search results for a given query	User satisfaction
Advertising	Which ad to display	Revenue from ads
Recommender systems	Which products to recommend	User satisfaction
Dynamic pricing	Product prices	Revenues
Procurement	Which items to buy	Utility from items and costs
Auction/market design	Which reserve price to use	Revenue
Crowdsourcing	Which tasks to give to which workers	Quality of completed tasks
Datacenter design	Which server to route the job to	Job completion time
Internet	Which TCP settings to use	Connection quality
Radio networks	Which radio frequency to use	Rate of successful transmission

There are numerous variants of the classical multi-armed bandit described above. Of particular importance to the OM community, the contextual bandit framework is a significant extension, allowing decision-makers to *personalize* decisions. In this setting, individuals at each time t are associated with a feature vector X_t that captures individual-specific information that may affect their response to the choice of the arm (e.g., customer or patient histories). Each arm is then associated with an unknown function $f : X \to Y$, which maps from the individual's feature vector to her observed reward. The most widely studied setting is where f is a linear (or generalized linear) model (Abbasi-Yadkori et al., 2011), but there has also been work studying nonparametric but smooth choices for f (Gur et al., 2019). Surprisingly, Bastani et al. (2020) show that when there is sufficient randomness in the observed features, the exploration-exploitation tradeoff disappears. This is because randomness in the features can induce *free exploration*, allowing a greedy algorithm to perform comparably to or better than bandit algorithms that explore.

7.5.1.1 Popular Variants

The bandit framework makes a number of assumptions that may not hold in practice. Thus, as bandit algorithms are increasingly being deployed in practice (for A/B testing, recommender systems, etc.), a number of variants have been proposed to bridge the gap between theory and practice.

For instance, the rewards of arms may *change* over time (e.g., news articles or fashion products may become outdated). Policies that "forget" old data have been designed for this non-stationary environment (Besbes et al., 2014; Cheung et al., 2018). In mobile health applications, users may become "habituated" to recently taken actions, reducing the expected reward for that action; this necessitates adapting existing bandit algorithms to additionally model the underlying habituation and recovery dynamics (Cheung et al. 2018).

Outcomes may not be observed immediately; for example, in a clinical trial, it may be many months before the patient's outcome is observed (Anderer et al., 2019). Good policies must account for assignments that are already in the pipeline but are yet to be observed when designing their exploration strategy (Joulani et al., 2013).

The observed individual-level features may be *high-dimensional*. In this case, one generally cannot design good policies unless there is additional structure. A popular assumption to impose is that the arm rewards are *sparse*—i.e., only a subset of the many observed features is predictive of the rewards. Then, Bastani and Bayati (2020) bridge high-dimensional estimation and bandit to design good policies in this setting.

In many recommender systems, the arms may not be a single product but a combinatorial *assortment* over a set of products. In this case, whether or not the user clicks on an item depends not only on the item but also on the other items in the assortment set. This type of feedback has been studied in the classical MNL choice model. Agrawal et al. (2019) bring these ideas to the bandit setting. Another issue with recommender systems is that users may *disengage* from the platform if they are initially offered poor recommendations. Bastani et al. (2018) show that it may be favorable in these instances to use customer information to constrain exploration upfront.

In practice, there may be a number of constraints that govern the decision-making process. For instance, in ad allocations, a firm may request the platform for a minimum expected click-through rate, or in resource allocation problems, the decision-maker may face capacity or budget constraints. Agrawal and Devanur (2019) study policies under general global convex constraints and concave objective functions.

7.5.1.2 Dynamic Pricing

Consider a monopolist that seeks to dynamically price a new product with unknown market demand. This problem suffers from the semi-bandit feedback: if a customer purchases a product at a price p, one can infer that she would have purchased it at any lower price $p' < p$, but we do not observe her purchase decision for higher prices $p' > p$; conversely, if a customer does *not* purchase a product at price p, we do not know if she would have purchased it for any lower prices. Thus, the decision-maker must navigate an exploration-exploitation tradeoff in her pricing decisions to learn the market demand and converge to an optimal price. This particular problem and its variants have received significant attention in the OM community (Keskin & Zeevi, 2014; Kleinberg & Leighton, 2003).

In collaboration with the fashion e-retailer Rue La La, Ferreira et al. (2016), which we have discussed in Sect. 7.3.3, also demonstrates the potential economic value of dynamic pricing policies in practice, particularly for new products with uncertain demand and stringent inventory constraints. However, in practice, a large platform must solve the pricing problem over a large number of products. In this case, one may wish to leverage contextual information in the form of product features (Cohen et al., 2020). However, product demand variation may not be captured by product features alone: for example, there may be different demand for two different black dresses due to factors that are hard to measure, such as fit or style. For these settings, Bastani et al. (2019) adopt an empirical Bayes approach to learn a shared prior across demand parameters for related products.

7.5.2 *Reinforcement Learning*

In the multi-armed bandit setting, while the actions taken by the decision-maker affect the data they observe, they do not affect the world. However, this assumption does not hold in many settings. For instance, if a platform shows too many advertisements to a consumer, she may decide to leave the platform. In this case, decisions made at the current step have long-term consequences beyond the immediate reward collected. Thus, decision-makers not only need to address the exploration-exploitation tradeoff but must also account for how their actions affect the underlying state of the world. This property is characteristic of many practical problems, including queuing (where the state encodes the current capacity of the queue), inventory management (where the state encodes the amount of inventory currently available), and dynamic pricing (where the state encodes the remaining inventory). Reinforcement learning algorithms are designed to solve these kinds of problems (Dai & Shi, 2019; Gijsbrechts et al., 2019).

The standard framework for formalizing a reinforcement learning problem is a *Markov decision process (MDP)*. At a high level, an MDP consists of a set of states representing the world's possible states. For instance, the state might represent whether the customer has left the platform. Similar to multi-armed bandits, an MDP also has a set of actions that the decision-maker can take. It also has a reward function; in contrast to the multi-armed bandits setting, rewards now depend not only on the action taken but also on the system's current state. For instance, if the customer has already left the platform, then the reward is zero regardless of what action is taken. Finally, an MDP also has a (probabilistic) transition function that describes how the state changes depending on the action taken. For instance, the customer might leave the platform with a higher probability if they are shown an advertisement.

The goal of reinforcement learning is to compute the optimal policy, which specifies the action to take in each state in a way that maximizes the cumulative reward collected over the time horizon of the problem. For infinite-horizon problems, a discount factor is applied to future rewards to ensure that the cumulative reward collected is finite. When the MDP reward function and transition function are known, the decision-maker observes the current state, and the state and action spaces are finite and small; thus, we can efficiently solve for the optimal policy using value iteration (also known as dynamic programming) (Bellman, 1957). At a high level, this approach characterizes the optimal policy in terms of the value function encoding the optimal cumulative reward achievable at each state, establishes a recursive equation, known as Bellman's equation, characterizing the value function, and then solves this equation using an iterative procedure that is guaranteed to converge.

There are three reasons that this approach may no longer work. The first is due to the *curse of dimensionality*. When the state space is very large or continuous, then value iteration is no longer computationally tractable. In this case, approximate dynamic programming algorithms for solving the MDP have been studied; these algorithms are not guaranteed to compute the optimal policy but often work very well in practice. Continuous states remain a major challenge but are common in predictive analytics applications; for instance, they might encode the current customers' attributes that can be used to predict the probability they will leave the platform.

The second is due to *partial observability*. The decision-maker may not always observe the state of the world; for instance, they might not know immediately whether the customer has left the platform or temporarily become unresponsive. In this case, the problem must instead be formalized as a *partially observed MDP (POMDP)*. Algorithms exist for solving for the optimal policy in a POMDP, though they do not scale nearly as well as value iteration.

The third reason is that the transition and reward functions are unknown. For instance, the decision-maker might not know ahead of time the probability that the customer will leave the platform if shown an advertisement. Instead, the decision-maker must learn this information by taking exploratory actions; thus, this setting combines bandit feedback with MDPs. Reinforcement learning typically refers to this setting; however, as we discuss below, specific reinforcement learning algorithms can be useful for addressing the previous two issues as well.

One can divide reinforcement learning algorithms into two approaches: model-based and model-free. Intuitively, a model-based algorithm first estimates the MDP transition and reward functions and then uses value iteration to compute the optimal policy based on these estimates. As the estimates converge to the true transition and reward functions, the computed policy converges to the true optimal policy. Most algorithms that provide theoretical guarantees are model-based. Kearns and Singh (2002) introduced the E^3 algorithm, which was the first provable near-optimal polynomial-time algorithm for learning in MDPs. Brafman and Tennenholtz (2002) proposed the much simpler R-MAX algorithm, which formally justified a solution strategy similar to bandits, based on optimism under uncertainty. This work then paved the way for improved algorithms for reinforcement learning based on UCB (Auer et al., 2009) and Thompson Sampling (Agrawal & Jia, 2017).

In contrast, model-free algorithms avoid estimating the transitions and rewards; instead, they directly learn a representation of the policy. These algorithms tend to be less sample-efficient compared to model-based algorithms. However, a key benefit of these approaches is that they are very general since they are agnostic to the structure of the MDP; for instance, they readily apply to MDPs with large or continuous state spaces. Model-free algorithms can furthermore be subdivided into two kinds. First, Q-learning Watkins and Dayan (1992) is an algorithm that aims to learn the Q-function, which encodes the cumulative reward achieved by taking an action in a given state and then acting optimally thereafter. The Q-function implicitly encodes the optimal policy since we can greedily choose the action with the highest value according to the Q-function in the current state. The Q-function can be learned using the method of temporal differences (Sutton, 1988), which establishes a recursive formula for the Q-function based on Bellman's equation. In the finite state setting, there has been recent work proving that Q-learning can efficiently recover the optimal policy (Jin et al., 2018; Strehl et al., 2006). Second, policy optimization algorithms rely on directly optimizing the policy. A classical approach is to use a parametric policy class such as neural networks and then to use gradient descent on to optimize these parameters (Williams, 1992). Recent work has proposed additional improvements, including actor-critic approaches that combine policy optimization with Q-learning (Konda & Tsitsiklis, 2000; Mnih et al., 2016; Sutton et al., 2000) and algorithms that rely on trust-region optimization (Schulman et al., 2015). Policy optimization algorithms are very general; for instance, unlike Q-learning, they can be applied to POMDPs. The drawback of these algorithms is that they are highly susceptible to local minima since the optimization problem tends to be highly non-convex.

7.6 Future Directions

We envision that the increasing availability of data will continue to drive the development of ML-based research in OM. Before we close this chapter, we identify several research areas at the intersection of ML and OM that we believe will continue to attract more research attention. We will start with supervised learning.

First, a large amount of observational data from actual business practice is being accumulated in many business disciplines and is gradually shared with business researchers (Shen et al., 2019; Zhang et al., 2020). Such data often include a large number of covariates available to describe the context of the data. Combined with advanced ML techniques, we think that the causal inference literature will focus increasingly on heterogeneous treatment effects (HTE) and provide personalized decision-making in operations, such as individualized medical choices or personalized assortment optimization/pricing. Two major difficulties are how to utilize ML tools' representation power to infer treatment effects for heterogeneous individuals that can overcome the endogeneity issue universally found in observational data and how to overcome the high-dimensionality in data. Previously mentioned work Wang et al. (2017) and Wang et al. (2018) aim to address the first issue. However, there is still much room for new developments. For example, existing approaches in HTE analysis deal mainly with cross-sectional settings, while a large body of causal inference literature has demonstrated the value of exploiting temporal variation on an individual level for average treatment effect analysis. Therefore, an important research direction is to develop ML-based HTE estimators tailored to *panel data*. Moreover, most work in HTE analysis uses tree-based methods. Can other techniques—e.g., *deep learning*—that are known to be more powerful when more training data are available be used for such purposes? Furthermore, advancements have been made recently in applying ML techniques to identify critical covariates in *high-dimensional data* for causal inference, such as those discussed in Chernozhukov et al. (2018). Can we tailor these methods to OM problems?

Second, we also expect that OM researchers will utilize more recent ML developments to improve traditional optimization techniques. In Sect. 7.3.3, we discussed the literature on incorporating specific ML models into optimal decision-making. Nevertheless, other ML models, especially those developed recently with more prediction power, can also be considered for such purposes. For example, it is sensible that deep learning models can better describe consumer choice behaviors than such classical choice models as MNL. However, it is far from trivial to figure out solution techniques for optimization problems such as assortment optimization or pricing under such models.

Third, we also anticipate that OM researchers will contribute to the ML literature by developing prescriptive systems with more business constraints. Price fairness (Bertsimas et al., 2011) and discrimination (Cui et al., 2020) have been long considered in the OM literature. Such topics become more and more essential in developing prediction and optimization algorithms using ML since essential decisions in our society, such as information acquisitions and hiring, are increasingly made by algorithms. Therefore, we believe that OM researchers will contribute to the ML literature by working on business applications that utilize supervised learning methods with business and ethnics constraints, such as fairness and privacy.

About supervised learning, a promising research direction is to utilize its power in learning representation and clustering to improve field experiment analyses. While field experiments have been the "gold standard" in getting causal inference towards business and policy questions, experiments on platforms, mostly two-sided platforms with limited demand or supply, or social networks suffer from interactions between units (Doudchenko et al., 2020; Johari et al., 2020; Ye et al., 2020). One exploration in this direction is found in Ugander and Yin (2020). It considers the estimation of the local average treatment effect in the presence of network inference. While unbiased and consistent estimators have been constructed for this problem, these estimators suffer from extreme variance when the experiment design is flawed. The authors propose a randomized graph cluster randomization that enables substantial mean squared error reduction in the estimator compared with existing approaches.

In terms of dynamic learning (both multi-armed bandits and reinforcement learning), one significant challenge is to satisfy safety constraints—i.e., how can we ensure that exploration does not lead to damaging or irrecoverable outcomes? Several different notions of safety have been studied. One natural notion applied to platforms is specifying a set of states that should not be reached—e.g., we want to ensure that a customer does not leave the platform with high probability (Bastani et al., 2018). Fairness can also be thought of as a safety constraint—i.e., ensuring that the algorithm does not unfairly discriminate against minorities (Hardt et al., 2016). For instance, recent work has shown that in certain settings, tradeoffs exist between exploring and ensuring fairness (Kleinberg, 2018). Finally, in the setting of multi-armed bandits, recent work that has studied algorithms under the constrained exploration is *conservative*—i.e., it is guaranteed to outperform a baseline policy for the entire time horizon (Wu et al., 2016). In general, characterizing the tradeoffs between exploration and satisfying practical constraints remains an important challenge in the field.

Another important challenge in dynamic learning is *policy evaluation*, of which the goal is to estimate the performance of a policy from historical data. Policy evaluation is needed to understand how well the bandit is doing compared to alternative approaches or baseline strategies. This line of work builds on the causal inference literature (Swaminathan and Joachims, 2015) to devise algorithms that produce unbiased estimates of the performance of the policy. A closely related problem is *offline learning* (or *batch learning*), where we want to learn the policy from observational data—i.e., data collected from another, possibly unknown, policy. For instance, we might collect patient outcomes from a doctor's actions; and, we want to learn a treatment policy based on these data without any active exploration. This approach is also related to safety since, in many domains, exploration is highly constrained due to ethical considerations (e.g., healthcare or legal and financial decision-making).

References

Abbasi-Yadkori, Y., Pál, D., & Szepesvári, C. (2011). Improved algorithms for linear stochastic bandits. In *Advances in Neural Information Processing Systems* (pp. 2312–2320).

Agrawal, S., Avadhanula, V., Goyal, V., & Zeevi, A. (2019). MNL-bandit: A dynamic learning approach to assortment selection. *Operations Research, 67*(5), 1453–1485.

Agrawal, S., & Devanur, N. R. (2019). Bandits with global convex constraints and objective. *Operations Research, 67*(5), 1486–1502.

Agrawal, S., & Jia, R. (2017) Optimistic posterior sampling for reinforcement learning: Worst-case regret bounds. In *Advances in Neural Information Processing Systems* (pp. 1184–1194).

Agrawal, R., Imieliński, T., & Swami, A. (1993). Mining association rules between sets of items in large databases. In *Proceedings of the 1993 ACM SIGMOD International Conference on Management of Data* (pp. 207–216).

Alley, M., Biggs, M., Hariss, R., Herrmann, C., Li, M., & Perakis, G. (2019). *Pricing for heterogeneous products: Analytics for ticket reselling*. Working paper, Pennsylvania State University

Anderer, A., Bastani, H., & Silberholz, J. (2019). *Adaptive clinical trial designs with surrogates: When should we bother?* Working paper, University of Pennsylvania.

Ang, E., Kwasnick, S., Bayati, M., Plambeck, E. L., & Aratow, M. (2016). Accurate emergency department wait time prediction. *Manufacturing & Service Operations Management, 18*(1), 141–156.

Angrist, J. D., & Pischke, J. S. (2008). M*ostly harmless econometrics: An empiricist's companion*. Princeton, NJ: Princeton University Press.

Athey, S., & Imbens, G. (2016). Recursive partitioning for heterogeneous causal effects. *Proceedings of the National Academy of Sciences, 113*(27), 7353–7360.

Auer, P., Jaksch, T., & Ortner, R. (2009). Near-optimal regret bounds for reinforcement learning. In *Advances in Neural Information Processing Systems* (pp. 89–96).

Auer, P., & Ortner, R. (2010). UCB revisited: Improved regret bounds for the stochastic multi-armed bandit problem. *Periodica Mathematica Hungarica, 61*(1–2), 55–65.

Baardman, L., Levin, I., Perakis, G., & Singhvi, D. (2017). *Leveraging comparables for new product sales forecasting*. Working paper, University of Michigan – Ann Arbor.

Bastani, H. (2021). Predicting with proxies: Transfer learning in high dimension. *Management Science, 67*(5), 2964–2984. INFORMS.

Bastani, H., & Bayati, M. (2020). Online decision making with high-dimensional covariates. *Operations Research, 68*(1), 276–294.

Bastani, H., Bayati, M., & Khosravi, K. (2020). Mostly exploration-free algorithms for contextual bandits. *Management Science*, Forthcoming.

Bastani, H., Harsha, P., Perakis, G., & Singhvi, D. (2018). *Sequential learning of product recommendations with customer disengagement*. Working paper, University of Pennsylvania.

Bastani, H., Simchi-Levi, D., & Zhu, R. (2019). *Meta dynamic pricing: Learning across experiments*. Working paper, University of Pennsylvania.

Baum, L. E., & Petrie, T. (1966). Statistical inference for probabilistic functions of finite state Markov chains. *The Annals of Mathematical Statistics, 37*(6):1554–1563.

Bellman, R. (1957). A Markovian decision process. *Journal of Mathematics and Mechanics, 6*(5), 679–684.

Bengio, Y., Courville, A., & Vincent, P. (2013). Representation learning: A review and new perspectives. *IEEE Transactions on Pattern Analysis and Machine Intelligence, 35*(8), 1798–1828.

Bengio, Y., Ducharme, R., Vincent, P., & Jauvin, C. (2003). A neural probabilistic language model. *Journal of Machine Learning Research, 3*, 1137–1155.

Berger, J. O. (2013). *Statistical decision theory and Bayesian analysis*. New York, NY: Springer Science & Business Media.

Bernstein, F., Modaresi, S., & Sauré, D. (2019). A dynamic clustering approach to data-driven assortment personalization. *Management Science, 65*(5), 2095–2115.

Bertsimas, D., Farias, V. F., & Trichakis, N. (2011). The price of fairness. *Operations Research, 59*(1), 17–31.

Bertsimas, D., & Kallus, N. (2020). From predictive to prescriptive analytics. *Management Science, 66*(3), 1025–1044.

Bertsimas, D., Kallus, N., Weinstein, A. M., & Zhuo, Y. D. (2017). Personalized diabetes management using electronic medical records. *Diabetes Care, 40*(2), 210–217.

Besbes, O., Gur, Y., & Zeevi, A. (2014). Stochastic multi-armed-bandit problem with non-stationary rewards. In *Advances in Neural Information Processing Systems* (pp. 199–207).

Bezdek, J. C. (1973). *Fuzzy mathematics in pattern classification*. PhD Thesis, Cornell University, Ithaca, NY.

Biggs, M., & Hariss, R. (2018). *Optimizing objective functions determined from random forests*. Working paper, University of Virginia.

Bishop, C. M. (2006). *Pattern recognition and machine learning*. Berlin: Springer

Boute, R. N., Gijsbrechts, J., & Van Mieghem, J. A. (2022). Digital lean operations: Smart automation and artificial intelligence in financial services. In Babich, V., Birge, J., & Hilary, G. (Eds.), *Innovative technology at the interface of Finance and Operations*. Springer Series in Supply Chain Management. Springer Natures.

Box, G. E.P., Jenkins, G., Reinsel, G. C. (1970). *Time series analysis, forecasting and control*. San Francisco, CA: Holden-Day.

Brafman, R. I., & Tennenholtz, M. (2002). R-max—a general polynomial time algorithm for near-optimal reinforcement learning. *Journal of Machine Learning Research, 3*, 213–231.

Breiman, L. (1996a). Bagging predictors. *Machine Learning, 24*(2), 123–140.

Breiman, L. (1996b). Heuristics of instability and stabilization in model selection. *The Annals of Statistics, 24*(6), 2350–2383.

Breiman, L. (2001). Random forests. *Machine Learning, 45*(1), 5–32.

Breiman, L., Friedman, J., Stone, C. J., & Olshen, R. A. (1984). *Classification and regression trees*. Monterey, CA: Wadsworth and Brooks.

Breunig, M. M., Kriegel, H. P., Ng, R. T., & Sander, J. (2000). LOF: identifying density-based local outliers. In: *Proceedings of the 2000 ACM SIGMOD International Conference on Management of Data* (pp. 93–104).

Buhmann, M. D. (2003). *Radial basis functions: theory and implementations* (vol. 12). Cambridge, UK: Cambridge University Press.

Burlig, F., Knittel, C., Rapson, D., Reguant, M., & Wolfram, C. (2020). Machine learning from schools about energy efficiency. *Journal of the Association of Environmental and Resource Economists, 7*(6), 1181–1217.

Chen, Y. C., & Mišić, V. V. (2019). *Decision forest: A nonparametric approach to modeling irrational choice*. Working paper, University of California at Los Angeles.

Chen, F., Liu, X., Proserpio, D., & Troncoso, I. (2020). *Product2vec: Understanding product-level competition using representation learning*. Working paper, University of South Carolina.

Cheung, W. C., Simchi-Levi, D., & Zhu, R. (2018). Hedging the drift: Learning to optimize under non-stationarity. Available at SSRN 3261050.

Chernozhukov, V., Chetverikov, D., Demirer, M., Duflo, E., Hansen, C., Newey, W., & Robins, J. (2018). Double/debiased machine learning for treatment and structural parameters. *The Econometrics Journal, 21*(1), C1–C68.

Chipman, H. A., George, E. I., McCulloch, R. E. (2010). Bart: Bayesian additive regression trees. *The Annals of Applied Statistics, 4*(1), 266–298.

Ciocan, D. F., & Mišić, V. V. (2020). Interpretable optimal stopping. *Management Science*. https://doi.org/10.1287/mnsc.2020.3592

Cleveland, W. S. (1979). Robust locally weighted regression and smoothing scatterplots. *Journal of the American Statistical Association, 74*(368), 829–836.

Cleveland, W. S., & Devlin, S. J. (1988) Locally weighted regression: an approach to regression analysis by local fitting. *Journal of the American Statistical Association, 83*(403), 596–610.

Cohen, M., Jiao, K., & Zhang, R. P. (2019). *Data aggregation and demand prediction*. Working paper, McGill University.

Cohen, M. C., Lobel, I., & Paes Leme, R. (2020). Feature-based dynamic pricing. *Management Science, 66*(11), 4921–4943. INFORMS.

Cortes, C., & Vapnik, V. (1995). Support-vector networks. *Machine Learning, 20*(3), 273–297.

Croston, J. D. (1972). Forecasting and stock control for intermittent demands. *Journal of the Operational Research Society, 23*(3), 289–303.

Cui, R., Gallino, S., Moreno, A., & Zhang, D. J. (2018). The operational value of social media information. *Production and Operations Management, 27*(10), 1749–1769.

Cui, R., Li, J., & Zhang, D. J. (2020). Reducing discrimination with reviews in the sharing economy: Evidence from field experiments on Airbnb. *Management Science, 66*(3), 1071–1094.

Dai, J., & Shi, P. (2019). Inpatient overflow: An approximate dynamic programming approach. *Manufacturing & Service Operations Management, 21*(4), 894–911.

Day, N. E. (1969). Estimating the components of a mixture of normal distributions. *Biometrika, 56*(3), 463–474.

Dempster, A. P., Laird, N. M., & Rubin, D. B. (1977). Maximum likelihood from incomplete data via the EM algorithm. *Journal of the Royal Statistical Society: Series B (Methodological), 39*(1), 1–22.

Deng, J., Dong, W., Socher, R., Li, L. J., Li, K., Fei-Fei, L. (2009). ImageNet: A large-scale hierarchical image database. In *2009 IEEE Conference on Computer Vision and Pattern Recognition* (pp. 248–255). IEEE.

Doudchenko, N., Zhang, M., Drynkin, E., Airoldi, E., Mirrokni, V., Pouget-Abadie, J. (2020). *Causal inference with bipartite designs*. Working paper, Massachusetts Institute of Technology.

Elmachtoub, A. N., & Grigas, P. (2017). *Smart "predict, then optimize"*. Working paper, Columbia University.

Elmachtoub, A. N., Liang, J. C. N., & McNellis, R. (2020). *Decision trees for decision-making under the predict-then-optimize framework*. Working paper, Columbia University.

Ester, M., Kriegel, H. P., Sander, J., & Xu, X. (1996). A density-based algorithm for discovering clusters in large spatial databases with noise. In *Kdd* (vol. 96, pp. 226–231).

Farias, V. F., Jagabathula, S., & Shah, D. (2013). A nonparametric approach to modeling choice with limited data. *Management Science, 59*(2), 305–322.

Farias, V. F., & Li, A. A. (2019). Learning preferences with side information. *Management Science, 65*(7), 3131–3149.

Ferreira, K. J., Lee, B. H. A., & Simchi-Levi, D. (2016). Analytics for an online retailer: Demand forecasting and price optimization. *Manufacturing & Service Operations Management, 18*(1), 69–88.

Fix, E. (1951). *Discriminatory analysis: nonparametric discrimination, consistency properties*. San Francisco, CA: USAF School of Aviation Medicine.

Freund, Y. (1995). Boosting a weak learning algorithm by majority. *Information and Computation, 121*(2), 256–285.

Friedman, J., Hastie, T., & Tibshirani, R. (2001). *The elements of statistical learning*. New York, NY: Springer Series in Statistics.

Friedman, N., Geiger, D., & Goldszmidt, M. (1997) Bayesian network classifiers. *Machine Learning, 29*(2–3), 131–163.

Fukushima, K. (2013). Training multi-layered neural network neocognitron. *Neural Networks, 40*, 18–31.

Gardner Jr, E. S. (1985). Exponential smoothing: The state of the art. *Journal of Forecasting, 4*(1), 1–28.

Gijsbrechts, J., Boute, R. N., Van Mieghem, J. A., & Zhang, D. (2019). *Can deep reinforcement learning improve inventory management? Performance on dual sourcing, lost sales and multi-echelon problems*. Working paper, Católica Lisbon School of Business and Economics.

Gittins, J. C. (1979). Bandit processes and dynamic allocation indices. *Journal of the Royal Statistical Society: Series B (Methodological), 41*(2), 148–164.

Glaeser, CK., Fisher, M., & Su, X. (2019). Optimal retail location: Empirical methodology and application to practice. *Manufacturing & Service Operations Management, 21*(1), 86–102.

Glorot, X., Bordes, A., & Bengio, Y. (2011). Deep sparse rectifier neural networks. In *Proceedings of the Fourteenth International Conference on Artificial Intelligence and Statistics* (pp. 315–323).

Goodfellow, I., Bengio, Y., Courville, A., & Bengio, Y. (2016). *Deep learning* (vol. 1). Cambridge, MA: MIT Press.

Goodfellow, I., Pouget-Abadie, J., Mirza, M., Xu, B., Warde-Farley, D., Ozair, S., Courville, A., & Bengio, Y. (2014). Generative adversarial nets. In *Advances in Neural Information Processing Systems* (pp. 2672–2680).

Govindarajan, A., Sinha, A., & Uichanco, J. (2021). Distribution-free inventory risk pooling in a multilocation newsvendor. *Management Science, 67*(4), 2272–2291. INFORMS.

Gur, Y., Momeni, A., & Wager, S. (2019). *Smoothness-adaptive stochastic bandits*. Technical Report, Stanford University.

Hardt, M., Price, E., & Srebro, N. (2016). Equality of opportunity in supervised learning. In *Advances in Neural Information Processing Systems* (pp. 3315–3323).

Hastie, T. J., & Tibshirani, R. J. (1990). *Generalized additive models* (vol. 43). London, UK: Chapman and Hall.

He, K., Zhang, X., Ren, S., & Sun, J. (2016). Deep residual learning for image recognition. In *Proceedings of the IEEE Conference on computer Vision and Pattern Recognition* (pp. 770–778).

Hinton, G. E., Osindero, S., & Teh, Y. W. (2006). A fast learning algorithm for deep belief nets. *Neural Computation, 18*(7), 1527–1554.

Ho, T. K. (1995). Random decision forests. In *Proceedings of 3rd International Conference on Document Analysis and Recognition* (vol. 1, pp. 278–282). IEEE.

Hochreiter, S., & Schmidhuber, J. (1997). Long short-term memory. *Neural Computation, 9*(8), 1735–1780.

Hoerl, A. E., & Kennard, R. W. (1970). Ridge regression: Biased estimation for nonorthogonal problems. *Technometrics, 12*(1), 55–67.

Hopfield, J. J. (1982). Neural networks and physical systems with emergent collective computational abilities. *Proceedings of the National Academy of Sciences, 79*(8), 2554–2558.

Hu, K., Acimovic, J., Erize, F., Thomas, D. J., & Van Mieghem, J. A. (2019). Forecasting new product life cycle curves: Practical approach and empirical analysis. *Manufacturing & Service Operations Management, 21*(1), 66–85.

Ibrahim, R., & Kim, S. H. (2019). Is expert input valuable? The case of predicting surgery duration. *Seoul Journal of Business, 25*(2), 1–34. The Institute of Management Research, SNU.

Ibrahim, R., Kim, S. H., & Tong, J. (2021). Eliciting human judgment for prediction algorithms. *Management Science, 67*(4), 2314–2325. INFORMS.

Jacob, F., Zhang, D., Liu, X., & Zhang, N. (2018). Customer choice models versus machine learning: Finding optimal product displays on Alibaba. *Operations Research*, Working Paper. Washington University in St. Louis.

Jagabathula, S., & Rusmevichientong, P. (2017). A nonparametric joint assortment and price choice model. *Management Science, 63*(9), 3128–3145.

Jagabathula, S., & Vulcano, G. (2018). A partial-order-based model to estimate individual preferences using panel data. *Management Science, 64*(4), 1609–1628.

Jagabathula, S., Subramanian, L., & Venkataraman, A. (2018). A model-based embedding technique for segmenting customers. *Operations Research, 66*(5), 1247–1267.

Jin, C., Allen-Zhu, Z., Bubeck, S., & Jordan, M. I. (2018). Is q-learning provably efficient? In *Advances in Neural Information Processing Systems* (pp. 4863–4873).

Johari, R., Li, H., & Weintraub, G. (2020). *Experimental design in two-sided platforms: An analysis of bias*. Working paper, Stanford University.

Joulani, P., Gyorgy, A., Szepesvári, C. (2013). Online learning under delayed feedback. In *International Conference on Machine Learning* (pp. 1453–1461).

Kaufman, L., & PJ, R. (1987). *Clustering by means of medoids*. Delft university of technology technical report, Delft University of Technology.

Kearns, M., & Singh, S. (2002). Near-optimal reinforcement learning in polynomial time. *Machine Learning, 49*(2–3), 209–232.

Keskin, N. B., & Zeevi, A. (2014). Dynamic pricing with an unknown demand model: Asymptotically optimal semi-myopic policies. *Operations Research, 62*(5), 1142–1167.

Kleinberg, J. (2018). Inherent trade-offs in algorithmic fairness. In *Abstracts of the 2018 ACM International Conference on Measurement and Modeling of Computer Systems* (pp. 40–40).

Kleinberg, R., & Leighton, T. (2003). The value of knowing a demand curve: Bounds on regret for online posted-price auctions. In *Proceedings of the 44th Annual IEEE Symposium on Foundations of Computer Science, 2003* (pp. 594–605). IEEE.

Knorr, E. M., Ng, R. T., & Tucakov, V. (2000). Distance-based outliers: Algorithms and applications. *The VLDB Journal, 8*(3–4), 237–253.

Konda, V. R., & Tsitsiklis, J. N. (2000). Actor-critic algorithms. In *Advances in Neural Information Processing Systems* (pp. 1008–1014).

Kramer, M. A. (1991). Nonlinear principal component analysis using autoassociative neural networks. *AIChE Journal, 37*(2), 233–243.

Kroer, C., & Stier-Moses, N. E. (2022). Market equilibrium models in large-scale internet markets. In Babich, V., Birge, J., & Hilary, G. (Eds.), *Innovative technology at the interface of Finance and Operations*. Springer Series in Supply Chain Management. Springer Natures, Forthcoming.

LeCun, Y., Boser, B., Denker, J. S., Henderson, D., Howard, R. E., Hubbard, W., & Jackel, L. D. (1989). Backpropagation applied to handwritten zip code recognition. *Neural Computation, 1*(4), 541–551.

Lewis, D. D., & Ringuette, M. (1994). A comparison of two learning algorithms for text categorization. In *Third Annual Symposium on Document Analysis and Information Retrieval* (vol. 33, pp. 81–93).

Li, K. J., Fong, D. K., & Xu, S. H. (2011). Managing trade-in programs based on product characteristics and customer heterogeneity in business-to-business markets. *Manufacturing & Service Operations Management, 13*(1), 108–123.

Liu, S., He, L., & Shen, Z. J. M. (2018). On-time last mile delivery: Order assignment with travel time predictors. *Management Science*, Forthcoming.

Loughran, T., & McDonald, B. (2011). When is a liability not a liability? Textual analysis, dictionaries, and 10-ks. *The Journal of Finance, 66*(1), 35–65.

Lu, Z., Pu, H., Wang, F., Hu, Z., & Wang, L. (2017). The expressive power of neural networks: A view from the width. In *Advances in Neural Information Processing Systems* (pp. 6231–6239).

MacQueen, J. (1967). Some methods for classification and analysis of multivariate observations. In *Proceedings of the Fifth Berkeley Symposium on Mathematical Statistics and Probability*, Oakland, CA, USA, 14 (pp. 281–297).

Mandi, J., Demirović, E., Stuckey, P., & Guns, T. (2019). *Smart predict-and-optimize for hard combinatorial optimization problems*. Working paper, Vrije Universiteit Brussel.

Marr, B. (2016). *A short history of machine learning–every manager should read*. http://tinyurl.com/gslvr6k

McCarthy, J., & Feigenbaum, E. A. (1990). In memoriam: Arthur Samuel: Pioneer in machine learning. *AI Magazine, 11*(3), 10–10.

Mikolov, T., Chen, K., Corrado, G., & Dean, J. (2013). *Efficient estimation of word representations in vector space*. Preprint arXiv:13013781.

Mnih, V., Badia, A. P., Mirza, M., Graves, A., Lillicrap, T., Harley, T., Silver, D., & Kavukcuoglu, K. (2016). Asynchronous methods for deep reinforcement learning. In *International Conference on Machine Learning* (pp. 1928–1937).

Montoya, R., & Gonzalez, C. (2019). A hidden Markov model to detect on-shelf out-of-stocks using point-of-sale data. *Manufacturing & Service Operations Management, 21*(4), 932–948.

Moon, T. K. (1996). The expectation-maximization algorithm. *IEEE Signal Processing Magazine, 13*(6), 47–60.

Morales, D. R., & Wang, J. (2010). Forecasting cancellation rates for services booking revenue management using data mining. *European Journal of Operational Research, 202*(2), 554–562.

Mintz, Y., Aswani, A., Kaminsky, P., Flowers, E., & Fukuoka, Y. (2020). Nonstationary bandits with habituation and recovery dynamics. *Operations Research, 68*(5), 1493–1516. INFORMS.

Mišić, V.V. (2020). Optimization of tree ensembles. *Operations Research, 68*(5), 1605–1624.

Nelder, J. A., & Wedderburn, R. W. (1972). Generalized linear models. *Journal of the Royal Statistical Society: Series A (General), 135*(3), 370–384.

Pan, S. J., & Yang, Q. (2009). A survey on transfer learning. *IEEE Transactions on Knowledge and Data Engineering, 22*(10), 1345–1359.

Pearson, K. (1901). LIII. on lines and planes of closest fit to systems of points in space. *The London, Edinburgh, and Dublin philosophical Magazine and Journal of Science, 2*(11), 559–572.

PwC (2020). *Internet advertising revenue report: Full year 2019 results & q1 2020 revenues*. https://www.iab.com/wp-content/uploads/2020/05/FY19-IAB-Internet-Ad-Revenue-Report_Final.pdf

Queenan, C., Cameron, K., Snell, A., Smalley, J., & Joglekar, N. (2019). Patient heal thyself: Reducing hospital readmissions with technology-enabled continuity of care and patient activation. *Production and Operations Management, 28*(11), 2841–2853.

Rumelhart, D. E., Hinton, G. E., & Williams, R. J. (1986). Learning representations by back-propagating errors. *Nature, 323*(6088), 533–536.

Rusmevichientong, P., Shen, Z. J. M., & Shmoys, D. B. (2010). Dynamic assortment optimization with a multinomial logit choice model and capacity constraint. *Operations Research, 58*(6), 1666–1680.

Russo, D. J., Van Roy, B., Kazerouni, A., Osband, I., & Wen, Z. (2018). *A tutorial on Thompson sampling* (vol. 11). Hanover, MA: Now Publishers.

van Ryzin, G., & Vulcano, G. (2015). A market discovery algorithm to estimate a general class of nonparametric choice models. *Management Science, 61*(2), 281–300.

van Ryzin, G., & Vulcano, G. (2017). An expectation-maximization method to estimate a rank-based choice model of demand. *Operations Research, 65*(2), 396–407.

Sahami, M., Dumais, S., Heckerman, D., & Horvitz, E. (1998). A Bayesian approach to filtering junk e-mail. In *Learning for Text Categorization: Papers from the 1998 Workshop* (pp. 98–105).

Schapire, R. E. (1990). The strength of weak learnability. *Machine Learning, 5*(2), 197–227.

Scherer, D., Müller, A., & Behnke, S. (2010). Evaluation of pooling operations in convolutional architectures for object recognition. In *International Conference on Artificial Neural Networks* (pp. 92–101). Springer.

Schulman, J., Levine, S., Abbeel, P., Jordan, M., & Moritz, P. (2015). Trust region policy optimization. In *International Conference on Machine Learning* (pp. 1889–1897).

Shen, H., & Huang, J. Z. (2008). Interday forecasting and intraday updating of call center arrivals. *Manufacturing & Service Operations Management, 10*(3), 391–410.

Shen, Z. J. M., Tang, C. S., Wu, D., Yuan, R., & Zhou, W. (2019). *Jd. com: Transaction level data for the 2020 MSOM data driven research challenge*. Working paper, University of California at Berkeley.

Şimşek, A. S., & Topaloglu, H. (2018). An expectation-maximization algorithm to estimate the parameters of the Markov chain choice model. *Operations Research, 66*(3), 748–760.

Slivkins, A. (2019). *Introduction to multi-armed bandits*. Technical Report, Microsoft Research, working Paper.

Strehl, A. L., Li, L., Wiewiora, E., Langford, J., & Littman, M. L. (2006). Pac model-free reinforcement learning. In *Proceedings of the 23rd International Conference on Machine Learning* (pp. 881–888).

Sun, L., Lyu, G., Yu, Y., & Teo, C. P. (2020). Cross-border e-commerce data set: Choosing the right fulfillment option. *Manufacturing & Service Operations Management*. https://doi.org/10.1287/msom.2020.0887

Sutton, R. S. (1988). Learning to predict by the methods of temporal differences. *Machine Learning, 3*(1), 9–44.

Sutton, R. S., McAllester, D. A., Singh, S. P., & Mansour, Y. (2000). Policy gradient methods for reinforcement learning with function approximation. In *Advances in Neural Information Processing Systems* (pp. 1057–1063).

Swaminathan, A., & Joachims, T. (2015). Counterfactual risk minimization: Learning from logged bandit feedback. In *International Conference on Machine Learning* (pp. 814–823).

Taigman, Y., Yang, M., Ranzato, M., & Wolf, L. (2014). DeepFace: Closing the gap to human-level performance in face verification. In *Proceedings of the IEEE Conference on Computer Vision and Pattern Recognition* (pp. 1701–1708).

Talluri, K., & Van Ryzin, G. (2004). Revenue management under a general discrete choice model of consumer behavior. *Management Science, 50*(1), 15–33.

Thompson, W. R. (1933). On the likelihood that one unknown probability exceeds another in view of the evidence of two samples. *Biometrika, 25*(3/4), 285–294.

Tibshirani, R. (1996). Regression shrinkage and selection via the lasso. *Journal of the Royal Statistical Society: Series B (Methodological), 58*(1), 267–288.

Ugander, J., & Yin, H. (2020). *Randomized graph cluster randomization*. Working paper, Stanford University.

Varian, H. R. (2016). Causal inference in economics and marketing. *Proceedings of the National Academy of Sciences, 113*(27), 7310–7315.

Vulcano, G., Van Ryzin, G., & Ratliff, R. (2012). Estimating primary demand for substitutable products from sales transaction data. *Operations Research, 60*(2), 313–334.

Wager, S., & Athey, S. (2018). Estimation and inference of heterogeneous treatment effects using random forests. *Journal of the American Statistical Association, 113*(523), 1228–1242.

Wang, G., Li, J., & Hopp, W. J. (2017). *Personalized health care outcome analysis of cardiovascular surgical procedures*. Working paper, The University of Texas at Dallas.

Wang, G., Li, J., & Hopp, W. J. (2018). *An instrumental variable tree approach for detecting heterogeneous treatment effects in observational studies*. Working paper, The University of Texas at Dallas.

Ward Jr, J. H. (1963). Hierarchical grouping to optimize an objective function. *Journal of the American Statistical Association, 58*(301), 236–244.

Watkins, C. J. C. H. (1989). *Learning from delayed rewards*. PhD Thesis, King's College, Cambridge, UK.

Watkins, C. J., & Dayan, P. (1992). Q-learning. *Machine learning, 8*(3–4), 279–292.

Williams, R. J. (1992). Simple statistical gradient-following algorithms for connectionist reinforcement learning. *Machine Learning, 8*(3–4), 229–256.

Wu, Y., Shariff, R., Lattimore, T., Szepesvári, C. (2016). Conservative bandits. In *International Conference on Machine Learning* (pp. 1254–1262).

Wylie, C. (2018). *The history of neural networks and AI: Part II*. https://opendatascience.com/the-history-of-neural-networks-and-ai-part-ii

Ye, Z., Zhang, D., Zhang, H., Zhang, R. P., Chen, X., Xu, Z. (2020). *Cold start on online advertising platforms: Data-driven algorithms and field experiments*. Working paper, University of Illinois at Urbana-Champaign.

Zhang, B., Hsu, M., & Dayal, U. (1999). *K-harmonic means-a data clustering algorithm*. Hewlett-Packard labs Technical Report HPL-1999-124, Hewlett-Packard.

Zhang, D., Hu, M., Liu, X., Wu, Y., & Li, Y. (2020). NetEase cloud music data. *Manufacturing & Service Operations Management*. https://doi.org/10.1287/msom.2020.0923

Zhang, S., Lee, D., Singh, P. V., & Srinivasan, K. (2016). *How much is an image worth? An empirical analysis of property's image aesthetic quality on demand at Airbnb*. Working paper, Carnegie Mellon University.

Chapter 8
Artificial Intelligence and Fraud Detection

Yang Bao, Gilles Hilary, and Bin Ke

8.1 Introduction and Motivation

Fraud exists in all walks of life. It is an economically significant issue. For example, some studies suggest that losses associated with credit card fraud in the United States alone are close to $17 billion.[1]The recent development in artificial intelligence (AI) in general, and machine learning in particular, has opened potential new venues to tackle fraud. However, recent research by the software firm SAS and the Association of Certified Fraud Examiners suggests that a mere 13% of organizations across industries take advantage of these technologies to detect and deter fraud.[2]

We thank Kai Guo for research assistance.

[1]https://www.wsj.com/articles/borrower-beware-credit-card-fraud-attempts-rise-during-the-coronavirus-crisis-11,590,571,800

[2]https://www.technologyreview.com/2019/11/18/131912/6-essentials-for-fighting-fraud-with-machine-learning/

Y. Bao
Antai College of Economics and Management, Shanghai Jiao Tong University, Shanghai, People's Republic of China
e-mail: baoyang@sjtu.edu.cn

G. Hilary (✉)
McDonough School of Business, Georgetown University, Washington, DC, USA

B. Ke
Department of Accounting, NUS Business School, National University of Singapore, Singapore, Singapore
e-mail: bizk@nus.edu.sg

V. Babich et al. (eds.), *Innovative Technology at the Interface of Finance and Operations*, Springer Series in Supply Chain Management 11,
https://doi.org/10.1007/978-3-030-75729-8_8

There are different reasons for this relative lack of implementation. Indeed, not all types of fraudulent activities are equally suited for AI treatment. For example, credit card fraud is a good setting for experimenting with machine learning algorithms. The high frequency of credit card transactions provides large datasets required for training, backtesting, and validation of machine learning algorithms.[3]Since a fraudulent activity is rather unambiguously defined, it facilitates the labeling of historical data to train classification algorithms. The historical datasets contain a diversified set of features that can be potentially incorporated in models, ranging from transaction characteristics, cardholder, or transaction history. In contrast, the detection of money laundering activities is more challenging. For example, it is much more difficult to determine whether an activity can be legally characterized as money laundering. They may involve multiple parties operating outside the perimeter of the firm. Given the sensitivity of the data involved, financial institutions may be more reluctant to share data (even in pseudo-anonymized format). Unsurprisingly, more progress has been achieved in deploying machine learning techniques to combat credit card fraud than to address money-laundering activities.

Generally, machine learning still struggles with more complex problems. The technology has recently made tremendous progress with facial, voice, and text recognition. In these cases, data are abundant. Some progress has also been achieved in using machine learning to categorize certain events that can be reasonably easily classified by humans. For example, algorithms to detect spam or doctored documents are now reasonably mature. Importantly, as we discuss subsequently, this does not mean that organizations do not face issues when they deploy systems to automate these tasks. In contrast, machine learning may not work well in more complex social situations, especially if they occur over extended periods. In this case, simple rules or human judgment may be more effective. For example, in Salganik et al. (2020), a large group of social scientists (160 teams) tried to predict six life outcomes (e.g., child's grade point average and whether a family would be evicted from their home) using machine learning methods. The first five waves of data and part of the sixth were available to the researchers; the goal was to predict outcomes in the sixth. The dataset contained close to 13,000 variables for over 4000 families for 15 years. Data collection included in-depth interviews and in-home observations repeated several times over many years. However, machine learning tools offered little improvement over standard methods in social science (Garip, 2020). Overall, the algorithms barely explained more than a linear regression based on four variables.

We discuss several of these challenges in this chapter. We do not attempt to review the entire literature on fraud, nor do we cover artificial intelligence or even machine learning in depth. The primary objective of the chapter is to identify the opportunities and challenges associated with deploying machine learning techniques to combat fraud, both from practical and academic perspectives. Many of our

[3]See Boute et al. (2022) for a more in-depth discussion on the use of AI in financial services.

statements apply to fraud detection in general. However, to better contextualize our discussion, we will often refer to a specific form of fraud, financial statement manipulation (i.e., accounting fraud).

We focus on financial statement manipulation for several reasons. First, accounting fraud is a worldwide problem. Well-known accounting fraud cases include Parmalat in Europe, Enron in the United States, and Sino-Forest in China. Second, the consequences of corporate accounting fraud are quite severe. Shareholders, creditors, customers, suppliers, employees, and audit firms all suffer. Karpoff et al. (2008) find that, on average, the fraudulent firms lose 38% of their market values when news of their misconduct is reported.[4] The revelation of accounting fraud cases could also create a significant spillover effect on many innocent companies. For example, Darrough et al. (2020) show that fraud allegations of some Chinese concept stocks result in strong negative spillover effects on the non-fraudulent Chinese concept stocks. Distinguishing between seemingly similar cases is, therefore, important.

Because of the significant costs and externalities associated with fraud, it is important to prevent and detect accounting fraud on a timely basis so that the damages of accounting fraud can be eliminated or mitigated. For example, external auditors are responsible for detecting material fraud in the Statement on Auditing Standards of some jurisdictions.[5] However, as we explain subsequently, accounting fraud detection is a very challenging task for various reasons. Prior research also suggests that existing fraud detection technologies lag, despite the increased frequency and costs of accounting fraud (KPMG, 1998; Ernst & Young, 2010). However, the significant advances in machine learning and AI technologies offer exciting opportunities to develop more powerful fraud prediction models in recent years.

The rest of the chapter is as follows. In Sect. 8.2, we review some of the challenges associated with fraud detection. In Sect. 8.3, we use a framework (data, method, and evaluation criterion) to review some of the practical considerations that affect the implementation of machine learning models to predict fraud. In Sect. 8.4, we review select papers in the academic literature that can help address some of the challenges discussed in Sect. 8.2 and provide a discussion of future directions for this line of research. We conclude in Sect. 8.5.

[4] In a 10-year review of corporate accounting fraud commissioned by the Committee of Sponsoring Organization of the Treadway Commission (COSO), Beasley et al. (2010) find that the total cumulative misstatement or misappropriation of nearly $120 billion across 300 fraud cases with available information (mean of nearly $400 million per case) (Beasley et al., 1999).

[5] See SAS no. 99 (American Institute of Certified Public Accountants, 2002) for a discussion of this issue in a U.S. context.

8.2 Challenges of Fraud Detection

We start this discussion by reviewing the empirical challenges that are specific to fraud detection using machine learning.

8.2.1 *Problems with Fraud and Machine Learning in General*

First, detected fraud cases are rare. For example, the U.S.'s rate of credit card fraud in 2015 was below 0.1%.[6]Most machine learning algorithms work best when the number of samples in each class is approximately equal because most algorithms are designed to maximize accuracy and reduce error. It is hard for algorithms to learn when samples are really unbalanced as they do not frequently encounter fraud cases. The existing literature is aware of this problem and has resorted to various methods to deal with this challenge.

Second, fraud is adversarial. Machine learning techniques work best when patterns are stable and important data are not omitted systematically or, worse, manipulated. In many applications of machine learning, parties are cooperating with the system to facilitate its learning (e.g., medical applications) or, at worst, are neutral toward it. In the case of fraud, perpetrators try to prevent the learning. For example, fraudsters may open accounts in different financial institutions in different jurisdictions to prevent an effective network analysis. Furthermore, fraudsters are constantly imagining new schemes. Thus, there may not be a precedent for algorithms to detect a new type of fraud.

8.2.2 *Problems that Are Specific to Accounting Fraud and Machine Learning*

Aside from these general concerns, specific types of fraud can have specific issues. We focus on accounting fraud to present examples of domain-specific issues.

First, many accounting fraud cases remain undetected or at least take a long time to be recognized. Most credit card frauds can be quickly identified and a determination of the existence of fraud after a complaint is straightforward in most cases. In contrast, determining the existence of an accounting fraud requires significant investigative resources in many instances, and the distinction between creative but legitimate practices and fraud may be difficult to ascertain. Models that explicitly consider the fact that fraud may be undetected are rare. Further,

[6]https://www.federalreserve.gov/publications/files/changes-in-us-payments-fraud-from-2012-to-2016-20181016.pdf

accounting fraud cases are often detected by regulators. In contrast, other types of fraud may be identified by the victim. To the extent that regulators are ineffective or biased, models of fraud detection will be ineffective and biased. For example, Dyck et al. (2020) estimate that only about half of severe financial reporting violation cases are detected by the Security Exchange Commission (SEC). This issue is likely to be even more serious in less developed countries with weaker institutional environments.

Second, if a firm commits accounting fraud, it tends to misstate accounting reports for several years before being caught. Most existing fraud prediction studies do not consider this serial fraud feature in model building. Instead, they tend to treat each firm-year as an independent observation, ignoring the time series dependence of serial fraud cases. Studies that consider the serial fraud issue sidestep this problem by using only the initial fraudulent year (e.g., Amiram et al., 2015) or removing the serial fraud observations in the training year or test year (e.g., Brown et al., 2020).

Finally, due to the time variation in managerial incentives and monitoring intensity, accounting fraud behavior exhibits regime shifts both over time and cross-sectionally (Beasley et al., 1999; Beasley et al., 2010). Prior research (Dechow et al., 2011) shows that the frequency of accounting fraud varies significantly across industries. Except for Abbasi et al. (2012), the existing accounting fraud prediction models have not incorporated such regime shifts in model building.

8.3 Practical Considerations in Model Building

As noted by Abbasi et al. (2012), building any fraud prediction model requires a researcher to make important decisions on the following three crucial components: (a) What data inputs (predictors) and data outputs (fraud labels) should be used for the model? (b) What specific machine learning methods should be used for the prediction task? (c) What evaluation criteria should be used to judge the performance of a fraud prediction model? Subsequently, we elaborate on each of the abovementioned three components of model building.

8.3.1 Data

8.3.1.1 Data and Fraud

Data quality is crucial for AI to be effective. As systems go from rules to simple structural models, from structural models to machine learning, and from machine learning to deep learning, the amount and quality of data that models require increases. This creates several challenges.

Quantity

The first challenge is the quantity of data. This issue is progressively solved as the cost of acquiring and storing structured data in data warehouses and unstructured data in data lakes decreases. However, for smaller organizations, infrequent situations, or extremely complex estimations, this can remain an issue.

Quality

A second issue is the quality, integrity, and comprehensiveness of data. A torrential flow of data emerging from heterogeneous sources has no utility if it is not structured properly.[7] Data maintenance alone is a challenge. Indeed, many financial institutions have to contact thousands of customers every month to refresh Know-Your-Customer (KYC) documents and update information that is incorrect or missing in their databases. This issue is a particularly vexing problem if the validation must happen in continuous time. In addition, dealing with a legacy system can be difficult. A good example is the Michigan Unemployment Insurance Agency's (UIA) switch from a 30-year-old mainframe system running COBOL to a new system dubbed Michigan Integrated Data Automated System (MiDAS). After spending over $44 million and 26 months on the project, the UIA launched MiDAS in October 2013. Soon after, the number of persons suspected of unemployment fraud grew fivefold compared to the average number found using the old system. The use of MiDAS generated savings close to $70 million for the agency.[8] Unfortunately, the error rate of the new system was staggering (around 90%). In August 2015, the agency stopped using the system without human intervention, but by then, MiDAS may have already falsely accused at least 20,000 people. The problem was at least partly rooted in the transfer of scanned documents to the new system.[9]

More generally, legacy systems typically suffer from integration problems when they need to interact with machine learning platforms. Their workflow, data management, and change controls are often poorly aligned with the needs of a modern machine learning system. This problem is mitigated when the machine learning system is deployed in parallel (e.g., ex post analysis of transactions to meet anti-money laundering requirements) but exacerbated when directly integrated into the workflow (e.g., in a payment process).

One may assess the quality of big data along four dimensions: volume, velocity, variety, and veracity. Unfortunately, the first three dimensions can impede the last. For example, heterogeneous data formats can affect data consistency. Firms nor-

[7] See Zhang et al. (2015) for a good discussion of these issues.

[8] https://spectrum.ieee.org/riskfactor/computing/software/michigans-midas-unemployment-system-algorithm-alchemy-that-created-lead-not-gold

[9] https://www.freep.com/story/news/local/michigan/2017/07/30/fraud-charges-unemployment-jobless-claimants/516332001/

mally decide what data to collect primarily based on legal and operational grounds. It is common for different operational entities within the same organization to develop their own policies for capturing, cleansing, normalizing, storing, searching, sharing, analyzing, and retaining data. Datasets are often segregated logically and physically across departments and geographical regions. Legal considerations may prevent the smooth integration of these datasets. For example, laws protecting national security typically prohibit the export of any data that falls within their scope, even if the data are shared within the same organization. China's state secret laws, which make the export of any state secret a criminal act, are examples of this type of regulation. Naturally, sharing across organizations is even more complicated. For example, the UK Data Protection Act allows for the storage and exchange of data between organizations. If a credit fraud-checking agency detects an anomaly between a new application for a lender and previous applications for other lending institutions, the agency can make each institution aware of the concern. In contrast, Ireland has not authorized this type of information sharing.[10]

Even absent legal issues, data integration can be difficult for technical reasons. The sheer size and complexity of datasets can make them difficult to manage and process using available database management tools. Nonstandard data structures, overlapping production cycles, and fragmented sources make data aggregation across legal entities, subsidiaries, and vendors difficult. Furthermore, data encryption and data stored on blockchains pause additional challenges.

Data that need to be moved and shared across departments or locations are generally provided in a summarized format and are limited to supporting specific functions, such as finance (e.g., invoicing and payment) or operations (e.g., shipping). These records are not necessarily the most relevant for fraud detection. For example, transactional data (e.g., phone call records) may not be readily available across departments.

Data mapping and traceability become key factors, and computer-assisted solutions have been designed to facilitate these processes, but naturally, they have their limitations. For example, while most enterprise resource planning (ERP) systems have certain fraud prevention and detection capabilities, systems often turn off controls to function more efficiently.[11]

Excess of Data

A third issue is (somewhat paradoxically) an excess of data. Over time, a legal structure has been developed to regulate the collection and storage of information. For example, the General Data Protection Regulation (GDPR) is a European data regulation that carries a maximum fine of the greater of €20 million or 4% of annual

[10] http://www.eurofinas.org/uploads/documents/Non-visible/Eurofinas-Accis_ReportOnFraud_WEB.pdf

[11] https://www.corporatecomplianceinsights.com/the-growing-problem-of-corporate-fraud/

global turnover for noncompliance. One of its provisions is that organizations are responsible for securing the data they collect. The British data regulator, Information Commissioner's Office (ICO), proposed a £183 m fine in 2019 for a 2018 breach. In the United States, a patchwork of state regulations has also gradually increased the disclosure requirements (see Chen et al. (2020) for an analysis of these laws). Aside from protecting the data once they have been collected, the organization needs first to pay attention to the legality of the data collection. For example, the Internet regulator in China investigated smartphone applications to determine whether they collect users' information illegally or excessively. The Ministry Industry and Information Technology targeted several popular applications such as Tencent's QQ and QQ Reading, Xiaomi's digital finance app Xiaomi Finance, and the intercity delivery service FlashEX in 2019.[12]In this context, the ever-increasing collection of data to feed the algorithms is not necessarily optimal. A standard cost-benefit analysis should be applied to data collection and storage and reflect the regulatory and reputation risk in case of breaches or misuses.

Biases

Finally, biases can be a significant issue.[13]Labeled training data can be biased because individuals have treated them with implicit or explicit biases. Ethnic biases have been well-publicized. For example, a recent NIST study reports the presence of demographic effects in the U.S. face recognition algorithms due to biases in the type of photos used.[14]Employing socially diverse individuals may mitigate this issue.

However, biases may also be introduced into algorithms if they learn from a third-party dataset contaminated by bias. For example, the Equal Credit Opportunity Act (ECOA) prohibits credit discrimination based on race, color, religion, national origin, sex, marital status, age, or because a person receives public assistance. If a company created a score to make credit decisions based on consumers' Zip Codes, resulting in a "disparate impact" on particular ethnic groups, this would likely be an illegal practice under ECOA.[15]This algorithm would also be contaminated if this score was subsequently incorporated in a dataset used in fraud detection.

However, the issue of biases is broader than the illegal ones. For example, if an algorithm analyzes official communication in a bank, there may be a tendency for traders who want to engage in nefarious activities to communicate through private

[12]https://technode.com/2019/12/19/tencent-xiaomi-apps-called-out-for-illegal-data-collection/

[13]Supervised models "learn" from labeled data. To train a supervised model, one presents both fraudulent and non-fraudulent records that have been labeled as such. Unsupervised models ask the model to "learn" the data structure on its own.

[14]https://nvlpubs.nist.gov/nistpubs/ir/2019/NIST.IR.8280.pdf

[15]https://www.ftc.gov/news-events/blogs/business-blog/2020/04/using-artificial-intelligence-algorithms

channels. This would then create potential biases in the analysis by systematically omitting important information.

8.3.1.2 Data and Financial Statement Fraud

Most financial statement fraud prediction studies employ supervised learning that requires data on both fraud labels (the dependent variable) and fraud predictors (the independent variables). The first critical decision one needs to make in building a fraud prediction model is to select an appropriate accounting fraud database. There are a variety of input data one could use to build fraud prediction models. Many studies utilize one data source only. For example, Dechow et al. (2011) focus on readily available accounting data, Cecchini et al. (2010) and Purda and Skillicorn (2015) use textual data only, while Dong et al. (2018) combine textual and network data together. However, few studies have attempted to combine all available input data of different kinds in building a unifying fraud prediction model.

Partially reflecting the ambiguity about what constitutes fraud, prior research has used different terms to describe fraud or alleged fraud, such as fraud, misconduct, irregularities, misreporting, and misrepresentation. Accordingly, the existing accounting fraud literature has used various databases to measure fraud, including the Government Accountability Office (GAO), Audit Analytics databases of restatement announcements, the Stanford Securities Class Action Clearinghouse (SCAC) database of securities class action lawsuits, and the SEC Accounting and Auditing Enforcement Releases. Karpoff et al. (2017) provide a detailed comparison of the pros and cons of using the four different databases for financial misconduct research. They find that the results from empirical tests can depend on which database is accessed and offer suggestions for researchers using these databases.

The second critical decision one has to make in building fraud prediction models is to select the list of fraud predictors. With the explosion of big data in the past decade, there exists a variety of predictors one could use to build accounting fraud prediction models. One may be tempted to throw in as many predictors as possible into a machine learning model for training and prediction, but Bao et al. (2020) confirm that more predictors do not necessarily improve prediction performance. Also, more costs are incurred when using more data, and the prediction model would be less generalizable to different countries and industries. Hence, a cost-benefit framework is also warranted in selecting the fraud predictors.

Following the cost-benefit framework, we could classify the fraud predictors based on the nature of the input data: structured data (e.g., accounting numbers) versus unstructured data (e.g., text, video, and voice). Unstructured data such as text or video are much harder to process than structured data and hence more costly. In addition, the useful information embedded in unstructured data could be already contained in the structured data. Given the increasing availability of many structured data sources, it makes sense to first extract as much useful information from structured data sources as possible before turning to the unstructured data sources for fraud prediction.

One could also classify the fraud predictors based on the causal motivation-ability-opportunity framework from the criminology literature. If one believes that the motivation-ability-opportunity framework is relatively comprehensive in explaining accounting fraud behavior, one could build powerful fraud prediction models based on theory-motivated input data as predictors. Past studies have developed many proxies for motivation (e.g., Burns & Kedia, 2006) and ability/personal traits (e.g., Davidson et al., 2015), while others have developed proxies for opportunity (e.g., Beasley, 1996; Larcker et al., 2007). Hence, researchers could select such theory-motivated fraud predictors in model building.

8.3.2 Methods

As analysts and researchers typically code fraud into a binary variable, logistic regressions have traditionally been the most popular learning method in the business literature before the rise of the machine learning field (e.g., Dechow et al., 2011). With the increasing availability of many unstructured databases and the emergence of methodological breakthroughs, researchers and analysts start to employ more sophisticated learning methods to train and predict accounting fraud. For example, Cecchini et al. (2010) and Perols et al. (2017) use support vector machines (SVM) to train a fraud prediction model. Amiram et al. (2015) apply Benford's Law to fraud prediction.

8.3.3 Evaluation Metrics

8.3.3.1 Evaluation Metrics in General

One issue with algorithms is what they should be maximizing. Often, the objective is to maximize accuracy under the assumption that efficient algorithms can both minimize false positives and false negatives. However, the two categories of errors need not entail similar private or social costs. More complex loss functions can be designed and incorporated into the algorithms. These different trade-offs need to be analyzed before algorithms are defined.

However, the definition of the loss function is more than a technical one. For example, organizations need to balance detection and customer experience. An algorithm that provides better classifications but requires intrusive data requests may be suboptimal. This concern becomes more relevant as regulation imposes more constraints on what kind of data organizations can collect, and future regulations may also impose constraints on the algorithm loss function. This potential disconnection between algorithm design and production constraints may explain why some statistics suggest that only 50% of all models developed ever make it into production.[16]

8.3.3.2 Evaluation Metrics for Accounting Fraud Prediction Models[17]

There are different ways to assess the performance of prediction models. The first classification performance metric considered is *accuracy*, defined as $\frac{TP+TN}{TP+FN+FP+TN}$, where TP (true positive) is the number of fraudulent firm-years that are correctly classified as fraud; FN (false negative) is the number of fraudulent firm-years that are misclassified as non-fraud; TN (true negative) is the number of non-fraudulent firm-years that are correctly classified as nonfraud; and FP (false positive) is the number of non-fraudulent firm-years that are misclassified as fraud. Bao et al. (2020) rejected *accuracy* as appropriate due to the imbalanced nature of our fraud versus non-fraud data. Over the period 1979–2014, the frequency of fraud detected by U.S. regulators is very low, typically <1% of all firms per year. Hence, a naive strategy of classifying all firm-years as nonfraud in their sample would lead to an accuracy of better than 99% based on *accuracy*. However, such seemingly high-performance fraud prediction models are of little value in our fraud prediction task because we care about both the true negative rate (i.e., *Specificity*) and the true positive rate (i.e., *Sensitivity*).

To properly gauge the performance of a fraud prediction model, Bao et al. (2020) also considered but rejected balanced accuracy (*BAC*) as an alternative performance evaluation metric (He & Ma, 2013). *BAC* is defined as the average of the fraud prediction accuracy within fraudulent observations and the nonfraud prediction accuracy within non-fraudulent observations. Specifically, $\mathrm{BAC} = \frac{1}{2} * (\mathit{Sensitivity} + \mathit{Specificity})$, where $Sensitivity = \frac{TP}{TP+FN}$ and $Specificity = \frac{TN}{TN+FP}$. Larcker and Zakolyukina (2012) note two important limitations of *BAC* as a performance evaluation metric. First, BAC is constructed based on a specific predicted fraud probability threshold of a given classifier, and the threshold is usually automatically determined by the classifier to maximize the BAC. In the absence of any knowledge of the costs of misclassifying false positives versus the costs of misclassifying false negatives, one cannot determine the optimal predicted fraud probability threshold for the purposes of classifying fraud and nonfraud. Second, measures such as S*ensitivity* are very sensitive to the relative frequency of positive and negative instances in the sample (i.e., data imbalance).

To avoid BAC's limitations, Bao et al. (2020) adopt AUC as one performance evaluation metric, following Larcker and Zakolyukina (2012). AUC is the area under the Receiver-Operating Characteristics (ROC) curve. A ROC curve is a two-dimensional depiction of a classifier's performance that combines the true positive rate (i.e., *Sensitivity*) and the false-positive rate (i.e., 1-*specificity*) in one graph

[16]https://mit-insights.ai/6-essentials-for-fighting-fraud-with-machine-learning/

[17]This section heavily relies on Bao et al. (2020).

(Fawcett, 2006). *BAC* represents only one point in the ROC curve. Many fraud prediction models use *AUC* as the primary performance evaluation metric.

Recall that the average frequency of detected accounting fraud among publicly listed U.S. firms is <1%. Therefore, even a top-performing fraud prediction model (e.g., Cecchini et al., 2010) would generate a large number of false positives. Table 7 in Cecchini et al. (2010) illustrates this point: Their SVM with a financial kernel correctly classifies 80% of the fraud observations and 90.6% of the non-fraudulent observations in the out-of-sample test period, the best among the competing models considered in their study. However, applying the Cecchini et al. model to the test period 2003–2008 considered by Bao et al. (2020) would result in too many false positives. Specifically, fraud occurred in only 237 of the 30,883 firm-years during the test period 2003–2008. Cecchini et al.'s method, however, would mislabel 2881 ((1–90.6%) × (30,883–237)) non-fraudulent observations as fraud—a serious overestimate of the number of actual cases of fraud in the test period.

To deal with this problem, Bao et al. (2020) introduce a new performance evaluation metric to the fraud prediction literature by treating the fraud prediction task as a ranking problem. Specifically, we can limit the out-of-sample performance evaluation to only a small number of firm-years with the highest predicted probability of fraud. In this scenario, the performance of a fraud prediction model can be measured by the following performance evaluation metric for ranking problems: Normalized Discounted Cumulative Gain at the position *k* (NDCG@k). NDCG@k is a widely used metric for evaluating ranking algorithms such as web search engine algorithms and recommendation algorithms (Järvelin & Kekäläinen, 2002) and has been theoretically proven effective (Wang et al., 2013). The values of NDCG@k are bounded between 0 and 1.0, and a higher value represents a model's better ranking performance. NDCG@k avoids the aforementioned problem of investigating too many false-positive cases by limiting the investigation to no more than a given number *k* of firm-years with the highest predicted fraud probability in the test period. As the average frequency of detected accounting fraud among publicly listed U.S. firms is <1%, Bao et al. (2020) set *k* equal to the top 1% of the firm-years in the test period.

8.3.4 Caveats about ML Models

Machine learning can be useful in the context of combating fraud in three ways: detection and interdiction, litigation, and prevention. An example of detection and interdiction is when a financial institution blocks credit card transactions in real time in case of suspicious activity. Litigation is a situation in which machine learning analysis is used to build a legal case. Prevention is an approach in which an organization uses machine learning insights to conduct a root cause analysis, reorganize its operations, and minimize the fraud risk in the first place. Each approach comes with its own set of issues.

In the case of detection and interdiction, the output of many algorithms is a score that predicts the risk level associated with a situation. However, users have to be clear about what is being predicted. In many cases, the algorithm will detect anomalous transactions (i.e., those that are different from an expected benchmark), but an anomalous transaction does not necessarily mean a problematic transaction. If the analysis is not conditioned properly, the lack of apparent anomaly can be problematic. For example, Parmalat (the largest European accounting fraud case to date) had very stable accounting ratios before the fraud was revealed.

Furthermore, what is normal can be unstable. For example, changes in the regulatory environment or socioeconomic environment (e.g., COVID-19) can modify people's behavior and require a new benchmarking.[18] Naturally, algorithms can learn, but the adjustment is unlikely to be immediate. Also, many algorithms are based on nonlinear statistics that yield unstable models. For example, several studies have shown that including an incongruous element (e.g., the picture of an elephant) can lead neural networks that otherwise detect and categorize objects (e.g., a person, a couch, and a television) with high confidence to miscategorize the objects completely.[19]

Another issue with the fraud prediction score is explainability. Current machine learning algorithms are notoriously bad at dealing with this issue. The importance of this weakness varies with the objective of fraud detection. If the objective is prevention through interdiction (e.g., credit card), the need for explainability can be lower. However, even in this situation, the issue cannot be ignored. For example, the European GDPR requires "the data subject shall have the right to obtain from the controller [. . .] information [about] the existence of automated decision-making, including profiling, [. . .] and, at least in those cases, meaningful information about the logic involved, as well as the significance and the envisaged consequences of such processing for the data subject." Human intervention is key, and processes must allow for a review by someone who has the appropriate authority and capability to change the decision generated by the system. An overtly complex algorithm may hinder compliance in that respect.

If the objective is to prevent fraud through litigation, the motivation of the classification becomes central, and there is a need for due process in an electronic context (e.g., Citron, 2008). It is also important in these cases to distinguish between aggressive (but legal) and fraudulent (and illegal cases) situations. While the difference can be clear-cut in some cases (e.g., the card owner authorized the payment or not), the difference between the two can be difficult to elucidate in complex cases (e.g., accounting fraud). Although machine learning can also conceivably help tackle this question, this analysis introduces an additional layer of complexity in the classification.

[18]https://www.technologyreview.com/2020/05/11/1001563/covid-pandemic-broken-ai-machine-learning-amazon-retail-fraud-humans-in-the-loop/

[19]https://arxiv.org/abs/1808.03305

If the objective is to prevent fraud through anticipation (e.g., process reengineering), the motivation for the classification has to be deeply understood so that a root cause analysis can be conducted and remedial actions implemented. This process may involve analyzing operational data (e.g., internal incentives) that are typically not included in many current fraud detection algorithms. Furthermore, going from a cluster of suspect cases generated through machine learning to a change in processes and organizations may be difficult. For example, it is well known that humans in general, and auditors in particular, have limited ability to process large amounts of information required for complex decision-making (e.g., Iselin, 1988). Prior research (e.g., Ashton, 1974) has shown that large volumes of accounting information can lead to suboptimal financial and auditing judgments. In this context, machine learning algorithms can act as data reduction tools to economize mental resources. However, the ability of individuals to combine cues from multiple sources is also limited (e.g., Benbasat & Taylor, 1982). The cognitive integration of black-box results from algorithms with complex organizational structures is poorly understood currently, but it seems plausible that this integration may bring new challenges.

8.3.5 Distinction between Prediction and Causal Inference[20]

Causal inference and prediction are fundamentally different problems. The objective of causal inference is to use statistical tools to test causal relationships. In contrast, the objective of prediction is to apply a statistical model or data mining algorithm to data for the purpose of predicting *new observations* (Hastie et al., 2009; Shmueli, 2010; Kleinberg et al., 2015).

The distinction between prediction and causal inference is significant because most existing accounting and finance academic research focuses on causal inference, while practitioners may be more interested in prediction. Causal inference studies are relevant for decision-makers who wish to design effective policy remedies to prevent and mitigate accounting fraud. However, there are many important decisions (e.g., whether or not to invest in a high-growth stock) that require an accurate and timely prediction of whether a firm is or is not engaged in fraud (i.e., a prediction problem). Furthermore, causal inference and prediction are not mutually exclusive. For example, Varian (2014) argues that predictive modeling can also benefit causal inference research because predictive modeling can provide a low-cost estimate of unobservable counterfactuals in causal inference (i.e., the outcome that would have happened without the policy intervention). Varian (2014) even argues that a good predictive model can be better than a randomly chosen control group due to the imperfection of the randomization process.

[20]This section borrows heavily from the online appendix of Bao et al. (2020).

The distinction between prediction and causal inference has a few important implications. First, causal inference emphasizes the unbiasedness of regression coefficients, but prediction may deliberately increase the bias of a regression coefficient in order to minimize the out-of-sample prediction error. Hence, for prediction purposes, a "wrong" model could produce better performance than a correctly specified model. Second, while causal modeling requires that f represent an underlying causal function, predictive modeling requires only an association between x and y. That is, an input variable that is not causal (e.g., raw financial data items that may have no obvious economic interpretation) could be included in a prediction model. Third, the choice of f could be different for causal inference and prediction problems. While f is carefully chosen based on theory and causal relationship for causal inference problems, f is often constructed from data and could take on more flexible and complex functional forms.

8.4 A Brief Overview of Existing Academic Research on Fraud Detection

Fraud prediction is highly interdisciplinary literature. We divide this literature into two streams by discipline: (a) studies that focus on fraud prediction out of sample using machine learning methods in the nonaccounting academic fields (e.g., computer science) and (b) studies in the accounting academic literature that focus on causal inference. Because these two types of literature often use different methodologies and emphasize different aspects (causal inference vs. prediction), we review the two literature streams separately. We adopt the conceptual framework in Sect. 8.3 (data, method, and evaluation criterion) to organize the literature overview.

8.4.1 Fraud Prediction Using Machine Learning in the Nonaccounting Academic Fields

Sections 8.2 and 8.3 have outlined some of the challenges associated with fraud detection through machine learning. The machine learning literature in the nonaccounting fields has proposed various solutions to some of the aforementioned challenges. These models attempt to predict different types of fraud, such as credit card fraud, insurance fraud, and e-commerce fraud. Interestingly, we find no study in the machine learning academic literature outside the accounting field that examines accounting fraud detection. The building of these models usually follows a similar conventional supervised machine learning pipeline. Specifically, fraud detection is treated as a binary classification problem. The prediction model is trained using off-the-shelf supervised machine learning algorithms, including but not limited to Logistic Regression, Support Vector Machine (SVM), Decision Tree, Neural

Network, and Random Forests. Since these conventional models have already been summarized in previous survey papers (Ngai et al., 2011; Dutta et al., 2017; Hajek & Henriques, 2017), we only highlight some recent fraud detection models in the nonaccounting fields that have significant methodological contributions addressing the challenges of fraud detection.

First, as noted in Sect. 8.2, detected fraud is typically a rare event. One commonly used method to deal with rarity is to reduce the imbalance of fraud and nonfraud observations by matching (e.g., Green & Choi, 1997; Lin et al., 2003; Whiting et al., 2012; Fletcher et al., 2011; Humpherys et al., 2011; Cecchini et al., 2010). While it is appropriate to use a smaller matched sample of fraud and nonfraud for model training, it is problematic to use only the matched fraudulent and non-fraudulent firm-years in the holdout test sample to evaluate the out-of-sample performance of a prediction model. This is because doing so would invite look-ahead bias.

Second, fraud detection is difficult because many fraud cases remain hidden. While the rare fraud case issue can be addressed reasonably well by combining imbalance learning and ensemble learning, the hidden fraud issue is seldom considered. To handle these two issues, Li et al. (2014) propose to detect fake reviews by using positive-unlabeled (PU) learning (Bekker & Davis, 2020). PU learning is a naturally suitable method for addressing the two issues simultaneously because it can be used to learn a binary classifier by only using positive examples (i.e., true fraud cases) and unlabeled examples (i.e., unknown cases that could be either fraud or non-fraud). In addition to PU learning, the other possible methods are one-class classification, unsupervised learning, transfer learning, and adversarial learning. For example, de Roux et al. (2018) propose an unsupervised machine learning model for detecting fraudulent taxpayers without using any labeled data. Zheng et al. (2019) propose a one-class classification model based on generative adversarial networks that use only one class of samples (i.e., fraud cases) for fraud detection. Zhu et al. (2020) propose a transfer learning framework for cross-domain fraud detection by transferring knowledge from existing domains with abundant labeled fraud cases to improve the new domain's performance with rare labeled fraud cases. Fiore et al. (2019) propose improving credit card fraud detection by using generative adversarial networks for generating minority class examples (i.e., pseudo fraud cases).

Third, serial fraud, where a fraudster commits fraud in several consecutive periods before being caught, is quite common due to delay in detection. Almost all existing models treat each fraud period as an independent fraud incidence and ignore the time series dependence of serial fraud cases. To address this issue, Guo et al. (2018) adapt the commonly used recurrent neural network model Long Short-Term Memory (LSTM) to extract the useful features from serial fraud behaviors. Oentaryo et al. (2014) also find that the extracted time-series features can improve fraud detection performance.

Fourth, fraud evolves over time, and fraudsters are highly adaptive because they learn from the detected fraud cases. To build adaptive fraud detection models, Abbasi et al. (2012) propose a meta-learning framework that can be learned in a self-adaptive manner to improve prediction accuracy. Xu et al. (2017) propose an online learning algorithm for reputation fraud campaign detection, which can be efficiently updated based on the new fraud cases for adaptively capturing the regime shift.

Last but not least, there is a growing body of research on using multimodal machine learning (Baltrušaitis et al., 2018) for improving fraud detection. In addition to the accounting data, there are various heterogeneous data types (e.g., text, image, audio, video, and network) that could contain useful information for fraud detection. Representative examples include text-based fraud detection (Cecchini et al., 2010; Humpherys et al., 2011; Purda & Skillicorn, 2015; Wang & Xu, 2018) and network-based fraud detection (Beutel et al., 2015; Van Vlasselaer et al., 2017; Shah et al., 2017; Yuan et al., 2017; Dong et al., 2018; Cao et al., 2019; Hu et al., 2019; Liang et al., 2019; Liu et al., 2019; Wang et al., 2019a, 2019b; Zhong et al., 2020).

8.4.2 Fraud Prediction in the Accounting Literature

There is a long literature in accounting on fraud prediction. However, most accounting fraud prediction studies deal with causal inference (i.e., what factors causally affect the incidence of accounting fraud) rather than fraud prediction. Even if some studies use the term "fraud prediction," they often mean fraud prediction *in sample* rather than out of sample (e.g., Brazel et al., 2009; Hobson et al., 2012).

Because many fraud prediction studies in the accounting field deal with causal inference, we adopt the well-known motivation-ability-opportunity framework from criminology to organize our review. The criminology framework considers three crucial factors in explaining an individual's criminal activities: (a) whether the person has the motive to commit a crime, referred to as incentive variables; (b) whether the person has the ability to commit a crime (e.g., does the person have a gun?); and (c) whether the person has the opportunity to commit a crime (e.g., whether the person is at the crime scene).

One could measure any of the abovementioned three classes of factors using nonaccounting data. For example, one could measure a person's incentive to commit fraud using the person's compensation contract details. As accounting data reflects a firm's business activities, one could also use accounting data to construct indirect proxies for the three classes of factors. For example, one could test whether growth firms are more likely to commit fraud by using a firm's sales growth or market-to-book ratio to measure firm growth.

The existing business literature has considered all three classes of factors to explain firms' accounting fraud behavior. In terms of motivation factors, prior research has considered the effects of both capital markets (e.g., incentives to increase a firm's stock price) and contracts (e.g., incentives to mitigate the constraints imposed by explicit business contracts). Representative research in the first category includes Dechow et al. (1996), Beneish (1999), Burns and Kedia (2006), Efendi et al. (2007), and Johnson et al. (2009). Representative research in the second category includes Healy (1985), Dechow et al. (1995), Dechow et al. (1996), and Burns and Kedia (2006). In terms of ability factors, representative research includes Beneish (1997), who shows that high lagged accruals can help identify earnings manipulation firms. High-lagged accruals are thought to indicate that managers have exhausted legitimate techniques for earnings management. In terms of opportunity factors, prior research has considered the role of corporate governance variables in explaining accounting fraud. Representative research includes Beasley (1996), Dechow et al. (1996), and Larcker et al. (2007).

Much existing accounting research uses readily available financial statement data (e.g., Dechow et al., 2011). Recent years have also witnessed accounting researchers' increasing usage of textual data (e.g., Cecchini et al., 2010; Larcker & Zakolyukina, 2012; Purda & Skillicorn, 2015; Brown et al., 2020) and network data sources for fraud prediction (e.g., Dong et al., 2018).

As accounting fraud is treated as a binary variable in most prior accounting research and most studies in this field focus on causal inference, logistic regressions are the most common statistical method in explaining the determinants of accounting fraud. True out-of-sample prediction studies are still relatively rare in the accounting literature. However, there has been a surging interest among accounting researchers in using interdisciplinary methods to predict accounting fraud out of sample. Representative research includes Cecchini et al. (2010), Larcker and Zakolyukina (2012), Abbasi et al. (2012), Purda and Skillicorn (2015), Perols et al. (2017), Dong et al. (2018), Brown et al. (2020), and Bao et al. (2020).

8.4.3 Future Research Directions

We believe that it would be a fruitful avenue for future research to combine the knowledge and expertise from both the accounting and machine learning domains to develop more powerful and adaptive learning models. In particular, we believe that the following interdisciplinary challenges deserve special attention by researchers interested in such problems.

First, it is important to incorporate regime shifts in prediction models. Existing research in other disciplines has already developed various methods based on adaptive learning (e.g., Brazdil et al., 2008; Abbasi et al., 2012). Another possible approach is to employ "online" learning algorithms to dynamically adapt to the recent new fraud patterns (Xu et al., 2017). Online learning is an important family of machine learning algorithms in which data arrive in sequential order, and the model is updated incrementally (Hoi et al., 2018). This approach is different from the traditional "off-line" machine learning algorithms that learn on the entire training data at once.

Second, undetected accounting fraud is a worldwide problem, especially in emerging markets. Hence, future researchers must develop models that can uncover such undetected fraud cases so that relevant decision-makers can take necessary intervention actions to deter and uncover fraudulent behavior. Existing research usually ignores this challenging problem and simply treats undetected accounting fraud cases as clean non-fraud cases. The possible direction for future research is to use unsupervised, semi-supervised, and positive-unlabeled learning algorithms (Bekker & Davis, 2020) to learn fraud detection models from truly clean fraud and non-fraud cases.

Third, future researchers could also explore the possibility of building more powerful models by infusing causal theories into machine learning. As noted in Sect. 8.4.2, the accounting literature has identified many causal determinants of accounting fraud. For example, Beasley (1996) finds that firms with larger proportions of outside members on the board of directors are less likely to commit accounting fraud. While existing research has attempted to use causal theories in selecting the fraud prediction models' input data, we are not aware of any existing study that incorporates the direction of a causal relation between an input variable and the output variable (i.e., accounting fraud) in building machine learning models to predict accounting fraud.

Fourth, considering the fact that serial fraud is prevalent in reality, future researchers could consider whether it is possible to build more accurate fraud prediction models by considering the time-series dependence of accounting fraud in model building. It seems promising to manually construct time-series of fraud features and feed them into conventional fraud prediction models (Oentaryo et al., 2014) or use time-series models such as recurrent neural networks for modeling serial fraud behavior directly (Guo et al., 2018).[21]

Fifth, publicly listed firms are required to produce many reports. The easy-to-process financial statements alone contain hundreds of accounting accounts. Existing research has only utilized a small portion of these data. Hence, it is potentially fruitful to employ powerful machine learning models such as deep learning to extract more useful information from such raw accounting data for fraud prediction (Zhang et al., 2019). It is also an interesting research direction to learn better fraud detection models from multimodal data, including but not limited to multilingual texts, images, audios, videos, and networks.

As we have illustrated in the previous sections, modeling fraud prediction is an interdisciplinary task that requires the close collaboration of accounting domain experts and machine learning experts. Hence, we strongly encourage experts across disciplines to come together to build better quality fraud prediction models that can be readily adopted by companies. We strongly believe that such interdisciplinary collaboration will have a better potential to generate breakthrough fraud prediction models.

As noted in Sect. 8.3, it is not a trivial task to define accounting fraud and assemble a large sample of accounting fraud. Hence, we also encourage the fraud prediction research community to work together to build a common and better accounting fraud database so that future researchers do not have to repeat the dirty

[21]Recurrent neural networks are artificial neural networks where connections between nodes form a directed graph along a temporal sequence.

work of data collection and cleaning datasets repeatedly. By having a common database, future research can more easily compare the different fraud prediction models' performance.

8.5 Conclusion

Deploying machine learning to detect anomalies, errors, and fraud is a promising and growing research field. In this chapter, we discuss the most critical challenges in fraud detection and highlight many important empirical considerations in fraud prediction model building. We also provide a broad overview of the state-of-the-art approaches to predicting fraud in the extant literature and suggest promising future research directions.

The ideas and algorithms discussed in this chapter should be of interest to academic researchers and decision-makers in many organizations. For example, machine learning platforms may allow organizations to monitor transactions in nearly real-time. These platforms may allow for a comprehensive analysis (rather than sampling) and faster remediation. Textual analysis can be delegated to a greater extent. For example, machine learning platforms can already read and analyze complex lease agreements to determine their appropriate accounting classification. In turn, this will allow for cleaner and faster closings of the books while providing a better audit trail to detect internal anomalies. Textual analysis can identify relevant documents through terabytes of data through Topic segmentation and keyword analysis. For example, the British Serious Fraud Office (SFO) exposed large-scale bribery and corruption at Rolls-Royce. They used machine learning to sift through 30 million documents, processing up to 600,000 every day. In contrast, the Chief Technology Officer (CTO) of the SFO indicated that the average processing rate of lawyers is 300 documents a day with lower accuracy and consistency.[22]These documents can also be automatically translated and summarized. Sentiment analysis can, for example, allow for the detection of stress, a predictor of fraud. Internal networks of communication can be easily mapped. As new data sources emerge (e.g., Internet of Things and drones), new internal controls can be designed. For example, one can envision that automatic treatment of videos could allow for the continuous physical monitoring of inventory and their reconciliation with accounting records. External sources of data can also be integrated. For example, video and images of physical assets from Google Earth and other geographic information system applications can help assert the plausibility of different assumptions. Social network analysis can allow for the anticipation of product issues.

However, the deployment of these tools in organizations remains challenging. Aside from the technical issues outlined in this chapter, these tools will challenge

[22]https://www.cio.com/article/3525877/serious-fraud-office-cto-ben-denison-reveals-how-ai-is-transforming-legal-work.html

existing practices and require change management skills. As fraud detection goes from an experience-based approach to a data-driven approach, the articulation of domain expertise with machine learning will need refinement. For example, algorithms often rely on three types of anomalies to detect fraud: those based on outliers in distribution (e.g., transactions above a certain threshold), those that are anomalous because of the context (e.g., a high withdrawal in a period of low economic activity), and those that are anomalous when multiple observations are analyzed jointly (e.g., ATM transactions from two continents over a short period of time). The first type of anomalies can probably be detected with minimal domain expertise. However, the second and third types often require domain expertise to be effective.

Furthermore, analytical processes must be analyzed and maintained regularly, adding layers of complexity to the organizational system. Other types of failures in the control system (e.g., cyber-risk) will have to be considered. Privacy issues (with different legal standards across jurisdictions) are likely to become increasingly important. All the requirements necessitate new skills that may be in short supply at the moment. This may explain why, according to some statistics, 85% of AI projects fail.[23]

Despite all the challenges, we believe that using machine learning to combat fraud remains a promising direction of inquiry for both researchers and industry practitioners. We look forward to more innovative approaches from future research to tackle this important problem facing our societies.

References

Abbasi, A., Albrecht, C., Vance, A., & Hansen, J. (2012). Metafraud: A meta-learning framework for detecting financial fraud. *MIS Quarterly*, 1293–1327.

American Institute of Certified Public Accountants (2002) Consideration of fraud in a financial statement audit. Statement on Auditing Standards No. 99. New York.

Amiram, D., Bozanic, Z., & Rouen, E. (2015). Financial statement errors: Evidence from the distributional properties of financial statement numbers. *Review of Accounting Studies, 20*, 1540–1593.

Ashton, R. H. (1974). Behavioral implications of information overload in managerial accounting reports. *Cost and Management, 48*(4), 37–40.

Baltrušaitis, T., Ahuja, C., & Morency, L. P. (2018). Multimodal machine learning: A survey and taxonomy. *IEEE Transactions on Pattern Analysis and Machine Intelligence, 41*(2), 423–443.

Bao, Y., Ke, B., Li, B., Yu, Y. J., & Zhang, J. (2020). Detecting accounting fraud in publicly traded US firms using a machine learning approach. *Journal of Accounting Research, 58*(1), 199–235.

Beasley, M. S. (1996). An empirical analysis of the relation between the board of director composition and financial statement fraud. *The Accounting Review, 71*, 443–465.

Beasley, M. S., Carcello, J. V., and Hermanson, D. R. (1999). Fraudulent financial reporting: 1987–1997: An Analysis of U.S. Public Companies. Sponsored by the Committee of Sponsoring Organizations of the Treadway Commission (COSO).

[23]https://customerthink.com/why-85-of-the-artificial-intelligence-projects-fail/

Beasley, M. S., Carcello, J. V., Hermanson, D. R., and Neal, T. L. (2010). Fraudulent financial reporting: 1998–2007: An Analysis of U.S. Public Companies." Sponsored by the Committee of Sponsoring Organizations of the Treadway Commission (COSO).

Bekker, J., & Davis, J. (2020). Learning from positive and unlabeled data: A survey. *Machine Learning, 109*(4), 719–760.

Beneish, M. D. (1997). Detecting GAAP violation: Implications for assessing earnings management among firms with extreme financial performance. *Journal of Accounting and Public Policy, 16*, 271–309.

Beneish, M. D. (1999). The detection of earnings manipulation. *Financial Analysts Journal, 55*, 24–36.

Benbasat, I., & Taylor, R. N. (1982). Behavioral aspects of information processing for the design of management information systems. *IEEE Transactions on Systems, Man, and Cybernetics, 12*(4), 439–450.

Beutel, A., Akoglu, L., & Faloutsos, C. (2015). Graph-based user behavior modeling: from prediction to fraud detection. *Proceedings of the 21th ACM SIGKDD international conference on knowledge discovery and data mining*. pp. 2309–2310.

Brazdil, P., Carrier, C. G., Soares, C., & Vilalta, R. (2008). *Metalearning: Applications to data mining*. Springer Science & Business Media.

Boute, R. N., Gijsbrechts, J., & Van Mieghem, J. A. (2022). Digital lean operations: Smart automation and artificial intelligence in financial services. In V. Babich, J. Birge, & G. Hilary (Eds.), *Innovative technology at the interface of finance and operations. Springer Series in Supply Chain Management*. Springer Nature.

Brazel, J. F., Jones, K. L., & Zimbelman, M. F. (2009). Using nonfinancial measures to assess fraud risk. *Journal of Accounting Research, 47*(5), 1135–1166.

Brown, N. C., Crowley, R. M., & Elliott, W. B. (2020). What are you saying? Using topic to detect financial misreporting. *Journal of Accounting Research, 58*, 237–291.

Burns, N., & Kedia, S. (2006). The impact of performance-based compensation on misreporting. *Journal of Financial Economics, 79*, 35–67.

Cao, S., Yang, X., Chen, C., Zhou, J., Li, X., & Qi, Y. (2019). TitAnt: Online real-time transaction fraud detection in ant financial. *arXiv. preprint arXiv:1906.07407*.

Chen, X., Hilary, G. and Tian, X. (2020). Mandatory data breach transparency and insider trading, working paper.

Cecchini, M., Aytug, H., Koehler, G. J., & Pathak, P. (2010). Making words work: Using financial text as a predictor of financial events. *Decision Support Systems, 50*(1), 164–175.

Citron, D. K. (2008). Technological due process. *Wash UL Rev, 85*, 1249.

Darrough, M., Huang, R., & Zhao, S. (2020). Spillover effects of fraud allegations and investor sentiment. *Contemporary Accounting Research, 37*, 982–1014.

Davidson, R., Dey, A., & Smith, A. (2015). Executives' Boff-the-job^ behavior, corporate culture, and financial reporting risk. *Journal of Financial Economics, 117*(1), 5–28.

de Roux, D., Perez, B., Moreno, A., Villamil, M. D. P., & Figueroa, C. (2018) Tax fraud detection for under-reporting declarations using an unsupervised machine learning approach. *Proceedings of the 24th ACM SIGKDD International Conference on Knowledge Discovery & Data Mining*. pp. 215–222.

Dechow, P. M., Sloan, R. G., & Sweeney, A. P. (1995). Detecting earnings management. *The Accounting Review, 70*(2), 193–226.

Dechow, P. M., Sloan, R. G., & Sweeney, A. P. (1996). Causes and consequences of earnings manipulation: An analysis of firms subject to enforcement actions by the SEC. *Contemporary Accounting Research, 13*, 1–36.

Dechow, P. M., Ge, W., Larson, C. R., & Sloan, R. G. (2011). Predicting material accounting misstatements. *Contemporary Accounting Research, 28*(1), 17–82.

Dong, W., Liao, S., & Zhang, Z. (2018). Leveraging financial social media data for corporate fraud detection. *Journal of Management Information Systems, 35*(2), 461–487.

Dutta, I., Dutta, S., & Raahemi, B. (2017). Detecting financial restatements using data mining techniques. *Expert Systems with Applications, 90*, 374–393.

Dyck, A., Morse, A., & Zingales, L. (2020). *How pervasive is corporate fraud*. University of Toronto. working paper.

Efendi, J., Srivastava, A., & Swanson, E. P. (2007). Why do corporate managers misstate financial statements? The role of option compensation and other factors. *Journal of Financial Economics, 85*, 667–708.

Ernst & Young (2010). Driving ethical growth—New markets, new challenges. 11th Global Fraud Survey. from https://linomartins.files.wordpress.com/2011/12/2011th_global_fraud_survey.pdf.

Fawcett, T. (2006). An introduction to roc analysis. *Pattern Recognition Letters, 27*, 861–874.

Fiore, U., De Santis, A., Perla, F., Zanetti, P., & Palmieri, F. (2019). Using generative adversarial networks for improving classification effectiveness in credit card fraud detection. *Information Sciences, 479*, 448–455.

Fletcher, H., Glancy, & Yadav, S. B. (2011). A computational model for financial reporting fraud detection. *Decision Support Systems, 50*(3), 595–601.

Garip, F. (2020). What failure to predict life outcomes can teach us. *Proceedings of the National Academy of Sciences, 117*(15), 8234–8235.

Green, P., & Choi, J. H. (1997). Assessing the risk of management fraud through neural network technology. *Auditing: A Journal of Practice & Theory, 16*, 14–29.

Guo, J., Liu, G., Zuo, Y., & Wu, J. (2018). Learning sequential behavior representations for fraud detection. *2018 IEEE international conference on data mining (ICDM)*. IEEE, pp. 127–136.

Hajek, P., & Henriques, R. (2017). Mining corporate annual reports for intelligent detection of financial statement fraud–a comparative study of machine learning methods. *Knowledge-Based Systems, 128*, 139–152.

Hastie, T., Tibshirani, R., & Friedman, J. H. (2009). *The elements of statistical learning*. Springer.

He, H., & Ma, Y. (2013). *Imbalanced learning: Foundations, algorithms, and applications*. Wiley.

Healy, P. M. (1985). The effect of bonus schemes on accounting decisions. *Journal of Accounting and Economics, 7*(1), 85–107.

Hobson, J. L., Mayew, W. J., & Venkatachalam, M. (2012). Analyzing speech to detect financial misreporting. *Journal of Accounting Research, 50*(2), 349–392.

Hoi, S. C., Sahoo, D., Lu, J., & Zhao, P. (2018). Online learning: A comprehensive survey. *arXiv preprint arXiv:1802.02871*.

Hu, B., Zhang, Z., Shi, C., Zhou, J., Li, X., & Qi, Y. (2019). Cash-out user detection based on attributed heterogeneous information network with a hierarchical attention mechanism. *Proceedings of the AAAI Conference on Artificial Intelligence*. pp. 946–953.

Humpherys, S. L., Moffitt, K. C., Burns, M. B., Burgoon, J. K., & Felix, W. F. (2011). Identification of fraudulent financial statements using linguistic credibility analysis. *Decision Support Systems, 50*(3), 585–594.

Iselin, E. R. (1988). The effects of information load and information diversity on decision quality in a structured decision task. *Accounting, Organizations and Society, 13*(2), 147–164.

Järvelin, K., & Kekäläinen, J. (2002). Cumulated gain-based evaluation of IR techniques. *ACM Transactions on Information Systems, 20*, 422–446.

Johnson, S. A., Ryan, H. E., & Tian, Y. S. (2009). Managerial incentives and corporate fraud: The sources of incentives matter. *Review of Finance, 13*, 115–145.

Karpoff, J. M., Lee, D. S., & Martin, G. S. (2008). The costs to firms of cooking the books. *Journal of Financial and Quantitative Analysis, 43*(03), 581–612.

Karpoff, J. M., Koester, A., Lee, D. S., & Martin, G. S. (2017). Proxies and databases in financial misconduct research. *The Accounting Review, 92*(6), 129–163.

Kleinberg, J., Ludwig, J., Mullainathan, S., & Obermeyer, Z. (2015). Prediction policy problems. *American Economic Review: Papers & Proceedings, 105*(5), 491–495.

KPMG. Peat Marwick (1998). *Fraud Survey*. KPMG Peat Marwick.

Larcker, D. F., Richardson, S. A., & Tuna, I. (2007). Corporate governance, accounting outcomes, and organizational performance. *The Accounting Review, 82*(4), 963–1008.

Larcker, D., & Zakolyukina, A. A. (2012). Detecting deceptive discussion in conference calls. *Journal of Accounting Research, 50*, 495–540.

Li, H., Liu, B., Mukherjee, A., & Shao, J. (2014). Spotting fake reviews using positive-unlabeled learning. *Computación y Sistemas, 18*(3), 467–475.

Liang, C., Liu, Z., Liu, B., Zhou, J., Li, X., and Yang, S. (2019). Uncovering Insurance Fraud Conspiracy with Network Learning. *Proceedings of the 42nd International ACM SIGIR Conference on Research and Development in Information Retrieval*. pp. 1181–1184.

Lin, J., Hwang, M., & Becker, J. (2003). A fuzzy neural network for assessing the risk of fraudulent financial reporting. *Managerial Auditing Journal, 18*, 657–665.

Liu, S., Hooi, B., & Faloutsos, C. (2019). A contrast metric for fraud detection in rich graphs. *IEEE Transactions on Knowledge and Data Engineering, 31*(12), 2235–2248.

Ngai, E. W., Hu, Y., Wong, Y. H., Chen, Y., & Sun, X. (2011). The application of data mining techniques in financial fraud detection: A classification framework and an academic review of literature. *Decision Support Systems, 50*(3), 559–569.

Oentaryo, R., Lim, E.-P., Finegold, M., Lo, D., Zhu, F., Phua, C., et al. (2014). Detecting click fraud in online advertising: A data mining approach. *The Journal of Machine Learning Research, 15*(1), 99–140.

Perols, J. L., Bowen, R. M., Zimmermann, C., & Samba, B. (2017). Finding needles in a haystack: Using data analytics to improve fraud prediction. *The Accounting Review, 92*, 221–245.

Purda, L., & Skillicorn, D. (2015). Accounting variables, deception, and a bag of words: Assessing the tools of fraud detection. *Contemporary Accounting Research, 32*(3), 1193–1223.

Salganik, M., Lundberg, I., Kindel, A., Ahearn, C., Al-Ghoneim, K. Almaatouq, A., Altschul, D., Brand, J., Carnegie, N., Compton, R, Datta, D., Davidson, T., Filippova, A., Gilroy, C., Goode, B., Jahani, E., Kashyap, R., Kirchner, A., Mckay, S. (2020). Measuring the predictability of life outcomes with a scientific mass collaboration. Proceedings of the National Academy of Sciences. 117.

Shah, N., Lamba, H., Beutel, A., & Faloutsos, C. (2017). The many faces of link fraud. *2017 IEEE International Conference on Data Mining (ICDM)*. IEEE, pp. 1069–1074.

Shmueli, G. (2010). To explain or to predict. *Statistical Science, 25*, 289–310.

Van Vlasselaer, V., Eliassi-Rad, T., Akoglu, L., Snoeck, M., & Baesens, B. (2017). Gotcha! Network-based fraud detection for social security fraud. *Management Science, 63*(9), 3090–3110.

Varian, H. R. (2014). Big data: New tricks for econometrics. *Journal of Economic Perspectives, 28*, 3–28.

Wang, D., Lin, J., Cui, P., Jia, Q., Wang, Z., Fang, Y., et al. (2019a). A Semi-supervised Graph Attentive Network for Financial Fraud Detection. *2019 IEEE International Conference on Data Mining (ICDM)*. IEEE, pp. 598–607.

Wang Y., Wang L., Li Y., He D., Chen W., Liu T.-Y. (2013). A Theoretical Analysis of NDCG Ranking Measures. In *Proceedings of the 26th Annual Conference on Learning Theory*.

Wang, J., Wen, R., Wu, C., Huang, Y., & Xion, J. (2019b). Fdgars: Fraudster detection via graph convolutional networks in online app review system. *Companion Proceedings of The 2019 World Wide Web Conference*. pp. 310–316.

Wang, Y., & Xu, W. (2018). Leveraging deep learning with LDA-based text analytics to detect automobile insurance fraud. *Decision Support Systems, 105*, 87–95.

Whiting, D. G., Hansen, J. V., McDonald, J. B., Albrecht, C., & Albrecht, W. S. (2012). Machine learning methods for detecting patterns of management fraud. *Computational Intelligence, 28*, 505–527.

Xu, C., Zhang, J., & Sun, Z. (2017). Online reputation fraud campaign detection in user ratings. *IJCAI*, 3873–3879.

Yuan, S., Wu, X., Li, J., & Lu, A. (2017) Spectrum-based deep neural networks for fraud detection. *Proceedings of the 2017 ACM on Conference on Information and Knowledge Management*. pp. 2419–2422.

Zhang, J., Yang, X., & Appelbaum, D. (2015). Toward effective big data analysis in continuous auditing. *Accounting Horizons, 29*(2), 469–476.

Zhang, Y.-L., Zhou, J., Zheng, W., Feng, J., Li, L., Liu, Z., et al. (2019). Distributed deep forest and its application to automatic detection of cash-out fraud. *ACM Transactions on Intelligent Systems and Technology (TIST), 10*(5), 1–19.

Zheng, P., Yuan, S., Wu, X., Li, J., & Lu, A. (2019) One-class adversarial nets for fraud detection. *Proceedings of the AAAI Conference on Artificial Intelligence*. pp. 1286–1293.

Zhong, Q., Liu, Y., Ao, X., Hu, B., Feng, J., Tang, J., et al. (2020). Financial defaulter detection on online credit payment via multi-view attributed heterogeneous information network. *Proceedings of The Web Conference 2020*. pp. 785–795.

Zhu, Y., Xi, D., Song, B., Zhuang, F., Chen, S., Gu, X., et al. (2020) Modeling Users' Behavior Sequences with Hierarchical Explainable Network for Cross-domain Fraud Detection. *Proceedings of The Web Conference 2020*. pp. 928–938.

Chapter 9
AI in Financial Portfolio Management: Practical Considerations and Use Cases

Joseph Byrum

9.1 Three Basic Goals for AI in Financial Portfolio Management

Generally, there are three basic goals for the application of AI-based technology in financial portfolio management. The types of AI most suitable for each application area may differ and these differences will also be highlighted subsequently.

The first goal is to **optimize the investment process** to achieve higher portfolio returns for clients at lower or similar risk levels, thereby achieving the highest possible returns given the client's risk tolerance. This is covered in Sect. 9.3.

The second goal is to **increase operational efficiency** to lower the costs of portfolio and fund management, benefiting both the client in a lower administration cost and making the fund more competitive versus other higher cost funds. This is covered in Sect. 9.4.

And the third goal is to **enhance the customer experience**, in particular to provide higher levels of personalization and customization at lower costs than could be provided by expensive, high-end human advisors. This is covered in Sect. 9.5.

In the following pages, after explaining some basic concepts in portfolio management, we will delve into each of these three goals to show current applications.

J. Byrum (✉)
Principal Financial Group, Des Moines, IA, USA
e-mail: jrbyrum@umich.edu

V. Babich et al. (eds.), *Innovative Technology at the Interface of Finance and Operations*, Springer Series in Supply Chain Management 11,
https://doi.org/10.1007/978-3-030-75729-8_9

9.2 Using AI in Portfolio Management: How it Works

The use of AI in financial portfolio management is a natural step in the evolution of investment. The investment industry has long made use of sophisticated statistical techniques, motivated by the ongoing search for higher portfolio returns. Linear regression models and data visualization have indeed been part of the normal stock-in-trade of investment professionals for a long time. Similarly, the investment industry has long been supported by various advanced forms of information technology, given the large quantities of data that have to be exchanged and managed, and the high-value decisions that need to be made. And exchanges themselves—the infrastructure hosting the purchase and sale of securities and commodities—have evolved from live settings to a world that is almost entirely virtual. But despite this legacy, today's AI technologies are a game changer for the industry, enabling new insights and workflow innovations that could not be contemplated with conventional statistical techniques or ordinary computer programming.

9.2.1 Introduction to the Various Types of AI Used in Financial Asset and Portfolio Management

Artificial intelligence is a very broad term that includes any type of computer programming that acts "intelligently" in the sense that it can "reason" in ways that we previously believed only humans could. As such, the definition of AI keeps changing with our expectations and as we get used to increasingly more sophisticated AI.

Proponents of more AI use in investment decisions also hope that dispassionate machine-generated strategies may help investors to avoid well-known behavioral biases such as *loss aversion*[1] or *confirmation bias*[2] that often cause human investors to act irrationally (Connected Wealth, 2018).

Paradoxically, however, the newest AI innovations do not so much counteract the worst tendencies of the human mind as emulate the best ones. This is where neural networks come in.

Neural networks, a type of AI that is inspired by the architecture of the brain and (crudely) mimics it, have been around for decades but have really come to the fore in the last decade or two. Their recent success has been made possible by large increases in computing power, an explosion in the amount of data (big data) available to analyze, and the ability to perform such analyses offsite in huge server farms (the cloud).

[1]The preference for avoiding losses over generating equivalent gains.

[2]The interpretation of new information to confirm preexisting beliefs.

Most of the current excitement around AI focuses on neural networks in their various forms. (However, neural networks are not the whole story as we will explain later.) A neural network is implemented mathematically by means of an algorithm that involves a form of *matrix multiplication*. Essentially values in the input layer are multiplied by a set of values in the inside layer to provide values in the output layer. Neural networks with multiple inside layers—and therefore multiple, successive matrix multiplications—are more powerful, and this "deeper" topology is referred to as *deep learning*. Some of the most remarkable recent achievements with AI involve deep learning.

Machine learning (ML)[3] refers to the process by which neural networks develop algorithms that establish a relationship between their data input and output. Machine learning usually entails functions like *prediction*, *optimization*, and *categorization*. For example, machine learning could be used to predict whether the debt of a particular company will be investment grade or high yield at some future date. The patterns established by machine learning may sometimes resemble classic linear regression algorithms, but the power of neural networks is that they are not constrained to the typical linear functions that are used to dominate financial analysis.

Step-by-step programming, the way all computer programs were written before, works fine if humans fully understand the rules that the algorithm should follow, and can define the desired relationships between the input and output data. But in many situations, humans cannot articulate the rules or do not know the relationships. Machine learning is a way for us to neatly circumvent this problem. Because a neural network can learn by inference, it frees us from the need to explicitly program the machine. Neural networks can learn, or be taught, in a few different ways that lend themselves to different situations and applications:

- ***Supervised learning*** requires a training dataset that is labeled with the correct outcomes. For example, in transaction fraud detection applications the dataset will contain transactions both known to be fraudulent and not. The algorithm will infer a general rule for identifying fraudulent transactions by being trained on this dataset. The larger and more representative the dataset, the better the algorithm will be.
- In contrast, ***unsupervised learning*** involves a training dataset that is not labeled. The algorithm will detect patterns in the data and identify records or observations that have similar characteristics, grouping them into clusters. For example, an algorithm could be asked to look for securities similar to a particular illiquid security that is hard to price. Once a cluster of securities is identified, prices of other securities in the cluster may be used to help price the targeted illiquid security.
- ***Reinforced learning*** is a combination of supervised and unsupervised learning, where the neural network algorithm is fed unlabeled data (as in unsupervised

[3]While machine learning is imprecise used these days as a synonym for AI, it is more correctly a subset of AI, and represents a specific approach to AI.

learning) and provides output based on that data, but then receives feedback on its output (as in supervised learning) which allows it to learn and tweak the algorithm.

Natural language processing **(NLP)** is when AI is used to analyze the way that humans naturally speak or write. It enables conversational interfaces whereby customers' speech as spoken to a call center (voice recognition) or text messages entered in a chat window can be understood by a computer. NLP may also be used to read documents like contracts to find particular terms or look for patterns and similarities, relieving humans of the tedium associated with that, and saving substantial labor costs.

JP Morgan Chase has an AI solution called the Contract Intelligence (COiN) platform designed to analyze legal documents and extract important clauses. COiN is based on a machine-learning system powered by a private cloud network. It uses image recognition and NLP to review the bank's contracts. The bank claims that in one of its first implementations, the AI could extract 150 relevant attributes from commercial credit agreements in seconds compared to the 360,000 person-hours that a human manual reviews take for the same task (Georgiou, 2019).

Evolutionary computation (EC) is another type of AI (altogether different from neural networks) that includes techniques such as *genetic algorithms (GAs)* and *genetic programming (GP)*. It is inspired by Darwin's process of natural selection, whereby successful traits are propagated through successive generations while unsuccessful traits are culled (Epstein, 2017). A genetic algorithm is a heuristic process designed to find an optimal solution through an iterative computer program that mimics evolution. It starts with a random selection of the potential solution population, which is modified through successive generations, each candidate solution generation is then evaluated for fitness, and kept or eliminated. The candidate solutions that are kept are further optimized in each successive generation. A measure of fitness is therefore necessary.

One early mover in this space was Sentient Investment Management, a small hedge fund (less than $100 m) started in 2016. Sentient developed a platform that used genetic algorithms and deep learning to examine historical and current trading datasets in search of successful investment strategies. After less than 2 years in operation, it folded after only earning 4% in its first year (Kishan & Barr, 2018).

9.2.2 *Key Portfolio Optimization Concepts*

Nasdaq defines portfolio optimization as: "determination of weights of securities in a portfolio such that it best suits a given objective, e.g. maximize return for a given risk."

An exhaustive description of the mathematics of portfolio optimization is beyond the scope of this paper. Instead, this paper will briefly review some of the key theories and formulas informing portfolio management in modern times to provide a reference framework for explaining AI developments in this area.

In the last several decades, the portfolio optimization problem has largely been defined by *Modern Portfolio Theory* (MPT) pioneered by Nobel laureate Harry Markowitz in the 1950s (Markowitz, 1952). The goal of MPT is to find an optimal allocation of capital among a possible set of financial assets by at the same time maximizing the return and minimizing the risk of the investments (see Fig. 9.1).

In the theoretical case of linear constraints, the problem can be solved by some form of linear programming or quadratic programming. But in reality, a financial market will impose nonlinear constraints such as a limitation to the number of assets that can be held in a portfolio, minimum transaction lots, which force the holding of assets in multiples of minimum lots, and transaction costs. This is where AI algorithms, which do not require linear relationships, can be of great help.

Markowitz's *mean-variance* (M-V) model is the original and best-known framework for optimal asset allocation. It describes an optimization problem where the inputs are the returns to N risky assets, and the output is an N-dimensional real vector with weights signifying the fraction held in each asset. The objective is to simultaneously maximize the portfolio mean while minimizing the variance. All feasible solutions of this problem describe a curve in the plane (with axes being the return vs. the volatility or risk as in Fig. 9.1) called the *efficient frontier*. In this model, volatility (risk) is measured as a standard deviation. The *Capital Market Line* (CML) represents portfolios that optimally combine risk and return. The tangential

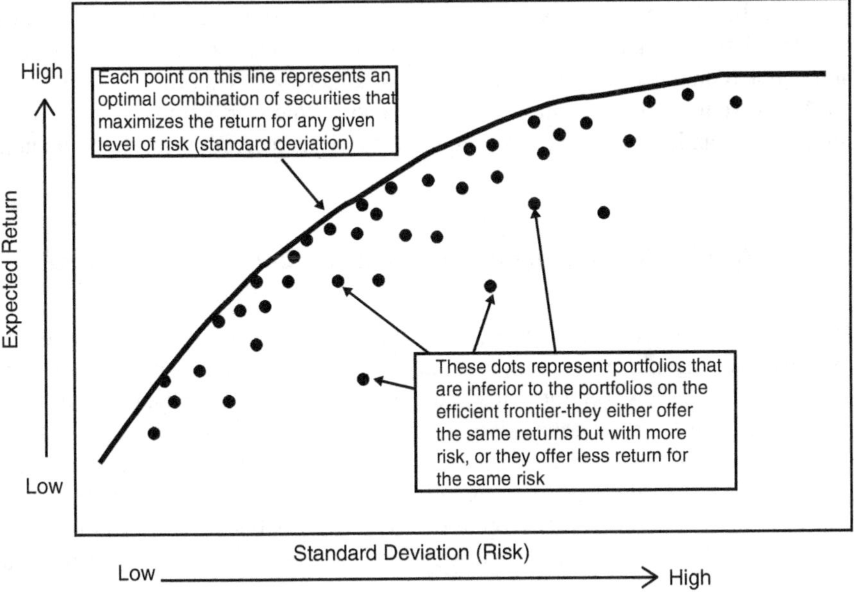

Fig. 9.1 Markowitz's efficient frontier (Honchar, 2020)

intercept point of the CML and the efficient frontier would result in the most efficient portfolio called the *tangency portfolio*.

A related concept is the *Sharpe ratio,* which is the average return earned in excess of the risk-free rate, divided by the standard deviation (volatility) of the excess return (Sharpe, 1964). The Sharpe ratio is the most widely used method for calculating risk-adjusted returns. It is useful because it shows whether a portfolio's excess return was due to smart investment decisions or just taking on more risk.

Two key metrics frequently used to specify the performance of an investment portfolio are alpha and beta. *Alpha* (α) is the return of the investment in comparison to the market index or other benchmark. *Beta* (β) is a measure of the volatility of the investment and a proxy for its relative risk.

The *Capital Asset Pricing Model (CAPM)* developed by Sharpe and Lintner builds on Markowitz by recognizing that investors expect to be compensated more for taking on more risk. CAPM is widely used in finance for pricing risky securities and establishing the expect return for financial assets given the risk and cost of capital. CAPM is defined by the formula $\boldsymbol{ERi = Rf + \beta i(ERm - Rf)}$ where ERi = the expected return of investment; Rf = the risk-free rate; βi = the beta of the investment; and $ERm - Rf$ = the market risk premium, which is the return expected from the market above the risk-free rate (Lintner, 1965). The risk-free rate is typically taken as the rate offered by a U.S. Treasury security that is held to maturity since default by the U.S. government is considered highly unlikely.

The most popular quantitative risk measure is JP Morgan's *Value-at-Risk (VaR)*, which signifies the maximum loss of the portfolio value at a certain confidence level. The three standard approaches for calculating VaR are the parametric approach (also known as the variance-covariance method because it assumes a normal distribution and calculates the standard deviation around an expected return value), historical simulation (constructing a histogram with past frequency of occurrences to estimate the future value with a certain confidence), and Monte Carlo simulation (running hundreds of random trials to estimate outcomes within a certain confidence range).

9.2.3 Brief Reference to Optimization Regimes Enabled by AI

Due to the proprietary and competitive nature of models used in the investment industry, industry players do not generally disclose what optimization algorithms they are running. However, the academic literature sheds light on the most common AI and machine-learning techniques used in asset optimization.

Rifki and Ono surveyed portfolio optimization approaches using genetic algorithms (GA),[4] heuristic algorithms based on survival of the fittest and concluded that GAs are useful for portfolio optimization under nonlinear conditions (Rifki & Ono, 2012). Unlike traditional solutions, GAs start with a random set of candidate

[4] A form of evolutionary computation—see Sect. 9.2.1.

solutions, called a *population* comprised of *chromosomes* which evolve through successive iterations called *generations*. GA-based optimization can be described as follows: Each chromosome represents a possible solution. During each generation, new chromosomes called *offspring* are created by merging potential pairs of *parents* as determined by a *crossover operator* and slightly changed via the *mutation operator*. The offspring replace the parents in the next generation to keep the population size constant. A *fitness function* is defined to assess the quality of each chromosome. The iteration is terminated when a prespecified number of generations have been modeled, or after the fitness has stabilized.

Aguilar-Rivera, Valenzuela-Rendón, and Rodríguez-Ortiz reviewed the use of GAs to solve financial problems relative to other evolutionary approaches. As mentioned, a GA is only one type of evolutionary computing (EC) (Aguilar-Rivera et al., 2015). The larger EC family includes genetic algorithms, genetic programming, learning classifier systems, multi-objective evolutionary algorithms, coevolutionary algorithms, and evolutionary estimation of distribution algorithms. The authors found that GAs are the most widely used of the evolutionary (Darwinian) approaches.

Paiva, Cardoso, Hanaoka, and Duarte developed a decision-making model for day trading on the stock market, using a machine-learning approach that combined the support vector machine (SVM) method with the mean variance (MV) of portfolio selection, and evaluated it with data from the São Paulo Stock Exchange Index (Ibovespa) using historical data from 2002 to 2016 covering 3716 trading days (Paiva et al., 2019). The SVM + MV model evaluated showed superior 3-year returns compared to other models of the Ibovespa index.

Oh, Kim, and Min demonstrated that index funds could improve their performance using a GA (Oh et al., 2005). Index funds attempt to copy a benchmark index such as the Dow Jones Industrial Average with a relatively small number of stocks and without owning all stock in the index. Thus, the performance of an index fund depends on picking the right subset of stocks. Using an index fund designed to track the Korean stock index (KOSPI 200) the researchers found clear advantages of the GA approach over conventional portfolio mechanisms.

Ban, Karoui, and Lim adapted two respective machine-learning models—*performance-based regularization* (PBR) and performance-based *cross-validation*—to portfolio optimization using real data subject to estimation issues and concluded that PBR has a promise as a model for handling uncertainty (Ban et al., 2018).

Lin and Liu presented three possible GA models for portfolio selection with minimum transaction lots and demonstrated that the portfolios obtained with these algorithms are close to optimal (very close to the Markowitz efficient frontier) (Lin & Liu, 2008).

Yan, Sewel, and Clack performed a head-to-head evaluation of two machine-learning techniques—genetic programming (GP)[5] and the more popular support vector machines (SVM)—to a real-world stock selection problem for hedge funds

[5]A form of evolutionary computation—see Sect. 9.2.1

(Yan et al., 2008). They found GP to be superior to SVM in terms of return on investment and robustness in volatile and unpredictable markets.

Note: Real-world AI-fund performance cannot be categorized by AI optimization method (as explained earlier, such methods are kept under wraps), but it can be categorized by fund. Backend Benchmarking publishes *The Robo Report* and a *Robo Ranking* covering the most well-known robo-advisors. They open, and fund, investment accounts with specific portfolio goals, which enable them to observe and track the actual holdings as well as the investment performance of the accounts. The Q4 2019 rated Fidelity Go as the best overall robo-advisor with Vanguard in second place and an honorable mention for TD Ameritrade.

9.3 Investment Process Optimization

Most major applications for AI in investment management are on the buy side where AI is employed to search for predictive signals in the noise and to increase alpha. As such, asset portfolio management is one of the major applications of AI in investment management, and we will start with that.

It is hoped that AI can breathe new life into active investment management. In 2019, the financial world marked the "end of an era" when index funds and exchange-traded funds surpassed active funds in assets under management-nearly \$4.3 trillion in passive funds versus a little over \$4.2 trillion in actively management funds, says Morningstar. Actively managed funds may regain in popularity or may continue to fall into relative decline. A deciding factor will be the use of AI to enhance the returns on actively managed funds.

9.3.1 New Alpha-Generation Strategies for the Portfolio

One of the major uses of AI in investment management is supporting higher returns for actively managed portfolios. This entails generating superior alpha-generating strategies by acquiring greater amounts of data and constructing new decision-making models from these. The deployment of AI by asset managers across broader and deeper datasets, therefore, includes the utilization of unstructured data through aggregating and processing such data sources. It also enables the much more rapid analysis of structured datasets, such as corporate financials, and the generation of research summaries using NLP techniques (Doshi et al., 2019). NLP can, for example, detect when CEOs duck certain questions on earnings calls or identify fake news by checking the content of an article for clickbait wording (Healy, 2019).

According to a report by the international Financial Stability Board (Financial Stability Board, 2017), the application of AI in portfolio management includes identifying new signals on price movement and making more effective use of the massive amount of available data and market research than conventional analytical models. As always, the goal is to identify signals in the data that can be used to predict price or volatility. Quant funds, which are mostly hedge funds, are the most extensive users of machine learning in the asset management industry. Quant funds are estimated by the FSB to manage $1 trillion in assets. At least $10 billion in AUM was estimated to be attributed to pure-play AI funds in 2017, a number that has no doubt grown rapidly in the years since this estimate was made.

San Francisco-based Equibot offers pure-play AI-powered exchange-traded funds (ETFs) using proprietary AI and IBM Watson. Equibot's AI-Powered Equity ETF was launched in 2017. It assesses more than 6000 U.S. traded stocks every day and decides where to invest by considering regulatory filings, earnings, valuations, and other fundamentals. In mid-2019, according to an analysis by the *Financial Post,* this ETF was trading below its 2017 opening value (Ferreira, 2019). This seems to support the argument of portfolio managers who argue that human portfolio managers cannot be completely replaced by AI, largely because there are too many variables involved in stock picking that cannot be programmed into an algorithm. Pattern recognition AI such as machine learning would need to be shown thousands of examples of what a good portfolio is to recognize a pattern. A further problem is that all the AI's knowledge is based on learning from past data. In finance, the past is not necessarily a good guide to the future—as we know all too well from the recent unexpected market drops due to the exogenous event of COVID-19, which caused company performances to defy all previous predictions. Yet on the other hand, attempting to make the AI more sensitive to only current trends and trading patterns sharply reduces the size of the dataset that can be used to train it. And the fundamental problem remains that neither AI nor any other kind of algorithm can predict future events that do not closely resemble past events. That always requires human investment managers to make educated judgments about where the future trends are going, based partly on knowledge, and partly on intuition (Pozen & Ruane, 2019).

Machine learning is so good at finding patterns, that it will find patterns even when there are none, as is the case with very "noisy" financial data. Portfolio recommendations based on such fluke patterns will obviously be no more valid than a throw of the dice. Humans will always be needed to do a sanity test of patterns found by machines.

Another problem identified by skeptics is that machine learning requires a clear goal. That is straightforward when you are using AI to win a board game like AlphaGo or chess, but less obvious in finance and investment. Higher returns over time can be achieved by, for example, taking two times levered position in equity markets (i.e., by using debt and derivatives in an exchange-traded fund to amplify the moves of an index). On the other hand, higher risk-adjusted return can be achieved by adding bonds to diversify the portfolio. Fund founder and entrepreneur, Ewan Kirk, recently wrote in the *Financial Times* that after experimenting with genetic algorithms that generated (or "bred") thousands of artificial traders, he got thousands of AI traders just doing what quantitative funds have always been doing, which is not what he wanted. He sums up the difficulty of getting the AI to do something differently:

> Consequently, we have to tell the AI system something like: "Do not find me the returns that everybody knows about; just the subtle unknown ones." But this is hard to specify. Even if one can accurately specify the desired returns, it leads to a second problem: If the effect is subtle, it is likely to be small or short-lived, and thus hard to exploit at scale. Across the vast global investment industry, only a tiny proportion of funds will therefore ever likely benefit. (Kirk, 2020)

9.3.2 The Human in the Machine

The pragmatic combination of machine learning to supplement human judgment was expressed as follows: "Machine learning will never solve the market. Even so, it may help practitioners to find an edge in an increasingly competitive industry" (Connected Wealth, 2018). This requires investment management firms to invest in both technology and human talent, with some expectation that the AI can help lower total payroll by reducing the number of traditional analysts needed.

Vanguard's Personal Advisory Services (PAS) provides an example of how AI and human advisors can be combined. Vanguard PAS uses algorithms to analyze the investor's data and recommend a trading strategy that fits the investor's objectives, such as risk level, asset allocation, and time horizon, according to the PAS brochure (Vanguard, 2020). Human advisors first gather information from the client via a survey on financial goals, risk tolerance, existing investments and assets, sources of income, investment preferences, and risk tolerances. This information is analyzed by the AI, which recommends a trading track that optimally fits the client's objectives. According to an article in the *Harvard Business Review in 2018*, this automated investment advice is complemented with the advice of human advisers. While the PAS offering has taken over many of the traditional tasks of the investment advisor such as portfolio construction and rebalancing, tax-loss harvesting, and tax-efficient investment selection, the human Vanguard advisors now perform more of a coaching role that entails answering questions, encouraging healthy financial behavior, and preventing unwise investor behaviors under stress. PAS had quickly accumulated more than $80 billion assets under management (AUM), at lower cost to Vanguard than typical human-based advisory services, and with high customer satisfaction (Davenport & Ronanki, 2008).

9.3.3 Research Applications

Quantitative research before machine learning was mainly directed at finding linear relationships (i.e., trends) between input data (e.g., past company earnings, interest rates, and historical price movements) and output data (subsequent asset price movements) that can then be used to predict future prices. When practitioners apply machine learning, the new algorithms often rediscover some of the previously known trends that have been understood for years. However, the AI may also find subtler, nonlinear relationships between the input and output data that were previously undiscovered. This makes AI a good complement to the traditional tools (Robertson, 2018).

First, the ability of machine learning to, for example, tease out new patterns in existing datasets has already born fruit. For example, machine learning has been proven to be 10% more accurate than conventional models in predicting bond defaults (Barboza et al., 2017). Machine learning's proficiency in finding patterns can also be used to analyze CEO earnings calls of S&P 500 companies over the past 20 years, and use the patterns to generate insights from current statements made by CEOs. Blackrock claims to use such technology to analyze over 5000 earnings call transcripts every quarter and more than 6000 broker reports daily (Novick et al., 2019).

Second, the flood of new data being generated by individuals, companies, and the internet of things (IoT) presents many new research opportunities. AI can analyze such new forms of data. Machine learning is a powerful tool for extracting patterns and insights from such large, often unstructured data sources. Nonfinancial data can inform decisions in finance, including investment decisions. For example, satellite images can be used to track oil rig and shipping activity, or observe the number of cars parked at shopping malls on holiday weekends, or estimate crop yields in China; credit card transaction patterns can be used to analyze sales trends; social media activity can be used to gauge investor sentiment; GPS location of mobile phones can be used to analyze retail store foot traffic; and so on.

Portfolio managers can also use AI to gauge market sentiments in real time so as to better understand the movement of tradable assets and provide more sophisticated advice to their clients. Refinitiv by Reuters offers MarketPsyche indices which use AI to continuously scour over 2000 financial news sources, as well as over 800 blogs, stock message websites, and social media platforms to assess market perception on stocks, bonds, commodities, currencies, countries, and cryptocurrencies. These real-time insights give portfolio managers intelligence on how particular asset classes and securities are expected to perform.

Third, as mentioned in Sect. 9.2.1, machine learning can help to debias human investment decisions. It may, for example, by used to interrogate the historical trading patterns of portfolio managers and their analysts to surface patterns indicative of such biases. Once visible, this permits humans to build in checks into future investment decisions. Such bias checks should be conducted at every stage in the investment process: portfolio construction, security selection, and trading execution (Pozen & Ruane, 2019).

9.3.4 Trade Execution Improvements

As traditional over-the-counter trade execution has been replaced by electronic trading in most asset classes, the digitization of the trading lifecycle has created a vast dataset for trading teams to analyze.

AI can assist human traders in selecting the routing destination or execution method that optimizes the three key goals of trade execution:

- To buy the securities at the lowest possible price.
- To pay as little as possible in facilitation fees to minimize transaction cost.
- To minimize the market impact of the particular transaction.

For example, an AI trading model can analyze broker–dealer inventory, pricing data, and historical transactions to make a routing recommendation on counterparties and venues. These recommendations can be fed into and automated by (non-AI) programmed instructions with a smart order router, which displays suggestions to traders and sends the order out electronically.

AI can also greatly reduce the need for human labor in the area of trade reconciliation. AI "bots" can operate on the entire transaction process flow across the back, middle, and front offices to complete trade reconciliation, alerting human operators only in the case of exceptions or disputes.

A more ambitious application of AI in asset management is the idea of self-creating exchanges with complete price transparency. Analysts from Société Générale foresee a time with "AI bots on both ends of the transaction across back, middle and front office doing it all and alerting humans only in rare cases of disputes" (Launoy & Torchon, n.d.)

9.4 Operational Efficiency

An important operational application of AI in asset management is the quality checking, monitoring, and exception handling of large amounts of data on the financial instruments and securities that need to be managed. Improving data quality helps to reduce operational risks and protects clients. Doing this via AI lowers costs. For example, a machine-learning model could take known inputs such as an average stock price to check if the latest vendor price is in error.

A case in point is Blackrock's AI-powered Aladdin, which creates over a million risk and exposure reports on portfolios from huge datasets each day. Since most data errors are systematic (such as missing or out-of-date data), machine-learning systems can provide great leverage to data teams who have to do error checking and cleansing.

Blackrock's Aladdin is also an example of a trend in operational efficiency identified by the World Economic Forum, which is that the back office can be transformed from a cost center to a profit center (World Economic Forum, 2018).

AI-enabled services can provide such high levels of operational excellence that they are not only a competitive advantage for the firm that owns the services but also can be sold to other firms in the same industry for deployment.

9.4.1 *Front Office*

In addition to complementing alpha-seeking models, machine learning's great strength is its ability to crunch large volumes of data faster and more efficiently than traditional analytical techniques. This analytical power greatly increases the ability of investment managers to rapidly process market information and draw insights from it. One such application is finding the most efficient channels for the execution of client trades (Robertson, 2018).

9.4.2 *Middle Office*

Asset management firms now analyze text and voice communications with NLP and other AI techniques. This helps them to pick up policy breaches in conversations and to provide AI-assisted responses to common operations questions. According to McKinsey, a leading asset manager deployed a solution which automatically upload documents to a central repository where NLP could extract required over four million unique data elements into a searchable reporting interface. This enabled a 60% reduction in report preparation time (Doshi et al., 2019).

9.4.3 *Back Office*

The main back-office applications of machine learning are flagging anomalies in execution log, detecting fraudulent transactions, and supporting risk management in general. Regulatory compliance is another application for AI-based analytics in asset management.

Asset managers are reporting that machine learning is better at detecting risks than even experienced human experts looking at the same documents. Asset managers who have deployed forensic analytics to monitor traders, cross-checking transactions and communications with personal data to catch ethical breaches and other anomalies have seen significant operational savings in surveillance activities—between 55% and 85% in time spent—as well as improved detection (Novick et al., 2019).

9.5 Customer Experience: Major Consumer Trends Driving the Adoption of AI

9.5.1 How the Shift to Digital and Mobile Intersects with AI to Create New Service Models

In investment, and wealth management, in particular, there has been steady growth in the number of digital financial advisor apps in recent years, with different plays being executed in the business-to-consumer (B2C) and business-to-business (B2B) spaces. (Note: The niche of financial technology (fintech) aimed at the wealth-management space, is sometimes called *wealthtech*. However, this is also the name of a company offering algorithmic financial planning and advice, and we will generally avoid the term.)

Robo-advisory services started with automated client-facing (B2C) solutions. B2C robo-advisors cut client costs by lowering asset-management fees but also make the investor fully liable for his or her own portfolio management performance. As such these solutions are most attractive to clients who cannot afford a financial advisor. As such, these services were initially marketed only to individual customers, rather than to businesses (B2B). The thinking was that while it is not cost-effective to use humans to manage small amounts of wealth, large complex portfolios comprising a variety of investment products that are managed for high-net-worth individuals still require the human touch of a trusted advisor (Soloshchuk, 2017).

For example, the online-only company Betterment is one of the oldest and largest independent robo-advisors with over $14 billion AUM and more than 400,000 customers. The Betterment portfolio is mostly made up of stock and bond exchange-traded funds (ETFs) and its algorithms use MPT to maximize return while minimizing risk.

B2B solutions arose as offshoots of the B2C solutions. They present professionals such as banks and independent advisors with a technology toolkit to scale their investment businesses. For example, the Motif Advisor platform is aimed at advisors with $100 M or less of AUM. It offers a selection of asset allocation models and the ability to construct and rebalance portfolios based on clients' life goals. It also comes with a design-your-own option and a full set of tools like dashboards and white-labeled client portals.

Advisor Engine is an all-in-one B2B platform that offers a white-label solution, which includes client portals, basic workflows, integration with popular trading platforms, electronic records, and digital compliance.

The VestmarkONE platform is a B2B platform that helps financial advisors provide superior service and solutions to their clients.

9.5.2 *The Drive for Convenience*

Customer preferences to use different channels for different needs are constantly evolving. McKinsey's latest *Retail Banking Consumer Survey* of over 45,000 consumers in 20 countries found that digital channels are increasingly important and have now become the dominant channel worldwide. In countries where digitization has moved faster, more than 85% of bank customers use them at least once a month. As a result, branch visits have drastically declined. Yet, the presence of a nearby branch is still a major factor when choosing a bank, and customers see branches as places where they can get face-to-face help on complex issues, like making choices among multiple financial options, or getting advice on complex products (Dallerup et al., 2020).

One of the main actions that banks can take after pushing simple interactions to digital is to offer new human-digital channels such as remote advisory: Customers are increasingly happy to conduct conversations from their homes—a trend that will no doubt be accelerated by the COVID-19 lockdowns.

Only 44% of high-net-worth (HNW) individuals interviewed by CapGemini in 2019 said they connected very well with their wealth managers. Main reasons given were lack of emotional intelligence from advisors, few value-added services, and insufficient face time. The promise of AI is that it will not only drive costs down but also improve the performance of wealth managers, in particular, to make it more consistent. The time saved by AI can allow for more interaction time with clients (Capgemini, 2020).

The median age of HNW individuals is declining, with wealthy millennials expecting an omnichannel experience, hyper-personalization, and niche portfolios that cater to their preferences, such as sustainable investment. Financial institutions increasingly use AI to deliver on hyper-personalization. Younger HNW individuals are tech-savvy and willing to use automated tools if that gets them a better, more personalized user experience.

Commerzbank uses machine-learning technology from the startup, IDnow, to verify customers' identities via smartphone or PC. This convenience results in a 50% higher conversion rate of prospects to clients. Thirty percentage of Commerzbank customers now verify their identities through IDnow (IDnow, n.d.).

Barclays Wealth and Investment Management (W&IM) use a voice biometrics recognition system based on NLP from Nuance Communications, helping Barclays customer agents to automatically detect the identity of the person calling, and to either rapidly authenticate the client or reject the call (Nuance, n.d.). After implementing voice authentication, Barclays experienced a 90% reduction in complaints about its security service, and a 15% reduction in average call times, allowing them to field more client queries in less time.

Voice biometrics powered by AI has additional benefits: Clients appreciate not having to remember passwords anymore, and fraud rates can be expected to decline as voice authentication is more unique to clients than passwords or security question answers that are easily compromised.

9.5.3 *Personalization Enabled by AI Technology Resulting in Mass Customization*

AI-based tools can take into account a user's age, income, risk tolerances, and target retirement income to help the user select an asset allocation mix that is optimal for meeting his/her financial goals. In addition, this technology can also support tax-loss harvesting, and portfolio allocation rebalancing. AI thereby enables robo-advisors to provide personalized investment advice at much lower cost than traditional human advisory models. Another potential application of AI is to help portfolio managers select the right clients and group them with like-minded investors.

Blackrock provides a number of AI-powered user-interface platforms that can be used by a wide range of professional services, from large institutions to individual wealth managers. Aladdin Wealth, targeted at wealth management firms and banks, includes portfolio analysis and construction capabilities as well as enterprise-level business and risk oversight. iRetire targets financial advisors specializing in retirement to quickly build plans for their clients. FutureAdvisor is a digital wealth management solution that helps financial institutions to onboard and service new client segments in a highly scalable way (Novick et al., 2019).

A 2019 report by the CFA Institute examined the trends and use cases of AI and big data technologies in investment management (CFA Institute, 2019). One of the major findings was that relatively few of the investment professionals surveyed are currently fully exploiting AI and big data tools. The CFA Institute is of the opinion that an AI + HI (human intelligence) model is the future of the industry. In this model, AI augments human intelligence, enabling higher levels of performance from human investment managers by freeing from the routine tasks and leveraging the "collective intelligence of machines and humans."

9.6 Business Outcomes

So far in this paper we have discussed how AI technologies help investment portfolio managers to better perform three existing tasks, that is, optimizing the investment process (covered in Sect. 9.3); increasing operational efficiency (covered in Sect. 9.4); and enhancing the customer experience (covered in Sect. 9.5). However, AI technologies also allow incumbent financial institutions and new entrants to create innovative new service and business models and to pursue investment strategies that could not be completed previously.

9.6.1 New Service Models

A major reason for poor investment returns for individual investors is their own poor decision-making. Financial firms like Personal Capital use behavioral prompts powered by AI to help customers make better financial decisions (Constable, 2020). For example, data-driven analyses of spending patterns or monthly cashflow result in prompts to invest cash in lying in low-yield deposit accounts to higher yield accounts. The advisory firm Betterment uses prompts to dissuade customers from making the mistake of panic selling during market downturns. AI is also a tool that can help financial advisors offer better services. For example, AI provides financial advisors at Financial Freedom Wealth Management Group, a wealth-management firm, with alerts that prompt the advisor to reach out to clients individually or in groups when it picks up abnormal patterns of account activity such as unusually high login volumes.

Charles Schwab offers a robo-advisor service for automated investing. Called Schwab Intelligent Portfolios®, the premium version of this product includes the advisory services of a Certified Financial Planner (CFP). The platform is aimed at investors with fairly standard needs. In late 2019, Schwab and TD Ameritrade announced a merger deal whereby the former would acquire the latter. The merger, which was planned to close in Q2 2020, is currently under regulatory review and subject to lawsuits (Horowitz, 2020).

9.6.2 New Business Models and Offerings

The Canadian robo-advisor company, Wealthsimple, is an online investment service company that focuses on younger customers. It charges a low management fee for its basic offering, which includes an investment up to $100 K in a personalized portfolio with automatic rebalancing and dividend reinvestments, as well as financial advisor assistance on demand. It offers a socially responsible portfolio particularly appealing to the younger generation. This startup has been attracting a lot of interest from large incumbents: In 2019, the tech investment fund of the German insurer, Allianz, acquired 10% of Wealthsimple as part of a $100 million (CDN) financing round. Previously, Quebec-based Power Financial Corp controlled by the Desmarais company had acquired 65% of Wealthsimple. Paul Desmarais III, the chairman of Wealthsimple, said "We believe the coming together of large incumbent companies that understand how to build global asset managers, with innovative, digital-first companies, is the future of financial services" (Rastello, 2019).

Blackrock's Aladdin Risk Platform is an end-to-end, cloud-based solution (Blackrock calls it an "operating system") for investment professionals in financial institutions. Aladdin employs machine learning in its risk analytics and portfolio management tools. It includes the ability to test thousands of risk scenarios and an optimizer to rebalance portfolios. A notable early client is the Oregon State

Treasury (OST) which in 2015 equipped its staff with Aladdin to manage the state's $90 billion investment portfolio. Blackrock has also set up a center in Palo Alto, California (the heart of Silicon Valley) dedicated to AI research, reflecting the appetite among asset managers for ever more sophisticated analysis methods (Wigglesworth & Flood, 2018).

Traditional banks use their deposit and lending relationships with clients to upsell them investment management services. New financial players (nonbank competition) are following a similar strategy, but this time in the digital realm where the pace of client acquisition is much faster. An example of this is Ant Financial: In 2004, the Alibaba Group founded by Jack Ma launched the mobile payment platform Alipay in China. By 2008, Alipay already had 150 million users with annual transaction volume of about $100 million. In 2014, a new parent company of Alipay, Ant Financial headquartered in Hangzhou, China, was established to "bring inclusive financial services to the world." The goal of Ant Financial was to use Alipay as a springboard to offer a wider range of financial services. By 2018, Yu'e Bao, Ant's money market fund, became the largest money market fund in the world with $168 billion AUM. By 2019, all of China's mutual fund managers were using the Ant Marketplace (Ant Fortune) platform with reach of over 180 million users (Capgemini, 2020).

9.6.3 New Investment Strategies

In a 2019 white paper, Allianz Global Investors (North America) take a measured view of the potential of AI in portfolio management (Heldmann & McCormick, 2019). Investors are advised to see AI as another (powerful) tool that fund managers can employ in their investment processes. But they caution against an overreliance on AI alone to improve alpha. There are two ways of applying AI to increase alpha: One is to ask the AI to identify outperformance signals and create new alpha strategies based on them from scratch. The other is to use AI to replicate and enhance an already established investment strategy. For example, you can train a neural network to operate a momentum investing strategy.

AI can be directed to crunch traditional structured financial data like reports, sell-side estimates, holdings, market, and macro data in order to create an excess-return model, and then to construct a portfolio and risk model. Alternatively, as mentioned earlier in Part 4 on the Investment Process, AI can be directed to large alternative datasets such as social media, web scraping, mobile phone, satellite images, and IoT data. Machine learning can then convert the unstructured data to structured data, after which the machine learning or a traditional statistical analysis can be used to create an excess-return model (Heldmann & McCormick, 2019).

One challenge facing the use of neural networks is data paucity. While price data on U.S. equities is available from the late 1920s onward, good quality fundamental data is only available from the 1960s on. Emerging markets have a data history not much longer than 20 years. While the available data contain millions of observations, it takes billions of observations to properly train neural networks. Machine learning is successfully used to analyze credit card purchasing patterns with tens of billions of annual transactions. But 30 years of good quality data for 10,000 global stocks produce 1.2 million observations, hardly enough for sophisticated machine learning insights.

9.7 Further Considerations

9.7.1 Regulatory Compliance and Security

It is important to keep in mind that the provision of investment advice is highly regulated. Any new tools, such as robo-advisors, are still subject to the same regulatory framework as human advisors.

When AI technologies have access to confidential client information, robust cybersecurity is paramount. This should include data encryption, business continuity planning, and cybersecurity insurance.

9.7.2 Algorithmic Bias

A major concern with using AI in asset management is the *black box* nature of the algorithms, which are not understood by portfolio managers, yet the managers are supposed to follow the direction given by the machines. Human portfolio managers may not understand how and why the trades prescribed by the AI will yield the expected investment returns.

The black box problem would not matter if algorithms were infallible, but they are not. While AI has the potential to de-bias human decisions, it has been known to add its own bias, sometimes in totally unexpected ways. Bias in machine learning is a known problem, which often starts with the dataset used (Jones, 2019):

- *Sample bias* occurs when the data are inadequate or unrepresentative.
- *Prejudicial bias* occurs when the dataset includes identity markers that may not be considered (e.g., race or strongly race-correlated data in loan applications).
- *Exclusion bias* occurs when the data cleaning removes important information that was considered not relevant.
- Lastly, *algorithmic bias* does not come from the dataset used to train the model, but from the model development itself and/or training methods used.

Human data scientists therefore need to integrate machine-learning insights with existing knowledge to prevent new biases.

9.7.3 *Transparency and Control*

Portfolio managers must be able to understand and interpret the inputs and outputs of AI systems. The greater the complexity of the machine-learning techniques applied, the more challenging this will be.

When portfolio managers use third-party AI solutions, they need to ensure clarity on the obligations of the solution provider and perform due diligence on the solution. The quality of any data sources used needs to be vetted too. Any AI used for trading should have robust development management, pre-trade controls, and the ability for human managers to shut down the system.

9.8 Conclusion

In financial portfolio management, various types of AI may be used to respectively achieve higher portfolio returns, increase operational efficiency, and enhance the customer experience.

Neural networks offer powerful new ways of discerning signal from noise in analyzing vast amounts of research data, particularly new sources of unstructured data. While it is a powerful new tool in the hands of the portfolio manager, machine learning always needs to be supplemented by human judgment; not least because past data patterns may not be a good guide to the future. Genetic algorithms (GAs), a form of evolutionary computation, are the most widely used type of AI to optimize investment returns through portfolio fund selection. The drawback of GAs is that they may be unoriginal, effectively replicating what traders have done before. AI can aid trading execution by reducing the need for human labor in the front, middle, and back offices. It can optimize order routing, perform trade reconciliations, find data errors, and support regulatory compliance.

On the B2C customer experience side, a type of AI called natural language processing (NLP) can support voice and text-based customer interactions, offering increased convenience and response times while saving on labor cost. AI-enhanced platforms and toolkits support professionals serving B2B customers with infrastructure like client portals, workflows, and electronic and compliance recordkeeping. AI also supports mass customization, including individual portfolio construction with low levels of human involvement.

AI is not a panacea and has potential flaws of its own, like algorithmic bias which may go undetected because of the black box nature of AI algorithms. Since portfolio management is highly regulated, any new tools like AI are still subject to the same rules as human advisors, which makes the transparency of any AI solution (whether in-house developed or acquired) essential. Successful AI usage will always involve an optimum mix of machine-provided and human-based services, where the AI enhances and accelerates human portfolio decision-making and saves labor costs. In this evolving partnership, human judgment will remain paramount.

References

Aguilar-Rivera, R., Valenzuela-Rendón, M., & Rodríguez-Ortiz, J. J. (2015). Genetic algorithms and Darwinian approaches in financial applications: A survey. *Expert Systems with Applications, 42*(21), 7. 684-7,697.

Ban, G.-Y., El Karoui, N., & Lim, A. E. B. (2018). Machine learning and portfolio optimization. *Management Science, 64*(3), 1136–1154.

Barboza, F.; Kimura, H. and Altman, E. "Machine learning models and bankruptcy prediction," Expert Systems with Applications, Vol. 83, Mar. 2017, pp. 405-417.

Capgemini Research Institute (2020). World Fintech Report 2020.

Capgemini (2020). Top trends in wealth management 2020.

CFA Institute (2019). AI pioneers in investment management.

Connected Wealth. Machine learning meets investment portfolio management. SEE IT Market, May 24, 2018.

Constable, S. These robots want to make sure you don't do anything stupid with your money. The Wall Street Journal, April 5, 2020.

Dallerup, K., Delzi, F., Ferreira, N., Niza, G., & Lasa, A. N. (2020). *Customer preferences spur retail banking channel evolution*. McKinsey & Company.

Davenport, T. H., & Ronanki, R. (2008). *Artificial intelligence for the real world*. Harvard Business Review.

Doshi, S., Kwek, J.-H., & Lai, J. (2019). *Advanced analytics in asset management: Beyond the buzz*. McKinsey & Company.

Epstein, J. Transcript of interview with Charlotte Parker, Jellyfish, Aug 3, 2017.

Fama, E. F. (1968). Risk, return, and equilibrium—Some clarifying comments. *Journal of Finance, 23*, 29–40.

Ferreira, V. Artificial intelligence can now pick stocks and build portfolios. Are human managers about to be replaced? Financial Post, June 3, 2019.

Financial Stability Board, Artificial intelligence and machine learning in financial services, Nov.1, 2017.

Georgiou, M. (2019). AI in banking: a JP Morgan case study and how your business can benefit. imaginovation, Dec. 4.

Healy, R. (2019). The future of asset management: AI in asset management. Liquidnet, July 9.

Heldmann, M. and McCormick, C. (2019). Artificial Intelligence in portfolio management: a tool, not a destination. Allianz Global Investors.

Honchar, A. (2020). AI for portfolio management: From Markowitz to reinforcement learning, Apr. 12.

Horowitz, J. (2020). TD Ameritrade shareholder sues to stop merger with Schwab. Advisorhub, March 19.

IDnow (n.d.), Case study: Commerzbank, https://www.idnow.io/docs/case-study/IDnow-CaseStudy_Commerzbank_EN.pdf.

Jones, T. (2019). Machine learning and bias. IBM Developer, Aug. 27.

Kirk, E. (2020). Don't believe the hype about AI and fund management. Financial Times, Mar. 2.

Kishan, S. and Barr, A. (2018). AI Hedge fund is said to liquidate after less than two years. Bloomberg, Sept. 7.

Launoy, L. and Torchon, J. (n.d.). The future of artificial intelligence in asset management. Societe Generale Tech Magazine.

Lin, C.-C., & Liu, Y.-T. (2008). Genetic algorithms for portfolio selection problems with minimum transaction lots. *European Journal of Operational Research, 185*(1), 393–404.

Lintner, J.. "The valuation of risk assets and the selection of risky investments in stock portfolios and capital budgets," Review of Economics and Statistics, Vol. 47, Feb. 1965, pp. 13.-37.

Markowitz, H. (1952). Portfolio selection. *The Journal of Finance, 7*(1), 77–79.

Novick, B., Mayston, D., Marcus, S. et al., Artificial intelligence and machine learning in asset management, Blackrock. Oct. 2019.

Nuance (n.d.). Barclays improves their customer experience, https://www.nuance.com/omni-channel-customer-engagement/case-studies/barclays.html

Oh, K. J., Kim, T. Y., & Min, S. (2005). Using genetic algorithm to support portfolio optimization for index fund management. *Expert Systems with Applications, 28*(2), 371–379.

Paiva, F. D., Cardoso, R. T. N., Hanaoka, G. P., & Duarte, W. M. (2019). Decision-making for financial trading: A fusion approach of machine learning and portfolio selection. *Expert Systems with Applications, 115*, 635–655.

Pozen, R. C. and Ruane, J. (2019). What machine learning will mean for asset managers. Harvard Business Review, Dec. 3.

Rastello, S. (2019). Wealthsimple adds Allianz as shareholder in 'major endorsement' of robo adviser. Financial Post, May 23.

Rifki, O. and Ono, H. (2012). A survey of computational approaches to portfolio optimization by genetic algorithms. 18th International Conference Computing in Economics and Finance, Society for Computational Economics.

Robertson, G. (2018). *Machine learning in investment management*. Man Institute.

Sharpe, W. F. "Capital asset prices: A theory of market equilibrium under conditions of risk," Journal of Finance, Vol.19, Sept. 1964, pp. 425-442.

Soloshchuk, V. (2017). B2C and B2B Robo-Advisory: Human Touch Is Still Required, but Not for Everyone. Advisorhub, Aug. 9.

Vanguard Personal Advisor Services Brochure, March 30, 2020, Vanguard Advisors Inc., https://personal.vanguard.com/pdf/vpabroc.pdf

Wigglesworth, R. and Flood, C. (2018). BlackRock bulks up research into artificial intelligence. Financial Times, Feb. 19.

World Economic Forum, The new physics of financial services. Understanding how artificial intelligence is transforming the financial ecosystem, Aug. 2018.

Yan, Wei; Sewell, Martin V.; and Clack, Christopher D. (2008). Learning to optimize profits beats predicting returns- comparing techniques for financial portfolio optimisation. Proceedings of the 10th annual conference on Genetic and evolutionary computation, pp. 1681-1688.

Chapter 10
Using Machine Learning to Demystify Startups' Funding, Post-Money Valuation, and Success

Yu Qian Ang, Andrew Chia, and Soroush Saghafian

10.1 Introduction

In the modern economy, startups and entrepreneurship are viewed almost synonymously, both resulting in technological innovation, economic growth, and jobs creation. Touted as both a panacea for solving unemployment and a catalyst for growth, it is unsurprising that major cities are vying to be the next Silicon Valley, competing to attract innovative ideas, entrepreneurial talents, technology-driven startups, and venture capital (VC) funding. Globally, startups have become an increasingly prominent feature in the world economy, both as creators of economic value and disruptors of existing industries. They also play significant roles in major cities as important drivers of innovation and sources of next-generation ideas, in a myriad of sectors, including healthcare, manufacturing, transportation, logistics, and finance. Having a vibrant startup ecosystem, thus, increases the attractiveness of a city for business investments that spur job growth or rejuvenate existing industries. It is, therefore, unsurprising that the popular media is often filled with against-all-odds success stories of startups. But are such startup success stories really against-all-odds? Or are there measurable factors that can help to correctly predict the future success of startups?

In recent years, academic research aimed at understanding the dynamics of entrepreneurship have proliferated due to the growing role that startups play (Shane & Ulrich, 2004), and financing/funding has been identified as a crucial

Y. Q. Ang
Massachusetts Institute of Technology, Cambridge, MA, USA
e-mail: yuqian@mit.edu

A. Chia · S. Saghafian (✉)
Harvard University, Cambridge, MA, USA
e-mail: andrewchia@g.harvard.edu; soroush_saghafian@hks.harvard.edu

V. Babich et al. (eds.), *Innovative Technology at the Interface of Finance and Operations*, Springer Series in Supply Chain Management 11,
https://doi.org/10.1007/978-3-030-75729-8_10

factor in any successful startup ecosystem. On the one hand, startups—especially technology-based firms—are often financially constrained (Carpenter & Petersen, 2002) requiring significant funding for research and development, customer acquisition, and marketing, among others. Startups that are well funded or VC-backed have been reported to outperform their non-funded counterparts (Gompers & Lerner, 2001; Denis, 2004). Obtaining financing such as VC investments or follow-up funding also contributes to the so-called signaling effect (Islam et al., 2018) helping early-stage startups gain credibility as they progress from conceptualization to commercialization. On the other hand, obtaining sufficient funding without early signs of traction is often impossible. Funding and startup success, hence, can be viewed as a chicken and egg problem.

This chicken and egg problem makes it often difficult to comprehend valuation of startups and identify the key factors contributing to their success. For example, will a startup with a given amount of Series A funding be eventually successful? Is it possible to predict such startup's likelihood of success with reasonable confidence, given that success stories are typically rare events with about 90% of startups failing on average? Answers to these types of questions can significantly assist various players and decision-makers in the startup ecosystem, including entrepreneurs, venture capitalists, policymakers, and researchers. For example, VCs are often perceived as entities that fill the void in the innovation and commercialization process. However, to ensure viability, VCs need to generate consistently superior returns on investments, a significant challenge given the inherently risky nature of early-stage companies. Since as high as 75% of venture-backed deals typically fail to return the investment (Hoque, 2020), VCs rely on a small number of portfolio investments to achieve outstanding paybacks—enough to cover for losses and still produce substantial profits. Therefore, any data-driven method that can yield superior investment decisions can be significantly valuable.

In this study, we review the entrepreneurial ecosystems and take stock of the key fundraising activities in major cities around the world. We then construct two models using modern machine learning approaches to predict startups' potential post-money valuation and probability of success using a dataset of funding activities across different regions, sectors of the economy, and funding stages, observed over a 10-year period (2009–2018).

Our study makes several contributions to the existing literature on startup and entrepreneurship. First, we examine the startup financing landscape in the context of different geographical regions and funding stages. In the ubiquitous, globalized nature of modern technology-based startups and their products and services, there is a need for research to shed light on how fundraising activities vary across cities. This will also be beneficial for startups seeking funding as part of their internationalization strategy, and for venture funds targeting specific geographical regions and financing stages. We also provide insights into statistical aspects of funding raised in different regions and sectors of economy, including their distributional properties. Second, we make use of some machine learning approaches to develop strong prediction models that can (a) augment the myriad analysis and benchmarking typically done by venture funds, startups, or policymakers and (b) serve as basis for further academic studies.

In what follows, we first review the startup financing landscape and introduce our dataset. We then describe the methodology and approach behind our machine learning models, and discuss the insights gained by making use of them on our dataset. Finally, we conclude by (a) providing recommendations for various entities involved in the startup ecosystem, including entrepreneurs and policymakers, (b) identifying limitations of our work, and (c) summarizing potential avenues for future work.

10.1.1 Financing

Funding is a vital resource for startups; financing and equity investments through government grants, accelerators/incubators, angel investors, and venture funds are key resources that can shape a startup's development trajectory. These funds are typically utilized to support critical activities such as product development, marketing, research and development, and staffing. Recognizing the importance of financing, governments, and policymakers around the world have developed their own funding programs, such as independent government-sponsored funds (Alperovych et al., 2015), co-investment/co-financing vehicles, and grants, among the many instruments designed to catalyze the startup ecosystem. These accompany private entrepreneurial investments by venture capitalist, corporate venture capital funds, startup accelerators/incubators and angels, as well as relatively newer financing modalities such as equity crowdfunding (Drover et al., 2017). Naturally, most of the financing activities gravitate and converge towards major cities. The geographical region in which a startup is located, hence, can play an important role in the investment amounts it can attract.

Besides the geographical region, the investment amounts a startup can attract typically vary significantly across funding stages. In most geographical regions and entrepreneurial ecosystems, seed funding is usually the first institutional funding received by a startup, although many venture funds are now looking at pre-seed due to the competitive nature of seed investments. The name of this round, seed funding, is self-explanatory: it is used to take a startup from ideation to some early traction, such as initial product development, market research, or validation for product-market fit. A seed funding round typically ranges between $100,000 and $2 million, depending on the type of startup and the geographical region. The typical valuation for a startup raising seed ranges between $3 million and $6 million (Reiff, Nathan, 2020). Unfortunately, many startups run out of seed funding before they can gain sufficient traction. For example, data from the market research firm CB Insights obtained by tracking a cohort of 1100 startups that raised seed rounds in the USA shows that less than 50% managed to raise a second round of funding. Furthermore, only 15% of these startups eventually raised a fourth round (which corresponds to Series C), and 67% either ended up dead or became self-sustaining (CB Insights, 2017).

Once a seed stage startup gains sufficient traction—measured in terms of common key performance indicators such as revenue or user acquisition—it moves to raise Series A funding. In this round, startups are expected to have a viable business model and sufficient traction, since investors want to assure more substantive development and growth. As the name suggests, series funding consists of a series of startup funding rounds that follow one after the other (Yuen, 2020), generally with increased valuation in each subsequent round. Typical rounds include Series A, B, C, D and sometimes E and F, and these rounds of funding are typically raised through venture capital firms (or other institutional investors). The different rounds are intended to also reflect the startup's status, performance, and valuation (Williams et al., 2013). A prospering and well-performing startup will have its company stock valued higher in a Series B round than A, and higher still in a Series C round. A startup not performing well may still obtain Series financing rounds, but subsequent Series rounds will often value the company at a lower stock price (a "downround"). Currently, the mean Series A funding round is valued at around $10–$15 million in the USA, a figure that has been growing steadily (Fundz Research, 2020). The mean Series B round currently stands at around $32 million, with a median pre-money valuation of $58 million (Fundz Research, 2020). However, these overall averages are highly contextualized and differ significantly across countries, different regions (even within the same country), and startup types.

Although the exact juncture is not specifically defined, typically after the second and/or third capital injection, startups enter a growth stage where funding serves to propel rapid growth and expansion rather than ignition. This usually entails internationalization (e.g., expansion to addition markets), diversification of product lines, aggressive marketing, or new manufacturing and production locations. With a commercially viable product and product-market-fit, a startup at this stage should have a good source of revenue and continue to attract new users/customers at breakneck speed. Very few startups eventually reach the Series D stage, and the amount raised by them as well as their valuations vary widely among them.

Finally, mezzanine financing and bridge loans are hybrid loan and equity financing mechanisms that prepare the startup for the final push for an exit. Mezzanine financing is typically perceived as being riskier than other types of startup financing due to higher interest rates. An initial public offering (IPO) is often the final stage of funding that a startup goes through before it becomes an established company. A startup may also be acquired along the way, regardless of funding stage, especially if it has novel technologies or has established significant user base or data that are of high value to the acquirer.

10.1.2 Post-Money Valuation

In the startup ecosystem, valuation is the process of quantifying the worth of a company at specific junctures. Valuation is important to founders for various reasons, including the fact that it determines the amount of equity they must give to investors in exchange for funds. Similarly, for investors, valuation helps to set the shares they should receive in lieu of their investments during a financing round (Miloud et al., 2012).

Valuation often has two stages: pre-money and post-money valuation. Pre-money valuation typically refers to the value of a company before—and not including—the latest funding round in question. Thus, pre-money valuation can be roughly described as how much a startup is worth prior to the current round of investments. Post-money valuation, however, refers to the value of the startup after receiving investments (Frei & Leleux, 2004). Both pre- and post-money valuation are usually affected by a variety of factors, including the sector of the economy the startup belongs to, its technology, revenue, reputation, and level of traction. Valuation methods can be broadly grouped into two main categories: qualitative and quantitative. The former—qualitative method—is more prevalent in assessing early-stage startups due to the lack of sufficient information at that point early on. The latter—quantitative method—is used more often in later stages, as more information (e.g., financial) becomes available at such stages.

One common method in valuation is the discounted cash flow method (Festel et al., 2013), which estimates how much cash flow the company is slated to produce. This estimation is obtained by making use of a reasonable, expected rate of investment return. A higher discount rate is typically associated with startups that have higher risks. This method relies partly on an investment analyst's ability to make sound and accurate assumptions on a startup's growth trajectory. A second popular method, which is usually utilized for pre-revenue and early-stage startups, is the Berkus Method, named after investor David Berkus (Berkus, 2016). This approach makes use of a general rule of thumb to estimate the value of the startup, since current pre-revenue forecasts rarely turned out to be accurate. Other commonly used methods include the First Chicago method, the venture capital method, the Comparables method, the Book Value method, the Scorecard method, and the Risk Factor Summation method (Nasser, 2017). As many valuation exercises are subjective, especially in early-stage investment, and the exact method utilized are often undisclosed, we avoid developing models that rely on any of these methods of valuation. Instead, we make use of machine learning algorithms and train them on actual post-money values in our data. These algorithms then learn to predict the post-money valuation of startups using their early-stage raw data.

10.1.3 Success

The definition of a successful startup is in general elusive and subjective. For investors, however, the notion of success is relatively straightforward, because they usually value return on investment. Thus, from an investor's perspective, the holy grail is a profitable exit, such as a successful acquisition or IPO. An exit is also often the only realistic way for professional or institutional investors to significantly profit from an investment. However, success is more complicated from the founders' perspective. Some founders, and especially serial entrepreneurs, seek financial gain, and pursue profitable exits after gaining significant visibility. Others value success on more introspective terms, such as creating social good. Moreover, there can be a long incubation time between the founding of a startup and its acquisition or IPO. Thus, labelling startups that are on their way to success but have not achieved it as unsuccessful is often an unfair assessment of their potential. These make studying success among startups a perplexing task.

For the goals of this study, we start by considering the conventional, investor-based definition of success: whether a startup will be acquired or will launch an IPO. We then expand our definition of success to also include startups that are able to raise follow-on funding amounts that are greater than their previous funding rounds, since such startups tend to grow over time. We make use of this definition of success to train a neural network model to classify startups into two categories: successful and unsuccessful. This classification is done based on predicting the probability of success using features such as geographic region, sector, stage, and funding, among others. Once it is trained, our neural network model is able to accurately predict if a startup (not included in the training data) will eventually be successful given its features.

10.2 Data

The primary dataset for this study comprises startup funding instances obtained from Crunchbase, with supplementary data on the companies, IPOs, and acquisitions. Crunchbase is a platform that aggregates business information about private and public companies. Originally built to track startups, Crunchbase now contains information on startups, venture funds, and companies on a global scale. Crunchbase sources their data through many channels, including an in-house data team, their venture program, and the community. We accessed Crunchbase data using a REpresentational State Transfer (REST) Application Programming Interface (API) user-key, to access compressed Tape Archive Files (TAR) that contains various raw data on companies and funding rounds globally, starting from 1915. The data from various files were matched using the unique identifier generated for each startup and investor. The resultant dataset reflects a 10-year period from 2009 to 2018, with a total of 290,707 observations of startups funding instances around the world. From these 290,707 observations, we retained 46,025 observations after (a) filtering for empty fields, mismatching, or corrupted data, and (b) focusing on observations related to one of the top 15 cities that have the highest number of startups. These allowed us to maintain a reasonable number of datapoints in each region, and consequently, perform analysis that are robust (and not affected by issues such as sparsity).

While there are other platforms and databases that tracks startup financing, including Pitchbook, AVCJ, and CB Insights, the data aggregating methodologies used in them are different. It is, therefore, unfeasible to simply merge data

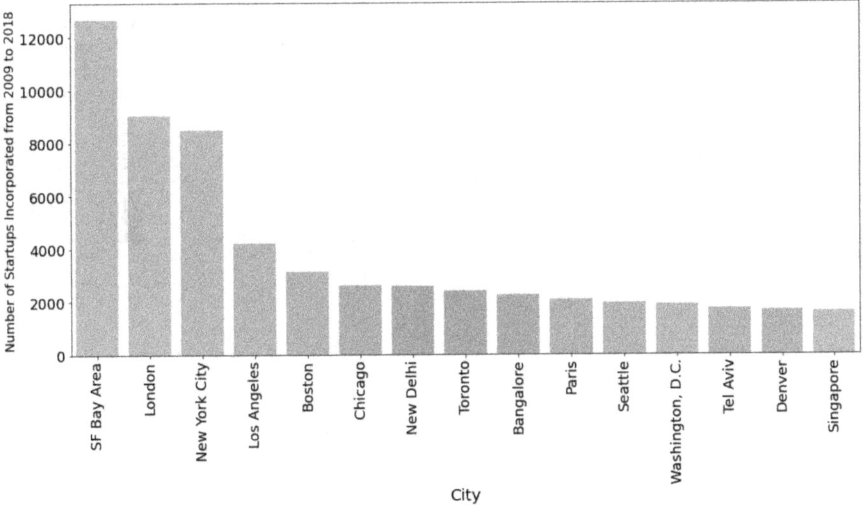

Fig. 10.1 Top 15 cities with the highest number of startups in our dataset

from different sources, especially if consistency is to be maintained. Furthermore, global financing data is often incomplete in practice, since a significantly number of transactions are undisclosed, and many startups operate in stealth mode for confidentiality. Therefore, we consider our Crunchbase dataset as relatively representative, even as the final dataset, after data wrangling, may be a relatively small sub-sample of the entire startup population.

Figure 10.1 shows the top 15 major cities with the highest number of startups in our dataset. In these cities, most startups are still operational, ranging from 83% of the startups in the San Francisco Bay Area to 92% in New Delhi. Figure 10.2 shows the status of startups in these major cities. Unsurprisingly, we see that San Francisco Bay Area not only has the largest number of startups but also the highest percentage of startups that are either acquired or have launched IPO (11%). Other cities with relatively high percentages of startups that were acquired or launched IPO include Toronto (11%) and Paris (10%).

Our preliminary exploratory analysis of the investment stage of startups revealed over 25 funding stages in our dataset, ranging from pre-seed stage to Series J and even post-IPO. Much of the data in many regions and in the later stages are sparse, containing very few data points. For consistency and rigor of our machine learning models, we used a subset of the overall data comprising funding information for the top 15 regions, as well as the following stages: grant, angel round, seed, series A, series B, series C, series D, and series E. Figure 10.3 shows the amount of funding raised based on region and funding stage.

To better understand the nature and properties of post-money valuations, we assessed their distributional properties across regions and funding stages using kernel density estimation (KDE). KDE is a non-parametric method commonly

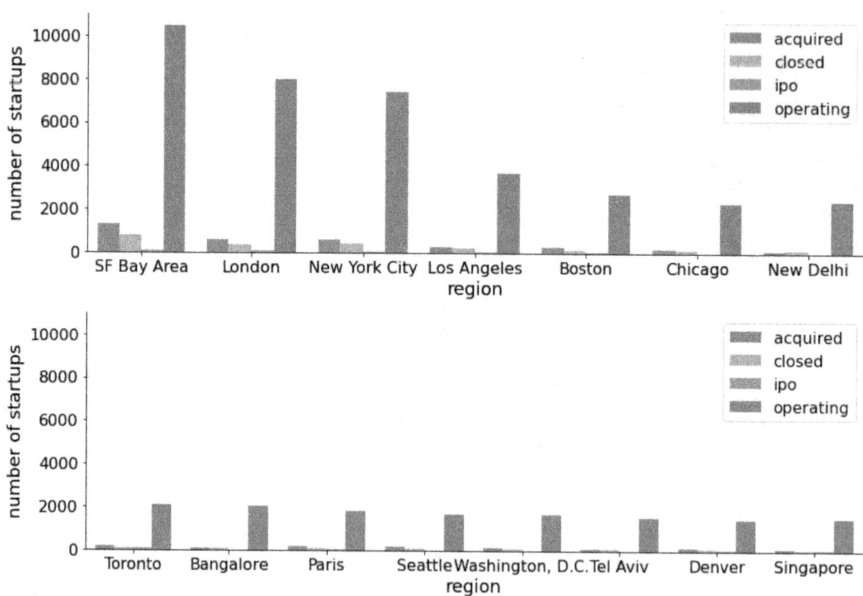

Fig. 10.2 Status of startups in the top 15 cities

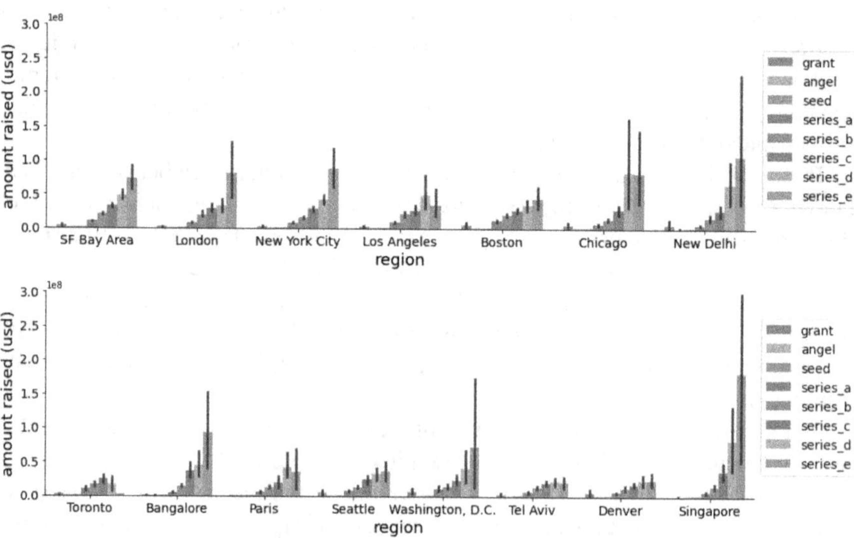

Fig. 10.3 Funding amount (USD) based on stage and region

employed to approximate the probability density function (PDF) of continuous values (Parzen, 1962) such as funding (Carayannis et al., 2018) or startup valuation (Quintero, 2019). Figures 10.4 and 10.5 show the KDE for the amount raised (on a logarithmic scale) based on region and funding stage, respectively. Funding

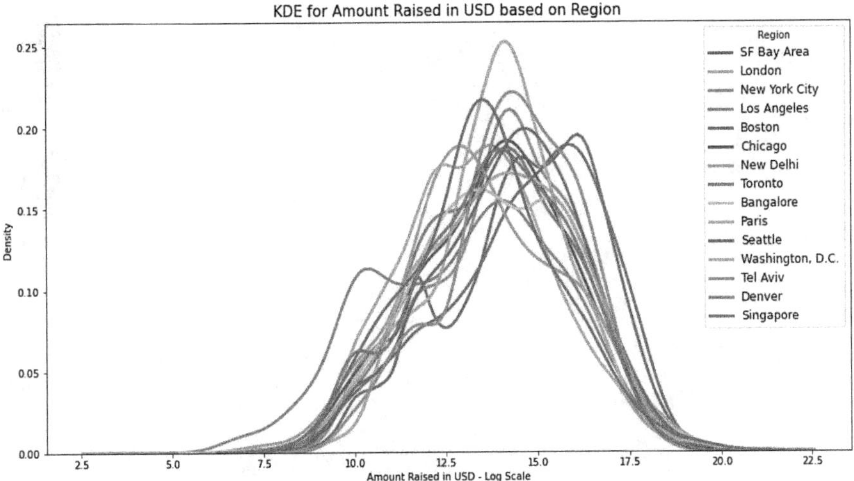

Fig. 10.4 KDE for funding amount raised (using numpy's logarithmic scale) based on region

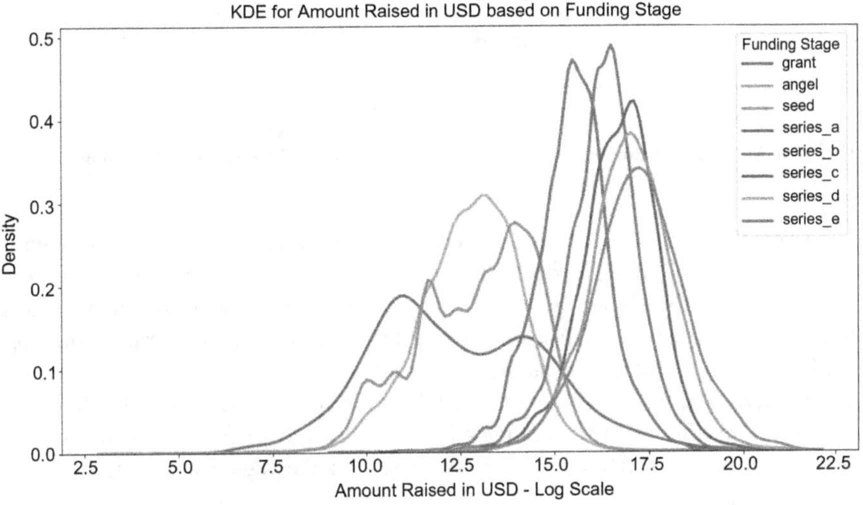

Fig. 10.5 KDE for funding amount raised (using numpy's logarithmic scale) based on funding stage

amount raised and post-money valuation in venture capital are typically power-law distributed (Korver, 2018), and may be subject to the "Babe Ruth Effect" (Dixon, 2015). While most funding raised and valuations are situated at lower values, there may exist a long tail of exceptionally high funding amount raised or post-money valuations (Quintero, 2019). Thus, the natural logarithm of these quantities is typically normally distributed. This also exemplifies the known fact that returns are highly concentrated on "home run" investments.

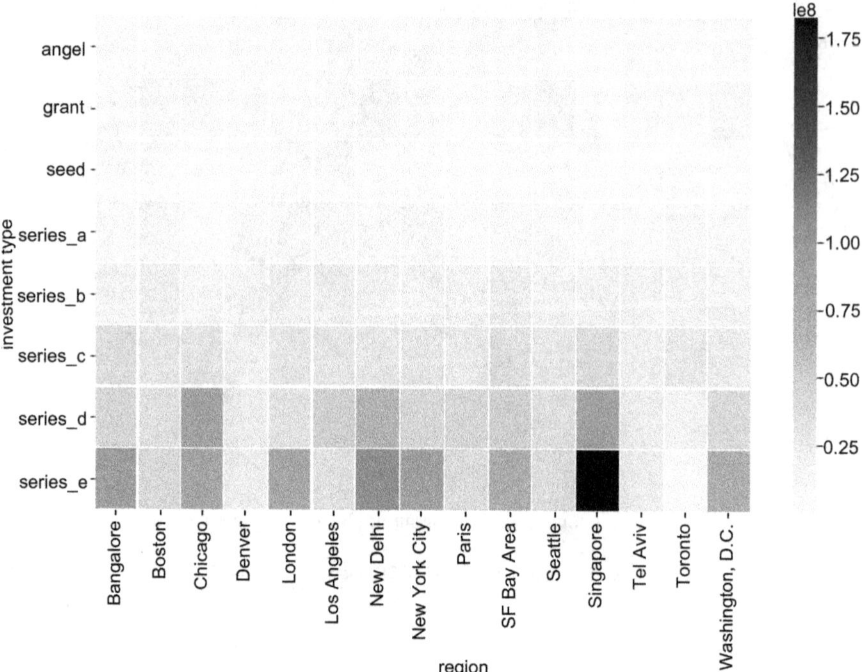

Fig. 10.6 Heatmap for funding amount (logarithmic scale) based on region and funding stage

Figure 10.6 illustrates the heatmap (in logarithmic scale) of funding stage and region. The darker colors represent higher funding amounts raised. As can be seen, the early-stage rounds are approximately similar, with New Delhi having more funding in terms of grants. Boston and San Francisco have more Series A funding, while Chicago, London, Singapore, and Bangalore have higher Series E funding compared to other cities. However, since the heatmap aggregates total funding over stages, the results could be dominated by outliers, e.g., a few companies raising significantly higher funding of startups based on the region and funding stage, respectively.

Figures 10.7 and 10.8 present the KDE of post-money valuations. First, most regions have a bimodal log-normal distribution, but it is evident that the second mode in San Francisco Bay Area has relatively higher density than the other regions. Second, there is significant overlap in post-money valuations between angel and seed rounds, as well as series C, series D, and series E. This suggests that while the differentiations between seed, and A and B funding rounds seem to be relatively clear, subsequent rounds for growth stage companies are relatively difficult to differentiate based on valuation alone. Quintero (2019) also provides a similar observation regarding the overlap between post-money valuation of startups in angel, pre-seed, and seed rounds. As Quintero (2019) discusses, this phenomenon

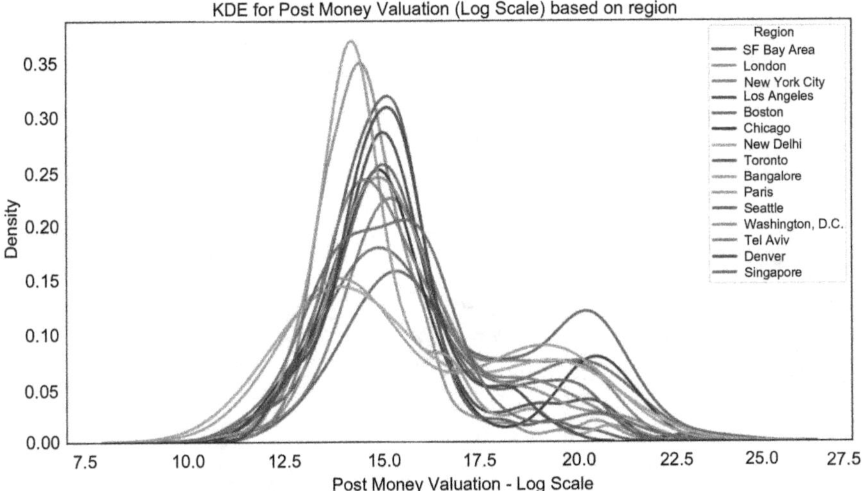

Fig. 10.7 KDE for post-money valuation (logarithmic scale) based on region

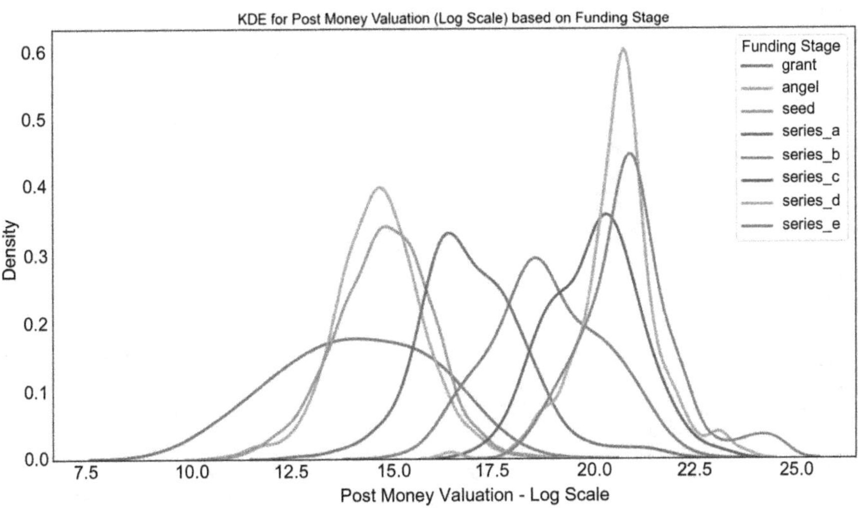

Fig. 10.8 KDE for post-money valuation (logarithmic scale) based on funding stage

is likely due to the changing definition of a seed round, and/or more institutional VCs participating in early-stage pre-seed rounds.

Finally, Fig. 10.9 illustrates the relationship between the post-money valuations (logarithmic scale) and the funding amount raised (logarithmic scale) separately for each region. Beyond the power-law connection, we observe from Fig. 10.9 that in general there is a positive relationship between the post-money valuation and

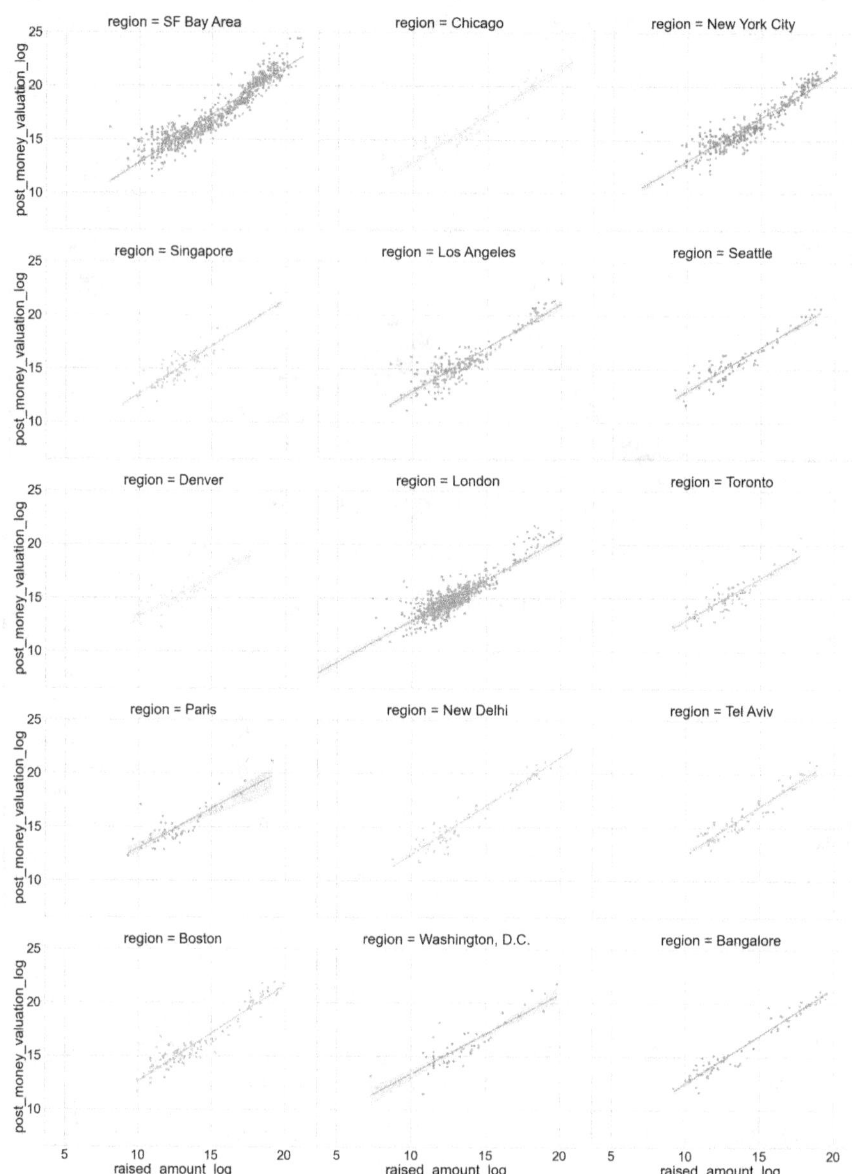

Fig. 10.9 Plots of funding amount raised with post-money valuations based on region, both on logarithmic scale

funding amount, and that the magnitude of this relationship is relatively consistent across different regions.

10.3 Methodology

10.3.1 Sectoral Clustering: Latent Dirichlet Allocation

While the dataset provides us with information on the sectors of economy each startup belongs to, the data in the category and description columns are manually entered or selected, with inconsistencies across the entire dataset. To overcome this issue, we employed a commonly used unsupervised learning approach in Natural Language Processing (NLP), topic modelling, and related fields: the Latent Dirichlet Allocation (LDA) method (Blei et al., 2003). LDA was first used in the context of population genetics (Pritchard et al., 2000). In machine learning, it is often viewed as a generative probabilistic model of a collection of composites of discrete parts/data such as text corpora. In particular, it is a three-level hierarchical Bayesian model, where each item in a collection is modelled as a finite mixture over an underlying set of topics, which is in turn modelled as an infinite mixture over an underlying set of topic probabilities (Blei et al., 2003).

LDA Algorithm

LDA (as introduced in Blei et al. 2003) involves the following generative process for each document in a corpus:

1. Choose $N \sim Poisson(\xi)$
2. Choose $\theta \sim Dir(\alpha)$
3. For each of the N words w_n:
   a. Choose a topic $z_n \sim Multinomial(\theta)$
   b. Choose a word w_n from $p(w_n|z_n, \beta)$, a multinomial probability conditioned on the topic z_n and model parameter β.

In the context of topic modelling, the composites are typically documents and the parts are words and/or phrase. Thus, LDA represents documents as mixtures of topics that churn out observable words based on random variables drawn from specific distributions (see the LDA algorithm above). For this study, we use LDA to group the startups into various sectoral clusters, based on (a) keywords in their categories or descriptions, and (b) probabilities of the keywords being associated with specific sectoral clusters. The optimal number of clusters is decided based on coherence scores for number of clusters (between 5 and 50). We then assign each startup to a cluster based on the LDA results and keyword probability assignments.

10.3.2 Predicting Post-money Valuation: ElasticNet

ElasticNet (Zou & Hastie, 2005) is a regularized linear model that employs both l_1-norm and l_2-norm penalization to achieve better mean-square prediction error performance compared to either pure Least Absolute Shrinkage and Selection Operator (LASSO) or Ridge regression. We use it to form a baseline model for predicting post-money valuations. The relative weight between l_1-norm and l_2-norm penalization as well as the overall penalization factor in ElasticNet are hyperparameters that we tune using five-fold cross-validation.

10.3.3 Predicting Post-money Valuation: XGBoost

XGBoost (Chen & Guestrin, 2016), short for eXtreme Gradient Boosting, is a recent optimized distributed gradient boosting technique that has been widely used in applied machine learning and online data science competitions, especially for structured or tabular data. XGBoost is an implementation of gradient boosted decision trees which is designed for enhanced speed and performance by making use of parallel tree boosting.

In this study, we deploy the XGBoost regressor to model the post-money valuation of startups in logarithmic scale. The feature set includes sector (obtained from LDA), region, funding amount raised, number of investors in the round, and funding stage as well as engineered features representing lag and growth.

10.3.3.1 Hyperparameter Tuning for XGBoost Using Bayesian Optimization

Common techniques for obtaining optimal hyperparameters include random search and grid search, but these techniques can be inefficient and slow. One reason is that they typically do not take advantage of the information learned during previous optimization rounds. For this study, we make use of Bayesian optimization (Snoek et al., 2012), which constantly learns from previous optimization stages to find the best set of hyperparameters. This gives Bayesian optimization the ability to require fewer samples and iterations to obtain the best set of hyperparameter values compared to some other methods (e.g., random search or grid search).

Bayesian optimization involves constructing a posterior distribution that improves as the number of observations grows. When used for hyperparameter tuning, the algorithm gets closer to the optimized set of hyperparameter values as the parameter space worth exploring shrinks. Bayesian optimization for hyperparameter tuning takes into account the classic exploration versus exploration paradigm and seeks to balance needs between both. A typical method is to fit a Gaussian process to the known samples for every iteration. The posterior distribution is then utilized to determine the next point to be explored.

In our test runs, where we used Bayesian optimization on XGBoost, our models generally converged in less than 10 iterations, compared with much longer search durations for cross-validated grid or randomized search. The resultant model accuracies were, however, approximately similar across cities. Nevertheless, we chose Bayesian optimization instead of typical methods of tuning such as cross-validated grid or randomized search due to its clear advantage in computational efficiency.

10.3.4 Predicting Success: Neural Network

To predict success of startups, we make use of a feed-forward neural network and train in it using our dataset. Mindful of the size our dataset, we restrict our neural network to two hidden layers. We also employ drop-out layers (Srivastava et al., 2014) between the dense layers to regularize our model and avoid over-fitting.

To train our neural network, we use two measures of startup success (as noted earlier). The first measure is based on whether a startup eventually make it to an exit by being acquired or by launching IPO. However, we also recognize that many startups in our study period may still be on their way being acquired or lunching IPO. Thus, we augment our definition of success by considering startups that are continuing to grow in terms of the amount of funding that they are able to raise. The second definition of success not only covers all firms that meet the first definition (being acquired or lunching IPO) but also includes all firms that have not exhibited signs of stagnation.

10.4 Results

10.4.1 Sectoral Clustering

Our LDA model found 16 sectoral clusters to be the optimal number of clusters. Figure 10.10 provides a wordcloud visualization of each sectoral cluster using the Python WordCloud package (Mueller, 2020). Words in this figure represent keywords with the highest probability of being in each sector cluster (generated by the LDA analysis) and the size of the font is proportional to this probability.

The sectors obtained using LDA and visualized in Fig. 10.10 are rather evident. For example, sectoral cluster one comprises startups in retail, fashion, and e-commerce. Similarly, sectoral cluster four comprises startups mainly in the domains of artificial intelligence, machine learning, and data analytics, while sectoral cluster fourteen comprises startups in medical technology, healthcare, and pharmaceuticals.

Fig. 10.10 Wordcloud for sectoral clusters found, with the larger fonts representing higher probabilities

However, since LDA is primarily an unsupervised approach, the results contain some keywords which do not fit quite well in particular clusters. An example is the inclusion of the word “insurance” in sector cluster six, which comprises primarily “energy” and “industrial” related startups.

Figure 10.11 shows the topic model visualization using the `pyLDAvis` package. The left visualization depicts the clustering of each of the topics, where the size of the circle is proportional to overall prevalence of the topic in the corpus. The distance between each of the topics is measured by calculating the Jensen-Shannon divergence, a measure of similarity between two probability distributions.

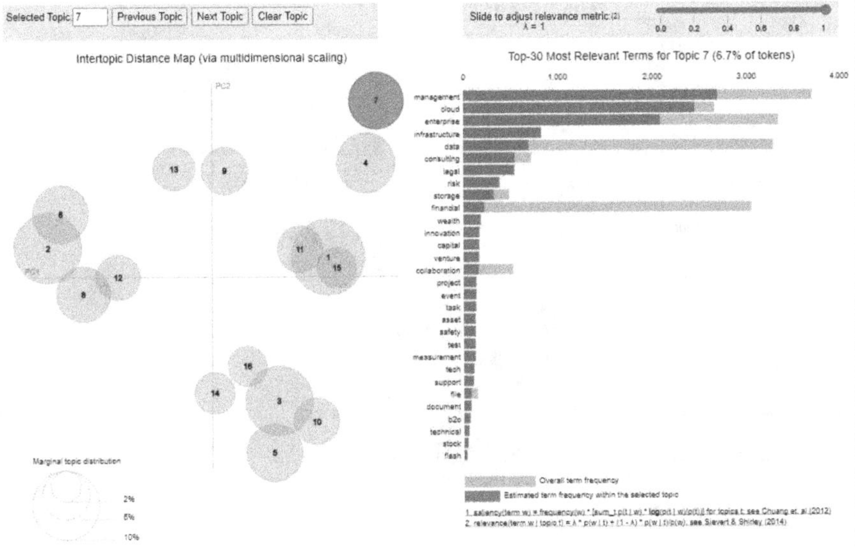

Fig. 10.11 `pyLDAvis` topic model visualization

Multidimensional scaling is used to project the distances onto two dimensions. It is desirable to have little to no overlap of the topic circles. The visualization on the right depicts the most important words of each topic.

10.4.2 Predicting Post-Money Valuation

Our ElasticNet model (tuned using cross-validation) chose an l_1-norm to l_2-norm ratio of 1.0, effectively representing a LASSO regression model. In addition, it chose a relatively low penalization rate of 0.00652. With these hyperparameters, the model was able to achieve an excellent accuracy of 96.275% and a mean absolute error of 0.589 on our test (i.e., out-of-sample) data.

We examined the coefficients of the predictors in our ElasticNet model to gain an initial understanding of the predictors that were the most important for the model. Figure 10.12 shows that (log) raised amount was the most decisive factor within the ElasticNet model, followed by the investment type. We also observe that the later series rounds types of investments have a positive association with post-money evaluation, while the earlier rounds investments have a negative association. Furthermore, the growth in raised amount as well as employee count seem to be positively associated with post-money valuation. However, the size of the coefficients depicted in Fig. 10.12 suggests that past performance and growth have a higher influence on the post-money valuation of a startup compared to the startup's size (measured by employee count).

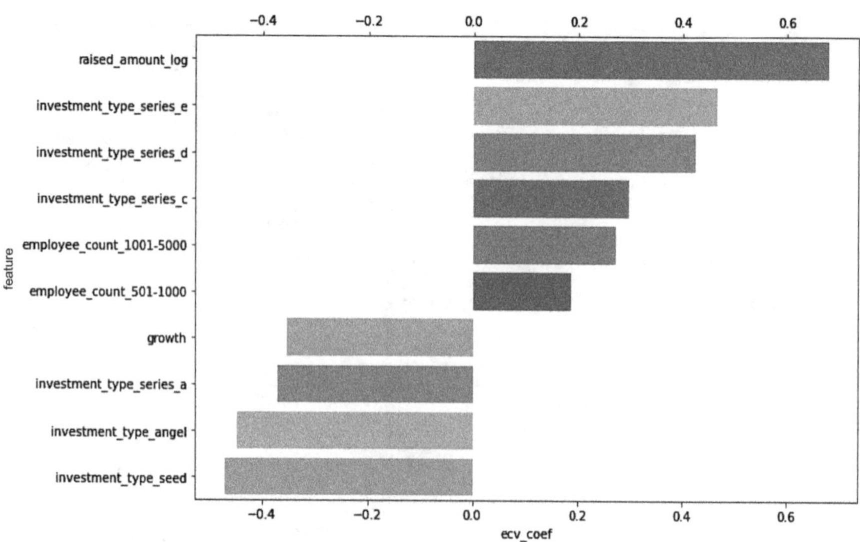

Fig. 10.12 Top 10 ElasticNet coefficients by size

Our tuned XGBoost model achieved an outstanding accuracy score of 96.45% and low mean absolute error of 0.550 on our test (i.e., out-of-sample) data. Figure 10.13 shows the plot of the true values (logarithm scale) and predicted values (logarithmic scale) in the test set (using our XGBoost model), with a high R^2 value of 0.9 when fitting a linear function. Our results indicate that our XGBoost model outperforms the ElasticNet approach. The increased accuracy and decreased mean absolute error achieved by the XGBoost model compared to ElasticNet suggest that the relationship between post-money valuation and its determinants is rather complex and most likely non-linear.

Using our XGBoost model, we next generate insights into the most important factors in predicting post-money valuation of startups. In Figs. 10.14 and 10.15, we illustrate a representative boosted tree and the feature importance of the predictors in the model, respectively. These figures show that funding amount raised is the most important predictor of post-money valuation, followed by the investor count. The observation that funding amount raised is the most important feature is consistent with the findings of our baseline ElasticNet model. The difference in second-most important feature (i.e., investor count in the XGBoost model versus the investment stage in the ElasticNet approach) could be due to a high correlation between investment stage and funding amount, which is accounted for in the XGBoost model in a non-parametric manner.

Finally, to test the robustness of our XGBoost model and its potential over-reliance on particular predictor(s), we first removed the top continuous predictors, and reran it. Between several runs, the resultant model only showed an accuracy decline of around 3–5%, with the LDA sectors remaining as the most important

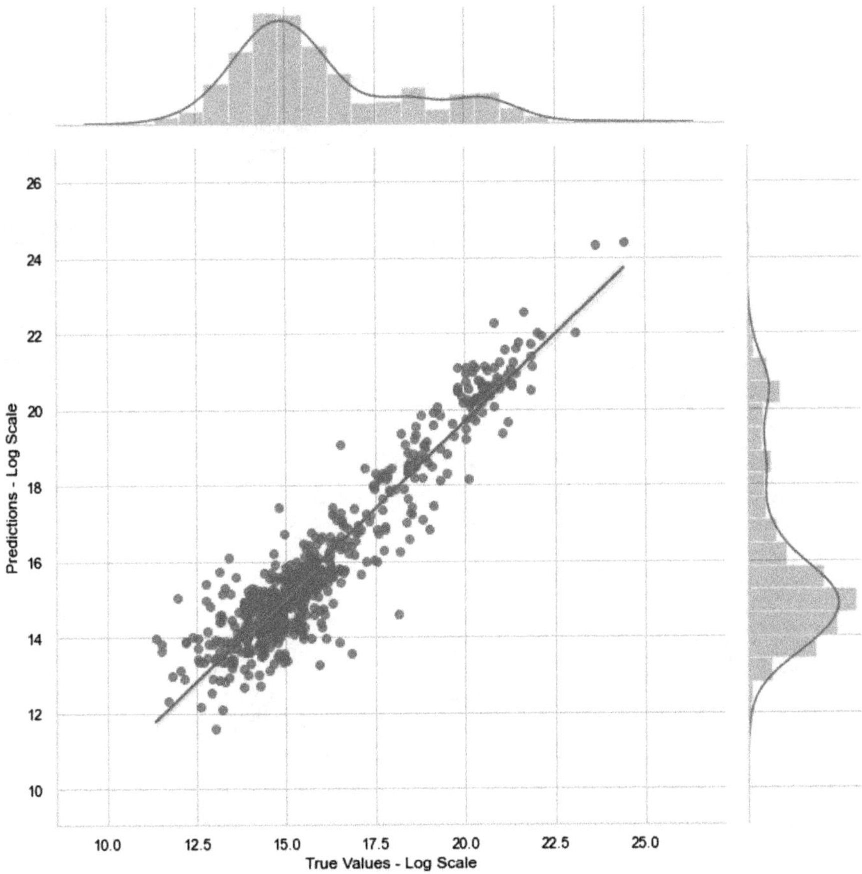

Fig. 10.13 True versus model predicted values in the test set

features. The resultant plot of true and predicted values in our test data is shown in Fig. 10.16, with a R^2 of 0.8 for the fitted linear function. As can be seen from this figure, the points are more widely scattered and dispersed across the values compared to our original XGBoost model (see Fig. 10.13, and compare with Fig. 10.16). Nonetheless, the low level of degradation in predictive power suggests that our XGBoost model can be used as an effective tool even in other datasets in which some of the important variables are not available.

10.4.3 Predicting Success

To test the performance of our neural network in predicating success, we first performed a random training/validation split of 80–20 on our data. After training

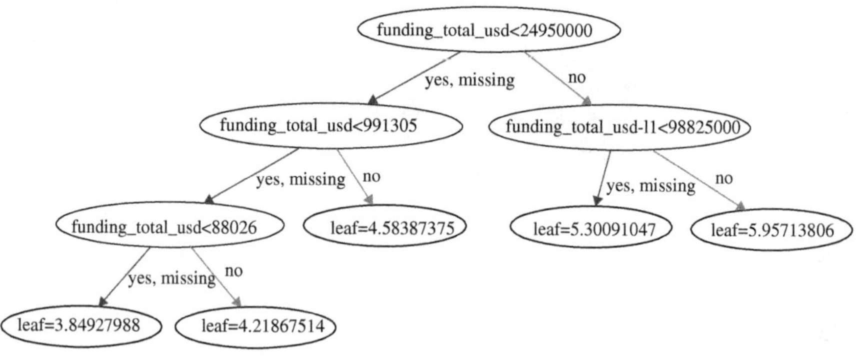

Fig. 10.14 Boosted tree example

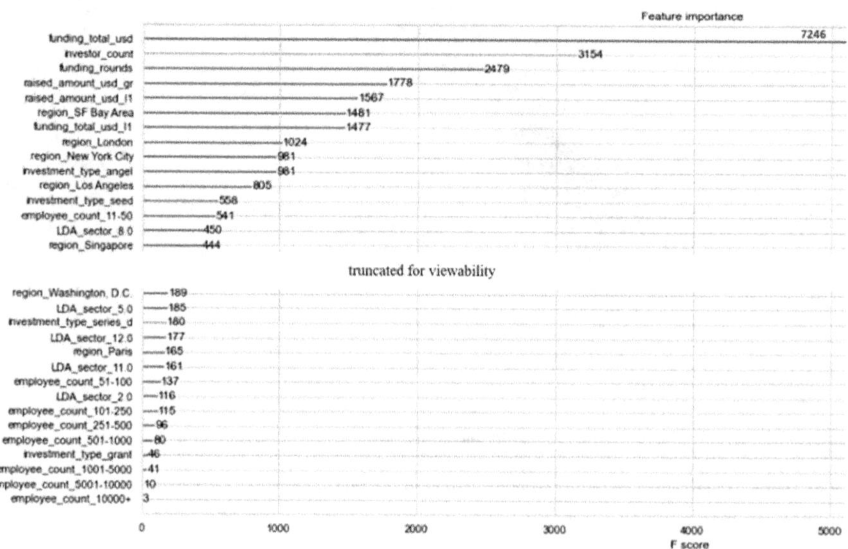

Fig. 10.15 Feature importance of XGBoost model

our neural network on the training part, we gauged its prediction accuracy on the validation set. We observed an accuracy of 92.48% when we used the first, stricter definition of success (i.e., defining success only based on acquisition or IPO). However, when we broadened the definition of success to startups that were still growing, we observed a prediction accuracy (on the validation set) of 81.21%. This reduction in prediction accuracy highlights the challenge of evaluating startup success. Specifically, focusing only on startups that eventually exit via an IPO or acquisition makes it difficult to make use of data on early-stage startups, and broadening the definition of success does not seem to help since the prediction performance suffers. This alludes to our earlier discussion in Sect. 10.3 that startup success is typically less straightforward to define.

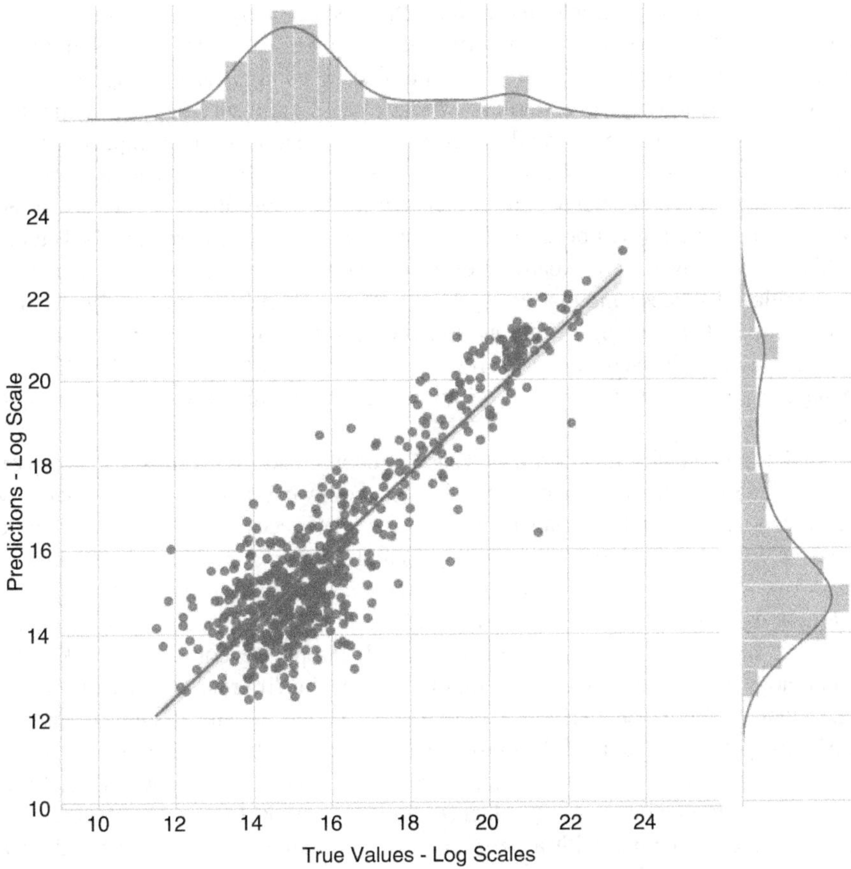

Fig. 10.16 True versus model predicted values in the test set with top predictors removed

10.5 Recommendations

In this section, we leverage our findings to provide broad recommendations for (a) entrepreneurs, (b) venture capital or investors, and (c) policymakers or governments seeking to improve the startup ecosystem. First, our results suggest that entrepreneurs seeking to maximize their post-money valuation should avoid trend-chasing (e.g., targeting a specific sector of economy) and instead focus on ideas or efforts that can generate the most amount of funding. Specifically, our findings suggest that trend-chasing may not maximize post-money valuation: no specific sector of economy is specifically significant in predicting post-money valuation, at least not compared to the total funding and investor counts. Besides the idea behind the startup, our findings suggest that fundraising efforts can also be significantly important in achieving high post-money valuation. Startups that are unable to gain and maintain momentum via fundraising activities are likely to suffer in their post-money valuation. Second, we observe that the investor count has a significant impact on post-money valuation, as exemplified by its high feature importance. A closer examination of some startups which raised significant amounts of funding also suggests that having "branded" investors can have a positive impact. This is most likely due to a "signaling effect:" investors often follow their high profile counterparts, since financial commitments from high profile investors are often interpreted by other investors as a sign of a startup's probable future success. Having a high profile investor on board or even leading the round leads to an increased probability of success and higher expected post-money evaluation. Finally, we also observe that there are significant agglomeration effects from being in top startup regions such as the San Francisco Bay Area or New York, although the effect of being in a particular region shows a diminishing rate of return as one moves through the list of top performing cities.

In the same vein as the above, we broadly recommend for startups to develop an internationalization strategy and consider expanding internationally at a relatively early stage, primarily for enhanced exposure, market access, and traction. It can be inferred from our exploratory data analysis and findings that domestic markets in most regions serve to be particularly advantageous only for certain sectors and for startups of certain sizes (or at certain stages). With the increasingly open nature of most startup ecosystems around the world, innovative companies backed by technology will be able to gain foothold quickly in different regions that place particular emphasis on the sector(s) that they belong to, and thereby obtain an early competitive advantage. Domestically, startups should gain access to credible reference customers in their respective sector(s) as early as possible, especially if they are developing innovative products or providing innovative services that require early adopters. Regions with a large base of multinational corporations and even small and medium-sized enterprises in the same sector can provide the necessary network effect to catalyze traction, which can in turn result in rapid revenue growth.

On the contrary, we recommend that venture funds (especially those dedicated to early-stage startups) focus their investments on specific areas/sectors of interest or expertise, rather than adopting a broad mandate which may potentially result in "thinning out" and subsequently hurt returns. Venture funds can be broadly classified as generalist, thesis-driven, or sector-focused. With the increased competition across funding stages and regions, it may be advantageous—especially for early-stage funds—to be sector specific. This coincides with our observation and analysis that apart from top startup hubs such as San Francisco Bay Area, different regions seem to "favor" different sectoral clusters. The key benefits of focusing on specific sectors are three-fold. First, sector-specific domain expertise and intelligence allow the fund to source for higher quality deal flows, and maximize value capture with the same dollar value. Within-sector network effects such as partnerships with corporates may also give these funds an edge over broad-based generalist VCs, and provide the fund an edge in sourcing for high potential startups to invest in. Second, unless the fund has celebrity or renowned General Partners (GP) or investors, having sector-specific domain intelligence and expertise will help the fund establish credibility and gain confidence from Limited Partners (LP)—a factor crucial in the hyper-competitive nature of this industry. Third, our feature importance analysis shows that the ability to predict startup success does not improve when we broaden our definition of success to take advantage of available data points related to early-stage startups. This suggests that it is difficult to assess the merits of early-stage startups using purely quantitative measures, which necessitates deeper subject matter or sectoral analysis.

In providing recommendations for policymakers (and more broadly, governments) we note that they often would like to develop vibrant ecosystems, boost job creation, and catalyze economic growth. Thus, they typically seek to promote the creation or attraction of startups that have high potential and can grow to provide substantial employment and/or value-add activities. Considering this, our results have a few implications for them. First, policymakers should consider setting up co-investment instruments or mechanisms with the private sector—while allowing the private sector to take the lead in investing—especially in areas where there are gaps in specific funding stages, or sectors which serve as important nodes linking various economic activity or supply chains. Similarly, our KDE plots show that there is some overlap between government grants and other funding mechanisms along the same angel and seed stage(s). It can be a signal that government grants are directed to the same space as private investments, which might not be the most efficient use of resources, and might not result in desirable outcomes. It will be worthwhile for policymakers and policy analysts to conduct further detailed analyses in this regard. Second, policymakers should design policy levers to further entrench well-performing (or priority) sectors, and anchor major players in the domain, including not just multinational corporations but also small and medium-sized startups with high-growth potential. Combining the two recommendations, policymakers should develop a strategy or implement a program to systematically cultivate top global entrepreneurial, technology, and investment talents, and attract them to establish startups or investment vehicles. The incentives to do these do not necessarily have to be directly monetary. For example, they could include a combination of market or technology access, financing, network, or other forms of support.

Finally, our findings on predicting post-money valuation indicate that in some cases, there may exist a disconnect between startup size and valuation. This can have a few different implications for public policy decisions depending on policymakers' objectives. If policymakers want to attract and encourage startups as a means of job creation, they must bear in mind that startups that generate the most jobs may not necessarily be those that are the most valued by the market. On the other hand, if their objective is to target high-value startups that can serve as anchors for a vibrant startup ecosystem, policymakers must accept that such a targeting strategy may not yield as many jobs, at least in the short-term.

10.6 Conclusions, Limitations, and Future Work

In this chapter, we analyzed the global startup landscape. We did so first by providing descriptive statistical analyses and visualizations and then by building predictive models using machine learning techniques. Our contribution lies in (a) a novel processing of sectoral level data through collating text-based descriptions into sectors of the economy, (b) making use of machine learning methods to predict post-money valuation and startup success, and (c) identifying the most important predictors of startups' performance.

Our machine learning models enable predicting (within reasonable confidence) a startup's post-money valuation and success based on various variables such as region, sector, and funding amount raised. Through our analysis of variable importance, we find that startups across different regions performed relatively similar in terms of post-money valuation. Thus, region is not a significant predictor of startup performance. In contrast, however, startups' post-money valuations differ based on some other important features. Specifically, our results indicate that two most important predictors of post-money valuation are the amount of funding raised and investor count. As is expected, we also observe that startups' post-money valuation mildly differs based on the sector of economy and the funding stage. However, we find that these variables (sector of economy and funding stage) are not strong predictors of future performance of startups.

An entrepreneur, venture capital analyst, or policymaker can use our models to predict the post-money valuation and success of a startup by simply specifying features such as the region, sector, and funding amount raised. This prediction, in turn, can be used to make better investment decisions, design more appropriate economic policies, and/or implement superior evidence-based mechanisms that can boost the overall startup ecosystem.

In closing, we note that our work has some important limitations that future research can address. First, as we noted earlier, measuring performance of startups, defining what success is, and how it can be quantified are perplexing tasks. We used a few measures of performance and success that we could quantify based on our data. We leave it to future work to validating our findings using other measures of startup performance. Second, our work is focused on developing predictive methods. Future research can combine our methods with prescriptive analyses to develop strong tools aimed at identify the causal drivers of startups' success. Third, we used a single source of data. Future work can enhance our analyses as well as the predictive power of our models by first combining this data with other sources, and then training our models on the resultant larger dataset. Finally, as more information about patents and the technical competency of startups become available, future work can (a) assess the role that different startups play in the technology translation process (e.g., from basic research to commercialization), and (b) determine mechanisms through which this translation process impacts their post-money valuation and success.

Acknowledgments The authors would like to thank Crunchbase for providing academic access to the data for this paper. The authors attest that there is no conflict of interest in this work.

References

Alperovych, Y., Hübner, G., & Lobet, F. (2015). How does governmental versus private venture capital backing affect a firm's efficiency? Evidence from Belgium. *Journal of Business Venturing, 30*(4), 508–525.

Berkus, D. (2016). *After 20 Years: Updating the Berkus Method of Valuation*. https://www.learnerslodge.com.sg/news/jc-cut-off-points-2018/. Accessed 9 June 2020.

Blei, D. M., Ng, A. Y., & Jordan, M. I. (2003). Latent Dirichlet allocation. *Journal of Machine Learning Research, 3*(Jan), 993–1022.

Carayannis, E. G., Dagnino, G. B., Alvarez, S., & Faraci, R. (2018). *Entrepreneurial ecosystems and the diffusion of startups*. Edward Elgar Publishing.

Carpenter, R. E., & Petersen, B. C. (2002). Capital Market Imperfections, High-tech Investment, and New Equity Financing. *The Economic Journal, 112*(477), F54–F72.

CB Insights (2017). *Venture Capital Funnel Shows Odds of Becoming a Unicorn Are Less than 1%*. March 29.

Chen, T., & Guestrin, C. (2016). Xgboost: A scalable tree boosting system. In *Proceedings of the 22nd ACM Sigkdd International Conference on Knowledge Discovery and Data Mining* (pp. 785–794).

Denis, D. J. (2004). Entrepreneurial finance: An overview of the issues and evidence. *Journal of Corporate Finance, 10*(2), 301–326.

Dixon, C. (2015). *Performance Data and the 'Babe Ruth' Effect in Venture Capital*. https://a16z.com/2015/06/08/performance-data-and-the-babe-ruth-effect-in-venture-capital/. Accessed 9 June 2020.

Drover, W., Busenitz, L., Matusik, S., Townsend, D., Anglin, A., & Dushnitsky, G. (2017). A review and roadmap of entrepreneurial equity financing research: Venture capital, corporate venture capital, angel investment, crowdfunding, and accelerators. *Journal of Management, 43*(6), 1820–1853.

Festel, G., Wuermseher, M., & Cattaneo, G. (2013). Valuation of early stage high-tech start-up companies. *International Journal of Business, 18*(3), 216.

Frei, P., & Leleux, B. (2004). Valuation—What you need to know. *Nature Biotechnology*.

Fundz Research (2020) *Series A, B, C Funding - The Ultimate Guide*. https://www.fundz.net/what-is-series-a-funding-series-b-funding-and-more. Accessed 8 June 2020.

Gompers, P., & Lerner, J. (2001). The venture capital revolution. *Journal of Economic Perspectives, 15*(2), 145–168.

Hoque, F. (2020). *Why Most Venture-Backed Companies Fail*. https://www.fastcompany.com/3003827/why-most-venture-backed-companies-fail. Accessed 8 June 2020.

Islam, M., Fremeth, A., & Marcus, A. (2018). Signaling by Early stage startups: US government research grants and venture capital funding. *Journal of Business Venturing, 33*(1), 35–51.

Korver, C. (2018). *Picking winners is a myth, but the PowerLaw is not*. https://medium.com/ulu-ventures/successful-vcs-need-at-least-one-outlier-to-have-a-well-performing-fund-c122c799dfb3. Accessed 9 June.

Miloud, T., Aspelund, A., & Cabrol, M. (2012). Startup valuation by venture capitalists: an empirical study. *Venture Capital, 14*(2–3), 151–174.

Mueller, A. (2020). *WordCloud for Python*. http://amueller.github.io/word_cloud/. Accessed 9 June.

Parzen, E. (1962). On estimation of a probability density function and mode. *The Annals of Mathematical Statistics, 33*(3), 1065–1076.

Pritchard, J. K., Stephens, M., & Donnelly, P. (2000). Inference of population structure using multilocus genotype data. *Genetics, 155*(2), 945–959.
Quintero, S. (2019). *An Empirical Perspective on Startup Valuations*. Radicle Working Paper.
Reiff, N. (2020). *Investopedia: Series A, B, C Funding: How it Works*. https://www.investopedia.com/articles/personal-finance/102015/series-b-c-funding-what-it-all-means-and-how-it-works.asp
Shane, S. A., & Ulrich, K. T. (2004). 50th anniversary article: Technological innovation, product development, and entrepreneurship in management science. *Management Science, 50*(2), 133–144.
Snoek, J., Larochelle, H., & Adams, R. P. (2012). Practical Bayesian optimization of machine learning algorithms. In *Advances in Neural Information Processing Systems* (pp. 2951–2959).
Srivastava, N., Hinton, G., Krizhevsky, A., Sutskever, I., & Salakhutdinov, R. (2014). Dropout: A simple way to prevent neural networks from overfitting. *The Journal of Machine Learning Research, 15*(1), 1929–1958.
Stéphanieueller, N. A. (2017). *TechinAsia: 9 methods of startup valuation explained*. https://www.techinasia.com/talk/9-method-startup-valuation. Accessed 9 June.
Williams, D., Robbins, L. E., Marks, K. H., Funkhouser, J. P., & Fernandez, G. (2013). *The handbook of financing growth: Strategies, capital structure, and M & A transactions*. Wiley.
Yuen, S. (2020). *Entrepreneurial ecosystems and the diffusion of startups*. Marshall Cavendish Business.
Zou, H., & Hastie, T. (2005). Regularization and variable selection via the elastic net. *Journal of the Royal Statistical Society: Series B (Statistical Methodology), 67*(2), 301–320.